BUILDING SOILS FOR BETTER CROPS

SUSTAINABLE SOIL MANAGEMENT

THIRD EDITION
BY FRED MAGDOFF AND HAROLD VAN ES
HANDBOOK SERIES BOOK 10

Published in 2009 by the Sustainable Agriculture Research and Education (SARE) program,
with funding from the National Institute of Food and Agriculture, U.S. Department of Agriculture

This book was published by the Sustainable Agriculture Research and Education (SARE) program under cooperative agreements with USDA's National Institute of Food and Agriculture, University of Maryland and University of Vermont.

To order:
Online: Visit www.sare.org/WebStore
By check or purchase order: Make payable to Sustainable Agriculture Publications and send to:

SARE Outreach Publications
c/o International Fulfillment Corporation
3570 Bladensburg Rd.
Brentwood, MD 20722

Cost:
- $20.95 for orders of 1-9 books
- $15.71 for 10-24 books (a 25% discount)
- $10.47 for 25 or more books (a 50% discount)

Shipping:
- $6.95 for first book (within USA). Add $2 s/h for each additional book—up to nine books—shipped within USA.
- For s/h on orders of 10 or more books, call (301) 779-1007 or visit www.sare.org/WebStore.

International or credit card orders:
- Call (301) 779-1007 or visit www.sare.org/WebStore.

Library of Congress Cataloging-in-Publication Data
Magdoff, Fred, 1942-
    Building soils for better crops : sustainable soil management / by Fred Magdoff and Harold van Es. -- 3rd ed.
        p. cm. -- (Handbook series ; bk. 10)
    Includes bibliographical references and index.
    ISBN 978-1-888626-13-1
  1. Soil management. 2. Humus. I. Van Es, Harold, 1958- II. Sustainable Agriculture Research & Education (Program) III. Title. IV. Series: Sustainable Agriculture Network handbook series ; bk. 10.
    S592.8.M34 2009
    631.4--dc22
                                        2009031856

Authors: Fred Magdoff and Harold van Es
Contributing Writer (farmer profiles): Amy Kremen
Production Manager: Dena Leibman
Copy Editing: Jill Mason
Graphic Design: Kirsten Ankers
Cover Illustration: Frank Fretz
Indexing: Jill Mason
Printing: Printed by United Book Press on process-chlorine-free, 100% post-consumer-waste paper.

MIX
From responsible sources
FSC® C010236
FSC
www.fsc.org

CONTENTS

ABOUT THE AUTHORS

Fred Magdoff is emeritus professor of plant and soil science at the University of Vermont and adjunct professor at Cornell University. He was Plant and Soil Science Department chair for eight years and for two decades was the coordinator of the twelve-state Northeast Region for the U.S. Department of Agriculture's Sustainable Agriculture Research and Education (SARE) program. He is also a fellow of the American Society of Agronomy. He has worked on soil testing for nitrogen and phosphorus, the effects of manures on soil properties and crop yields, buffering of soil pH, and many other issues related to soil health. He lives in Burlington and Fletcher, Vermont, with his wife, dog, two cats, a large garden, an occasional flock of chickens, and a small herd of beef cows.

Harold van Es is a professor of soil science at Cornell University and serves as chair of the Department of Crop and Soil Sciences. Born in Amsterdam, Netherlands, he grew up in an environment where soil and water are critical issues. His current research focuses on soil health, computational agriculture, and environmental statistics. He teaches courses in soil management and space-time statistics and also leads an extension program. He is a fellow of the Soil Science Society of America and the American Society of Agronomy. He lives in Lansing, New York, with his wife, three children, and two cats.

ABOUT SARE

SARE is a grant-making and outreach program. Its mission is to advance—to the whole of American agriculture—innovations that improve profitability, stewardship, and quality of life by investing in groundbreaking research and education.

Since it began in 1988, SARE has funded more than 5,000 projects around the nation that explore innovations, from rotational grazing to direct marketing to cover crops—and many other best practices. Administering SARE grants are four regional councils composed of farmers, ranchers, researchers, educators, and other local experts, and coordinators in every state and island protectorate run education programs for ag professionals. SARE Outreach publishes practical books, bulletins, online resources, and other information for farmers and ranchers. All of SARE's activities are funded by the National Institute of Food and Agriculture, U.S. Department of Agriculture.

Guided by the belief that healthy soil is the foundation of healthy agriculture, SARE has made soil quality research and education a cornerstone of its project portfolio—and made *Building Soils for Better Crops* one of its signature handbooks. This new, all-color edition is an authoritative text on soil health, detailing the latest research and experiences of soil scientists—many of whom are SARE grant participants, including the book's authors. Some other SARE titles that might be of interest to *Building Soils* readers: (Books) *Managing Cover Crops Profitably*, third edition; *The New American Farmer*, second edition; *Crop Rotation on Organic Farms*; (Bulletins) *Diversifying Cropping Systems*; *Transitioning to Organic Production*; and *Smart Water Use on Your Farm or Ranch*.

For more information about SARE's grant-making program and information products, visit www.sare.org or contact: SARE Outreach, 1122 Patapsco Bldg., University of Maryland, College Park, MD 20742-6715; info@sare.org; (301) 405-8020.

SARE's four regional offices and outreach office work to advance sustainable innovations to the whole of American agriculture.

PREFACE

Used to be anybody could farm. All you needed was a strong back . . . but nowadays you need a good education to understand all the advice you get so you can pick out what'll do you the least harm.

—VERMONT SAYING, MID-1900s

We have written this book with farmers, farm advisors, students, and gardeners in mind, although we have also found copies of earlier editions on the bookshelves of many of our colleagues. *Building Soils for Better Crops* is a practical guide to ecological soil management that provides background information as well as details of soil-improving practices. This book is meant to give the reader a holistic appreciation of the importance of soil health and to suggest ecologically sound practices that help to develop and maintain healthy soils.

Building Soils for Better Crops has evolved over time. The first edition focused exclusively on the management of soil organic matter. If you follow practices that build and maintain good levels of soil organic matter, you will find it easier to grow healthy and high-yielding crops. Plants can withstand droughty conditions better and won't be as bothered by insects and diseases. By maintaining adequate levels of organic matter in soil, you have less reason to use as much commercial fertilizer, lime, and pesticides as many farmers now purchase. Soil organic matter is that important.

Organic matter management was also the heart of the second edition, but we decided to write a more comprehensive guide that includes other essential aspects of building healthy soils, such as managing soil physical properties and nutrients, as well as a chapter on evaluating soil health (chapter 22). In addition, we updated farmer case studies and added a new one. The case studies describe a number of key practices that enhance the health of the farmers' soils.

Many chapters were rewritten, expanded, and reorganized for the third edition—some completely. A chapter on physical properties and issues was divided into two (chapters 5 and 6), and chapters were added on the principles of ecological soil management (chapter 8) and on irrigation and drainage (chapter 17). The third edition, while still focusing on farming and soils in the United States, has a broader geographical scope; the book has evolved into a more comprehensive treatise of sustainable soil management for a global audience. We have, however, maintained the use of English units in the book for the convenience of our original target audience, although many readers outside North America—and scientists like us—would perhaps prefer the use of metric units.

A book like this one cannot give exact answers to problems on specific farms. In fact, we are purposely staying away from recipe-type approaches. There are just too many differences from one field to another, one farm to another, and one region to another, to warrant blanket recommendations. To make specific suggestions, it is necessary to know the details of the soil, crop, climate, machinery, human considerations, and other variable factors. Good soil management needs to be adaptive and is better achieved through education and understanding than with simple recommendations.

Over many centuries, people have struggled with the same issues we struggle with today. We quote some of these people in many of the epigraphs at the beginning of each chapter in appreciation for those who have come before. *Vermont Agricultural Experiment Station Bulletin No. 135,* published in 1908, is especially fascinating; it contains an article by three scientists about the importance of soil organic matter that is strikingly modern in many ways. The message of Edward Faulkner's *Plowman's Folly*—that reduced tillage and increased use of organic residues are essential to improving soil—is as valid today as in 1943 when it was first published. And let's not forget the first textbook of soil management, Jethro Tull's *A Horse-Hoeing Husbandry, or an Essay on the Principles of Tillage and Vegetation,* first published in 1731. Although it discusses now-refuted concepts, like the need for intensive tillage, it contains the blueprints for modern seed drills. The saying is right— what goes around comes around. Sources are cited at the end of each chapter and at the end of the book, although what's provided is not a comprehensive list of references on the subject.

Many people reviewed individual chapters or the entire manuscript at one stage or another and made very useful suggestions. We would like to thank George Abawi, William Brinton, Andy Clark, Bill Cox, Karl

Czymmek, Heather Darby, Addy Elliott, Charles Francis, Tim Griffin, Joel Gruver, Karl Hammer, Jon Hanson, Ellen Harrison, John Havlin, Robert L. Hill, Bruce Hoskins, Bill Jokela, Doug Karlen, Ann Kennedy, Charles Mitchell, Jr., Tom Morris, John Peters, Stu Pettygrove, Marianne Sarrantonio, John Sawyer, Eric Sideman, Gene Stevens, Jeff Strock, and Ray Weil.

We recognize colleagues who provided photos in the figure captions, and we are grateful for their contribution. All other photos are our own or in the public domain. We also acknowledge some of our colleagues— Bob Schindelbeck, George Abawi, David Wolfe, Omololu (John) Idowu, Ray Weil, and Rich Bartlett (deceased)— whose ideas and insights have helped shape our understanding of the subject. And we thank our wives, Amy Demarest and Cindy van Es, for their patience and encouragement during the writing of this book. Any mistakes are, of course, ours alone.

— Fred Magdoff
Professor Emeritus
Department of Plant & Soil Science
University of Vermont

— Harold van Es
Professor and Chair
Department of Crop & Soil Sciences
Cornell University

June 2009

INTRODUCTION

... it is our work with living soil that provides sustainable alternatives to the triple crises of climate, energy, and food. No matter how many songs on your iPod, cars in your garage, or books on your shelf, it is plants' ability to capture solar energy that is at the root of it all. Without fertile soil, what is life?

—VANDANA SHIVA, 2008

Throughout history, humans have worked the fields, and land degradation has occurred. Many civilizations have collapsed from unsustainable land use, including the cultures of the Fertile Crescent in the Middle East, where the agricultural revolution first occurred about 10,000 years ago. The United Nations estimates that 2.5 billion acres have suffered erosion since 1945 and that 38% of global cropland has become seriously degraded since then. In the past, humankind survived because people developed new lands. But a few decades ago the total amount of agricultural land actually began to decline as new land could no longer compensate for the loss of old land. The exhaustive use of land is combined with increasing populations; greater consumption of animal products produced in large-scale facilities, which creates less efficient use of crop nutrients; expanding acreages for biofuel crops; and the spread of urban areas, suburban and commercial development, and highways onto agricultural lands. We have now reached a point where we are expanding into marginal lands—like shallow hillsides and arid areas—that are very fragile and can degrade rapidly (figure I.1). Another area of agricultural expansion is virgin tropical rainforests, which are the last remnants of unspoiled and biologically rich land. The rate of deforestation at this time is very disconcerting; if continued at this level, there will be little virgin forest left by the middle of the century. We must face the reality that we are running out of land. We have already seen hunger and civil strife—especially in Africa—over limited land resources and productivity, and a global food crisis

Figure I.1. Reaching the limits: Marginal rocky land is put into production in Africa.

break out in 2008. Some countries with limited water or arable land are purchasing or renting land in other countries to produce food for the "home" market.

Nevertheless, human ingenuity has helped us overcome many agricultural challenges, and one of the truly modern miracles is our agricultural system, which produces abundant food. High yields often come from the use of improved crop varieties, fertilizers, pest control products, and irrigation, which have resulted in food security for much of the developed world. At the same time, mechanization and the ever-increasing capacity of field equipment allow farmers to work increasing acreage. Despite the high productivity per acre and per person, many farmers, agricultural scientists, and extension specialists see severe problems associated with our intensive agricultural production systems. Examples abound:

- With conventional agricultural practices heavily dependent on fossil fuels, the increase in the price of

BUILDING SOILS FOR BETTER CROPS: SUSTAINABLE SOIL MANAGEMENT

energy—as well as the diversion of crops to produce ethanol and biodiesel and other trends—will cause food prices to be higher in the future, resulting in a worldwide upsurge in hunger.

• Too much nitrogen fertilizer or animal manure sometimes causes high nitrate concentrations in groundwater. These concentrations can become high enough to pose a human health hazard. Many of the biologically rich estuaries and the parts of seas near river inflows around the world, including the Gulf of Mexico, are hypoxic (have low oxygen levels) during late summer months due to nitrogen enrichment from agricultural sources.

• Phosphate and nitrate in runoff and drainage water enter water bodies and degrade their quality by stimulating algae growth.

• Antibiotics used to fight diseases in farm animals can enter the food chain and may be found in the meat we eat. Perhaps even more important, their overuse on farms where large numbers of animals are crowded together has resulted in outbreaks of human illness from strains of disease-causing bacteria that have become resistant to many antibiotics.

• Erosion associated with conventional tillage and lack of good rotations degrades our precious soil and, at the same time, causes the silting up of reservoirs, ponds, and lakes.

• Soil compaction reduces water infiltration and increases runoff, thereby increasing flooding, while at the same time making soils more drought prone.

• In some parts of the country groundwater is being used for agriculture faster than nature can replenish this invaluable resource. In addition, water is increasingly diverted for urban growth in dry regions of the country, lessening the amount available for irrigated agriculture.

The whole modern system of agriculture and food is based on extensive use of fossil fuels—to make and power large field equipment, produce fertilizers and pesticides, dry grains, process food products, and transport them over long distances. With the price of energy so much greater than just a few years ago, the economics of the "modern" agricultural system may need to be reevaluated.

The food we eat and our surface and groundwaters are sometimes contaminated with disease-causing organisms and chemicals used in agriculture. Pesticides used to control insects and plant diseases can be found in foods, animal feeds, groundwater, and surface water running off agricultural fields. Farmers and farm workers are at special risk. Studies have shown higher cancer rates among those who work with or near certain pesticides. Children in areas with significant usage of pesticides are also at risk of having developmental problems. When considered together, these inadvertent by-products of agriculture are huge. The costs of all these negative effects on wildlife, natural resources, human health, and biodiversity in the United States is estimated at between $6 billion and $17 billion per year. The general public is increasingly demanding safe, high-quality food that is produced without excessive damage to the environment—and many are willing to pay a premium to obtain it.

To add to the problems, farmers are in a perpetual struggle to maintain a decent standard of living. As consolidations and other changes occur in the agriculture input (seeds, fertilizers, pesticides, equipment, etc.), food processing, and marketing sectors, the farmer's bargaining position weakens. For many years the high cost of purchased inputs and the low prices of many agricultural commodities, such as wheat, corn, cotton, and milk, caught farmers in a cost-price squeeze that made it hard to run a profitable farm. At the time of writing this edition, the prices for many agricultural commodities have recently seen sharp increases and then a rapid decrease. On the other hand, the costs of purchased inputs also increased greatly but then did not decrease as much as crop prices did. The wide swings in prices of crops and animal products have created a lot of stress among farmers.

Given these problems, you might wonder if we should

continue to farm in the same way. A major effort is under way by farmers, extension educators, and researchers to develop and implement practices that are both more environmentally sound than conventional practices and, at the same time, more economically rewarding for farmers. As farmers use management skills and better knowledge to work more closely with the biological world and the consumer, they frequently find that there are ways to increase profitability by decreasing the use of inputs purchased off the farm and selling direct to the end-user.

SOIL HEALTH INTEGRAL TO SUSTAINABLE AGRICULTURE

With the new emphasis on sustainable agriculture comes a reawakening of interest in soil health. Early scientists, farmers, and gardeners were well aware of the importance of soil quality and organic matter to the productivity of soil. The significance of soil organic matter, including living organisms in the soil, was understood by scientists at least as far back as the 17th century. John Evelyn, writing in England during the 1670s, described the importance of topsoil and explained that the productivity of soils tended to be lost with time. He noted that their fertility could be maintained by adding organic residues. Charles Darwin, the great natural scientist of the 19th century who developed the modern theory of evolution, studied and wrote about the importance of earthworms to the cycling of nutrients and the general fertility of the soil.

Around the turn of the 20th century, there was again an appreciation of the importance of soil health. Scientists realized that "worn-out" soils, whose productivity had drastically declined, resulted mainly from the depletion of soil organic matter. At the same time, they could see a transformation coming: Although organic matter was "once extolled as the essential soil ingredient, the bright particular star in the firmament of the plant grower, it fell like Lucifer" under the weight of "modern" agricultural ideas (Hills, Jones, and Cutler, 1908). With the availability of inexpensive fertilizers and

larger farm equipment after World War II, and the availability of cheap water for irrigation in some parts of the western United States, many people working with soils forgot or ignored the importance of organic matter in promoting high-quality soils.

"[Organic matter was] once extolled as the essential soil ingredient, the bright particular star in the firmament of the plant grower . . ."

As farmers and scientists were placing less emphasis on soil organic matter during the last half of the 20th century, farm machinery was getting larger. More horsepower for tractors allowed more land to be worked by fewer people. Large four-wheel-drive tractors allowed farmers to do field work when the soil was wet, creating severe compaction and sometimes leaving the soil in a cloddy condition, requiring more harrowing than otherwise would be needed. The use of the moldboard plow, followed by harrowing, broke down soil structure and left no residues on the surface. Soils were left bare and very susceptible to wind and water erosion. New harvesting machinery was developed, replacing hand harvesting of crops. As dairy herd size increased, farmers needed bigger spreaders to handle the manure. More passes through the field with heavier equipment to spread fertilizer and manure, prepare a seedbed, plant, spray pesticides, and harvest created the potential for significant amounts of soil compaction.

A new logic developed that most soil-related problems could be dealt with by increasing external inputs. This is a reactive way of dealing with soil issues—you react after seeing a "problem" in the field. If a soil is deficient in some nutrient, you buy a fertilizer and spread it on the soil. If a soil doesn't store enough rainfall, all you need is irrigation. If a soil becomes too compacted and water or roots can't easily penetrate, you use an implement, such as a subsoiler, to tear it open. If a plant disease or insect infestation occurs, you apply a pesticide.

Are low nutrient status; poor water-holding capacity; soil compaction; susceptibility to erosion; and disease, nematode, or insect damage really individual and unrelated problems? Perhaps they are better viewed as symptoms of a deeper, underlying problem. The ability to tell the difference between what is the underlying problem and what is only a symptom of a problem is essential to deciding on the best course of action. For example, if you are hitting your head against a wall and you get a headache—is the problem the headache and aspirin the best remedy? Clearly, the real problem is your behavior, not the headache, and the best solution is to stop banging your head against the wall!

What many people think are individual problems may just be symptoms of a degraded, poor-quality soil.

What many people think are individual problems may just be symptoms of a degraded, poor-quality soil. These symptoms are usually directly related to depletion of soil organic matter, lack of a thriving and diverse population of soil organisms, and compaction caused by use of heavy field equipment. Farmers have been encouraged to react to individual symptoms instead of focusing their attention on general soil health management. A new approach is needed to help develop farming practices that take advantage of the inherent strengths of natural systems. In this way, we can prevent the many symptoms of unhealthy soils from developing, instead of reacting after they develop. If we are to work together with nature, instead of attempting to overwhelm and dominate it, the buildup and maintenance of good levels of organic matter in our soils are as critical as management of physical conditions, pH, and nutrient levels.

A skeptic might argue that the challenges described above are simply the result of basic economic forces, including the long-run inexpensive cost of fossil fuel and crop inputs (although this is changing), and the fact that environmental consequences and long-term impacts are not internalized into the economic equation. It could then be argued that matters will not improve unless the economic incentives are changed. We argue that those economic motivations are already present, that sustainable soil management is profitable, and that such management will cause profitability to increase with greater scarcity of resources and higher prices of crop inputs.

This book has four parts. Part 1 provides background information about soil health and organic matter: what it is, why it is so important, the importance of soil organisms, and why some soils are of higher quality than others. Part 2 includes discussions of soil physical properties, soil water storage, and nutrient cycles and flows. Part 3 deals with the ecological principles behind—and practices that promote—building healthy soil. It begins with chapters that place a lot of emphasis on promoting organic matter buildup and maintenance. Following practices that build and maintain organic matter may be the key to soil fertility and may help solve many problems. Practices for enhancing soil quality include the use of animal manures and cover crops; good residue management; appropriate selection of rotation crops; use of composts; reduced tillage; minimizing soil compaction and enhancing aeration; better nutrient and amendment management; good irrigation and drainage; and adopting specific conservation practices for erosion control. Part 4 discusses how you can evaluate soil health and combine soil-building management strategies that actually work on the farm, and how to tell whether the health of your soils is improving.

SOURCES

Hills, J.L., C.H. Jones, and C. Cutler. 1908. Soil deterioration and soil humus. In *Vermont Agricultural Experiment Station Bulletin 135*, pp. 142–177. Burlington: University of Vermont, College of Agriculture.

Montgomery, D. 2007. *Dirt: The Erosion of Civilizations*. Berkeley: University of California Press.

Tegmeier, E.M., and M.D. Duffy. 2004. External costs of agricultural production in the United States. *International Journal of Agricultural Sustainability* 2: 1–20.

ORGANIC MATTER—THE KEY TO HEALTHY SOILS

Photo by Dennis Nolan

Chapter 1

HEALTHY SOILS

All over the country [some soils are] worn out, depleted, exhausted, almost dead.
But here is comfort: These soils possess possibilities and may be restored to high
productive power, provided you do a few simple things.

—C.W. BURKETT, 1907

It should come as no surprise that many cultures have considered soil central to their lives. After all, people were aware that the food they ate grew from the soil. Our ancestors who first practiced agriculture must have been amazed to see life reborn each year when seeds placed in the ground germinated and then grew to maturity. In the Hebrew Bible, the name given to the first man, Adam, is the masculine version of the word "earth" or "soil" (*adama*). The name for the first woman, Eve (or Hava in Hebrew), comes from the word for "living." Soil and human life were considered to be intertwined. A particular reverence for the soil has been an important part of the cultures of many civilizations, including American Indian tribes.

Although we focus on the critical role soils play in growing crops, it's important to keep in mind that soils also serve other important purposes. Soils govern whether rainfall runs off the field or enters the soil and eventually helps recharge underground aquifers. When a soil is denuded of vegetation and starts to degrade,

excessive runoff and flooding are more common. Soils also absorb, release, and transform many different chemical compounds. For example, they help to purify wastes flowing from the septic system fields in your back yard. Soils also provide habitats for a diverse group of organisms, many of which are very important—such as those bacteria that produce antibiotics. Soil organic matter stores a huge amount of atmospheric carbon. Carbon, in the form of carbon dioxide, is a greenhouse gas associated with global warming. So by increasing soil organic matter, more carbon can be stored in soils, reducing the global warming potential. We also use soils as a foundation for roads, industry, and our communities.

WHAT KIND OF SOIL DO YOU WANT?

Soil consists of four important parts: mineral solids, water, air, and organic matter. Mineral solids are sand, silt, and clay and mainly consist of silicon, oxygen, aluminum, potassium, calcium, and magnesium. The soil water, also called the soil solution, contains dissolved

Photo by Dan Anderson

nutrients and is the main source of water for plants. Essential nutrients are made available to the roots of plants through the soil solution. The air in the soil, which is in contact with the air above ground, provides roots with oxygen and helps remove excess carbon dioxide from respiring root cells. When mineral and organic particles clump together, aggregates are formed. They create a soil that contains more spaces, or pores, for storing water and allowing gas exchange as oxygen enters for use by plant roots and soil organisms and the carbon dioxide (CO_2) produced by organisms leaves the soil.

Farmers sometimes use the term *soil health* to describe the condition of the soil. Scientists usually use the term *soil quality*, but both refer to the same idea— how good is the soil in its role of supporting the growth of high-yielding, high-quality, and healthy crops? How would you know a high-quality soil from a lower-quality soil? Most farmers and gardeners would say that they know one when they see one. Farmers can certainly tell you which of the soils on their farms are of low, medium, or high quality. They know high-quality soil because it generates higher yields with less effort. Less rainwater runs off, and fewer signs of erosion are seen on the better-quality soils. Less power is needed to operate machinery on a healthy soil than on poor, compacted soils.

The first thing many might think of is that the soil should have a sufficient supply of nutrients throughout the growing season. But don't forget, at the end of the season there shouldn't be too much nitrogen and phosphorus left in highly soluble forms or enriching the soil's surface. Leaching and runoff of nutrients are most likely to occur after crops are harvested and before the following year's crops are well established.

We also want the soil to have good tilth so that plant roots can fully develop with the least amount of effort. A soil with good tilth is more spongy and less compact than one with poor tilth. A soil that has a favorable and stable soil structure also promotes rainfall infiltration and water storage for plants to use later. For good root growth and drainage, we want a soil with sufficient depth before a compact soil layer or bedrock is reached.

We want a soil to be well drained, so it dries enough in the spring and during the following rains to permit timely field operations. Also, it's essential that oxygen is able to reach the root zone to promote optimal root health—and that happens best in a soil without a drainage problem. (Keep in mind that these general characteristics do not hold for all crops. For example, flooded soils are desirable for cranberry and paddy rice production.)

We want the soil to have low populations of plant disease and parasitic organisms so plants grow better. Certainly, there should also be low weed pressure, especially of aggressive and hard-to-control weeds. Most soil organisms are beneficial, and we certainly want high amounts of organisms that help plant growth, such as earthworms and many bacteria and fungi.

THINK LIKE A ROOT!

If you were a root, what would *you* like from an ideal soil? Surely you'd want the soil to provide adequate nutrients and to be porous with good tilth, so that you could easily grow and explore the soil and so that soil could store large quantities of water for you to use when needed. But you'd also like a very biologically active soil, with many beneficial organisms nearby to provide you with nutrients and growth-promoting chemicals, as well as to keep potential disease organism populations as low as possible. You would not want the soil to have any chemicals, such as soluble aluminum or heavy metals, that might harm you; therefore, you'd like the pH to be in a proper range for you to grow. You would also not want any subsurface layers that would restrict your growth deep into the soil.

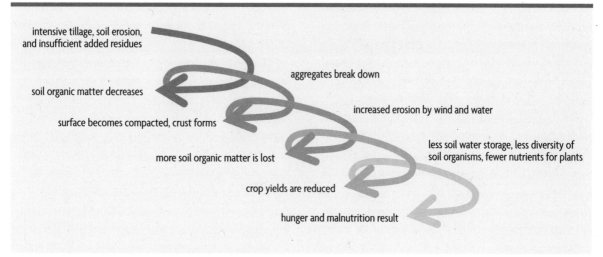

intensive tillage, soil erosion, and insufficient added residues

aggregates break down

soil organic matter decreases

increased erosion by wind and water

surface becomes compacted, crust forms

less soil water storage, less diversity of soil organisms, fewer nutrients for plants

more soil organic matter is lost

crop yields are reduced

hunger and malnutrition result

Figure 1.1. The downward spiral of soil degradation. Modified from Topp et al. (1995).

A high-quality soil is free of chemicals that might harm the plant. These can occur naturally, such as soluble aluminum in very acid soils or excess salts and sodium in arid soils. Potentially harmful chemicals also are introduced by human activity, such as fuel oil spills or application of sewage sludge with high concentrations of toxic elements.

A high-quality soil should resist being degraded. It also should be resilient, recovering quickly after unfavorable changes like compaction.

THE NATURE AND NURTURE OF SOILS

Some soils are exceptionally good for growing crops, and others are inherently unsuitable; most are in between. Many soils also have limitations, such as low organic matter content, texture extremes (coarse sand or heavy clay), poor drainage, or layers that restrict root growth. Iowa's loess-derived prairie soils are naturally blessed with a combination of silt loam texture and high organic matter content. By every standard for assessing soil health, these soils—in their virgin state—would rate very high.

The way we care for, or *nurture*, a soil modifies its inherent nature. A good soil can be abused through

years of poor management and turn into one with poor health, although it generally takes a lot of mistreatment to reach that point. On the other hand, an innately challenging soil may be very "unforgiving" of poor management and quickly become even worse. For example, a heavy clay loam soil can be easily compacted and turn into a dense mass. Both naturally good and poor soils can be productive if they are managed well. However, they will probably never reach parity, because some limitations simply cannot be completely overcome. The key idea is the same that we wish for our children—we want our soils to reach their fullest potential.

HOW DO SOILS BECOME DEGRADED?

Although we want to emphasize healthy, high-quality soils because of their ability to produce high yields of crops, it is also crucial to recognize that many soils in the U.S. and around the world have become degraded—they have become what many used to call "worn-out" soils. Degradation most commonly occurs when erosion and decreased soil organic matter levels initiate a downward spiral resulting in poor crop production (figure 1.1). Soils become compact, making it hard for water to infiltrate and roots to develop properly. Erosion contin- ues, and nutrients decline to levels too low for good crop growth. The development of saline (too salty) soils under irrigation in arid regions is another cause of reduced soil health. (Salts added in the irrigation water need to be leached beneath the root zone to avoid the problem.)

Historically, soil degradation caused significant harm to many early civilizations, including the drastic loss of productivity resulting from soil erosion in Greece and many locations in the Middle East (such as present-day Israel, Jordan, Iraq, and Lebanon). This led either to colonial ventures to help feed the citizenry or to the decline of the culture.

Tropical rainforest conditions (high temperature and rainfall, with most of the organic matter near the soil surface) may cause significant soil degradation within two or three years of conversion to cropland. This is the reason the "slash and burn" system, with people moving to a new patch of forest every few years, developed in the tropics. After farmers depleted the soils in a field, they would cut down and burn the trees in the new patch, allowing the forest and soil to regenerate in previously cropped areas.

The westward push of U.S. agriculture was stimu- lated by rapid soil degradation in the East, originally a zone of temperate forest. Under the conditions of the humid portion of the Great Plains (moderate rainfall and temperature, with organic matter distributed deeper in the soil), it took many decades for the effects of soil degradation to become evident.

The extent of erosion on a worldwide basis is staggering—it is estimated that erosion has progressed far enough to decrease yields on an estimated 16% of all the world's agricultural soils. The value of annual crop loss due to soil degradation by erosion is around $1 bil- lion. And erosion is still a major global problem, robbing people of food and each year continuing to reduce the productivity of the land.

HOW DO YOU BUILD A HEALTHY, HIGH-QUALITY SOIL?

Some characteristics of healthy soils are relatively easy to achieve—for example, an application of limestone will make a soil less acid and increase the availability of many nutrients to plants. But what if the soil is only a few inches deep? In that case, there is little that can be done within economic reason, except on a very small, garden-size plot. If the soil is poorly drained because of a restricting subsoil layer of clay, tile drainage can be installed, but at a significant cost.

We use the term *building soils* to emphasize that the nurturing process of converting a degraded or low-quality soil into a truly high-quality one requires understand- ing, thought, and significant actions. This is also true for maintaining or improving already healthy soils. Soil organic matter has a positive influence on almost all of the characteristics we've just discussed. As we will discuss in chapters 2 and 8, organic matter is even critical for managing pests—and improved soil management should be the starting point for a pest reduction program on

> ...what now remains of the formerly rich land is like the skeleton of a sick man, with all the fat and soft earth having wasted away and only the bare framework remaining. Formerly, many of the mountains were arable. The plains that were full of rich soil are now marshes. Hills that were once covered with forests and produced abundant pasture now produce only food for bees. Once the land was enriched by yearly rains, which were not lost, as they are now, by flowing from the bare land into the sea. The soil was deep, it absorbed and kept the water in the loamy soil, and the water that soaked into the hills fed springs and running streams everywhere. Now the abandoned shrines at spots where formerly there were springs attest that our description of the land is true.
>
> —PLATO, 4TH CENTURY B.C.E.

EVALUATING YOUR SOILS

Score cards and laboratory tests have been developed to help farmers assess their soils, using scales to rate the health of soils. In the field, you can evaluate the presence of earthworms, severity of erosion, ease of tillage, soil structure and color, extent of compaction, water infiltration rate, and drainage status. Then you rate crops growing on the soils by such characteristics as their general appearance, growth rates, root health, degree of resistance to drought, and yield. It's a good idea for all farmers to fill out such a score card for every major field or soil type on their farms every few years, or, alternatively, to send in soil to a lab that offers soil health analyses. But even without doing that, you probably already know what a really high-quality and healthy soil—one that would consistently produce good yields of high-quality crops with minimal negative environmental impact—would be like. You can read more on evaluating soil health in chapter 22.

every farm. Appropriate organic matter management is, therefore, the foundation for high-quality soil and a more sustainable and thriving agriculture. It is for this reason that so much space is devoted to organic matter in this book. However, we cannot forget other critical aspects of management—such as trying to lessen compaction by heavy field equipment and good nutrient management.

Although the details of how best to create high-quality soils differ from farm to farm and even field to field, the general approaches are the same—for example:

- Implement a number of practices that add organic materials to the soil.
- Add diverse sources of organic materials to the soil.
- Minimize losses of native soil organic matter.
- Provide plenty of soil cover—cover crops and/or surface residue—to protect the soil from raindrops and temperature extremes.
- Minimize tillage and other soil disturbances.
- Whenever traveling on the soil with field equipment, use practices that help develop and maintain good soil structure.
- Manage soil fertility status to maintain optimal pH levels for your crops and a sufficient supply of nutrients for plants without resulting in water pollution.
- In arid regions, reduce the amount of sodium or salt in the soil.

Later in the book we will return to these and other practices for developing and maintaining healthy soils.

A LARGER VIEW

In this book we discuss the ecological management of soils. And although the same basic principles discussed here apply to all soils around the world, the problems may differ in specifics and intensity and different mixes of solutions may be needed on any particular farm or in any ecological zone. It is estimated that close to half the people in the world are deficient in nutrients and vitamins and that half the premature deaths that occur globally are associated with malnutrition. Part of the problem is the low amount of nutrient-rich foods such as vegetables and fruits in diets. When grains form too large a part of the diet, even if people obtain sufficient calories and some protein, the lack of other nutrients results in health problems. Although iron, selenium, cobalt, and iodine deficiencies in humans are rare in the U.S., they may occur in developing countries whose soils are depleted and nutrient poor. It frequently is an easier and healthier solution to get these nutrients into people's diets by increasing plant content through adding these essential elements to the soil (or through irrigation water for iodine) rather than to try to provide everyone with supplements. Enhancing soil health—in

7

all its aspects, not just nutrient levels—is probably one of the most essential strategies for providing nutritious food to all the people in the world and ending the scourge of hunger and malnutrition.

SOURCES

den Biggelaar, C., R. Lal, R.K. Wiebe, H. Eswaran, V. Breneman, and P. Reich. 2004. The global impact of soil erosion on productivity. II: Effects on crop yields and production over time. *Advances in Agronomy*, vol. 81: 49–95.

Doran, J.W., M. Sarrantonio, and M.A. Liebig. 1996. Soil health and sustainability. In *Advances in Agronomy*, vol. 56, pp. 1–54. San Diego, CA: Academic Press, Inc.

Graham, R.D., R.M. Welch, D.A. Saunders, I. Ortiz-Monasterio, H.E. Bouis, M. Bonierbale, S. de Haan, G. Burgos, G. Thiele, R. Liria, C.A. Meisner, S.E. Beebe, M.J. Potts, M. Kadian, P.R.

Hobbs, R.K. Gupta, and S. Twomlow. 2007. Nutritious subsistence food systems. In *Advances in Agronomy*, vol. 92, pp. 1–74. San Diego, CA: Academic Press, Inc.

Hillel, D. 1991. *Out of the Earth: Civilization and the Life of the Soil*. Berkeley: University of California Press.

Spillman, W.J. 1906. *Renovation of Worn-out Soils*. Farmers' Bulletin No. 245. Washington, DC: USDA; Government Printing Office.

Topp, G.C., K.C. Wires, D.A. Angers, M.R. Carter, J.L.B. Culley, D.A. Holmstrom, B.D. Kay, G.P. Lafond, D.R. Langille, R.A. McBride, G.T. Patterson, E. Perfect, V. Rasiah, A.V. Rodd, and K.T. Webb. 1995. Changes in soil structure. In *The Health of Our Soils: Toward Sustainable Agriculture in Canada*, ed. D.F. Acton and L.J. Gregorich, chapter 6. Centre for Land and Biological Resources Research. Research Branch, Agriculture and Agri-Food Canada. Publication 1906/E. http://web.archive.org/web/20040324063604/res2.agr.gc.ca/publications/hs/index_e.htm.

Chapter 2

ORGANIC MATTER: WHAT IT IS AND WHY IT'S SO IMPORTANT

*Follow the appropriateness of the season, consider well the nature and conditions
of the soil, then and only then least labor will bring best success. Rely on one's own idea
and not on the orders of nature, then every effort will be futile.*

—JIA SI XIE, 6TH CENTURY, CHINA

As we will discuss at the end of this chapter, organic matter has an overwhelming effect on almost all soil properties, although it is generally present in relatively small amounts. A typical agricultural soil has 1% to 6% organic matter. It consists of three distinctly different parts—living organisms, fresh residues, and well-decomposed residues. These three parts of soil organic matter have been described as the *living*, the *dead*, and the *very dead*. This three-way classification may seem simple and unscientific, but it is very useful.

The living part of soil organic matter includes a wide variety of microorganisms, such as bacteria, viruses, fungi, protozoa, and algae. It even includes plant roots and the insects, earthworms, and larger animals, such as moles, woodchucks, and rabbits, that spend some of their time in the soil. The living portion represents about 15% of the total soil organic matter. Microorganisms, earthworms, and insects feed on plant residues and

manures for energy and nutrition, and in the process they mix organic matter into the mineral soil. In addition, they recycle plant nutrients. Sticky substances on the skin of earthworms and other substances produced by fungi help bind particles together. This helps to stabilize the soil aggregates, clumps of particles that make up good soil structure. Organisms such as earthworms and some fungi also help to stabilize the soil's structure (for example, by producing channels that allow water to infiltrate) and, thereby, improve soil water status and aeration. Plant roots also interact in significant ways with the various microorganisms and animals living in the soil. Another important aspect of soil organisms is that they are in a constant struggle with each other (figure 2.1). Further discussion of the interactions between soil organisms and roots, and among the various soil organisms, is provided in chapter 4.

A multitude of microorganisms, earthworms, and

Photo by Christine Markoe

9

insects get their energy and nutrients by breaking down organic residues in soils. At the same time, much of the energy stored in residues is used by organisms to make new chemicals as well as new cells. How does energy get stored inside organic residues in the first place? Green plants use the energy of sunlight to link carbon atoms together into larger molecules. This process, known as *photosynthesis,* is used by plants to store energy for respiration and growth.

The fresh residues, or "dead" organic matter, consist of recently deceased microorganisms, insects, earthworms, old plant roots, crop residues, and recently added manures. In some cases, just looking at them is enough to identify the origin of the fresh residues (figure 2.2). This part of soil organic matter is the active, or easily decomposed, fraction. This active fraction of soil organic matter is the main supply of food for various organisms—microorganisms, insects, and earthworms—living in the soil. As organic materials are decomposed by the "living," they release many of the nutrients needed by plants. Organic chemical compounds produced during the decomposition of fresh residues also help to bind soil particles together and give the soil good structure.

Organic molecules directly released from cells of fresh residues, such as proteins, amino acids, sugars, and starches, are also considered part of this fresh organic matter. These molecules generally do not last long in the soil because so many microorganisms use them as food.

The well-decomposed organic material in soil, the "very dead," is called *humus*. Some use the term *humus* to describe all soil organic matter; some use it to describe just the part you can't see without a microscope. We'll use the term to refer only to the well-decomposed part of soil organic matter. Because it is so stable and complex, the average age of humus in soils is usually more than 1,000 years. The already well-decomposed humus is not a food for organisms, but its very small size and chemical properties make it an important part of the soil. Humus holds on to some essential nutrients, storing them for slow release to plants. Humus also can surround certain potentially harmful chemicals and prevent them from causing damage to plants. Good amounts of soil humus can both lessen drainage and compaction problems that occur in clay soils and improve water retention in sandy soils by enhancing aggregation, which reduces soil density, and by holding on to and releasing water.

Another type of organic matter, one that has gained a lot of attention lately, is usually referred to as *black carbon*. Almost all soils contain some small pieces of

Figure 2.1. A nematode feeds on a fungus, part of a living system of checks and balances. Photo by Harold Jensen.

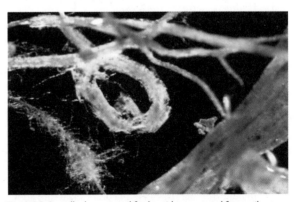

Figure 2.2. Partially decomposed fresh residues removed from soil. Fragments of stems, roots, and fungal hyphae are all readily used by soil organisms.

BIOCHAR AS A SOIL AMENDMENT

It is believed that the unusually productive "dark earth" soils of the Brazilian Amazon region were produced and stabilized by incorporation of vast amounts of charcoal over the years of occupation and use. Black carbon, produced by wildfires as well as human activity and found in many soils around the world, is a result of burning biomass at around 700 to 900°F under low oxygen conditions. This incomplete combustion results in about half or more of the carbon in the original material being retained as char. The char, also containing ash, tends to have high amounts of negative charge (cation exchange capacity), has a liming effect on soil, retains some nutrients from the wood or other residue that was burned, stimulates microorganism populations, and is very stable in soils. Although many times increases in yield have been reported following biochar application—probably a result of increased nutrient availability or increased pH—sometimes yields suffer. Legumes do particularly well with biochar additions, while grasses are frequently nitrogen deficient, indicating that nitrogen may be deficient for a period following application.

Note: The effects of biochar on raising soil pH and immediately increasing calcium, potassium, magnesium, etc., are probably a result of the ash rather than the black carbon itself. These effects can also be obtained by using more completely burned material, which contains more ash and little black carbon.

charcoal, the result of past fires, of natural or human origin. Some, such as the black soils of Saskatchewan, Canada, may have relatively high amounts of char. However, the interest in charcoal in soils has come about mainly through the study of the soils called dark earths (*terra preta de indio*) that are on sites of long-occupied villages in the Amazon region of South America that were depopulated during the colonial era. These dark earths contain 10–20% black carbon in the surface foot of soil, giving them a much darker color than the surrounding soils. The soil charcoal was the result of centuries of cooking fires and in-field burning of crop residues and other organic materials. The manner in which the burning occurred—slow burns, perhaps because of the wet conditions common in the Amazon—produces a lot of char material and not as much ash as occurs with more complete burning at higher temperatures. These soils were intensively used in the past but have been abandoned for centuries. Still, they are much more fertile than the surrounding soils—partially due to the high inputs of nutrients in animal and plant residue—and yield better crops than surrounding soils

typical of the tropical forest. Part of this higher fertility—the ability to supply plants with nutrients with very low amounts of leaching loss—has been attributed to the large amount of black carbon and the high amount of biological activity in the soils. Charcoal is a very stable form of carbon and apparently helps maintain relatively high cation exchange capacity as well as biological activity. People are beginning to experiment with adding large amounts of charcoal to soils—but we'd suggest waiting for results of the experiments before making large investments in this practice. The quantity needed to make a major difference to a soil is apparently huge—many tons per acre—and may limit the usefulness of this practice to small plots of land.

Normal organic matter decomposition that takes place in soil is a process that is similar to the burning of wood in a stove. When burning wood reaches a certain temperature, the carbon in the wood combines with oxygen from the air and forms carbon dioxide. As this occurs, the energy stored in the carbon-containing chemicals in the wood is released as heat in a process called oxidation. The biological world, including humans, animals, and microorganisms, also makes use of the energy inside carbon-containing molecules. This process of converting sugars, starches, and other compounds into a directly usable form of energy is also a type of oxidation. We usually call it respiration. Oxygen is used, and carbon dioxide and heat are given off in the process.

Soil carbon is sometimes used as a synonym for *organic matter*. Because carbon is the main building block of all organic molecules, the amount in a soil is strongly related to the total amount of all the organic matter—the living organisms plus fresh residues plus well-decomposed residues. When people talk about soil carbon instead of organic matter, they are usually referring to organic carbon. The amount of organic matter in soils is about twice the organic carbon level. However, in many soils in glaciated areas and semiarid regions it is common to have another form of carbon in soils—limestone, either as round concretions or dispersed evenly throughout the soil. Lime is calcium carbonate, which contains calcium, carbon, and oxygen. This is an *inorganic* carbon form. Even in humid climates, when limestone is found very close to the surface, some may be present in the soil.

WHY SOIL ORGANIC MATTER IS SO IMPORTANT

A fertile and healthy soil is the basis for healthy plants, animals, and humans. And soil organic matter is the very foundation for healthy and productive soils. Understanding the role of organic matter in maintaining a healthy soil is essential for developing ecologically sound agricultural practices. But how can organic matter, which only makes up a small percentage of most soils, be so important that we devote the three chapters in this section to discuss it? The reason is that organic matter positively influences, or modifies the effect of, essentially all soil properties. That is the reason it's so important to our understanding of soil health and how to manage soils better. Organic matter is essentially the heart of the story, but certainly not the only part. In addition to functioning in a large number of key roles that promote soil processes

and crop growth, soil organic matter is a critical part of a number of global and regional cycles.

It's true that you can grow plants on soils with little organic matter. In fact, you don't have to have any soil at all. (Although gravel and sand hydroponic systems without soil can grow excellent crops, large-scale systems of this type are usually neither economically nor ecologically sound.) It's also true that there are other important issues aside from organic matter when considering the quality of a soil. However, as soil organic matter decreases, it becomes increasingly difficult to grow plants, because problems with fertility, water availability, compaction, erosion, parasites, diseases, and insects become more common. Ever higher levels of inputs—fertilizers, irrigation water, pesticides, and machinery—are required to maintain yields in the face of organic matter depletion. But if attention is paid to proper organic matter management, the soil can support a good crop without the need for expensive fixes.

The organic matter content of agricultural topsoil is usually in the range of 1–6%. A study of soils in Michigan demonstrated potential crop-yield increases of about 12% for every 1% organic matter. In a Maryland experiment, researchers saw an increase of approximately 80 bushels of corn per acre when organic matter increased from 0.8% to 2%. The enormous influence of organic matter on so many of the soil's properties—biological, chemical, and physical—makes it of critical importance to healthy soils (figure 2.3). Part of the explanation for this influence is the small particle size of the well-decomposed portion of organic matter—the humus. Its large surface area–to–volume ratio means that humus is in contact with a considerable portion of the soil. The intimate contact of humus with the rest of the soil allows many reactions, such as the release of available nutrients into the soil water, to occur rapidly. However, the many roles of living organisms make soil life an essential part of the organic matter story.

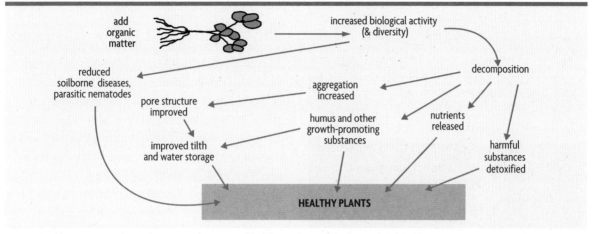

Figure 2.3. Adding organic matter results in many changes. Modified from Oshins and Drinkwater (1999).

Plant Nutrition

Plants need eighteen chemical elements for their growth—carbon (C), hydrogen (H), oxygen (O), nitrogen (N), phosphorus (P), potassium (K), sulfur (S), calcium (Ca), magnesium (Mg), iron (Fe), manganese (Mn), boron (B), zinc (Zn), molybdenum (Mo), nickel (Ni), copper (Cu), cobalt (Co), and chlorine (Cl). Plants obtain carbon as carbon dioxide (CO_2) and oxygen partially as oxygen gas (O_2) from the air. The remaining essential elements are obtained mainly from the soil. The availability of these nutrients is influenced either directly or indirectly by the presence of organic matter. The elements needed in large amounts—carbon, hydrogen, oxygen, nitrogen, phosphorus, potassium, calcium, magnesium, sulfur—are called macronutrients. The other elements, called micronutrients, are essential elements needed in small amounts. (Sodium [Na] helps many plants grow better, but it is not considered essential to plant growth and reproduction.)

Nutrients from decomposing organic matter. Most of the nutrients in soil organic matter can't be used by plants as long as those nutrients exist as part of large organic molecules. As soil organisms decompose organic matter, nutrients are converted into simpler, inorganic, or mineral forms that plants can easily use. This process, called mineralization, provides much of the nitrogen that plants need by converting it from organic forms. For example, proteins are converted to ammonium (NH_4^+) and then to nitrate (NO_3^-). Most plants will take up the majority of their nitrogen from soils in the form of nitrate. The mineralization of organic matter is also an important mechanism for supplying plants with such nutrients as phosphorus and sulfur and most of the

WHAT MAKES TOPSOIL?

Having a good amount of topsoil is important. But what gives topsoil its beneficial characteristics? Is it because it's on TOP? If we bring in a bulldozer and scrape off one foot of soil, will the exposed subsoil now be topsoil because it's on the surface? Of course, everyone knows that there's more to topsoil than its location on the soil surface. Most of the properties we associate with topsoil—good nutrient supply, tilth, drainage, aeration, water storage, etc.—are there because topsoil is rich in organic matter and contains a huge diversity of life.

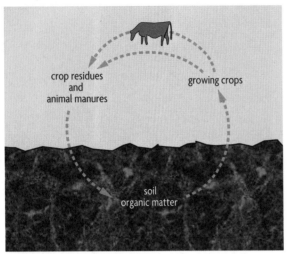

Figure 2.4. The cycle of plant nutrients.

micronutrients. This release of nutrients from organic matter by mineralization is part of a larger agricultural nutrient cycle (see figure 2.4). For a more detailed discussion of nutrient cycles and how they function in various cropping systems, see chapter 7.

Addition of nitrogen. Bacteria living in nodules on legume roots convert nitrogen from atmospheric gas (N_2) to forms that the plant can use directly. A number of free-living bacteria also fix nitrogen.

Storage of nutrients on soil organic matter. Decomposing organic matter can feed plants directly, but it also can indirectly benefit the nutrition of the

plant. A number of essential nutrients occur in soils as positively charged molecules called cations (pronounced cat-eye-ons). The ability of organic matter to hold on to cations in a way that keeps them available to plants is known as cation exchange capacity (CEC). Humus has many negative charges. Because opposite charges attract, humus is able to hold on to positively charged nutrients, such as calcium (Ca^{++}), potassium (K^+), and magnesium (Mg^{++}) (see figure 2.5a). This keeps them from leaching deep into the subsoil when water moves through the topsoil. Nutrients held in this way can be gradually released into the soil solution and made available to plants throughout the growing season. However, keep in mind that not all plant nutrients occur as cations. For example, the nitrate form of nitrogen is negatively charged (NO_3^-) and is actually repelled by the negatively charged CEC. Therefore, nitrate leaches easily as water moves down through the soil and beyond the root zone.

Clay particles also have negative charges on their surfaces (figure 2.5b), but organic matter may be the major source of negative charges for coarse and medium-textured soils. Some types of clays, such as those found in the southeastern United States and in the tropics, tend to have low amounts of negative charge. When those clays are present, organic matter may be the major source of negative charges that bind nutrients,

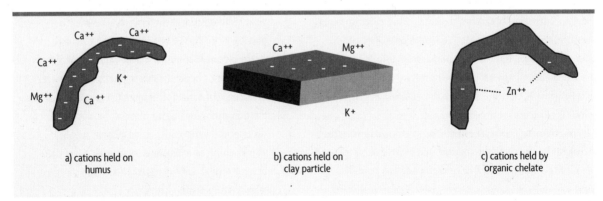

a) cations held on
humus

b) cations held on
clay particle

c) cations held by
organic chelate

Figure 2.5. Cations held on negatively charged organic matter and clay.

even for fine-textured (high-clay-content) soils.

Protection of nutrients by chelation. Organic molecules in the soil may also hold on to and protect certain nutrients. These particles, called "chelates" (pronounced key-lates) are by-products of the active decomposition of organic materials and are smaller than the particles that make up humus. In general, elements are held more strongly by chelates than by binding of positive and negative charges. Chelates work well because they bind the nutrient at more than one location on the organic molecule (figure 2.5c). In some soils, trace elements, such as iron, zinc, and manganese, would be converted to unavailable forms if they were not bound by chelates. It is not uncommon to find low-organic-matter soils or exposed subsoils deficient in these micronutrients.

Other ways of maintaining available nutrients. There is some evidence that organic matter in the soil can inhibit the conversion of available phosphorus to forms that are unavailable to plants. One explanation is that organic matter coats the surfaces of minerals that can bond tightly to phosphorus. Once these surfaces are covered, available forms of phosphorus are less likely to react with them. In addition, humic substances may chelate aluminum and iron, both of which can react with phosphorus in the soil solution. When they are held as chelates, these metals are unable to form an insoluble mineral with phosphorus.

Beneficial Effects of Soil Organisms

Soil organisms are essential for keeping plants well supplied with nutrients because they break down organic matter. These organisms make nutrients available by freeing them from organic molecules. Some bacteria fix nitrogen gas from the atmosphere, making it available to plants. Other organisms dissolve minerals and make phosphorus more available. If soil organisms aren't present and active, more fertilizers will be needed to supply plant nutrients.

ORGANIC MATTER INCREASES THE AVAILABILITY OF NUTRIENTS . . .

Directly

- As organic matter is decomposed, nutrients are converted into forms that plants can use directly.
- CEC is produced during the decomposition process, increasing the soil's ability to retain calcium, potassium, magnesium, and ammonium.
- Organic molecules are produced that hold and protect a number of micronutrients, such as zinc and iron.

Indirectly

- Substances produced by microorganisms promote better root growth and healthier roots, and with a larger and healthier root system plants are able to take in nutrients more easily.
- Organic matter contributes to greater amounts of water retention following rains because it improves soil structure and thereby improves water-holding capacity. This results in better plant growth and health and allows more movement of mobile nutrients (such as nitrates) to the root.

A varied community of organisms is your best protection against major pest outbreaks and soil fertility problems. A soil rich in organic matter and continually supplied with different types of fresh residues is home to a much more diverse group of organisms than soil depleted of organic matter. This greater diversity of organisms helps insure that fewer potentially harmful organisms will be able to develop sufficient populations to reduce crop yields.

Soil Tilth

When soil has a favorable physical condition for growing plants, it is said to have good *tilth*. Such a soil is porous and allows water to enter easily, instead of running off

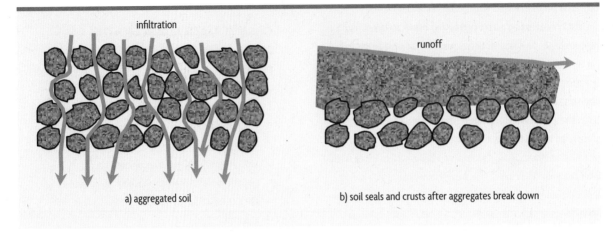

infiltration

runoff

a) aggregated soil

b) soil seals and crusts after aggregates break down

Figure 2.6. Changes in soil surface and water-flow pattern when seals and crusts develop.

the surface. More water is stored in the soil for plants to use between rains, and less erosion occurs. Good tilth also means that the soil is well aerated. Roots can easily obtain oxygen and get rid of carbon dioxide. A porous soil does not restrict root development and exploration. When a soil has poor tilth, the soil's structure deteriorates and soil aggregates break down, causing increased compaction and decreased aeration and water storage. A soil layer can become so compacted that roots can't grow. A soil with excellent physical properties will have numerous channels and pores of many different sizes.

Studies on both undisturbed and agricultural soils show that as organic matter increases, soils tend to be less compact and have more space for air passage and water storage. Sticky substances are produced during the decomposition of plant residues. Along with plant roots and fungal hyphae, they bind mineral particles together into clumps, or aggregates. In addition, the sticky secretions of mycorrhizal fungi—beneficial fungi that enter roots and help plants get more water and nutrients—are important binding material in soils. The arrangement and collection of minerals as aggregates and the degree of soil compaction have huge effects on plant growth (see chapters 5 and 6). The development of

aggregates is desirable in all types of soils because it promotes better drainage, aeration, and water storage. The one exception is for wetland crops, such as rice, when you want a dense, puddled soil to keep it flooded.

Organic matter, as residue on the soil surface or as a binding agent for aggregates near the surface, plays an important role in decreasing soil erosion. Surface residues intercept raindrops and decrease their potential to detach soil particles. These surface residues also slow water as it flows across the field, giving it a better chance to infiltrate into the soil. Aggregates and large channels greatly enhance the ability of soil to conduct water from the surface into the subsoil.

Most farmers can tell that one soil is better than another by looking at them, seeing how they work up when tilled, or even by sensing how they feel when walked on or touched. What they are seeing or sensing is really good tilth. For an example, see the photo on the back cover of this book. It shows that soil differences can be created by different management strategies. Farmers and gardeners would certainly rather grow their crops on the more porous soil depicted in the photo on the right.

Since erosion tends to remove the most fertile part of the soil, it can cause a significant reduction in crop yields. In some soils, the loss of just a few inches of top-soil may result in a yield reduction of 50%. The surface of some soils low in organic matter may seal over, or crust, as rainfall breaks down aggregates and pores near the surface fill with solids. When this happens, water that can't infiltrate into the soil runs off the field, carrying valuable topsoil (figure 2.6).

Large soil pores, or channels, are very important because of their ability to allow a lot of water to flow rapidly into the soil. Larger pores are formed in a number of ways. Old root channels may remain open for some time after the root decomposes. Larger soil organisms, such as insects and earthworms, create channels as they move through the soil. The mucus that earthworms secrete to keep their skin from drying out also helps to keep their channels open for a long time.

Protection of the Soil against Rapid Changes in Acidity

Acids and bases are released as minerals dissolve and organisms go about their normal functions of decomposing organic materials or fixing nitrogen. Acids or bases are excreted by the roots of plants, and acids form in the soil from the use of nitrogen fertilizers. It is best for plants if the soil acidity status, referred to as pH, does not swing too wildly during the season. The pH scale is a way of expressing the amount of free hydrogen (H^+) in the soil water. More acidic conditions, with greater amounts of hydrogen, are indicated by lower numbers. A soil at pH 4 is very acid. Its solution is ten times more acid than a soil at pH 5. A soil at pH 7 is neutral—there is just as much base in the water as there is acid. Most crops do best when the soil is slightly acid and the pH is around 6 to 7. Essential nutrients are more available to plants in this pH range than when soils are either more acidic or more basic. Soil organic matter is able to slow down, or buffer, changes in pH by taking free hydrogen out of solution as acids are produced or by giving off hydrogen as bases are produced. (For discussion about management of acidic soils, see chapter 20.)

Figure 2.7. Corn grown in nutrient solution with (right) and without (left) humic acids. Photo by R. Bartlett. In this experiment by Rich Bartlett adding humic acids to a nutrient solution increased the growth of tomatoes and corn as well as the amount and branching of roots.

Stimulation of Root Development

Microorganisms in soils produce numerous substances that stimulate plant growth. Humus itself has a directly beneficial effect on plants (figure 2.7). The reason for this stimulation has been found mainly to be due to making micronutrients more available to plants—causing roots to grow longer and have more branches, resulting in larger and healthier plants. In addition, many soil microorganisms produce a variety of root-stimulating substances that behave as plant hormones.

Darkening of the Soil

Organic matter tends to darken soils. You can easily see this in coarse-textured sandy soils containing light-colored minerals. Under well-drained conditions, a darker soil surface allows a soil to warm up a little faster in the spring. This provides a slight advantage for seed germination and the early stages of seedling development, which is often beneficial in cold regions.

Protection against Harmful Chemicals

Some naturally occurring chemicals in soils can harm plants. For example, aluminum is an important part of many soil minerals and, as such, poses no threat to

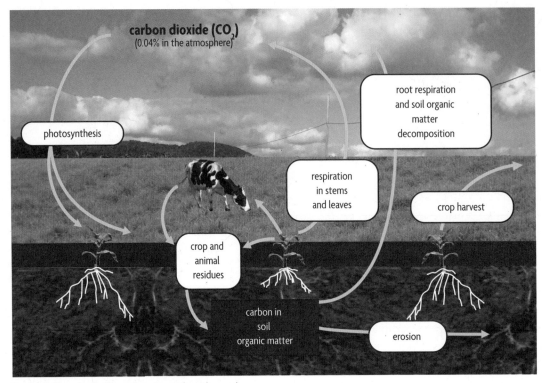

Figure 2.8. The role of soil organic matter in the carbon cycle.

plants. As soils become more acidic, especially at pH levels below 5.5, aluminum becomes soluble. Some soluble forms of aluminum, if present in the soil solution, are toxic to plant roots. However, in the presence of significant quantities of soil organic matter, the aluminum is bound tightly and will not do as much damage.

Organic matter is the single most important soil property that reduces pesticide leaching. It holds tightly on to a number of pesticides. This prevents or reduces leaching of these chemicals into groundwater and allows time for detoxification by microbes. Microorganisms can change the chemical structure of some pesticides, industrial oils, many petroleum products (gas and oils), and other potentially toxic chemicals, rendering them harmless.

ORGANIC MATTER AND NATURAL CYCLES
The Carbon Cycle

Soil organic matter plays a significant part in a number of global cycles. People have become more interested in the carbon cycle because the buildup of carbon dioxide in the atmosphere is thought to cause global warming. Carbon dioxide is also released to the atmosphere when fuels, such as gas, oil, and wood, are burned. A simple version of the natural carbon cycle, showing the role of soil organic matter, is given in figure 2.8. Carbon dioxide is removed from the atmosphere by plants and used to make all the organic molecules necessary for life. Sunlight provides plants with the energy they need to carry out this process. Plants, as well as the animals feeding on plants, release carbon dioxide back into the

COLOR AND ORGANIC MATTER

In Illinois, a hand-held chart has been developed to allow people to estimate percent of soil organic matter. Their darkest soils—almost black—indicate from 3.5 to 7% organic matter. A dark brown soil indicates 2 to 3%, and a yellowish brown soil indicates 1.5 to 2.5% organic matter. (Color may not be as clearly related to organic matter in all regions, because the amount of clay and the types of minerals also influence soil color.)

atmosphere as they use organic molecules for energy.

The largest amount of carbon present on the land is not in the living plants, but in soil organic matter. That is rarely mentioned in discussions of the carbon cycle. More carbon is stored in soils than in all plants, all animals, and the atmosphere combined. Soil organic matter contains an estimated four times as much carbon as living plants. In fact, carbon stored in all the world's soils is over three times the amount in the atmosphere. As soil organic matter is depleted, it becomes a source of carbon dioxide for the atmosphere. Also, when forests are cleared and burned, a large amount of carbon dioxide is released. A secondary, often larger, flush of carbon dioxide is emitted from soil from the rapid depletion of soil organic matter, following conversion of forests to agricultural practices. There is as much carbon in six inches of soil with 1% organic matter as there is in the atmosphere above a field. If organic matter decreases from 3% to 2%, the amount of carbon dioxide in the atmosphere could double. (Of course, wind and diffusion move the carbon dioxide to other parts of the globe.)

The Nitrogen Cycle

Another important global process in which organic matter plays a major role is the nitrogen cycle. It is of direct importance in agriculture, because there is frequently not enough available nitrogen in soils for plants to grow their best. Figure 2.9 shows the nitrogen cycle and how soil organic matter enters into the cycle. Some bacteria living in soils are able to "fix" nitrogen, converting nitrogen gas to forms that other organisms, including crop plants, can use. Inorganic forms of nitrogen, like ammonium and nitrate, exist in the atmosphere naturally, although air pollution causes higher amounts than normal. Rainfall and snow deposit inorganic nitrogen forms on the soil. Inorganic nitrogen also may be added in the form of commercial nitrogen fertilizers. These fertilizers are derived from nitrogen gas in the atmosphere through an industrial fixation process.

Almost all of the nitrogen in soils exists as part of the organic matter, in forms that plants are not able to use as their main nitrogen source. Bacteria and fungi convert the organic forms of nitrogen into ammonium, and different bacteria convert ammonium into nitrate. Both nitrate and ammonium can be used by plants.

Nitrogen can be lost from a soil in a number of ways. When crops are removed from fields, nitrogen and other nutrients also are removed. The nitrate (NO_3^-) form of nitrogen leaches readily from soils and may end up in groundwater at higher concentrations than may be safe for drinking. Organic forms of nitrate as well as nitrate and ammonium (NH_4^+) may be lost by runoff water and erosion. Once freed from soil organic matter, nitrogen may be converted to forms that end up back in the atmosphere. Bacteria convert nitrate to nitrogen (N_2) and nitrous oxide (N_2O) gases in a process called denitrification, which occurs in saturated soils. Nitrous oxide (also a "greenhouse gas") contributes strongly to global warming. In addition, when it reaches the upper atmosphere, it decreases ozone levels that protect the earth's surface from the harmful effects of ultraviolet (UV) radiation. So if you needed another reason not to

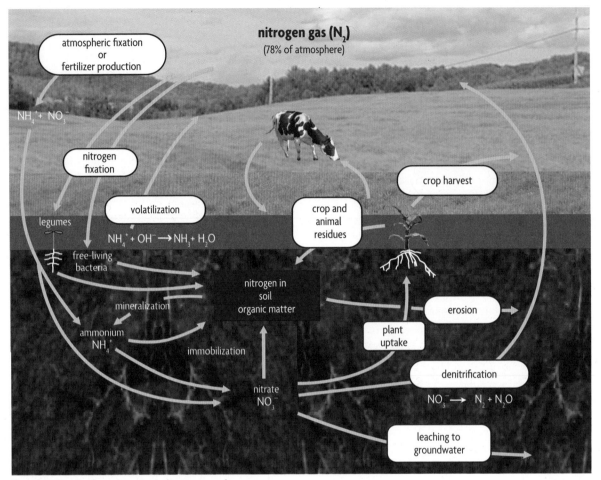

Figure 2.9. The role of organic matter in the nitrogen cycle.

apply excessive rates of nitrogen fertilizers or manures—in addition to the economic costs and the pollution of ground and surface waters—the possible formation of nitrous oxide should make you cautious.

The Water Cycle

Organic matter plays an important part in the local, regional, and global water cycles due to its role in promoting water infiltration into soils and storage within the soil. The water cycle is also referred to as the *hydrologic* cycle. Water evaporates from the soil surface and from living plant leaves as well as from the ocean and lakes. Water then returns to the earth, usually far from where it evaporated, as rain and snow. Soils high in organic matter, with excellent tilth, enhance the rapid infiltration of rainwater into the soil. This water may be available for plants to use or it may percolate deep into the subsoil and help to recharge the groundwater supply. Since groundwater is commonly used as a drinking water source for homes and for irrigation, recharging groundwater is important. When the soil's organic matter level is depleted, it is less able to accept water, and high levels of runoff and erosion result. This means less water for plants and decreased groundwater recharge.

VALUE OF SOIL ORGANIC MATTER

It is very difficult, if not impossible, to come up with a meaningful monetary value for the worth of organic matter in our soils. It positively affects so many different properties that taking them all into account and figuring out their dollar value is an enormous task. One study published in 2004 estimated the value of nitrogen contributions and the added water availability from increased organic matter. In 2008 dollars, their estimates for just those two aspects would amount to about $20 per acre per year for every extra percent of organic matter.

SUMMARY

Soil organic matter is the key to building and maintaining healthy soils because it has such great positive influences on essentially all soil properties—helping to grow healthier plants. It also plays a critical role in the water, nitrogen, and carbon cycles. Organic matter consists mainly of the living organisms in the soil ("the living"), the fresh residue ("the dead"), and the very well decomposed (or burned) material ("the very dead"). Each of these types of organic matter plays an important role in maintaining healthy soils.

SOURCES

Allison, F.E. 1973. *Soil Organic Matter and Its Role in Crop Production*. Amsterdam: Scientific Publishing Co.

Brady, N.C., and R.R. Weil. 2008. *The Nature and Properties of Soils*, 14th ed. Upper Saddle River, NJ: Prentice Hall.

Follett, R.F., J.W.B. Stewart, and C.V. Cole, eds. 1987. *Soil Fertility and Organic Matter as Critical Components of Production Systems*. Special Publication No. 19. Madison, WI: Soil Science Society of America.

Lehmann, J., D.C. Kern, B. Glaser, and W.I. Woods, eds. 2003. *Amazonian Dark Earths: Origin, Properties, Management*. Dordrecht, Netherlands: Kluwer Academic Publishing.

Lehmann, J., and M. Rondon. 2006. Bio-char soil management on highly weathered soils in the humid tropics. In *Biological Approaches to Sustainable Soil Systems*, ed. N. Uphoff et al., pp. 517–530. Boca Raton, FL: CRC Press.

Lucas, R.E., J.B. Holtman, and J.L. Connor. 1977. Soil carbon dynamics and cropping practices. In *Agriculture and Energy*, ed. W. Lockeretz, pp. 333–451. New York: Academic Press. See this source for the Michigan study on the relationship between soil organic matter levels and crop-yield potential.

Manlay, R.J., C. Feller, and M.J. Swift. 2007. Historical evolution of soil organic matter concepts and their relationships with the fertility and sustainability of cropping systems. *Agriculture, Ecosystems and Environment* 119: 217–233.

Oshins, C., and L. Drinkwater. 1999. *An Introduction to Soil Health*. A slide set available at the Northeast Region SARE website: www.uvm.edu/~nesare/slide.html.

Powers, R.F., and K. Van Cleve. 1991. Long-term ecological research in temperate and boreal forest ecosystems. *Agronomy Journal* 83: 11–24. This reference compares the relative amounts of carbon in soils with that in plants.

Stevenson, F.J. 1986. *Cycles of Soil: Carbon, Nitrogen, Phosphorus, Sulfur, Micronutrients*. New York: John Wiley & Sons. This reference compares the amount of carbon in soils with that in plants.

Strickling, E. 1975. Crop sequences and tillage in efficient crop production. *Abstracts of the 1975 Northeast Branch American Society Agronomy Meetings*, pp. 20–29. See this source for the Maryland experiment relating soil organic matter to corn yield.

Tate, R.L., III. 1987. *Soil Organic Matter: Biological and Ecological Effects*. New York: John Wiley & Sons.

Weil, R., and F. Magdoff. 2004. Significance of soil organic matter to soil quality and health. In *Soil Organic Matter in Sustainable Agriculture*, ed. F. Magdoff and R. Weil, pp. 1–43. Boca Raton, FL: CRC Press.

Chapter 3

AMOUNT OF ORGANIC MATTER IN SOILS

*The depletion of the soil humus supply is apt to be
a fundamental cause of lowered crop yields.*

—J.H. HILLS, C.H. JONES, AND C. CUTLER, 1908

The amount of organic matter in any particular soil is the result of a wide variety of environmental, soil, and agronomic influences. Some of these, such as climate and soil texture, are naturally occurring. Agricultural practices also influence soil organic matter levels. Tillage, crop rotation, and manuring practices all can have profound effects on the amount of soil organic matter. Hans Jenny carried out pioneering work on the effect of natural influences on soil organic matter levels in the U.S. more than sixty years ago.

The amount of organic matter in a soil is the result of all the additions and losses of organic matter that have occurred over the years (figure 3.1). In this chapter, we will look at why different soils have different organic matter levels. While we will be looking mainly at the total amount of organic matter, keep in mind that all three "types" of organic matter—the living, dead, and very dead—serve critical roles and the amount of each of these may be affected differently by natural factors and agricultural practices.

Anything that adds large amounts of organic residues to a soil may increase organic matter. On the other hand, anything that causes soil organic matter to decompose more rapidly or be lost through erosion may deplete organic matter.

Figure 3.1. Additions and losses of organic matter from soils.

STORAGE OF ORGANIC MATTER IN SOIL

Organic matter is protected in soils by:

- Formation of strong chemical organic matter—clay (and fine silt) bonds
- Being inside small aggregates (physically protected)
- Conversion into stable substances such as humic materials that are resistant to biological decomposition
- Restricted drainage, sometimes related to texture, that reduces the activity of the organisms that need oxygen to function
- Char produced by incomplete burning

Large aggregates are made up of many smaller ones that are held together by sticky substances and fungal hyphae. Organic matter in large aggregates—but outside of the small aggregates that make up the larger ones—and freely occurring particulate organic matter (the "dead") are available for soil organisms to use. However, poor aeration resulting from restricted drainage because of a dense subsurface layer, compaction, or being in the bottom of a slope may cause a low rate of use of the organic matter. So the organic matter needs to be in a favorable chemical form and physical location for organisms to use it; *plus,* the environmental conditions in the soil—adequate moisture *and* aeration—need to be sufficient for most soil organisms to use the residues and thrive.

If additions are greater than losses, organic matter increases. When additions are less than losses, there is a depletion of soil organic matter. When the system is in balance and additions equal losses, the quantity of soil organic matter doesn't change over the years.

NATURAL FACTORS

Temperature

In the United States, it is easy to see how temperature affects soil organic matter levels. Traveling from north to south, higher average temperatures lead to less soil organic matter. As the climate gets warmer, two things tend to happen (as long as rainfall is sufficient): More vegetation is produced because the growing season is longer, and the rate of decomposition of organic materials in soils increases because soil organisms work more rapidly and are active for longer periods of the year at higher temperatures. Faster decomposition with warmer temperatures becomes the dominant influence determining soil organic matter levels.

Rainfall

Soils in arid climates usually have low amounts of organic matter. In a very dry climate, such as a desert, there is little growth of vegetation. Decomposition is also low because of low amounts of organic inputs and low microorganism activity when the soil is dry. When it finally rains, a very rapid burst of decomposition of soil organic matter occurs. Soil organic matter levels generally increase as average annual precipitation increases. With more rainfall, more water is available to plants, and more plant growth results. As rainfall increases, more residues return to the soil from grasses or trees. At the same time, soils in high rainfall areas may have less organic matter decomposition than well-aerated soils—decomposition is slowed by restricted aeration.

Soil Texture

Fine-textured soils, containing high percentages of clay and silt, tend to have naturally higher amounts of soil organic matter than coarse-textured sands or sandy loams. The organic matter content of sands may be less than 1%; loams may have 2% to 3%, and clays from 4% to more than 5%. The strong chemical bonds that develop between organic matter and clay and fine silt protect organic molecules from attack and decomposition by microorganisms and their enzymes. Also, clay and fine silt combine with organic matter to form very small aggregates that in turn protect the organic matter inside from organisms and their enzymes. In addition, fine-textured soils tend to have smaller pores and less oxygen than coarser soils. This also limits decomposition rates, one of the reasons that organic matter levels in fine-textured soils are higher than in sands and loams.

Soil Drainage and Position in the Landscape

Decomposition of organic matter occurs more slowly in poorly aerated soils. In addition, some major plant compounds such as lignin will not decompose at all in anaerobic environments. For this reason, organic matter tends to accumulate in wet soil environments. When conditions are extremely wet or swampy for a very long period of time, organic (peat or muck) soils, with organic matter contents of over 20%, develop. When these soils are artificially drained for agricultural or other uses, the soil organic matter will decompose rapidly. When this happens, the elevation of the soil surface actually decreases. Homeowners on organic soils in Florida normally sink the corner posts of their houses below the organic level to provide stability. Originally level with the ground, some of those homes now perch on posts atop a soil surface that has decreased so dramatically that the owners can park their cars under their homes.

Soils in depressions at the bottom of hills receive runoff, sediments (including organic matter), and seepage from upslope and tend to accumulate more organic matter than drier soils farther upslope. In contrast, soils on a steep slope or knoll will tend to have low amounts of organic matter because the topsoil is continually eroded.

Type of Vegetation

The type of plants that grow on the soil as it forms can be an important source of natural variation in soil organic matter levels. Soils that form under grassland vegetation generally contain more organic matter and a deeper distribution of organic matter than soils that form under forest vegetation. This is probably a result of the deep and extensive root systems of grassland species (figure 3.2). Their roots have high "turnover"

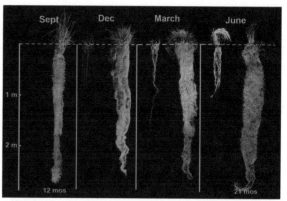

Figure 3.2. Root systems of annual wheat (at left in each panel) and wheatgrass, a perennial, at four times of the year. Approximately 25% to 40% of the wheatgrass root system dies back each year, adding considerable amounts of organic matter, and then grows back again. Compared to annual wheat, it has a longer growing season and has much more growth both above ground and below ground. Wheatgrass was 12 and 21 months old when the first and last photos were taken. Photo by the Land Institute.

rates, for root death and decomposition constantly occur as new roots are formed. Dry natural grasslands also frequently experience slow-burning fires from lightning strikes, which contribute biochar that is very resistant to degradation. The high levels of organic matter in soils that were once in grassland partly explain why these are now some of the most productive agricultural soils in the world. By contrast, in forests, litter accumulates on top of the soil, and surface organic layers commonly contain over 50% organic matter. However, subsurface mineral layers in forest soils typically contain less than 2% organic matter.

Acidic Soil Conditions

In general, soil organic matter decomposition is slower under acidic soil conditions than at a more neutral pH. In addition, acidic conditions, by inhibiting earthworm activity, encourage organic matter to accumulate at the soil surface, rather than distributing throughout the soil layers.

ROOT VS. ABOVEGROUND RESIDUE CONTRIBUTION TO SOIL ORGANIC MATTER

Roots, already being well distributed and in intimate contact with the soil, tend to contribute a higher percentage of their weight to the more persistent organic matter ("dead" and "very dead") than above-ground residues. In addition, compared to aboveground plant parts, many crop roots have higher amounts of materials such as lignin that decompose relatively slowly. One experiment with oats found that only one-third of the surface residue remained after one year, while 42% of the root organic matter remained in the soil and was the main contributor to particulate organic matter. In another experiment, five months after spring incorporation of hairy vetch, 13% of the aboveground carbon remained in the soil, while close to 50% of the root-derived carbon was still present. Both experiments found that the root residue contributed much more to particulate organic matter (active, or "dead") than did aboveground residue.

HUMAN INFLUENCES

Loss of topsoil that is rich in organic matter by erosion has dramatically reduced the total amount of organic matter stored in many soils after they were developed for agriculture. Crop production obviously suffers when part of the most fertile layer of the soil is removed. Erosion is a natural process and occurs on almost all soils. Some soils naturally erode more easily than others, and the problem is greater in some regions than others. However, agricultural practices accelerate erosion. It is estimated that erosion in the United States is responsible for annual losses of about a billion dollars in available nutrients and many times more in total soil nutrients.

Unless erosion is severe, a farmer may not even realize a problem exists. But that doesn't mean that crop yields are unaffected. In fact, yields may decrease by 5% to 10% when only moderate erosion occurs. Yields may suffer a decrease of 10–20% or more with severe erosion. The results of a study of three midwestern soils (referred to as Corwin, Miami, and Morley), shown in table 3.1, indicate that erosion greatly influences both organic matter levels and water-holding ability. Greater amounts of erosion decreased the organic matter content of these loamy and clayey soils. In addition, eroded soils stored less available water than minimally eroded soils.

Organic matter also is lost from soils when organisms decompose more organic materials during the year than are added. This occurs as a result of practices that accelerate decomposition, such as intensive tillage and crop production systems that return low amounts of residues. Much of the rapid loss of organic matter following the conversion of grasslands to agriculture has been attributed to large reductions in residue inputs, accelerated mineralization of organic matter because of plowing, and erosion.

Tillage Practices

Tillage practices influence both the amount of topsoil erosion and the rate of decomposition of organic matter. Conventional plowing and disking of a soil to prepare a smooth seedbed break down natural soil aggregates and

Table 3.1
Effects of Erosion on Soil Organic Matter and Water

Soil	Erosion	Organic Matter (%)	Available Water Capacity (%)
Corwin	slight	3.03	12.9
	moderate	2.51	9.8
	severe	1.86	6.6
Miami	slight	1.89	16.6
	moderate	1.64	11.5
	severe	1.51	4.8
Morley	slight	1.91	7.4
	moderate	1.76	6.2
	severe	1.60	3.6

Source: Schertz et al. (1985).

destroy large, water-conducting channels. The soil is left in a physical condition that is highly susceptible to wind and water erosion.

The more a soil is disturbed by tillage practices, the greater the potential breakdown of organic matter by soil organisms. During the early years of agriculture in the United States, when colonists cleared the forests and planted crops in the East and farmers later moved to the Midwest to plow the grasslands, soil organic matter decreased rapidly. In fact, the soils were literally mined of this valuable resource. In the Northeast and Southeast, it was quickly recognized that fertilizers and soil amendments were needed to maintain soil productivity. In the Midwest, the deep, rich soils of the tall-grass prairies were able to maintain their productivity for a long time despite accelerated loss of soil organic matter and significant amounts of erosion. The reason for this was their unusually high reserves of soil organic matter and nutrients at the time of conversion to cropland.

Rapid decomposition of organic matter by organisms usually occurs when a soil is intensively tilled. Incorporating residues with a moldboard plow, breaking aggregates open, and fluffing up the soil allow microorganisms to work more rapidly. It's something like opening up the air intake on a wood stove, which lets in more oxygen and causes the fire to burn hotter. In Vermont, we found a 20% decrease in organic matter after five years of growing corn on a clay soil that had previously been in sod for decades. In the Midwest, many soils lost 50% of their organic matter within forty years of beginning cropping. Rapid loss of soil organic matter occurs in the early years because of the high initial amount of active ("dead") organic matter available to microorganisms. After much of the active portion is lost, the rate of loss slows and what remains is mainly the already well-decomposed "passive" or "very dead" materials. With the current interest in reduced (conservation) tillage, growing row crops in the future should not have such a detrimental effect on soil organic matter. Conservation tillage practices leave more residues on the surface and cause less soil disturbance than conventional moldboard plow–and–disk tillage. In fact, soil organic matter levels usually increase when no-till planters place seeds in a narrow band of disturbed soil, leaving the soil between planting rows undisturbed. Residues accumulate on the surface because the soil is not inverted by plowing. Earthworm populations increase, taking some of the organic matter deeper into the soil and creating channels that also help water infiltrate into the soil. The beneficial effects of minimizing tillage on soil organic matter levels are often observed quickly at the soil surface; but deeper changes are much slower to develop, and depletion at depth is sometimes observed. In the upper Midwest there is conflicting evidence as to whether a long-term no-till approach results in greater accumulation of soil organic matter (SOM) than a conventional tillage system when the full profile is considered. In contrast, significant increases in profile SOM have been routinely observed under no-till in warmer locations.

Crop Rotations and Cover Crops

Levels of soil organic matter may fluctuate during the different stages of a crop rotation. SOM may decrease, then increase, then decrease, and so forth. While annual row crops under conventional moldboard-plow cultivation usually result in decreased soil organic matter, perennial legumes, grasses, and legume-grass forage crops tend to increase soil organic matter. The high amount of root production by hay and pasture crops, plus the lack of soil disturbance, causes organic matter to accumulate in the soil. This effect is seen in the comparison of organic matter increases when growing alfalfa compared to corn silage (figure 3.3). In addition, different types of crops result in different quantities of residues being returned to the soil. When corn grain is harvested, more residues are left in the field than after soybeans, wheat, potatoes, or lettuce harvests. Harvesting the same crop in different ways leaves

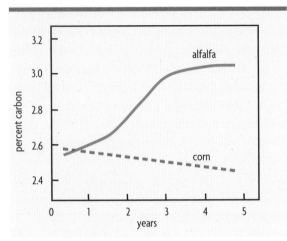

Figure 3.3. Organic carbon changes when growing corn silage or alfalfa. Redrawn from Angers (1992).

different amounts of residues. When corn grain is harvested, more residues remain in the field than when the entire plant is harvested for silage or stover is used for purposes like bioenergy (figure 3.4).

Soil erosion is greatly reduced and topsoil rich in organic matter is conserved when rotation crops, such as grass or legume hay, are grown year-round. The permanent soil cover and extensive root systems of sod crops account for much of the reduction in erosion.

Having sod crops as part of a rotation reduces loss of topsoil, decreases decomposition of residues, and builds up organic matter by the extensive residue addition of plant roots.

Use of Synthetic Nitrogen Fertilizer

Fertilizing very nutrient-deficient soils usually results in greater crop yields. A fringe benefit of this is a greater amount of crop residue—roots, stems, and leaves—resulting from larger and healthier plants. However, nitrogen fertilizer has commonly been applied at much higher rates than needed by plants, frequently by as much as 50%. Evidence is accumulating that having extra mineral nitrogen in soils actually helps organisms better decompose crop residues—resulting in decreased levels of soil organic matter. (See chapter 19 for a detailed discussion of nitrogen management.)

Use of Organic Amendments

An old practice that helps maintain or increase soil organic matter is to apply manures or other organic residues generated off the field. A study in Vermont during the 1960s and 1970s found that between 20 and 30 tons (wet weight, including straw or sawdust bedding)

a) corn silage

b) corn grain

Figure 3.4. Soil surface after harvest of corn silage or corn grain. Photos by Bill Jokela and Doug Karlen.

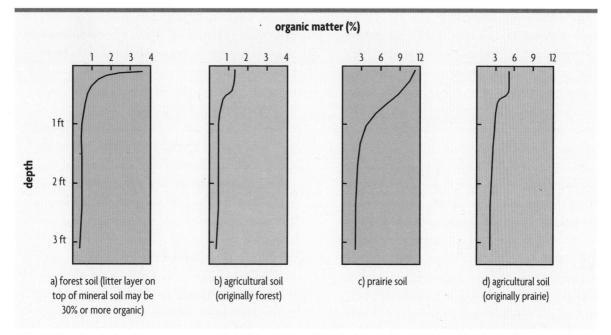

Figure 3.5. Examples of soil organic matter content with depth (note different scales for forest and prairie soils). Modified from Brady and Weil (2008).

of dairy manure per acre were needed to maintain soil organic matter levels when silage corn was grown each year. This is equivalent to one or one and a half times the amount produced by a large Holstein cow over the whole year. Varying types of manure—like bedded, liquid stored, digested, etc.—can produce very different effects on soil organic matter and nutrient availability. Manures differ in their initial composition and also are affected by how they are stored and handled in the field—for example, surface applied or incorporated.

ORGANIC MATTER DISTRIBUTION IN SOIL
With Depth in the Soil

In general, more organic matter is present near the surface than deeper in the soil (see figure 3.5). This is one of the main reasons that topsoils are more productive than subsoils exposed by erosion or mechanical removal of surface soil layers. Some of the plant residues that eventually become part of the soil organic matter are from the aboveground portion of plants. In most cases,

plant roots are believed to contribute more to a soil's organic matter than the crop's shoots and leaves. But when the plant dies or sheds leaves or branches, depositing residues on the surface, earthworms and insects help incorporate the residues on the surface deeper into the soil. The highest concentrations of organic matter, however, remain within 1 foot of the surface.

Litter layers that commonly develop on the surface of forest soils may have very high organic matter contents (figure 3.5a). Plowing forest soils after removal of the trees incorporates the litter layers into the mineral soil. The incorporated litter decomposes rapidly, and an agricultural soil derived from a sandy forest soil in the North or a silt loam in the South would likely have a distribution of organic matter similar to that indicated in figure 3.5b. Soils of the tall-grass prairies have a deeper distribution of organic matter (see figure 3.5c). After cultivation of these soils for 50 years, far less organic matter remains (figure 3.5d).

Organic Matter and Aggregates

Organic matter occurs outside of aggregates as living roots or larger organisms or pieces of residue from a past harvest. Some organic matter is even more intimately associated with soil. Humic materials may be adsorbed onto clay and small silt particles, and small to medium-size aggregates usually contain particles of organic matter. The organic matter inside very small aggregates is physically protected from decomposition because microorganisms and their enzymes can't reach inside. This organic matter also attaches to mineral particles and thereby makes the small particles stick together better. The larger soil aggregates, composed of many smaller ones, are held together primarily by the hyphae of fungi with their sticky secretions, by sticky substances produced by other microorganisms, and by roots and their secretions. Microorganisms are also found in very small pores within larger aggregates. This can sometimes protect them from their larger predators—paramecium, amoeba, and nematodes.

There is an interrelationship between the amount of fines (silt and clay) in a soil and the amount of organic matter needed to produce stable aggregates. The higher the clay and silt content, the more organic matter is needed to produce stable aggregates, because more is needed to occupy the surface sites on the minerals during the process of organic matter accumulation. In order to have more than half of the soil composed of water-stable aggregates, a soil with 50% clay may need twice as much organic matter as a soil with 10% clay.

ACTIVE ORGANIC MATTER

Most of the discussion in this chapter so far has been about the factors that control the quantity and location of total organic matter in soils. However, we should keep in mind that we are also interested in balancing the different types of organic matter in soils—the living, the dead (active), and the very dead (humus). We don't want just a lot of humus in soil, we also want a lot of active organic matter to provide nutrients and aggregating glues when it decomposes. It also supplies food to keep a diverse population of organisms present. As mentioned earlier, when forest or grassland soils were first cultivated, organic matter decreased rapidly. Almost the entire decline in organic matter was due to a loss of the active ("dead") part of the organic matter. Although it decreases fastest when intensive tillage is used, the active portion increases relatively quickly when practices such as reduced tillage, rotations, cover crops, and applying manures and composts are used to increase soil organic matter.

AMOUNTS OF *LIVING* ORGANIC MATTER

In chapter 4, we discuss the various types of organisms that live in soils. The weight of fungi present in forest soils is much greater than the weight of bacteria. In grasslands, however, there are about equal weights of the two. In agricultural soils that are routinely tilled, the weight of fungi is less than the weight of bacteria. The loss of surface residues with tillage lowers the number of surface-feeding organisms. And as soils become more compact, larger pores are eliminated first. To give some perspective, a soil pore that is 1/20 of an inch is considered large. These are the pores in which soil animals, such as earthworms and beetles, live and function, so the number of such organisms in compacted soils decreases. Plant root tips are generally about 0.1 mm (1/250 of an inch) in diameter, and very compacted soils that lost pores greater than that size have serious rooting problems. The elimination of smaller pores and the loss of some of the network of small pores with even more compaction is a problem for even small soil organisms.

The total amounts (weights) of living organisms vary in different cropping systems. In general, soil organisms are more abundant and diverse in systems with complex rotations that return more diverse crop residues and that use other organic materials such as cover crops, animal manures, and composts. Leaves and grass clippings may be an important source of organic residues for gardeners. When crops are rotated regularly, fewer parasite, disease, weed, and insect problems occur than when the same crop is grown year after year.

On the other hand, frequent cultivation reduces the populations of many soil organisms as their food supplies are depleted by decomposition of organic matter. Compaction from heavy equipment also causes harmful biological effects in soils. It decreases the number of medium to large pores, which reduces the volume of soil available for air, water, and populations of organisms—such as mites and springtails—that need the large spaces in which to live.

HOW MUCH ORGANIC MATTER IS ENOUGH?

As mentioned earlier, soils with higher levels of fine silt and clay usually have higher levels of organic matter than those with a sandier texture. However, unlike plant nutrients or pH levels, there are few accepted guidelines for adequate organic matter content in particular agricultural soils. We do know some general guidelines. For example, 2% organic matter in a sandy soil is very good and difficult to reach, but in a clay soil 2% indicates a greatly depleted situation. The complexity of soil organic matter composition, including biological diversity of organisms, as well as the actual organic chemicals present, means that there is no simple interpretation for total soil organic matter tests. We also know that soils higher in silt and clay need more organic matter to produce sufficient water-stable aggregates to protect soil from erosion and compaction. For example, to have an aggregation similar to that of a soil with 16% clay and 2% organic matter, a soil with close to 50% clay may need around 6% organic matter.

Organic matter accumulation takes place slowly and is difficult to detect in the short term by measurements of total soil organic matter. However, even if you do not greatly increase soil organic matter (and it might

> *The question will be raised, How much organic matter should be assigned to the soil? No general formula can be given. Soils vary widely in character and quality. Some can endure a measure of organic deprivation . . . others cannot. On slopes, strongly erodible soils, or soils that have been eroded already, require more input than soils on level lands.*
>
> —Hans Jenny, 1980

take years to know how much of an effect is occurring), improved management practices such as adding organic materials, creating better rotations, and reducing tillage will help maintain the levels currently in the soil. And, perhaps more important, continuously adding a variety of residues results in plentiful supplies of "dead" organic matter—the relatively fresh particulate organic matter—that helps maintain soil health by providing food for soil organisms and promoting the formation of soil aggregates. A recently developed soil test that oxidizes part of the organic matter is thought to provide a measure of active carbon. It is more sensitive to soil management than total organic matter and is thereby an earlier indicator for soil health improvement. Interpretation of the test is currently an active research area. (See chapter 22.)

THE DYNAMICS OF RAISING AND MAINTAINING SOIL ORGANIC MATTER LEVELS

It is not easy to dramatically increase the organic matter content of soils or to maintain elevated levels once they are reached. It requires a sustained effort that includes a number of approaches that add organic materials to soils and minimize losses. It is especially difficult to raise the organic matter content of soils that are very well aerated, such as coarse sands, because the potential for aggregation (which protects particles of organic matter) is limited, as are the fine minerals that form protective bonds with organic matter. Soil organic matter levels can be maintained with lower additions of organic residues in high-clay-content soils with restricted aeration than in coarse-textured soils because of the slower decomposition. Organic matter can be increased much more readily in soils that have become depleted of organic matter than in soils that already have a good amount of organic matter with respect to their texture and drainage condition.

When you change practices on a soil depleted in organic matter, perhaps one that has been intensively row-cropped for years and has lost a lot of its original aggregation, organic matter will increase slowly, as diagrammed in figure 3.6. At first any free mineral surfaces that are available for forming bonds with organic matter will form organic-mineral bonds. Small aggregates will also form around particles of organic matter. Then larger aggregates will form, made up of the smaller aggregates and held by a variety of means—frequently by mycorrhizal fungi and small roots. Once all possible

mineral sites have been occupied by organic molecules and all of the small aggregates have been formed around organic matter particles, organic matter accumulates mainly as free particles—within the larger aggregates or completely unaffiliated with minerals. This is referred to as free particulate organic matter. After you have followed similar soil-building practices (for example, cover cropping or applying manures) for some years, the soil will come into equilibrium with your management and the total amount of soil organic matter will not change from year to year. In a sense, the soil is "saturated" with organic matter as long as your practices don't change. All the sites that protect organic matter (chemical bonding sites on clays and physically protected sites inside small aggregates) are occupied, and only free particles of organic matter (POM) can accumulate. But because there is little protection for the free POM, it tends to decompose relatively rapidly under normal (oxydized) conditions.

When management practices are used that deplete organic matter, the reverse of what is depicted in figure 3.6 occurs. First free POM is depleted, and then as aggregates are broken down physically protected organic matter becomes available to decomposers. What usually remains after many years of soil-depleting practices is the organic matter that is tightly held by clay mineral particles.

Assuming that the same management pattern has occurred for many years, a fairly simple model can be used to estimate the percent of organic matter in a soil. It allows us to see interesting trends that reflect the real world. To use this model you need to assume reasonable values for rates of addition of organic materials and SOM decomposition rates in the soil. Without going through the details (see the appendix, p. 34, for sample calculations), the estimated percent of organic matter in soils for various combinations of addition and decomposition rates indicates some dramatic differences (table 3.2). It takes about 5,000 pounds of organic residues added annually to a sandy loam soil (with an estimated decomposition rate of 3% per year) to result eventually

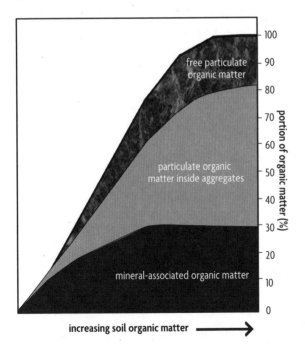

Figure 3.6. Organic matter changes in soil as practices favoring buildup are implemented. Redrawn and modified from Angers (1992).

Table 3.2
Estimated Levels of Soil Organic Matter after Many Years with Various Rates of Decomposition (Mineralization) and Residue Additions*

Annual organic material additions	Added to soil if 20% remains after one year	Annual rate of SOM decomposition (%)				
		Fine textured, poorly drained		⟵⟶	Coarse textured, well drained	
		1	2	3	4	5
-----lbs per acre per year-----		-----final % organic matter in soil -----				
2,500	500	2.5	1.3	0.8	0.6	0.5
5,000	1,000	5.0	2.5	1.7	1.3	1.0
7,500	1,500	7.5	3.8	2.5	1.9	1.5
10,000	2,000	10.0	5.0	3.3	2.5	2.0

*Assumes upper 6 inches of soil weighs 2 million pounds.

in a soil with 1.7% organic matter. On the other hand, 7,500 pounds of residues added annually to a well-drained, coarse-textured soil (with a soil organic matter mineralization, or decomposition, rate of 5% per year) are estimated to result after many years in only 1.5% soil organic matter.

Normally when organic matter is accumulating in soil, it will increase at the rate of tens to hundreds of pounds per acre per year—but keep in mind that the weight of organic material in 6 inches of soil that contains 1% organic matter is 20,000 pounds. Thus, the small annual changes, along with the great variation you can find in a single field, means that it usually takes years to detect changes in the total amount of organic matter in a soil.

In addition to the final amount of organic matter in a soil, the same simple equation used to calculate the information in table 3.2 can be used to estimate organic matter changes as they occur over a period of years or decades. Let's take a more detailed look at the case where 5,000 pounds of residue is added per year with only 1,000 pounds remaining after one year. Let's assume that the residue remaining from the previous year behaves the same as the rest of the soil's organic matter—in this case, decomposing at a rate of 3% per year. As we mentioned

above, with these assumptions, after many years a soil will end up having 1.7% organic matter. If a soil starts at 1% organic matter content, it will have an annual net gain of around 350 pounds of organic matter per acre in the first decade, decreasing to very small net gains after decades of following the same practices (figure 3.7a). Thus, even though 5,000 pounds per acre are added each year, the net yearly gain decreases as the soil organic matter content reaches a steady state. If it was a very depleted soil and the additions started when it was at only at 0.5% organic matter content, a lot of it might be bound to clay mineral surfaces and so help to form very small aggregates—preserving more organic matter each year. In this case, it is estimated that the net annual gain in the first decade might be over 600 pounds per acre (figure 3.7a).

The soil organic matter content rises more quickly for the very depleted soil (starting at 0.5% organic matter) than for the 1% organic matter content soil (figure 3.7b), because so much more organic matter can be stored in organo-mineral complexes and inside very small and medium-size aggregates. Once all the possible sites that can physically or chemically protect organic matter have done so, organic matter accumulates more slowly, mainly as free particulate (active) material.

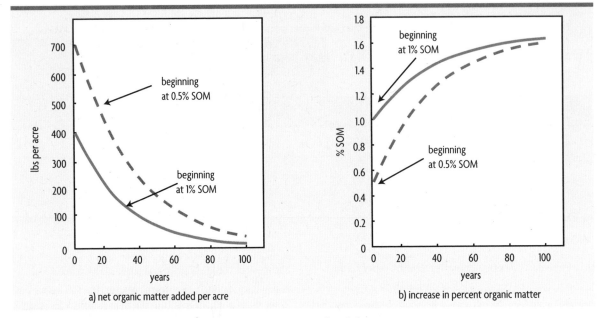

Figure 3.7. Net organic matter additions and changes in % organic matter content for soils.*

*Estimated for soil starting at 0.5% or 1% organic matter, receiving a total of 5,000 lbs of residue per acre per year; 20% remains after one year, and soil organic matter decomposes at the rate of 3% a year.

APPENDIX
Calculations for Table 3.2 and Figure 3.7
Using a Simple Equilibrium Model

The amount of organic matter in soils is a result of the balance between the gains and losses of organic materials. Let's use the abbreviation SOM as shorthand for soil organic matter. Then the change in soil organic matter during one year (the SOM change) can be represented as follows:

SOM change = gains – losses   [equation 1]

If gains are greater than losses, organic matter accumulates and the SOM change is positive. When gains are less than losses, organic matter decreases and SOM change is negative. Remember that gains refer not to the amount of residues added to the soil each year but rather to the amount of residue added to the more resistant pool that remains at the end of the year. This is the fraction (f) of the fresh residues added that do not decompose during the year multiplied by the amount of fresh residues added (A), or gains = (f)(A). For purposes of calculating the SOM percentage estimates in table 3.2 we have assumed that 20% of annual residue additions remain at the end of the year in the form of slowly decomposing residue.

If you follow the same cropping and residue or manure addition pattern for a long time, a steady-state situation usually develops in which gains and losses are the same and SOM change = 0. Losses consist of the percentage of organic matter that's mineralized, or decomposed, in a given year (let's call that k) multiplied by the *amount* of organic matter (SOM) in the surface 6 inches of soil. Another way of writing that is losses = k(SOM). The amount of organic matter that will remain in a soil under steady-state conditions can then be estimated as follows:

SOM change = 0 = gains – k(SOM)   [equation 2]

Because in steady-state situations gains = losses, then gains = k(SOM), or

SOM = gains/k   [equation 3]

A large increase in soil organic matter can occur when you supply very high rates of crop residues, manures, and composts or grow cover crops on soils in which organic matter has a very low rate of decomposition (k). Under steady-state conditions, the effects of residue addition and the rate of mineralization can be calculated using equation 3 as follows:

If k = 3% and 2.5 tons of fresh residue are added annually, 20% of which remains as slowly degradable following one year, then the gains at the end of one year = (5,000 lbs per acre)0.2 = 1,000 lbs per acre.

Assuming that gains and losses are happening only in the surface 6 inches of soil, then the amount of SOM after many years when the soil is at equilibrium equals gains/k = 1,000 lbs/0.03 = 33,333 lbs of organic matter in an acre to 6 inches.

The percent SOM = 100 (33,000 lbs organic matter/2,000,000 lbs soil).

The percent SOM = 1.7%.

SOURCES

Angers, D.A. 1992. Changes in soil aggregation and organic carbon under corn and alfalfa. *Soil Science Society of America Journal* 56: 1244–1249.

Brady, N.C., and R.R. Weil. 2008. *The Nature and Properties of Soils,* 14th ed. Upper Saddle River, NJ: Prentice Hall.

Carter, M. 2002. Soil quality for sustainable land management: Organic matter and aggregation—Interactions that maintain soil functions. *Agronomy Journal* 94: 38–47.

Carter, V.G., and T. Dale. 1974. *Topsoil and Civilization.* Norman: University of Oklahoma Press.

Gale, W.J., and C.A. Cambardella. 2000. Carbon dynamics of surface residue– and root-derived organic matter under simulated no-till. *Soil Science Society of America Journal* 64: 190–195.

Hass, H.J., G.E.A. Evans, and E.F. Miles. 1957. *Nitrogen and Carbon Changes in Great Plains Soils as Influenced by Cropping and Soil Treatments.* U.S. Department of Agriculture Technical Bulletin No. 1164. Washington, DC: U.S. Government Printing Office. This is a reference for the large decrease in organic matter content of Midwest soils.

Jenny, H. 1941. *Factors of Soil Formation.* New York: McGraw-Hill. Jenny's early work on the natural factors influencing soil organic matter levels.

Jenny, H. 1980. *The Soil Resource.* New York: Springer-Verlag.

Khan, S.A., R.L. Mulvaney, T.R. Ellsworth, and C.W. Boast. 2007. The myth of nitrogen fertilization for soil carbon sequestration. *Journal of Environmental Quality* 36: 1821–1832.

Magdoff, F. 2000. *Building Soils for Better Crops,* 1st ed. Lincoln: University of Nebraska Press.

Magdoff, F.R., and J.F. Amadon. 1980. Yield trends and soil chemical changes resulting from N and manure application to continuous corn. *Agronomy Journal* 72: 161–164. See this reference for further information on the studies in Vermont cited in this chapter.

National Research Council. 1989. *Alternative Agriculture.* Washington, DC: National Academy Press.

Puget, P., and L.E. Drinkwater. 2001. Short-term dynamics of root- and shoot-derived carbon from a leguminous green manure. *Soil Science Society of America Journal* 65: 771–779.

Schertz, D.L., W.C. Moldenhauer, D.F. Franz-meier, and H.R. Sinclair, Jr. 1985. Field evaluation of the effect of soil erosion on crop productivity. In *Erosion and Soil Productivity*, pp. 9–17. Proceedings of the National Symposium on Erosion and Soil Productivity, New Orleans, December 10–11, 1984. St. Joseph, MI: American Society of Agricultural Engineers, Publication 8–85.

Tate, R.L., III. 1987. *Soil Organic Matter: Biological and Ecological Effects.* New York: John Wiley.

Wilhelm, W.W., J.M.F. Johnson, J.L. Hatfield, W.B. Voorhees, and D.R. Linden. 2004. Crop and soil productivity response to corn residue removal: A literature review. *Agronomy Journal* 96: 1–17.

Chapter 4

THE LIVING SOIL

The plow is one of the most ancient and most valuable of man's inventions; but long before he existed the land was in fact regularly ploughed, and continues to be thus ploughed by earthworms.

—CHARLES DARWIN, 1881

When soil organisms and roots go about their normal functions of getting energy for growth from organic molecules, they "respire"—using oxygen and releasing carbon dioxide to the atmosphere. (Of course, as we take our essential breaths of air, we do the same.) An entire field can be viewed as breathing as if it is one large organism. The soil is like a living being in another way, too—it may get "sick" in the sense that it becomes incapable of supporting healthy plants.

The organisms living in the soil, both large and small, play a significant role in maintaining a healthy soil system and healthy plants. One of the main reasons we are interested in these organisms is because of their role in breaking down organic residues and incorporating them into the soil. Soil organisms influence every aspect of decomposition and nutrient availability. As organic materials are decomposed, nutrients become available to plants, humus is produced, soil aggregates are formed, channels are created for water infiltration and better aeration, and those residues originally on the surface are brought deeper into the soil.

We classify soil organisms in several different ways. Each can be discussed separately or all organisms that do the same types of things can be discussed as a group. We also can look at soil organisms according to their role in the decomposition of organic materials. For example, organisms that use fresh residues as their source of food are called primary (1°), or first-level, consumers of organic materials (see figure 4.1). Many of these primary consumers break down large pieces of residues into smaller fragments. Secondary (2°) consumers are organisms that feed on the primary consumers themselves or their waste products. Tertiary (3°) consumers then feed on the secondary consumers. Another way to treat organisms is by general size, such as very small, small, medium, large, and very large. This is how we will discuss soil organisms in this chapter.

There is constant interaction among the organisms living in the soil. Some organisms help others, as when bacteria that live inside the earthworm's digestive

Photo by Jerry DeWitt

37

BUILDING SOILS FOR BETTER CROPS: SUSTAINABLE SOIL MANAGEMENT

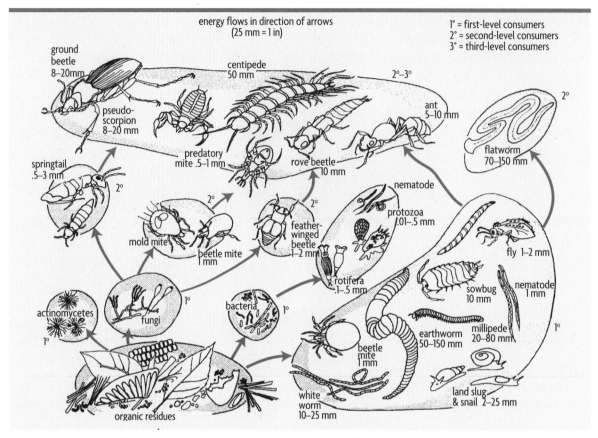

Figure 4.1. Soil organisms and their role in decomposing residues. Modified from D.L. Dindal (1972).

system help decompose organic matter. Although there are many examples of such mutually beneficial, or *symbiotic*, relationships, an intense competition occurs among most of the diverse organisms in healthy soils. Organisms may directly compete with each other for the same food. Some organisms naturally feed on others—nematodes may feed on fungi, bacteria, or other nematodes, and some fungi trap and kill nematodes. There are also fungi and bacteria that parasitize nematodes and completely digest their content.

Some soil organisms can harm plants, either by causing disease or by being parasites. In other words, there are "good" as well as "bad" bacteria, fungi, nematodes, and insects. One of the goals of agricultural production

systems should be to create conditions that enhance the growth of beneficial organisms, which are the vast majority, while decreasing populations of those few that are potentially harmful.

SOIL MICROORGANISMS

Microorganisms are very small forms of life that can sometimes live as single cells, although many also form colonies of cells. A microscope is usually needed to see individual cells of these organisms. Many more microorganisms exist in topsoil, where food sources are plentiful, than in subsoil. They are especially abundant in the area immediately next to plant roots (called the rhizosphere), where sloughed-off cells and chemicals released by roots provide ready food sources. These organisms are primary decomposers of organic matter, but they do other things, such as provide nitrogen through fixation to help growing plants, detoxify harmful chemicals (toxins), suppress disease organisms, and produce products that might stimulate plant growth. Soil microorganisms have had another direct importance for humans—they are the source of most of the antibiotic medicines we use to fight diseases.

Bacteria

Bacteria live in almost any habitat. They are found inside the digestive system of animals, in the ocean and fresh water, in compost piles (even at temperatures over 130°F), and in soils. Although some kinds of bacteria live in flooded soils without oxygen, most require well-aerated soils. In general, bacteria tend to do better in neutral pH soils than in acid soils.

In addition to being among the first organisms to begin decomposing residues in the soil, bacteria benefit plants by increasing nutrient availability. For example, many bacteria dissolve phosphorus, making it more available for plants to use.

Bacteria are also very helpful in providing nitrogen to plants, which they need in large amounts but is often deficient in agricultural soils. You may wonder how soils can be deficient in nitrogen when we are surrounded by it—78% of the air we breathe is composed of nitrogen gas. Yet plants as well as animals face a dilemma similar to that of the Ancient Mariner, who was adrift at sea without fresh water: "Water, water, everywhere nor any drop to drink." Unfortunately, neither animals nor plants can use nitrogen gas (N_2) for their nutrition. However, some types of bacteria are able to take nitrogen gas from the atmosphere and convert it into a form that plants can use to make amino acids and proteins. This conversion process is known as *nitrogen fixation*.

Some nitrogen-fixing bacteria form mutually beneficial associations with plants. One such symbiotic relationship that is very important to agriculture involves the nitrogen-fixing rhizobia group of bacteria that live inside nodules formed on the roots of legumes. These bacteria provide nitrogen in a form that leguminous plants can use, while the legume provides the bacteria with sugars for energy.

People eat some legumes or their products, such as peas, dry beans, and tofu made from soybeans. Soybeans, alfalfa, and clover are used for animal feed. Clovers and hairy vetch are grown as cover crops to enrich the soil with organic matter, as well as nitrogen, for the following crop. In an alfalfa field, the bacteria may fix hundreds of pounds of nitrogen per acre each

RELATIVE AMOUNTS OF BACTERIA AND FUNGI

All soils contain both bacteria and fungi, but they may have different relative amounts depending on soil conditions. The general ways in which you manage your soil—the amount of disturbance, the degree of acidity permitted, and the types of residues added—will determine the relative abundance of these two major groups of soil organisms. Soils that are disturbed regularly by intensive tillage tend to have higher levels of bacteria than fungi. So do flooded rice soils, because fungi can't live without oxygen, while many species of bacteria can. Soils that are not tilled tend to have more of their fresh organic matter at the surface and to have higher levels of fungi than bacteria. Because fungi are less sensitive to acidity, higher levels of fungi than bacteria may occur in very acid soils. Despite many claims, little is known about the agricultural significance of bacteria- versus fungal-dominated soil microbial communities, except that bacteria-prevalent soils are more characteristic of more intensively tilled soils that tend to also have high nutrient availability and enhanced nutrient levels as a result of more rapid organic matter decomposition.

year. With peas, the amount of nitrogen fixed is much lower, around 30 to 50 pounds per acre.

The actinomycetes, another group of bacteria, break large lignin molecules into smaller sizes. Lignin is a large and complex molecule found in plant tissue, especially stems, that is difficult for most organisms to break down. Lignin also frequently protects other molecules like cellulose from decomposition. Actinomycetes have some characteristics similar to those of fungi, but they are sometimes grouped by themselves and given equal billing with bacteria and fungi.

Fungi

Fungi are another type of soil microorganism. Yeast is a fungus used in baking and in the production of alcohol. Other fungi produce a number of antibiotics. We have all probably let a loaf of bread sit around too long only to find fungus growing on it. We have seen or eaten mushrooms, the fruiting structures of some fungi. Farmers know that fungi cause many plant diseases, such as downy mildew, damping-off, various types of root rot,

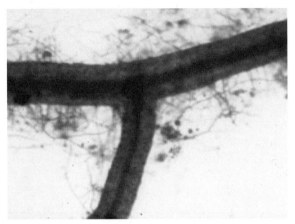

Figure 4.2. Root heavily infected with mycorrhizal fungi (note round spores at the end of some hyphae). Photo by Sara Wright.

and apple scab. Fungi also initiate the decomposition of fresh organic residues. They help get things going by softening organic debris and making it easier for other organisms to join in the decomposition process. Fungi are also the main decomposers of lignin and are less sensitive to acid soil conditions than bacteria. None are able to function without oxygen. Low soil disturbance resulting from reduced tillage systems tends to promote organic residue accumulation at and near the surface. This tends to promote fungal growth, as happens in many natural undisturbed ecosystems.

Many plants develop a beneficial relationship with fungi that increases the contact of roots with the soil. Fungi infect the roots and send out rootlike structures called *hyphae* (see figure 4.2). The hyphae of these *mycorrhizal* fungi take up water and nutrients that can then feed the plant. The hyphae are very thin, about 1/60 the diameter of a plant root, and are able to exploit the water and nutrients in small spaces in the soil that might be inaccessible to roots. This is especially important for phosphorus nutrition of plants in low-phosphorus soils. The hyphae help the plant absorb water and nutrients, and in return the fungi receive energy in the form of sugars, which the plant produces in its leaves and sends down to the roots. This symbiotic

MYCORRHIZAL FUNGI

Mycorrhizal fungi help plants take up water and nutrients, improve nitrogen fixation by legumes, and help to form and stabilize soil aggregates. Crop rotations select for more types of and better performing fungi than does mono cropping. Some studies indicate that using cover crops, especially legumes, between main crops helps maintain high levels of spores and promotes good mycorrhizal development in the next crop. Roots that have lots of mycorrhizae are better able to resist fungal diseases, parasitic nematodes, drought, salinity, and aluminum toxicity. Mycorrhizal associations have been shown to stimulate the free-living nitrogen-fixing bacteria azotobacter, which in turn also produce plant growth–stimulating chemicals.

interdependency between fungi and roots is called a mycorrhizal relationship. All things considered, it's a pretty good deal for both the plant and the fungus. The hyphae of these fungi help develop and stabilize larger soil aggregates by secreting a sticky gel that glues mineral and organic particles together.

Algae

Algae, like crop plants, convert sunlight into complex molecules like sugars, which they can use for energy and to help build other molecules they need. Algae are found in abundance in the flooded soils of swamps and rice paddies, and they can be found on the surface of poorly drained soils and in wet depressions. Algae may also occur in relatively dry soils, and they form mutually beneficial relationships with other organisms. Lichens found on rocks are an association between a fungus and an alga.

Protozoa

Protozoa are single-celled animals that use a variety of means to move about in the soil. Like bacteria and many fungi, they can be seen only with the help of a microscope. They are mainly secondary consumers of organic materials, feeding on bacteria, fungi, other protozoa, and organic molecules dissolved in the soil water. Protozoa—through their grazing on nitrogen-rich organisms and excreting wastes—are believed to be responsible for mineralizing (releasing nutrients from organic molecules) much of the nitrogen in agricultural soils.

SMALL AND MEDIUM-SIZE SOIL ANIMALS
Nematodes

Nematodes are simple multicellular soil animals that resemble tiny worms but are nonsegmented. They tend to live in the water films around soil aggregates. Some types of nematodes feed on plant roots and are well-known plant pests. Fungi such as *Pythium* and *Fusarium*, which may enter nematode-feeding wounds on the root, sometimes cause greater disease severity and more damage than the nematode itself. A number of plant-parasitic nematodes vector important and damaging plant viruses of various crops. However, there are many beneficial nematodes that help in the breakdown of organic residues and feed on fungi, bacteria, and protozoa as secondary consumers. In fact, as with the protozoa, nematodes feeding on fungi and bacteria help convert nitrogen into forms for plants to use. As much as 50% or more of mineralized nitrogen comes from nematode feeding. A number of nematodes alone or with special bacteria parasitize and kill insects such as the larvae of the cabbage looper and the grubs of the Japanese beetle. Finally, several nematodes infect animals and humans, causing serious diseases such as river blindness and heartworm.

Earthworms

Earthworms are every bit as important as Charles Darwin believed they were more than a century ago. They are keepers and restorers of soil fertility. Different types of earthworms, including the night crawler, field (garden) worm, and manure (red) worm, have different feeding habits. Some feed on plant residues that remain on the soil surface, while other types tend to feed on organic matter that is already mixed with the soil.

The surface-feeding night crawlers fragment and mix fresh residues with soil mineral particles, bacteria, and enzymes in their digestive system. The resulting material is given off as worm casts. Worm casts are generally higher in available plant nutrients, such as nitrogen, calcium, magnesium, and phosphorus, than the surrounding soil and, therefore, contribute to the nutrient needs of plants. They also bring food down into their burrows, thereby mixing organic matter deep into the soil. Earthworms feeding on debris that is already below the surface continue to decompose organic materials and mix them with the soil minerals.

A number of types of earthworms, including the

surface-feeding night crawler, make burrows that allow rainfall to easily infiltrate the soil. These worms usually burrow to 3 feet or more, unless the soil is saturated or very hard. Even those types of worms that don't normally produce channels to the surface help loosen the soil, creating channels and cracks below the surface that help aeration and root growth. The number of earthworms in the soil ranges from close to zero to over a million per acre. Just imagine, if you create the proper conditions for earthworms, you could have 800,000 small channels per acre that conduct water into your soil during downpours.

Earthworms do some unbelievable work. They move a lot of soil from below up to the surface—from about 1 to 100 tons per acre each year. One acre of soil 6 inches deep weighs about 2 million pounds, or 1,000 tons. So 1 to 100 tons is the equivalent of about .006 of an inch to about half an inch of soil. A healthy earthworm population may function as nature's plow and help replace the need for tillage by making channels and bringing up subsoil and mixing it with organic residues.

Earthworms do best in well-aerated soils that are supplied with plentiful amounts of organic matter. A study in Georgia showed that soils with higher amounts of organic matter contained higher numbers of earthworms. Surface feeders, a type we would especially like to encourage, need residues left on the surface. They are harmed by plowing or disking, which disturbs their burrows and buries their food supplies. Worms are usually more plentiful under no-till practices than under conventional tillage systems. Although many pesticides have little effect on worms, some insecticides are very harmful to earthworms.

Diseases or insects that overwinter on leaves of crops can sometimes be partially controlled by high earthworm populations. The apple scab fungus—a major pest of apples in humid regions—and some leaf miner insects can be partly controlled when worms eat the leaves and incorporate the residues deeper into the soil.

Although the night crawler is certainly beneficial in farm fields, this European introduction has caused problems in some northern forests. As fishermen have discarded unused worms near forest lakes, night crawlers have become adapted to the forests. They have in some cases reduced the forest litter layer almost completely, accelerating nutrient cycling and changing species composition of the understory vegetation. So some forest managers view this organism, considered so positively by farmers, as a pest!

Insects and Other Small to Large Soil Animals

Insects are another group of animals that inhabit soils. Common types of soil insects include termites, springtails, ants, fly larvae, and beetles. Many insects are secondary and tertiary consumers. Springtails feed on fungi and animal remains, and in turn they themselves are food for predacious mites. Many beetles, in particular, eat other types of soil animals. Some beetles feed on weed seeds in the soil. Termites, well-known feeders of woody material, also consume decomposed organic residues in the soil.

Other medium-size to large soil animals include millipedes, centipedes, mites, slugs, snails, and spiders. Millipedes are primary consumers of plant residues, whereas centipedes tend to feed on other organisms. Mites may feed on food sources like fungi, other mites, and insect eggs, although some feed directly on residues. Spiders feed mainly on insects and keep insect pests from developing into large populations.

VERY LARGE SOIL ANIMALS

Very large soil animals, such as moles, rabbits, woodchucks, snakes, prairie dogs, and badgers, burrow in the soil and spend at least some of their lives below ground. Moles are secondary consumers, their diet consisting mainly of earthworms. Most of the other animals exist on vegetation. In many cases, their presence is considered a nuisance for agricultural production or lawns and gardens. Nevertheless, their burrows may help conduct water away from the surface during downpours and thus decrease erosion. In the southern U.S., the burrowing action of crawfish, abundant in many somewhat poorly drained soils, can have a large effect on soil structure. (In Texas and Louisiana, some rice fields are "rotated" with crawfish production.)

PLANT ROOTS

Healthy plant roots are essential for good crop yields. Roots are clearly influenced by the soil in which they live and are good indicators of soil quality. If the soil is compact, is low in nutrients or water, includes high populations of root pathogens, or has other problems, plants will not grow well. On the other hand, plants also influence the soil in which they grow. The physical pressure of roots growing through soil helps form aggregates by bringing particles closer together. Small roots also help bind particles together. In addition, many organic compounds are given off, or exuded, by plant roots and provide nourishment for soil organisms living on or near the roots. The zone surrounding roots is one of especially great numbers and activity of organisms that live off root exudates and sloughed-off cells. This increased activity by microorganisms, plus the slight disruption caused as roots grow through the soil, enhances the use of active ("dead") organic matter by organisms—also enhancing nutrient availability to the plant. A sticky layer surrounding roots, called the mucigel, provides close contact between microorganisms, soil minerals, and the plant (figure 4.3). Plant roots also contribute

The soil population must be considered from the point of view of a biological complex; it is not sufficient to separate it into different constituent groups.

—S.A. WAKSMAN, 1923

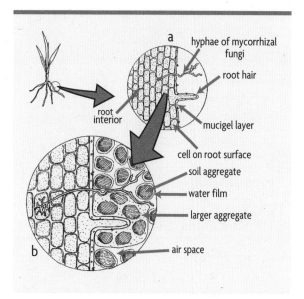

Figure 4.3. Close-up view of a plant root: (a) The mucigel layer is shown containing some bacteria and clay particles on the outside of the root. Also shown is a mycorrhizal fungus sending out its rootlike hyphae into the soil. (b) Soil aggregates are surrounded by thin films of water. Plant roots take water and nutrients from these films. Also shown is a larger aggregate made up of smaller aggregates pressed together and held in place by the root and hyphae.

greatly to organic matter accumulation. They are usually well distributed in the soil and may be slower to decompose than surface residues, even if incorporated by plowing or harrowing.

For plants with extensive root systems, such as grasses, the amount of living tissue below ground may actually weigh more than the amount of leaves and stems we see above ground.

BIOLOGICAL DIVERSITY, ABUNDANCE, AND BALANCE

A diverse biological community in soils is essential to maintaining a healthy environment for plant roots. There may be over 100,000 different types of organisms living in soils. Most are providing numerous functions that assist plants, such as making nutrients more available, producing growth-stimulating chemicals, and helping form soil aggregates. In a teaspoon of agricultural soils it

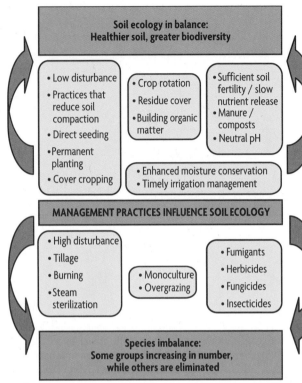

Figure 4.4. Management practices that influence soil life. Modified from Kennedy, Stubbs, and Schillinger (2004).

is estimated that there are from 100 million to 1 billion bacteria, several yards of fungi, and several thousand protozoa. It may hold 10 to 20 bacterial-feeding nematodes and a few fungal-feeding and plant parasitic nematodes. Arthropods can number up to 100 per square foot, and earthworms from 5 to 30 per square foot.

Of all the organisms in soils, only a small number of bacteria, fungi, insects, and nematodes might harm plants in any given year. Diverse populations of soil organisms maintain a system of checks and balances that can keep disease organisms or parasites from becoming major plant problems. Some fungi kill nematodes, and others kill insects. Still others produce antibiotics that kill bacteria. Protozoa feed on bacteria and may attack fungi. Some bacteria kill harmful insects. Many protozoa, springtails, and mites feed on disease-causing fungi and bacteria.

Beneficial organisms, such as the fungus *Trichoderma* and the bacteria *Pseudomonas fluorescens,* colonize plant roots and protect them from attack by harmful organisms. Some of these organisms, isolated from soils, are now sold commercially as biological control agents. The effects of bacteria and fungi that suppress plant disease organisms are thought to arise from competition for nutrients, production of antagonistic substances, and/ or direct parasitism. In addition, a number of beneficial soil organisms induce the immune systems of plants to defend the plants (*systemic acquired resistance*; see discussion in chapter 8). Also, roots of agronomic crops usually have their own characteristic microbial communities with numerous interactions.

Soil management can have dramatic effects on soil biological composition (see figure 4.4 for management effects on organisms). For example, the less a soil is disturbed by tillage, the greater the importance of fungi relative to bacteria. Thus, promotion of cropping practices that encourage abundance and diversity of soil organisms encourages a healthy soil. Crop rotations of plants from different families are recommended to keep microbial diversity at its maximum and to break up any potential damaging pest cycles. Additional practices that promote the diversity and activity of soil organisms include low amounts of soil disturbance, use of cover crops, maintaining pH close to neutral, and routine use of organic sources of slow-release fertility.

SUMMARY

Soils are alive with a fantastic number of many types of organisms, most of which help to grow healthy plants and protect them from pests. The food for all the soil's organisms originates with crop residues and organic materials added from off the field. These provide the fuel that powers the underground life that has such a positive effect on the soil's chemical and physical properties, as well as, of course, maintaining a system of equilibrium that helps regulate the populations of organisms. Soil organisms are associated with each other in a balance in which each type of organism performs specific roles and interacts with other organisms in complex ways. When there is an abundance of food and minimal soil disturbance, the complex food web that exists helps to maintain a self-regulation of organisms as bacteria and protozoa eat bacteria and some fungi, nematodes eat bacteria and fungi (as well as other nematodes and plant roots), fungi eat nematodes, and so on up the food web. We should be trying to use management practices that promote a thriving and diverse population of soil organisms.

SOURCES

Alexander, M. 1977. *Introduction to Soil Microbiology*, 2nd ed. New York: John Wiley.

Avisa, T.J., V. Gravelb, H. Antouna, and R.J. Tweddella. 2008. Multifaceted beneficial effects of rhizosphere microorganisms on plant health and productivity. *Soil Biology and Biochemistry* 40: 1733–1740.

Behl, R.K., H. Sharma, V. Kumar, and N. Narula. 2003. Interactions amongst mycorrhiza, *azotobacter chroococcum* and root characteristics of wheat varieties. *Journal of Agronomy & Crop Science* 189: 151–155.

Dindal, D. 1972. *Ecology of Compost*. Office of News and Publications, 122 Bray Hall, SUNY College of Environmental Science and Forestry, 1 Forestry Drive, Syracuse, NY.

Dropkin, V.H. 1989. *Introduction to Plant Nematology*. New York: John Wiley.

Garbeva, P., J.A. van Veen, and J.D. van Elsas. 2004. Microbial diversity in soil: Selection of microbial populations by plant and soil type and implications for disease suppressiveness. *Annual Review of Phytopathology* 42: 243–270.

Hendrix, P.F., M.H. Beare, W.X. Cheng, D.C. Coleman, D.A. Crossley, Jr., and R.R. Bruce. 1990. Earthworm effects on soil organic matter dynamics in aggrading and degrading agroecosystems on the Georgia Piedmont. *Agronomy Abstracts,* p. 250. Madison, WI: American Society of Agronomy.

Ingham, E.R., A.R. Moldenke, and C.A. Edwards. 2000. *Soil Biology Primer*. Soil and Water Conservation Society and USDA Natural Resource Conservation Service. http://soils.usda.gov/sqi/concepts/soil_biology/biology.html.

Kennedy, A.C., T.L. Stubbs, and W.F. Schillinger. 2004. Soil and crop management effects on soil microbiology. In *Soil Organic Matter in Sustainable Agriculture,* ed. F.R. Magdoff and R. Weil, pp. 295–326. Boca Raton, FL: CRC Press.

Paul, E.A., and F.E. Clark. 1996. *Soil Microbiology and Biochemistry,* 2nd ed. San Diego, CA: Academic Press.

Photo by Dennis Nolan

Chapter 5

SOIL PARTICLES, WATER, AND AIR

Moisture, warmth, and aeration; soil texture; soil fitness; soil organisms; its tillage, drainage,
and irrigation; all these are quite as important factors in the make up and maintenance of the fertility
of the soil as are manures, fertilizers, and soil amendments.

—J.L. HILLS, C.H. JONES, AND C. CUTLER, 1908

The physical condition of a soil has a lot to do with its ability to produce crops. A degraded soil usually has reduced water infiltration and percolation (drainage into the subsoil), aeration, and root growth. These conditions reduce the ability of the soil to supply nutrients, render harmless many hazardous compounds (such as pesticides), and maintain a wide diversity of soil organisms. Small changes in a soil's physical conditions can have a large impact on these essential processes. Creating a good physical environment, which is a critical part of building and maintaining healthy soils, requires attention and care.

Let's first consider the physical nature of a typical mineral soil. It usually contains about 50% solid particles and 50% pores on a volume basis (figure 5.1). We discussed earlier how organic matter is only a small, but a very important, component of the soil. The rest of a soil's particles are a mixture of variously sized minerals that define its texture. A soil's textural class—such as a clay, clay loam, loam, sandy loam, or sand—is perhaps its most fundamental inherent characteristic, as it affects many of the important physical, biological, and chemical processes in a soil and changes little over time.

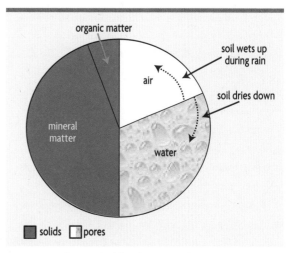

Figure 5.1. Distribution of solids and pores in soil.

Photo courtesy Ray Weil

49

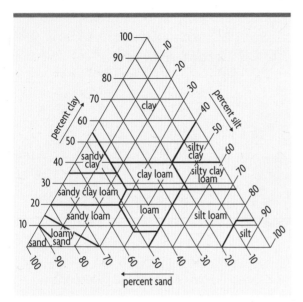

Figure 5.2. The percentages of sand, silt, and clay in the soil textural classes. From USDA-NRCS.

The textural class (figure 5.2) is defined by the relative amounts of sand (0.05 to 2 mm particle size), silt (0.002 to 0.05 mm), and clay (less than 0.002 mm). Particles that are larger than 2 mm are rock fragments (pebbles, cobbles, stones, and boulders), which are not considered in the textural class because they are relatively inert.

Soil particles are the building blocks of the soil skeleton. But the spaces (pores) between the particles and between aggregates are just as important as the sizes of the particles themselves. The total amount of pore space and the relative quantity of variously sized pores—large, medium, small, and very small—govern the important processes of water and air movement. Soil organisms live and function in pores, which is also where plant roots grow. Most pores in clay are small (generally less than 0.002 mm), whereas most pores in sandy soil are large (but generally still smaller than 2 mm).

The pore sizes are affected not only by the relative amounts of sand, silt, and clay in a soil, but also by the amount of aggregation. On the one extreme, we see that beach sands have large particles (in relative terms, at least—they're visible) and no aggregation due to a lack of organic matter or clay to help bind the sand grains. A good loam or clay soil, on the other hand, has smaller particles, but they tend to be aggregated into crumbs that have larger pores between them and small pores within. Although soil texture doesn't change •ver time, the total amount of pore space and the relative amount of variously sized pores are strongly affected by management practices—aggregation and structure may be destroyed or improved.

WATER AND AERATION

Soil pore space can be filled with either water or air, and their relative amounts change as the soil wets and dries (figures 5.1, 5.3). When all pores are filled with water, the soil is saturated, and the exchange of soil gases with atmospheric gases is very slow. During these conditions, carbon dioxide produced by respiring roots and soil organisms can't escape from the soil and atmospheric oxygen can't enter, leading to undesirable anaerobic (no oxygen) conditions. On the other extreme, a soil with little water may have good gas exchange but be unable to supply sufficient water to plants and soil organisms.

Water in soil is mostly affected by two opposing forces that basically perform a tug of war: Gravity pulls water down and makes it flow to deeper layers, but water also has a tendency to stay in a soil pore because it is attracted to a solid surface and has a strong affinity for other water molecules. The latter are the same forces that keep water drops adhering to glass surfaces,

Figure 5.3. A moist sand with pores between grains that contain water and air. The larger pores have partially drained and allowed air entry, while the narrower ones are still filled with water.

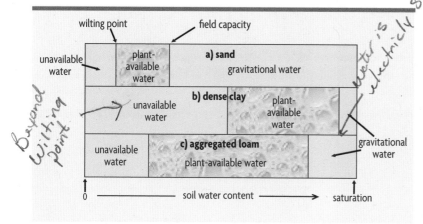

water is electrically stuck

Beyond wilting point

Figure 5.4. Water storage for three soils.

and their effect is stronger in small pores (figure 5.3) because of the closer contact with solids. Soils are a lot like sponges in the way they hold and release water (figure 5.4). When a sponge is fully saturated, it quickly loses water by gravity but will stop dripping after about 30 seconds. The largest pores drain rapidly because they are unable to retain water against the force of gravity. But when it stops dripping, the sponge still contains a lot of water, which would, of course, come out if you squeezed it. The remaining water is in the smaller pores, which hold it more tightly. The sponge's condition following free drainage is akin to a soil reaching field capacity water content, which in the field occurs after about two days of free drainage following saturation by a lot of rain or irrigation. If a soil contains mainly large pores, like a coarse sand, it loses a lot of water through quick gravitational drainage. This drainage is good because the pores are now open for air exchange. On the other hand, little water remains for plants to use, resulting in more frequent periods of drought stress. Coarse sandy soils have very small amounts of water available to plants before they reach their wilting point (figure 5.4a). On the other hand, a dense, fine-textured soil, such as a compacted clay loam, has mainly small pores, which tightly retain water and don't release it

as gravitational drainage (figure 5.4b). In this case, the soil has more plant-available water than a coarse sand, but plants will suffer from long periods of poor aeration following saturating rains.

These different effects of various pore sizes have great impacts: Leaching of pesticides and nitrates to groundwater is controlled by the relative amounts of different sizes of pores. The rapidly draining sands may more readily lose these chemicals in the percolating water, but this is much less of a problem with fine loams and clays. For the latter, the more common anaerobic conditions resulting from extended saturated conditions cause other problems, like gaseous nitrogen losses through denitrification, as we will discuss in chapter 19.

The ideal soil is somewhere between the two

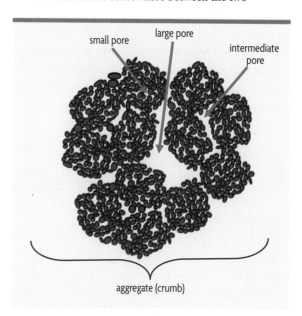

Figure 5.5. A well-aggregated soil has a range of pore sizes. This medium-size soil crumb is made up of many smaller ones. Very large pores occur between the medium-size aggregates.

Figure 5.6. Left: Corn root in a compacted soil cannot access water and nutrients from most of the soil volume. Right: Dense rooting allows for full exploration of soil water and nutrients.

extremes, and its behavior is typical of that exhibited by a well-aggregated loam soil (figures 5.4c, 5.5). Such a soil has a sufficient amount of large pore spaces between the aggregates to provide adequate drainage and aeration during wet periods, but also has enough small pores and water-holding capacity to provide water to plants and soil organisms between rainfall or irrigation events. Besides retaining and releasing water at near optimum quantities, such soils also allow for good water infiltration, thereby increasing plant water availability and reducing runoff and erosion. This ideal soil condition is therefore characterized by crumb-like aggregates, which are common in good topsoil.

AVAILABLE WATER AND ROOTING

There is an additional dimension to plant-available water capacity of soils: The water in the soil may be available, but roots also need to be able to access it, along with the nutrients contained in the water. Consider the soil from the compacted surface horizon in figure 5.6 (left), which was penetrated only by a single corn root with few fine lateral rootlets. The soil volume held sufficient water, which was in principle available to the corn plant, but the roots were unable to penetrate most of the hard soil. The corn plant, therefore, could

not obtain the moisture it needed. The corn roots on the right (figure 5.6) were able to fully explore the soil volume with many roots, fine laterals, and root hairs, allowing for better water and nutrient uptake.

Similarly, the depth of rooting can be limited by compaction. Figure 5.7 shows, on the right, corn roots from moldboard-plowed soil with a severe plow pan. The roots could not penetrate into the subsoil and were therefore limited to water and nutrients in the plow layer. The corn on the left was grown in soil that had been subsoiled, and the roots were able to reach about twice the depth. Subsoiling opened up more soil for

Figure 5.7. Corn roots on the right were limited to the plow layer due to a severe compaction pan. Roots on the left penetrated into deeper soil following subsoiling and could access more water and nutrients.

root growth and, therefore, more usable water and nutrients. Thus, plant water availability is a result of both the soil's water retention capacity (related to texture, aggregation, and organic matter) and potential rooting volume, which is influenced by compaction.

INFILTRATION VS. RUNOFF

An important function of soil is to absorb water at the land surface, and either store it for use by plants or slowly release it to groundwater through gravitational flow (figure 5.8). When rainfall hits the ground, most water will infiltrate the soil; but some may run off the surface, and some may stand in ruts or depressions before infiltrating or evaporating. The maximum amount of rainwater that can enter a soil in a given time, called *infiltration capacity*, is influenced by the soil type, structure, and moisture content at the start of the rain.

Early in a storm, water usually enters a soil readily, as it is literally sucked into the dry ground. As the soil wets up during a continuing intense storm, water entry into the soil is reduced and a portion of rainfall begins to run downhill over the surface to a nearby stream or wetland. The ability of a soil to maintain high infiltration rates, even when saturated, is related to the sizes of its pores. Since sandy and gravelly soils have more large pores than do fine loams and clays, they maintain better infiltration during a storm. But soil texture is also important in governing the number of pores and their sizes: When finer-textured soils have strong aggregates due to good management, they can also maintain high infiltration rates.

When rainfall exceeds a soil's infiltration capacity, runoff is produced. Rainfall or snowmelt on frozen ground generally poses even greater runoff concerns,

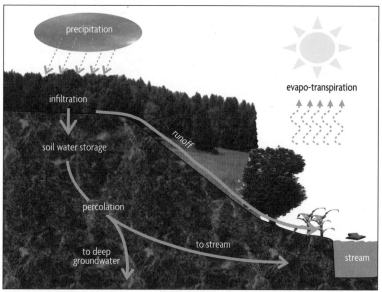

Figure 5.8. The fate of precipitation at the land surface determines whether water infiltrates or runs off the surface.

as pores are blocked with ice. Runoff happens more readily with poorly managed soils, because they lack strong aggregates that hold together against the force of raindrops and moving water and, therefore, have few large pores open to the surface to quickly conduct water downward. Such runoff can initiate erosion, with losses of nutrients and agrochemicals as well as sediment.

SOIL WATER AND AGGREGATION

Processes like erosion, soil settling, and compaction are affected by soil moisture conditions, and in turn affect soil hardness and the stability of aggregates. When soil is saturated and all pores are filled with water, the soil is very soft. (Fungal hyphae and small roots also serve to form and stabilize aggregates deeper in the soil.) Under these saturated conditions, the weaker aggregates may easily fall apart from the impact of raindrops and allow the force of water moving over the surface to carry soil particles away (figure 5.9). Supersaturated soil has no internal strength, and the positive water pressure in fact pushes particles apart (figure 5.10, left). This makes soil

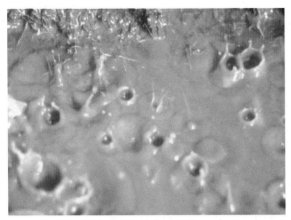

Figure 5.9. Saturated soil is soft, easily dispersed by raindrop impact, and readily eroded. Photo by USDA-NRCS.

very susceptible to erosion by water flowing over the surface or allows it to be pulled down by gravity as land (mud) slides.

As soil dries and becomes moist instead of wet, the pore water remaining in contact with solid surfaces becomes curved and pulls particles together, making the soil stronger and harder (figure 5.10, middle). But when soils low in organic matter and aggregation, especially sands, are *very* dry, the bonding between particles decreases greatly because there is little pore water left to hold the particles together. The soil then becomes loose

and susceptible to wind erosion (figure 5.10, right).

Strong aggregation is especially important during these moisture extremes, as it provides another source of cohesion that keeps the soil together. Good aggregation, or *structure*, helps to ensure a high-quality soil and prevents dispersion (figure 5.11). A well-aggregated soil also results in good *soil tilth*, implying that it forms a good seedbed after soil preparation. Aggregation in the surface soil is enhanced by surface residue and lack of tillage. Also, a continuous supply of organic materials, roots of living plants, and mycorrhizal fungi hyphae are needed to maintain good soil aggregation.

Surface residues and cover crops protect the soil from wind and raindrops and moderate the temperature and moisture extremes at the soil surface. On the other hand, an unprotected soil may experience very high soil temperatures at the surface and become extremely dry. Worms and insects will then move deeper into the bare soil, resulting in a surface zone that contains few active organisms. Many bacteria and fungi that live in thin films of water may die or become inactive, slowing the natural process of organic matter cycling. Large and small organisms promote aggregation in a soil that is protected by a surface layer of crop residue cover, mulch, or sod and has continuous supplies of organic

 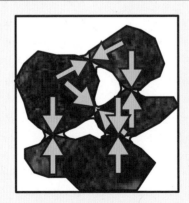 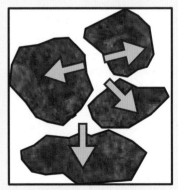

Figure 5.10. Pore water pushes soil particles apart in supersaturated soils (left). Moist soils are firm or hard because curved water-surface contacts of the pore water pull particles together (middle). Particles become loose in dry soil due to a lack of cohesion from pore water (right).

Figure 5.11. Well-aggregated soil from an organically managed field with a rye cover crop.

Figure 5.12. Drought and poor soil health created wind and water erosion during the Dust Bowl. Photo by USDA.

matter to maintain a healthy food chain. An absence of both erosion and compaction processes also helps maintain good surface aggregation.

The soil's chemistry also plays a role in aggregate formation and stability, especially in dry climates. Soils that have high sodium content (see chapters 6 and 20) pose particular challenges.

WHAT COMES FROM THE SKY: THE LIFEBLOOD OF ECOSYSTEMS

We need to take a short diversion from our focus on soils and briefly discuss climate. Various characteristics of precipitation affect the potential for crop production and the losses of water, sediment, and contaminants to the environment. These include the annual amount of precipitation (for example, arid vs. humid climate); the seasonal distribution and relation to the growing season (can rainfall supply the crops, or is irrigation routinely needed?); and the intensity, duration, and frequency of rain (regular gentle showers are better than infrequent intense storms that may cause runoff and erosion).

Precipitation patterns are hardly ever ideal, and most agricultural systems have to deal with shortages of water at some time during the growing season, which remains the most significant yield-limiting factor

worldwide. Water excess can also be a big problem, especially in humid regions or monsoonal tropics. The main problem, however, is not the excess water itself, but the lack of air exchange and oxygen. Many management practices focus on limiting the effects of these climatic deficiencies. Subsurface drainage and raised beds remove excess water and facilitate aeration; irrigation overcomes inadequate rainfall; aquatic crops like rice allow for grain production in poorly drained soil; and so forth. (See chapter 17 for a discussion of irrigation and drainage.)

So climate affects how soils function and the processes occurring in soils. What is perhaps less understood is that good soil management and healthy soils are important to reducing *susceptibility* to climatic vagaries and making the soil more resilient to weather extremes. The Great Plains area of the United States learned this during the Dust Bowl era of the 1930s (figure 5.12), when a decade of drought and unsustainable soil management practices resulted in excessive wind and water erosion, crop failures, the collapse of the agricultural industry, and massive human migrations out of the region. That devastating experience gave birth to the soil conservation movement, which has achieved much; but most soils, even in the U.S., are still in need of protection from erosion.

SOURCES

Brady, N.C., and R.R. Weil. 2008. *The Nature and Properties of Soils*, 14th ed. Upper Saddle River, NJ: Prentice Hall.

Hill, R.L. 1990. Long-term conventional and no-tillage effects on selected soil physical properties. *Soil Science Society of America Journal* 54: 161–166.

Karunatilake, U., and H.M. van Es. 2002. Temporal and spatial changes in soil structure from tillage and rainfall after alfalfa-corn conversion in a clay loam soil. *Soil and Tillage Research* 67: 135–146.

Kay, B.D. 1990. Rates of change of soil structure under cropping systems. *Advances in Soil Science* 12: 1–52.

Shepard, G., C. Ross, L. Basher, and S. Suggar. *Visual Soil Assessment*, vol. 2: *Soil Management Guidelines for Cropping and Pastoral Grazing on Flat to Rolling Country*. Palmerston North, New Zealand: Horizons.mw and Landcare Research.

Whitman, H., ed. 2007. *Healthy Soils for Sustainable Vegetable Farms: Ute Guide*. Clayton North, Victoria: Land and Water Australia, AUSVEG, Ltd.

Chapter 6

SOIL DEGRADATION: EROSION, COMPACTION, AND CONTAMINATION

Hard ground makes too great resistance, as air makes too little resistance, to the surfaces of roots.

—JETHRO TULL, 1733

EROSION

Soil loss during agricultural production is mainly caused by water, wind, and tillage. Additionally, landslides (gravitational erosion) may occur on very steep slopes. While water erosion and landslides occur under extremely wet soil conditions, wind erosion is a concern with very dry soil. Tillage erosion occurs on fields that are either steep or have undulating topography and is not affected by soil moisture conditions, because the soil movement downslope is caused by the action of farm implements.

Erosion is the result of the combination of an erosive force (water, wind, or gravity), a susceptible soil, and several other management- or landscape-related factors. A soil's inherent susceptibility to erosion (its erodibility) is primarily a function of its texture (generally, silts more than sands and clays), its aggregation (the strength and size of aggregates, which are related to the amount of organic matter), and soil water conditions. Many management practices can reduce soil erosion, although different types of erosion have different solutions.

Water Erosion

Water erosion occurs on bare, sloping land when intense rainfall rates exceed a soil's infiltration capacity and runoff begins. The water concentrates into tiny streamlets, which detach the saturated soil and transport the particles downhill. Runoff water gains more energy as it moves down the slope, scouring away more soil and also carrying more agricultural chemicals and nutrients, which end up in streams, lakes, and estuaries (figure 6.1). Reduced soil health in many of our agricultural and urban watersheds has resulted in increased runoff during intense rainfall and increased problems with flooding. Also, the lower infiltration capacity of degraded soils reduces the amount of water that is available to plants, as well as the amount that percolates through the soil into underground aquifers. This reduction in underground water recharge results in streams drying up during drought periods. Watersheds with degraded soils thus experience lower stream flow during dry seasons and increased flooding during times of high rainfall.

Soil erosion is of greatest concern when the surface

Photo by Jerry DeWitt

Figure 6.1. Left: Water erosion on clean-tilled soil in Bulgaria. Topsoil has been lost in the background field. Right: A stream in Guarico, Venezuela, contaminated with dispersed sediment.

is unprotected and directly exposed to the destructive energy of raindrops and wind (figure 6.1). While degraded soils tend to promote erosion, the process of erosion in turn leads to a decrease in soil quality. Thus, a vicious cycle is begun in which erosion degrades soils, which then leads to further susceptibility to erosion, and so on. Soil is degraded because the best soil material—the surface layer enriched in organic matter—is removed by erosion. Erosion also selectively removes the more easily transported finer soil particles. Severely eroded soils, therefore, become low in organic matter and have less favorable physical, chemical, and biological characteristics, leading to a reduced ability to sustain crops and increased potential for harmful environmental impacts.

Wind Erosion

The picture of wind erosion from the Dust Bowl era (figure 5.12, p. 55) provides a graphic illustration of land degradation. Wind erosion can occur when soil is dry and loose, the surface is bare and smooth, and the landscape has few physical barriers to wind. The wind tends to roll and sweep larger soil particles along the soil surface, which will dislodge other soil particles

SOIL AND WATER CONSERVATION IN HISTORICAL TIMES

Some ancient farming civilizations recognized soil erosion as a problem and developed effective methods for runoff and erosion control. Ancient terracing practices are apparent in various parts of the world, notably in the Andean region of South America and in Southeast Asia. Other cultures effectively controlled erosion using mulching and intercropping that protected the soil surface. Some ancient desert civilizations, such as the Anasazi in the southwestern U.S. (A.D. 600 to 1200), held back and distributed runoff water with check dams to grow crops in downhill depressions (see the picture of a now forested site). Their methods, however, were specific to very dry conditions. For most agricultural areas of the world today, erosion still causes extensive damage (including the spread of deserts) and remains the greatest threat to agricultural sustainability and water quality.

Figure 6.2. Wind erosion damaged young wheat plants through abrasion. Photo by USDA Wind Erosion Research Unit.

Figure 6.3. Sustained rains from Hurricane Mitch in 1998 caused super-saturated soils and landslides in Central America. Photo by Benjamin Zaitchik.

and increase overall soil detachment. The smaller soil particles (very fine sand and silt) are lighter and will go into suspension. They can be transported over great distances, sometimes across continents and oceans. Wind erosion affects soil quality through the loss of topsoil rich in organic matter and can cause crop damage from abrasion (figure 6.2). In addition, wind erosion affects air quality, which is a serious concern for nearby communities.

The ability of wind to erode a soil depends on how that soil has been managed, because strong aggregation makes it less susceptible to dispersion and transportation. In addition, many soil-building practices like mulching and the use of cover crops protect the soil surface from both wind and water erosion.

Landslides

Landslides occur on steep slopes when the soils have become supersaturated from prolonged rains. They are especially of concern in places where high population pressure has resulted in farming of steep hillsides (figure 6.3). The sustained rains saturate the soil (especially in landscape positions that receive water from upslope areas). This has two effects: It increases the weight of

the soil mass (all pores are filled with water), and it decreases the cohesion of the soil (see the compaction of wet soil in figure 6.10, right, p. 64) and thereby its ability to resist the force of gravity. Agricultural areas are more susceptible than forests because they lack large, deep tree roots that can hold soil material together. Pastures on steep lands, common in many mountainous areas, typically have shallow-rooted grasses and may also experience slumping. With certain soil types, landslides may becomes liquefied and turn into mudslides.

Tillage Erosion

Tillage degrades land even beyond promoting water and wind erosion by breaking down aggregates and exposing soil to the elements. It can also cause erosion by directly moving soil down the slope to lower areas of the field. In complex topographies—such as seen in figure 6.4—tillage erosion ultimately removes surface soil from knolls and deposits it in depressions (swales) at the bottom of slopes. What causes tillage erosion? Gravity causes more soil to be moved by the plow or harrow downslope than upslope. Soil is thrown farther downslope when tilling in the downslope direction than is thrown uphill when tilling in the upslope direction (figure 6.5a).

Figure 6.4. Effects of tillage erosion on soils. Photo by USDA-NRCS.

Downslope tillage typically occurs at greater speed than when traveling uphill, making the situation even worse. Tillage along the contour also results in downslope soil movement. Soil lifted by a tillage tool comes to rest at a slightly lower position on the slope (figure 6.5b). A more serious situation occurs when using a moldboard plow along the contour. Moldboard plowing is typically performed by throwing the soil down the slope, as better inversion is thus obtained than by trying to turn the furrow up the slope (figure 6.5c). One unique feature of tillage erosion compared to wind, water, and gravitational

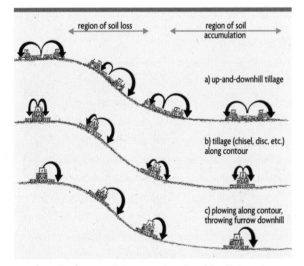

Figure 6.5. Three causes of erosion resulting from tilling soils on slopes.

erosion is that it is unrelated to extreme weather events and occurs gradually with every tillage operation.

Soil loss from slopes due to tillage erosion enhances the potential for further soil losses from water or wind erosion. On the other hand, tillage erosion does not generally result in off-site damage, because the soil is merely moved from higher to lower positions within a field. However, it is another reason to reduce tillage on sloping fields.

SOIL TILTH AND COMPACTION

A soil becomes more compact, or dense, when aggregates or individual particles of soil are forced closer together. Soil compaction has various causes and different visible effects. Compaction can occur either at or near the surface (surface compaction, which includes surface crusting as well as plow layer compaction) or lower down in the soil (subsoil compaction). See figure 6.6.

Surface Compaction

Plow layer compaction—compaction of the surface layer—has probably occurred to some extent in all intensively worked agricultural soils. It is the result of a loss of soil aggregation that typically has three primary causes—erosion, reduced organic matter levels, and force exerted by the weight of field equipment. The first two result in reduced supplies of sticky binding materials and a subsequent loss of aggregation.

Surface crusting has the same causes as plow layer compaction but specifically occurs when the soil surface is unprotected by crop residue or a plant canopy and the energy of raindrops disperses wet aggregates, pounding them apart so that particles settle into a thin, dense surface layer. The sealing of the soil reduces water infiltration, and the surface forms a hard crust when dried. If the crusting occurs soon after planting, it may delay or prevent seedling emergence. Even when the crust is not severe enough to limit germination, it can reduce water infiltration. Soils with surface crusts are prone to

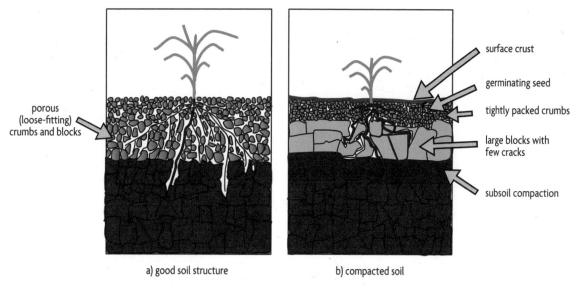

porous (loose-fitting) crumbs and blocks

surface crust

germinating seed

tightly packed crumbs

large blocks with few cracks

subsoil compaction

a) good soil structure

b) compacted soil

Figure 6.6. Plants growing in (a) soil with good tilth and (b) soil with all three types of compaction.

high rates of runoff and erosion. You can reduce surface crusting by leaving more residue on the surface and maintaining strong soil aggregation.

Compaction of soils by heavy equipment and tillage tools is especially damaging when soils are wet. This combination of factors is the primary cause for sub-soil compaction and one of the causes for plow layer compaction. To understand this, we need to know a little about soil *consistence*, or how soil reacts to external forces. At very high water contents, a soil may behave like a liquid (figure 6.7), because it has little internal cohesion (figure 5.10, left, p. 54). On a slope it can simply flow as a result of the force of gravity—as with mudslides during excessively wet periods. At slightly lower water contents, soil has somewhat more cohesion (figure 5.10, middle, p. 54), but it can still be easily molded and is said to be *plastic* (figure 6.7). Upon further drying, the soil will become *friable*—it will break apart rather than mold under pressure (figure 6.7).

The point between plastic and friable soil, the *plastic limit,* has important agricultural implications. When a soil is wetter than the plastic limit, it may become

seriously compacted if tilled or traveled on, because soil aggregates are pushed together into a smeared, dense mass. This compaction may be observed when you see shiny, cloddy furrows or deep tire ruts in a field (figure 6.8). When the soil is friable (the water content is below the plastic limit), it crumbles when tilled and aggregates resist compaction by field traffic. Thus, the potential for compaction is strongly influenced by the timing of field

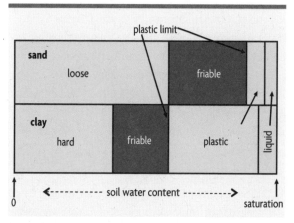

plastic limit

sand

loose

friable

clay

hard

friable

plastic

liquid

0

← - - - - - - - - - soil water content - - - - - - - - - →

saturation

Figure 6.7. Soil consistency states for a sand and a clay soil (friable soil is best for tillage).

Figure 6.8. Deep tire ruts in a hay field following harvest when soil was wet and plastic.

operations as related to soil moisture conditions.

A soil's consistency is strongly affected by its texture (figure 6.7). For example, as coarse-textured sandy soils drain, they rapidly change from being plastic to friable. Fine-textured loams and clays need longer drying periods to lose enough water to become friable. This extra drying time may cause delays when scheduling field operations.

Surface crusting and plow layer compaction are especially common with intensively tilled soils. Tillage operations often become part of a vicious cycle in which a compacted soil tills up very cloddy (figure 6.9a), and then requires extensive secondary tillage and packing trips to create a satisfactory seedbed (figure 6.9b). Natural aggregates break down, and organic matter decomposes in the process—contributing to more compaction in the future. Although the final seedbed may be ideal at the time of planting, rainfall shortly after planting may cause surface sealing and further settling (figure 6.9c), because few sturdy aggregates are present to

prevent the soil from dispersing. The result may be a soil with a dense plow layer and a crust at the surface. Some soils may hard-set like cement, even after the slightest drying, thereby slowing plant growth. Although the soil becomes softer when it re-wets, that moisture provides only temporary relief to plants.

Subsoil Compaction

Subsoil compaction—dense soil below the normally tilled surface layer—is usually referred to as a plow pan, although it is commonly caused by more than just plowing. Subsoil is easily compacted, because it is usually wetter, denser, higher in clay content, lower in organic matter, and less aggregated than topsoil. Also, subsoil is not loosened by regular tillage and cannot easily be amended with additions of organic materials, so compaction in the subsoil is more difficult to manage.

Subsoil compaction is the result of either direct loading or the transfer of compaction forces from the surface into deeper layers. Subsoil compaction occurs when farmers run heavy vehicles with poor weight distribution. The load exerted on the surface is transferred into the soil along a cone-shaped pattern (figure 6.10, p. 64). With increasing depth, the compaction force is distributed over a larger area, thereby reducing the pressure in deeper layers. When the loading force at the surface is small, say through foot or hoof traffic or a light tractor, the pressure exerted below the plow layer is minimal. But when the load is high from heavy equipment, the pressures at depth are sufficient to cause considerable soil compaction. When the soil is wet, the force causing compaction near the surface is more easily transferred to the subsoil. Clearly, the most severe compaction

CHECK BEFORE TILLING
To be sure that a soil is ready for equipment use, you can do the simple "ball test" by taking a handful of soil from the lower part of the plow layer and trying to make a ball out of it. If it molds easily and sticks together, the soil is too wet. If it crumbles readily, it is sufficiently dry for tillage or heavy traffic.

damage to subsoils occurs with the combination of heavy vehicle traffic and wet soil conditions.

Direct loading is also caused by the pressure of a tillage implement, especially a plow or disk, pressing on the soil below. Plows cause compaction because the weight of the plow plus the lifting of the furrow slices results in strong downward forces. Disks have much of their weight concentrated at the bottom of the disk and thereby cause pans. Subsoil compaction may also occur during moldboard plowing when a set of tractor wheels is placed in the open furrow, thereby applying wheel pressure directly to the soil below the plow layer.

CONSEQUENCES OF COMPACTION

As compaction pushes particles closer together, the soil becomes dense and pore space is lost. Notably, the larger pores are eliminated. Loss of aggregation from compaction is particularly harmful for fine- and medium-textured soils that depend on those pores for good infiltration and percolation of water, as well as air exchange with the atmosphere. Although compaction can also damage coarse-textured soils, the impact is less severe. They depend less on aggregation, because the pores between individual particles are sufficiently large to allow good water and air movement.

Compacted soil becomes hard when it dries, as it has many small pores that can hold water under high suction and pull particles tightly together. This can restrict root growth and the activity of soil organisms. Compacted soils typically have greater resistance to penetration at a given soil moisture level than a well-structured soil (figure 6.11, p. 65), which has large pores between aggregates that therefore easily pull apart. The resistance to penetration for a moist, high-quality soil is usually well below the critical level where root growth ceases for most crops—300 pounds per square inch (psi). As the soil dries, its strength increases, but a high-quality soil may not exceed the critical level for most (or all) of the moisture range. A compacted soil, on

a) Stage 1: Cloddy soil after tillage makes for a poor seedbed.

b) Stage 2: Soil is packed and pulverized to make a fine seedbed.

c) Stage 3: Raindrops disperse soil aggregates, forming a surface crust.

Figure 6.9. Three stages of tilth for a compacted soil that has become addicted to tillage.

SOME CROPS MORE SENSITIVE THAN OTHERS

Compaction doesn't affect all crops to the same extent. An experiment in New York found that direct-seeded cabbage and snap beans were more harmed by compaction than cucumbers, table beets, sweet corn, and transplanted cabbage. Much of the plant damage was caused by the secondary effects of compaction, such as prolonged soil saturation after rain, reduced nutrient availability or uptake, and greater pest problems.

the other hand, has a very narrow water content range for good root growth. The soil has increased resistance to penetration even in the wet range (the soil is hard). When it dries, a compacted soil hardens quicker than a well-structured soil, rapidly becoming so hard that it is well above the critical 300-psi level that restricts root growth.

Actively growing roots need large pores with diameters greater than about 0.1 mm, the size of most root tips. Roots must enter the pore and anchor themselves before continuing growth. Compacted soils that have few or no large pores don't allow plants to be effectively rooted—thus limiting water and nutrient uptake.

What happens when root growth is limited? The root system will probably develop short, thick roots and few fine roots or root hairs (figure 6.6). The few thick roots may be able to find some weak zones in the soil, often by following crooked patterns. These roots have thickened tissue and are not efficient at taking up water and nutrients. In many cases,

roots in degraded soils do not grow below the tilled layer into the subsoil (see figure 6.6)—it's just too dense and hard for them to grow. Deeper root penetration is especially critical under rain-fed agriculture. The limitation on deep root growth by subsoil compaction reduces the volume of soil from which plant roots can extract water and increases the probability of yield losses from drought stress.

There is also a more direct effect on plant growth, beyond the reduced soil volume for roots to explore. A root system that's up against mechanical barriers sends a hormonal signal to the plant shoot, which then slows down respiration and growth. This plant response appears to be a natural survival mechanism similar to what occurs when plants experience water stress. In fact, because some of the same hormones are involved—and mechanical resistance increases when the soil dries—it is difficult to separate the effects of compaction from those of drought.

THE WATER RANGE FOR BEST PLANT GROWTH

The limitations to plant growth caused by compaction and water extremes can be combined into the concept of the *optimum water range* for plant growth—the range of water contents under which plant growth is not reduced by drought, mechanical stress, or lack of

Figure 6.10. Forces of heavy loads are transferred deep into the soil, especially when the soil is wet.

depth of tillage

dry soil

wet soil

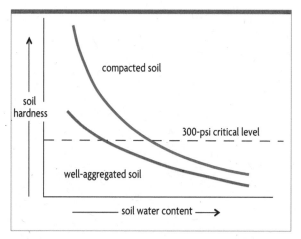

Figure 6.11. Compacted soils harden more quickly upon drying than well-aggregated soils.

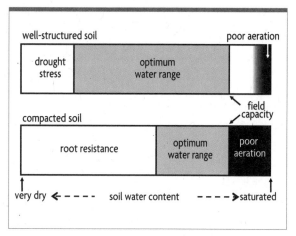

Figure 6.12. The optimum water range for crop growth for two different soils.

aeration (figure 6.12). This range, referred to by scientists as the *least-limiting water range,* is bounded on two sides—when the soil is too wet and when it's too dry.

The optimum water range in a well-structured soil has its *field capacity* on the wet end, as water above that moisture content is quickly drained out by gravity. On the dry end is the wilting point—beyond which the soil holds water too tightly to be used by plants. However, the soil water range for best growth in a compacted soil is much narrower. Even after a severely compacted soil drains to field capacity, it is still too wet because it lacks large pores and is poorly aerated. Good aeration requires at least 20% of the pore space (about 10% of the volume of the whole soil) to be air filled. On the dry end, plant growth in a compacted soil is commonly limited by soil hardness rather than by lack of available water. Plants in compacted soils therefore experience more stress during both wet and dry periods than plants in soils with good tilth. The effects of compaction on crop yields usually depend on the length and severity of excessive wet or dry periods and when those periods occur relative to critical times for plant growth.

CHEMICAL CONTAMINATION OF SOIL

Soils can be contaminated with chemicals—either naturally or by human activity—to such an extent that crops are adversely affected. In this section we'll start with a discussion of problems of saline and sodic (alkaline) soils, normally found in arid and semiarid regions. Then we'll discuss other types of chemical contamination.

Sodic and Saline Soils

Special soil problems are found in arid and semiarid regions, including soils that are high in salts, called saline soils, and those that have excessive sodium (Na^+), called sodic soils. Sometimes these go together and the result is a saline-sodic soil. Saline soils usually have good soil tilth, but plants can't get the water they need because the high salt levels in the soil inhibit water uptake. Sodic soils tend to have very poor physical structure because the high sodium levels cause clays to disperse, leading aggregates to break apart. As aggregates break down, these soils become difficult to work with and very inhospitable for plants because of compaction and greatly reduced aeration.

Aggregates of sodic soils disperse when they are saturated, and the solids then settle as individual particles and make the soil very dense (figure 6.13). When a sodic soil is fine textured, such poor structure develops—the consistency and appearance of a wet sodic clay soil are something like that of chocolate pudding—that there are serious problems with drainage, seedling emergence, and root development. A soil like that must be remediated before growing crops. Also, the ionic strength of the cations in the soil can affect aggregate stability. Some believe that soils with high magnesium-over-calcium ratios tend to have weaker aggregates and would benefit from calcium applications, but that is not supported by research, except in unusual situations.

Saline and sodic soils are commonly found in the semiarid and arid regions of the western U.S., with pockets of saline soils found near the coastline. They are common in similar climate zones in many countries around the world.

Although some soils are naturally saline or sodic or both, there are a number of ways that surface soils may become contaminated with salts and sodium. When irrigation water containing significant salt content is used—without applying extra water to leach out the salts—accumulation of salts can create a saline soil. Also, routine use of irrigation water with high sodium levels relative to calcium and magnesium will create a sodic soil over time. Over-irrigating, which often occurs

Figure 6.13. A sodic soil in Tasmania, Australia, that lacks aggregation and has problems with waterlogging when wet and with hardsetting when dry. Photo by Richard Doyle.

with conventional flood or furrow irrigation, can create salinity problems in the topsoil by raising water tables to within 2–3 feet of the surface. Shallow groundwater can then move by capillary action to the surface, where the water evaporates and the salts remain. Sometimes the extra moisture accumulated during a fallow year in semiarid regions causes field seeps, in which salty water high in sodium comes to the surface, leading to the development of saline and sodic patches.

Other Types of Chemical Contamination

Soils can become contaminated with all sorts of chemicals—from oil, gasoline, or pesticides to a variety of industrial chemicals and mining wastes. This contamination may occur through unintended spills, although in the past waste materials of these types were frequently disposed of by dumping on soils. In urban areas it is common to

---

SALINE SOIL.
Electrical conductivity of a soil extract is greater than 4 ds/m, enough to harm sensitive crops.

SODIC SOIL.
Sodium occupies more than 15% of the cation exchange capacity (CEC). Soil structure can significantly deteriorate in some soils at even lower levels of sodium.

SALT PRESENCE IN ALL SOILS

Salts of calcium, magnesium, potassium, and other cations—along with the common negatively charged anions chloride, nitrate, sulfate, and phosphate—are found in all soils. However, in soils in humid and subhumid (drier than humid, where most crops can be grown without irrigation) climates—with from 1–2 to well over 7 inches of water percolating beneath the root zone every year—salts don't usually accumulate to levels where they can be harmful to plants. Even when high rates of fertilizers are used, salts usually become a problem only when you place large amounts in direct contact with seeds or growing plants. Salt problems frequently occur in greenhouse potting mixes because growers regularly irrigate their greenhouse plants with water containing fertilizers and may not add enough water to leach the accumulating salts out of the pot.

find lead-contaminated soils as a result of the use of lead-based paint for decades. Lead, as well as other contaminants, frequently makes creating an urban garden a real challenge. Frequently, new topsoil is brought in, mixed with a large quantity of compost, and placed in raised beds so that plant roots grow above the contaminated soil. Agricultural soils that have a history of applications of sewage sludge (*biosolids* is the current term) may have received significant quantities of heavy metals such as cadmium, zinc, and chromium, as well as antibiotics and pharmaceutical drugs contained in the sludge.

There are a number of ways to remediate chemically contaminated soils. Sometimes adding manure or other organic amendments and growing crops stimulates soil organisms to break down organic chemicals into less harmless forms. Some plants are especially good at taking up certain metals from soil and are sometimes used to clean contaminated soil—but they then must be disposed of carefully.

SUMMARY

Soil degradation is one of the world's great environmental problems. At the same time as rivers are contaminated with sediments eroded from soils, severe erosion in many parts of the world results in a significant decrease in soil productivity. Although the immediate cause for water erosion may be intense rainfall, there are a number of reasons soil loss is especially severe in some situations. Susceptibility to erosion is influenced by soil type (silts are more susceptible), degree of aggregate stability, and extent of soil cover by residue and/or growing plants. Compaction, another form of soil degradation, can go unnoticed unless one looks for the symptoms, but it can have a damaging effect on plant growth. For a discussion of tried and true ways of reducing erosion and compaction, see chapters 14 and 15. And for how to reclaim saline, sodic, and saline-sodic soils, see chapter 20.

SOURCES

da Silva, A.P., B.D. Kay, and E. Perfect. 1994. Characterization of the least limiting water range of soils. *Soil Science Society of America Journal* 58: 1775–1781.

Letey, J. 1985. Relationship between soil physical properties and crop production. *Advances in Soil Science* 1: 277–294.

Ontario Ministry of Agriculture, Food, and Rural Affairs (OMA-FRA). 1997. *Soil Management*. Best Management Practices Series. Available from the Ontario Federation of Agriculture, Toronto, Ontario, Canada.

Soehne, W. 1958. Fundamentals of pressure distribution and soil compaction under tractor tires. *Agricultural Engineering* 39: 276–290.

Tull, J. 1733. The horse-hoeing husbandry: Or an essay on the principles of tillage and vegetation. Printed by A. Rhames, for R. Gunne, G. Risk, G. Ewing, W. Smith, & Smith and Bruce, Booksellers. Available online through the Core Historical Literature of Agriculture, Albert R. Mann Library, Cornell University, http://chla.library.cornell.edu.

Unger, P.W., and T.C. Kaspar. 1994. Soil compaction and root growth: A review. *Agronomy Journal* 86: 759–766.

Chapter 7

NUTRIENT CYCLES AND FLOWS

Increasingly . . . emphasis is being laid on the direction of natural forces, on the conservation
of inherent richness, on the acquirement of plant food supplies from the air and subsoil.

—J.L. HILLS, C.H. JONES, AND C. CUTLER, 1908

We used the term *cycle* earlier when discussing the flow of nutrients from soil to plant to animal to soil, as well as global carbon and nitrogen cycles (chapter 2). Some farmers minimize their use of nutrient supplements and try to rely more on natural soil nutrient cycles—as contrasted with purchased commercial fertilizers—to provide fertility to plants. But is it really possible to depend forever on the natural cycling of all the nutrients to meet a crop's needs? Let's first consider what a nutrient cycle is and how it differs from the other ways that nutrients move from one place to another.

When nutrients move from one place to another, that is a *flow*. There are many different types of nutrient flows that can occur. When you buy fertilizers or animal feeds, nutrients are "flowing" onto the farm. When you sell sweet corn, apples, alfalfa hay, meat, or milk, nutrients are "flowing" off the farm. Flows that involve products entering or leaving the farm gate are managed intentionally, whether or not you are thinking about

nutrients. Other flows are unplanned—for example, when nitrate is lost from the soil by leaching to groundwater or when runoff waters take nutrients along with eroded topsoil to a nearby stream.

When crops are harvested and brought to the barn to feed animals, that is a nutrient flow, as is the return of animal manure to the land. Together these two flows are a true cycle, because nutrients return to the fields from which they came. In forests and natural grassland, the cycling of nutrients is very efficient. In the early stages of agriculture, when almost all people lived near their fields, nutrient cycling was also efficient (figure 7.1a). However, in many types of agriculture, especially modern, "industrial-style" farming, there is little real cycling of nutrients, because there is no easy way to return nutrients shipped off the farm. In addition, nutrients in crop residues don't cycle very efficiently when the soil is without living plants for long periods, and nutrient runoff and leaching losses are much larger than from natural systems.

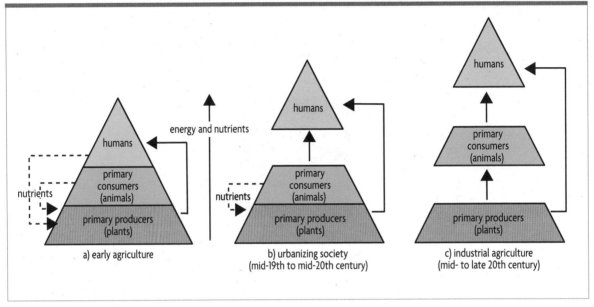

Figure 7.1. The patterns of nutrient flows change over time. From Magdoff, Lanyon, and Liebhardt (1997).

The first major break in the cycling of nutrients occurred as cities developed and nutrients began to routinely travel with farm products to feed the growing urban populations. It is rare for nutrients to travel many miles away from cities and return to the soils on which the crops and animals were originally raised (figure 7.1b,c). Thus, nutrients have accumulated in urban sewage and polluted waterways around the world. Even with the building of many new sewage treatment plants in the 1970s and 1980s, effluent containing nutrients still flows into waterways, and sewage sludges are not always handled in an environmentally sound manner.

The trend toward farm specialization, mostly driven by economic forces, has resulted in the second break in nutrient cycling by separating animals from the land that grows their feed. With specialized animal facilities (figure 7.1c), nutrients accumulate in manure while crop farmers purchase large quantities of fertilizers to keep their fields from becoming nutrient deficient.

DIFFERING FLOW PATTERNS

Different types of farms may have distinctly different nutrient flow patterns. Farms that exclusively grow grain or vegetables have a relatively high annual nutrient export (figure 7.2a). Nutrients usually enter the farm as either commercial fertilizers or various amendments and leave the farm as plant products. Some cycling of nutrients occurs as crop residues are returned to the soil and decompose. A large nutrient outflow is common, however, because a large portion of the crop is usually exported off the farm. For example, an acre of tomatoes or onions usually contains over 100 pounds of nitrogen, 20 pounds of phosphorus, and 100 pounds of potassium. For agronomic crops, the annual export of nutrients is about 100 pounds of nitrogen, 6 pounds of phosphorus, and 50 pounds of potassium per acre for corn grain and about 150 pounds of nitrogen, 20 pounds of phosphorus, and 130 pounds of potassium per acre for grass hay.

It should be fairly easy to balance inflows and out-flows on crop farms, at least theoretically. In practice, under good management, nutrients are depleted a bit by crop growth and removal until soil test levels fall too low, and then they're raised again with fertilizers or manures (see chapter 21).

A grass-fed beef operation that uses little to no imported feed should also be able to easily balance imports and exports because few nutrients leave the farm (as animals) and few nutrients are brought on to the farm (figure 7.2b). Most of the nutrients on this type of operation complete a true cycle on the farm—they are taken up from the soil by plants, which are eaten by the animals, and most of the nutrients are then returned to the soil as manure and urine. The same type of flows will occur on all integrated crop and livestock farms that produce all of their own feed.

A contrasting situation occurs on dairy farms if all of the forage is produced on the farm but grains and miner-als are purchased (figure 7.2c). Many dairy farms in the northeast U.S. do not have the land base to grow all the needed feed and tend to emphasize growing forage crops. In this situation, there are more sources of nutrients coming onto the farm—with concentrates (commonly mixtures containing corn grain and soy) and minerals usually comprising a larger source of nutrient inputs than fertilizers. In a study of forty-seven New York state dairy farms an average 76% of N came onto the farms as feeds and 23% as fertilizers. The percentages were pretty much the same for P (73% as feeds and 26% as fertiliz-ers). Most of the nutrients consumed by animals end up in the manure—from 60% to over 90% of the nitrogen, phosphorus, and potassium. Compared with crop farms, where a high percent of the crop grown is sold, fewer nutrients flow from dairy farms per acre. Under this situation, nutrients will accumulate on the farm and may eventually cause environmental harm from excess nitro-gen or phosphorus. This same problem exists for any ani-mal farm that imports a high percentage of its feed. To

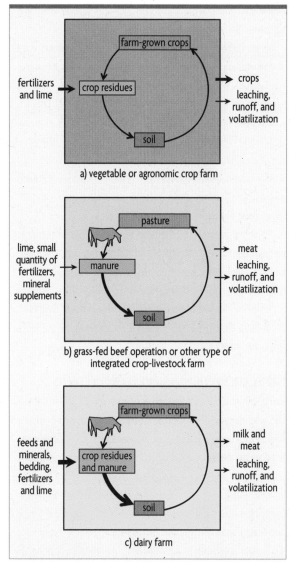

Figure 7.2. Nutrient flows and cycles on (a) crop farm, (b) grass-fed beef or other type of integrated crop-livestock farm, and (c) dairy farm.

put it another way, these farms have an inadequate land base to produce all their feed and therefore also have an inadequate land base on which to apply their manure at environmentally safe rates. Animal operations that import all feeds and have a limited land base to use the manure have the greatest potential to accumulate high amounts of nutrients. Contract growers of chickens are an example of this situation.

Two different nutrient flows occur when manure on livestock farms is applied to the fields used for growing the feeds. The nutrients in manure that came from farm-grown feed sources are completing a true cycle. The nutrients in manure that originally entered the farm as purchased feeds and mineral supplements are not participating in a true cycle. These nutrients are completing a flow that might have started in a far-away farm, mine, or fertilizer factory and are now just being transported from the barn to the field.

If there is enough cropland to grow most of the grain and forage needs, low amounts of imported nutrients and export per acre will result. Relatively low amounts of nutrients exported per acre as animal products make it easier to rely on nutrient cycling on a mixed livestock-crop farm that produces most of its feed than on a farm growing only crops.

IMPLICATIONS OF NUTRIENT FLOW PATTERNS

Long-distance transportation of nutrients is central to the way the modern food system functions. On average, the food we eat has traveled about 1,300 miles from field to processor to distributor to consumer. Exporting wheat from the U.S. Pacific Northwest to China involves an even longer distance, as does the import of apples from New Zealand to New York. The nutrients in concentrated commercial fertilizers also travel large distances from the mine or factory to distributors to the field. The specialization of the corn and soybean farms of the Midwest and the hog and chicken mega farms centralized in a few regions, such as Arkansas, the East Coast's Delmarva Peninsula, and North Carolina, has created a unique situation. The long-distance flows of nutrients from crop farms to animal farms require the purchase of fertilizers on the crop farms; meanwhile, the animal farms are overloaded with nutrients.

Of course, the very purpose of agriculture in the modern world—the growing of food and fiber and the use of the products by people living away from the farm—results in a loss of nutrients from the soil, even under the best possible management. In addition, leaching losses of nutrients, such as calcium, magnesium, and potassium, are accelerated by natural acidification, as well as by acidification caused by the use of fertilizers. Soil minerals—especially in the "young" soils of glaciated regions and in arid regions not subject to much leaching—may supply lots of phosphorus, potassium, calcium, and magnesium and many other nutrients. A soil with plentiful active organic matter also may supply nutrients for a long time. Eventually, however, nutrients will need to be applied to a continually cropped soil. Nitrogen is the only nutrient you can "produce" on the farm—legumes and their bacteria working together can remove nitrogen from the atmosphere and change it into forms that plants can use. However, sooner or later you will need to apply some phosphorus or potassium, even to the richest soils. If the farm is in a mixed crop-livestock system that exports only animal products, it may take a long time to deplete a rich soil, because so few nutrients per acre are exported with those products. For crop farms, especially in humid regions, the depletion occurs more rapidly, because more nutrients are exported per acre each year.

The issue eventually becomes not whether nutrients will be imported onto the farm, but rather, what source of nutrients you should use. Will the nutrients brought onto the farm be commercial fertilizers; traditional amendments (limestone); biologically fixed nitrogen; imported feeds or minerals for livestock; organic materials such as manures, composts, and sludges; or some combination of sources?

Three Different Flow Patterns

There are three main nutrient flow patterns, each one with implications for the long-term functioning of the farm and the environment: Imports of nutrients may be less than exports, imports may be greater than exports, or imports may equal exports.

Imports are less than exports. For farms "living off capital" and drawing down the supplies of nutrients from minerals and organic matter, nutrient concentrations continually decline. This can continue for a while, just like a person can live off savings in a bank account until the money runs out. At some point, the availability of one or more nutrients becomes so low that crop yields decrease. If this condition is not remedied, the farm becomes less and less able to produce food, and its economic condition will decline. This is clearly not a desirable situation for either the farm or the country. Unfortunately, the low productivity of much of Africa's agricultural lands is partially caused by this type of nutrient flow pattern, as increasing population pressure elevated land-use intensity, and fertilizer prices are too high for poor farmers. In previous times under the system of shifting cultivation, agricultural fields would have been allowed to return to forest for 20 or more years, during which time there would have been a replenishment of nutrients in the topsoil. One of the greatest challenges of our era is to increase the fertility of the soils of Africa, both by using fertilizers and by building up healthier soils.

Imports are larger than exports. Animal farms with inadequate land bases to produce all needed feed pose a different type of problem (figure 7.2c). As animal numbers increase relative to the available cropland and pasture, larger purchases of feeds (containing nutrients) are necessary. As this occurs, there is less land available—relative to the nutrient loads—to spread manure. Ultimately, the operation exceeds the capacity of the land to assimilate all the nutrients, and pollution of ground and surface waters occurs. For example, in a study of New York dairy farms, as animal density increased from around 1/4 of an animal unit (1 AU = one 1,000-pound animal, or a number of animals that together weigh 1,000 pounds) per acre to over 1 AU

per acre, the amount of N and P remaining on farms increased greatly. When there was 1/4 AU per acre, imports and exports were pretty much in balance. But at 1 AU per acre, around 150 pounds of N and 20 pounds of P remain on the farm per acre each year. The nutrient flow pattern on farms with high animal densities— with large imports, mainly as feeds, greatly exceeding exports—is not environmentally acceptable, although under current conditions it may be more economical than a more balanced pattern. In addition, some farmers, mainly organic ones, try to build up their soil organic matter and nitrogen supply by annual applications of manure or compost. This also causes an unacceptable buildup of nutrients in soils. In a survey from 2002 through 2004 of thirty-four organic farms from seven states in the Northeast, encompassing 203 fields, it was found that approximately a third of the soils had below-optimal levels of nutrients. However, about half of the fields were found to have excessive levels of P. Other ways need to be found to add organic matter through on-farm practices such as intensive use of cover crops and rotations with perennial forages.

Imports and exports are close to balanced. From the environmental perspective and for the sake of long-term soil health, fertility should be raised to—and then maintained at—optimal levels. The best way to keep desirable levels once they are reached is to roughly balance inflows and outflows. Soil tests can be very helpful in fine-tuning a fertility program and making sure that levels are not building up too high or being drawn down too low (see chapter 21). This can be a challenge and may not be economically possible for all farms. This is easier to do on a mixed crop-livestock farm than on either a crop farm or a livestock farm that depends significantly on imported feeds. As discussed above, because such a high percentage of the nutrients in feeds are excreted, animal products end up exporting relatively low amounts of nutrients off the farm. So if all the feeds are farm grown, adding an animal enterprise to a crop farm will tend to lower the nutrient exports.

In order to help balance nutrient imports and exports, routine soil tests should become a part of every farm's practices, because they will indicate whether nutrients are being depleted or accumulating to higher levels than needed.

SUMMARY

There is true nutrient cycling on most farms as crop residues or manures produced by animals fed crops grown on the farm are returned to the soil. However, there are potentially large flows of nutrients onto and off of farms, and we are concerned about cases where the flows are unbalanced. The inflow occurs as commercial and organic fertilizers and amendments as well as animal feeds are imported onto the farm and in manures and composts brought from off the farm. Exports are mainly in the form of crops and animal products. In general, larger amounts of nutrients are exported off the farm in vegetation (grains, forages, vegetables, etc.) than in animal products. This happens because a high percent of the nutrients in the feeds pass through the animal and are available as manure. And relatively few nutrients are exported per acre in the form of milk, meat, wool, etc., compared to the amount exported from crop farms. Nutrient flows are of such great concern because as nutrient levels decline, the soil rapidly degrades. On the other hand, when nutrients build up on the farm, they

tend to be more readily lost to the environment. Even midwestern U.S. cash grain farms that have balanced nutrient imports and exports lose nutrients. Nitrogen-leaching losses from these farms are having negative environmental effects on the Mississippi River and Gulf of Mexico ecosystems.

SOURCES

Anderson, B.H., and F.R. Magdoff. 2000. Dairy farm characteristics and managed flows of phosphorus. *American Journal of Alternative Agriculture* 15: 19–25.

Harrison, E., J. Bonhotal, and M. Schwarz. 2008. *Using Manure Solids as Bedding*. Report prepared by the Cornell Waste Management Institute (Ithaca, NY) for the New York State Energy Research and Development Authority.

Magdoff, F., L. Lanyon, and W. Liebhardt. 1997. Nutrient cycling, transformations, and flows: Implications for a more sustainable agriculture. *Advances in Agronomy* 60: 1–73.

Magdoff, F., L. Lanyon, and W. Liebhardt. 1998. *Sustainable Nutrient Management: A Role for Everyone*. Burlington, VT: Northeast Region Sustainable Agriculture Research and Education Program.

Morris, T.F. 2004. Survey of the nutrient status of organic vegetable farms. Search for project report LNE01-144 in the SARE project database, http://www.sare.org/projects.

Rasmussen, C.N., Q.M. Ketterings, G. Albrecht, L. Chase, and K.J. Czymmek. 2006. Mass nutrient balances: A management tool for New York dairy and livestock farms. In *Silage for Dairy Farms: Growing, Harvesting, Storing, and Feeding*, pp. 396–414. NRAES Conference, Harrisburg, PA, January 23–25.

Seiter, S., and W.R. Horwath. 2004. Strategies for managing soil organic matter to supply plant nutrients. In *Soil Organic Matter in Sustainable Agriculture*, ed. F. Magdoff and R.R. Weil, pp. 269–293. Boca Raton, FL: CRC Press.

ECOLOGICAL SOIL MANAGEMENT

Photo by Francesco Ridolfi

Chapter 8

SOIL HEALTH, PLANT HEALTH, AND PESTS

There are few farms in this or any country that are not capable of great improvement.

—LUCIUS D. DAVIS, 1830

SOIL PROPERTIES AND THEIR INTERRELATIONSHIPS

Healthy soils occur when their biological, chemical, and physical conditions are all optimal (figure 8.1), enabling high yields of crops. When this occurs, roots are able to proliferate easily, plentiful water enters and is stored in the soil, the plant has a sufficient nutrient supply, there are no harmful chemicals in the soil, and beneficial organisms are very active and able to keep potentially harmful ones in check as well as stimulate plant growth.

A soil's various properties are frequently related to one another, and the interrelationships should be kept in mind. For example, when a soil is compacted, there is a loss of the large pore spaces, making it difficult or impossible for some of the larger soil organisms to move or even survive. In addition, compaction may make the soil waterlogged, causing chemical changes such as when nitrate (NO_3^-) is denitrified and lost to the atmosphere as nitrogen gas (N_2). When soils contain a lot of sodium, common in arid and semiarid climates,

aggregates may break apart and cause the soils to have few pore spaces for air exchange. Plants will grow poorly in a soil that has degraded tilth even if it contains an optimum amount of nutrients. Therefore, to prevent problems and develop soil habitat that is optimal for plants, we can't just focus on one aspect of soil but must approach crop and soil management from a holistic point of view.

PLANT DEFENSES, MANAGEMENT PRACTICES, AND PESTS

Before discussing the key ecological principles and approaches to soil management, let's first see how amazing plants really are. They use a variety of systems to defend themselves from attack by insects and diseases. Sometimes they can just outgrow a small pest problem by putting out new root or shoot growth. Many plants also produce chemicals that slow down insect feeding. While not killing the insect, it at least limits the

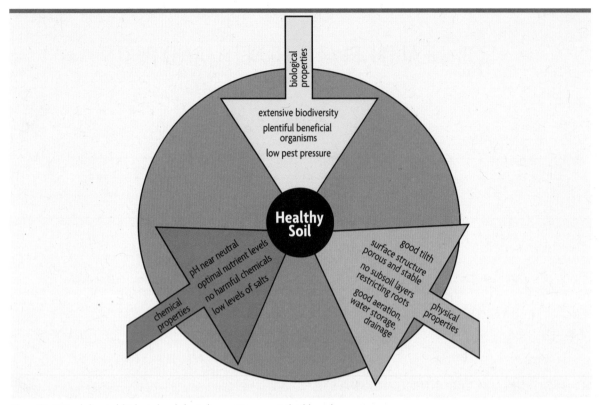

Figure 8.1. Optimal chemical, biological, and physical properties promote healthy soils.

damage. Beneficial organisms that attack and kill insect pests need a variety of sources of nutrition, usually obtained from flowering plants in and around the field. However, when fed upon—for example, by caterpillars—many plants produce a sticky sweet substance from the wounds, called "extra-floral nectar," which provides some attraction and food for beneficial organisms. Plants under attack by insects also produce airborne (volatile) chemicals that signal beneficial insects that the specific host it desires is on the plant. The beneficial insect, frequently a small wasp, then hones in on the chemical signal, finds the caterpillar, and lays its eggs inside it (figure 8.2). As the eggs develop, they kill the caterpillar. As one indication of how sophisticated this system is, the wasp that lays its eggs in the tomato hornworm caterpillar injects a virus along with the

eggs that deactivates the caterpillar's immune system. Without the virus, the eggs would not be able to develop and the caterpillar would not die. There is also evidence that plants near those with feeding damage sense the chemicals released by the wounded leaves and start making chemicals to defend themselves even before they are attacked.

Leaves are not the only part of the plant that can send signals when under attack that recruit beneficial organisms. When under attack by the western corn rootworm—a major pest—the roots of some varieties of corn have been shown to release a chemical that attracts a nematode that infects and kills rootworm larvae. During the process of breeding corn in the U.S., this ability to signal the beneficial nematode has apparently been lost. However, it is present in wild relatives and in European

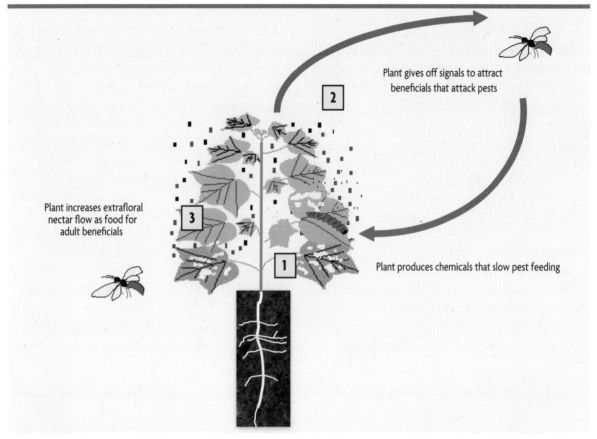

Figure 8.2. Plants use a number of defense strategies following damage by feeding insects. Modified from unpublished slide of W.J. Lewis.

corn varieties and is, therefore, available for reintroduction into U.S. corn varieties.

Plants also have defense systems to help protect them from a broad range of viral, fungal, and bacterial attacks. Plants frequently contain substances that inhibit a disease from occurring whether the plant is exposed to the disease organism or not. In addition, antimicrobial substances are produced when genes within the plant are activated by various compounds or organisms—or a pest—in the zone immediately around the root (the rhizosphere) or by a signal from an infection site on a leaf. This phenomenon is called "induced resistance." This type of resistance causes the plant to form various hormones and proteins that enhance the plant's defense

system. The resistance is called systemic because the entire plant becomes resistant to a disease, even far away from the site where the plant was stimulated.

There are two major types of induced resistance: systemic acquired resistance (SAR) and induced systemic resistance (ISR) (figure 8.3). SAR is induced when plants are exposed to a disease organism or even some organisms that do not produce disease. Once the plant is exposed to the organism, it will produce the hormone salicylic acid and defense proteins that protect the plant from a wide range of pests. ISR is induced when plant roots are exposed to specific plant growth–promoting rhizobacteria (PGPR) in the soil. Once the plants are exposed to these beneficial bacteria, hormones (jasmonate and ethylene) are produced that protect the plants from various pests. Some organic amendments have been shown to induce resistance in plants. Therefore, farmers who have very biologically active soils high in organic matter may already be taking advantage of induced resistance. However, there currently are no reliable and cost-effective indicators to determine whether a soil amendment or soil is enhancing a plant's defense mechanisms. More research needs to be conducted before induced resistance becomes a dependable form of pest management on farms. Although the mechanism works very differently from the way the human immune system works, the effects are similar—the system, once it's stimulated, offers protection from attack by a variety of pathogens and insects.

When plants are healthy and thriving, they are better able to defend themselves from attack and may also be less attractive to pests. When under one or more stresses, such as drought, nutrient limitations, or soil compaction, plants may "unwittingly" send out signals to pests saying, in effect, "Come get me, I'm weak." Vigorous plants are also better competitors with weeds, shading them out or just competing well for water and nutrients.

Many soil management practices discussed in this chapter and the other chapters in part 3 help to reduce the severity of crop pests. Healthy plants growing

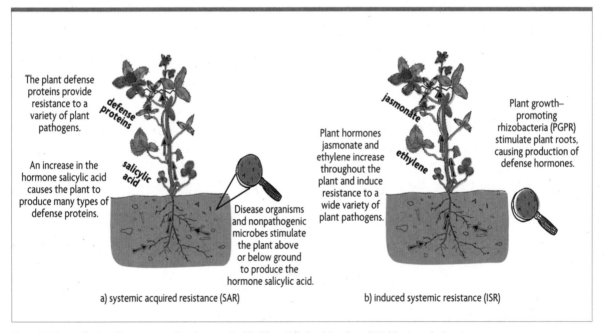

Figure 8.3. Types of induced resistance to plant diseases. Modified from Vallad and Goodman (2004) by Amanda Gervais.

on soils with good biological diversity can mount a strong defense against many pests. For examples of the effects of soil management on plant pests, see the box on the right. The issue of plant health is so critical to ecological soil and plant management because it also influences, as we have just seen, the ability of plants to resist pests. Developing optimal soil health is, therefore, the basis for management of crop pests on farms—it should be a central goal that underpins crop integrated pest management (IPM) programs.

ECOLOGICAL PRINCIPLES FOR AGRICULTURE

Approaching agriculture and soil management from an ecological point of view means first understanding the characteristics that comprise strong natural systems. Let's take a look at overall strategies that can contribute to similar strength of crops, animals, and farms. Then we'll briefly discuss practices that contribute to creating vital and strong agricultural systems (discussed in more detail in later chapters).

Ecological crop and soil management practices can be grouped under one or more of three overall strategies:
- grow healthy plants with strong defense capabilities
- stress pests
- enhance beneficial organisms

These overall strategies are accomplished by practices that maintain and enhance the habitat both above ground and in the soil. Ecological approaches call for designing the field and farm to take advantage of the inherent strengths of natural systems. Most of this is done prior to, and during, planting a crop and has the goal of preventing problems from developing by contributing to one or more of the three overall strategies. However, there are also routine management practices that occur during the season even if you have done a lot of preventive management. For example, irrigation is frequently needed for high-value crops such as fresh market vegetables—even in humid regions. Also, scouting for pest problems and beneficials should

MANAGING SOILS AND CROPS TO MINIMIZE PEST PROBLEMS

It is well established—and known by most farmers—that crop rotation can decrease many disease, insect, nematode, and weed pressures. A few other examples of management practices that reduce pest pressure follow:

- Insect damage can be reduced by avoiding excess inorganic nitrogen levels in soils by using better nitrogen management.

- Adequate nutrient levels reduce disease incidence. For example, calcium applications have reduced diseases in crops such as wheat, peanuts, soybeans, and peppers, while added potassium has reduced the incidence of fungal diseases in crops such as cotton, tomatoes, and corn.

- Damage from insect and disease (such as fungal diseases of roots) can be decreased by lessening soil compaction.

- Severity of root rots and leaf diseases can be reduced with composts that contain low levels of available nitrogen but still have some active organic matter.

- Many pests are kept under control by having to compete for resources or by direct antagonism from other insects (including the beneficials feeding on them). Good quantities of a variety of organic materials help maintain a diverse group of soil organisms.

- Root surfaces are protected from fungal and nematode attack by high rates of beneficial mycorrhizal fungi. Most cover crops help keep mycorrhizal fungi spore counts high and promote higher rates of infection by the beneficial fungi.

- Parasitic nematodes can be suppressed by selected cover crops.

- Weed seed numbers are reduced in soils that have a lot of biological activity, with both microorganisms and insects helping the process.

- Weed seed predation by ground beetles is encouraged by reduced tillage and maintenance of surface residues. Reduced tillage also keeps the weed seeds at the surface, where they are accessible to predation by other organisms, such as rodents, ants, and crickets.

- Residues of some cover crops, such as winter rye, produce chemicals that reduce weed seed germination.

STRONG ECOSYSTEM CHARACTERISTICS

Efficiency. Efficient energy flows are characteristic of natural systems. The sun's energy captured by green plants is used by many organisms, as fungi and bacteria decompose organic residues and are then fed upon by other organisms, which are themselves fed upon by others higher up the food web. Natural ecosystems also tend to be efficient in capturing and using rainfall and in mobilizing and cycling nutrients. This helps to keep the ecosystem from "running down" because of excessive loss of nutrients and at the same time helps maintain the quality of the groundwater and surface waters. Rainfall tends to enter the porous soil, rather than run off, providing water to plants as well as recharge to groundwater, slowly releasing water to streams and rivers.

Diversity. High biological diversity, both above ground and in the soil, characterizes many natural ecosystems in temperate and tropical regions. It provides nutrients to plants, checks on disease outbreaks, etc. For example, competition for resources and specific antagonisms (such as antibiotic production) from the multitude of soil organisms usually keep soilborne plant diseases from severely damaging a natural grassland or forest.

Self-sufficiency. A consequence of efficiency and diversity in natural terrestrial ecosystems is that they become self-sufficient—requiring only inputs of sunlight and rainfall.

Self-regulation. Because of the great diversity of organisms, outbreaks (or huge population increases) of diseases or insects that severely damage plants or animals are uncommon. In addition, plants have a number of defense mechanisms that help protect them from attack.

Resiliency. Disturbances, such as climate extremes, occur in all ecosystems—natural or not. The stronger ones are more resistant to disturbances and are able to bounce back more quickly.

—MODIFIED FROM MAGDOFF (2007).

be part of routine management during the season. If an unanticipated problem, such as an insect outbreak, arises, remedial action, such as applying the most ecologically sound pesticide or releasing purchased beneficials into the field, may be required to save the crop.

Ecological principles provide a good framework for sustainable management, but we must also recognize that crop production is inherently an "unnatural" process because we favor one organism (the crop plant) over the competing interests of others. With currently available pesticides, the temptation exists to simply wipe out competitors—for example through soil fumigation—but this creates dependency on purchased materials from off the farm and weakens the overall resiliency of the soil and cropping system. The goal of ecological crop

and soil management is to minimize the extent of reactive management (which reacts to unanticipated occurrences) by creating conditions that help grow healthy plants, promote beneficials, and stress pests. The discussion below and in the rest of this book focuses on ways to maintain and enhance habitat in order to promote one or more of the three strategies listed above.

ECOLOGICAL CROP AND SOIL MANAGEMENT

We'll discuss ecological crop and soil management practices as part of a general framework for approaching ecological crop management (figure 8.4). The heart of the matter is that the strength of the system is improved by creating improved habitat both above ground and in the soil. Although it is somewhat artificial to talk

82

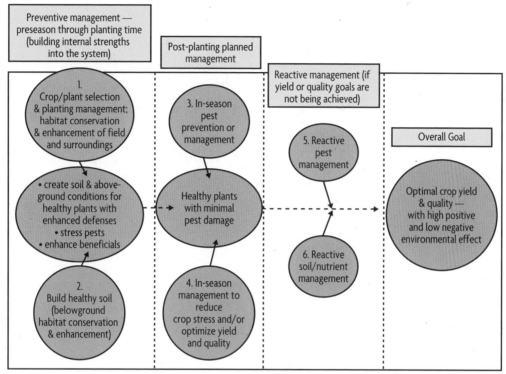

Figure 8.4. A whole-system approach to soil and crop management at the field level. Modified from Magdoff (2007).

separately about aboveground and soil habitat—many practices help both at the same time—it should make many issues clearer. Not all of the aboveground discussion refers directly to management of soil, but most does. In addition, the practices we'll discuss contribute to one or more of the overall strategies: (a) growing healthy plants with strong defense capabilities, (b) stressing pests, and (c) enhancing beneficial organisms.

Aboveground Habitat Management

There are numerous ways that the aboveground habitat can be improved to help grow healthy plants, stress pests, and enhance beneficial organisms:

- Select crops and varieties that are resistant to local pests (in addition to other qualities such as yield, taste, etc.).

- Use appropriate planting densities (and companion crops) to help crops grow vigorously, smother weeds, and (with companion crops) provide some protection against pests. In some cases, blends of two or more varieties of the same crop (one susceptible to a pest but with a higher yield potential, and one that's resistant) have shown potential for increasing total yields for wheat and rice. Even though the farmer is growing the same crop, increased genetic diversity due to using different varieties (cultivars) seems to provide some protection. Perhaps there are possibilities for growing mixes of other crops as well.

- Plant perimeter (trap) crops that are more attractive to a particular pest than the economic crop(s) growing in the middle of the field and so can intercept incoming insects. (This has been successfully practiced by planting blue Hubbard squash on the perimeter of summer squash fields to intercept the striped cucumber beetle.)

- Create field boundaries and zones within fields that are attractive to beneficial insects. This usually involves planting a mix of flowering plants around or as strips inside fields to provide shelter and food for beneficials.
- Use cover crops routinely for multiple benefits, such as providing habitat for beneficial insects, adding N and organic matter to the soil, reducing erosion and enhancing water infiltration into the soil, retaining nutrients in the soil, and much more. It is possible to supply all of the nitrogen to succeeding crops by growing a vigorous winter legume cover crop, such as crimson clover in the South and hairy vetch in the North.
- Use rotations that are complex, involve plants of different families, and, if at all possible, include sod crops such as grass/clover hay that remain without soil disturbance for a number of years.
- Reduce tillage. This is an important part of an ecological approach to agriculture. Tillage buries residues, leaving the soil bare and more susceptible to the erosive effects of rainfall, and at the same time breaks up natural soil aggregates that help infiltration, storage, and drainage of precipitation. (The use of practices that reduce erosion is critical to sustaining soil productivity.)

Some of these practices—use of cover crops and more complex rotations and reducing tillage—will also be mentioned below under "Enhancing Soil Habitat" and discussed in detail in later chapters.

Enhancing Soil Habitat

The general practices for improving the soil as a place for crop roots and beneficial organisms to thrive are the same for all fields and farms and are the focus of our discussions in the next chapters. However, the real questions are which ones are best implemented, and how are they implemented on a specific farm? These questions can only be answered by knowing the specific situation as well as the resources available on the farm. However, many practices are outlined below that may make the soil a better environment for growing healthy plants, stressing pests, and enhancing beneficial organisms:

- Add organic materials—animal manures, composts, tree leaves, cover crops, rotation crops that leave large amounts of residue, etc.—on a regular basis (see chapters 10 through 13).
- Use different types of organic materials because they have different positive effects on soil biological, chemical, and physical properties (chapter 9).
- Keep soil covered with living vegetation and/or crop residues by using cover crops, sod crops in rotation, and/or reduced tillage practices (chapters 10, 11, and 16). This encourages water infiltration, reduces erosion, promotes organisms that feed on weed seeds, and increases mycorrhizal numbers on the roots of the following crops.
- Reduce soil compaction to a minimum by keeping off fields when they are too wet, redistributing loads, using traffic lanes, etc. (chapter 15).
- Use practices to supply supplemental fertility sources, when needed, that better match nutrient availability to crop uptake needs (chapters 18 through 21). This helps to reduce both weed and insect damage as well as pollution of surface and groundwaters.
- For soils in arid and semiarid climates, reduce salt and sodium contents if they are high enough to interfere with plant growth (chapter 20).
- Evaluate soil health status (chapter 22) so that you can see improvement and know what other soil-improving practices might be appropriate.
- Use multiple practices that improve the soil habitat (chapter 23). Each one may have a positive effect, but there are synergies that come into play when a number of practices—such as reduced tillage and cover crops—are combined.

CONFLICTING DISEASE MANAGEMENT ADVICE?

In this book we promote reduced tillage and retention of crop residues at the soil surface. But farmers are often encouraged to incorporate crop residues because they can harbor disease organisms. Why the conflicting advice? The major difference is in the overall approach to soil and crop management. In a system that involves good rotations, conservation tillage, cover crops, other organic matter additions, etc., the disease pressure is reduced as soil biological diversity is increased, beneficial organisms are encouraged, and crop stresses are reduced. In a more traditional system, the susceptibility dynamics are different, and a disease organism is more likely to become a dominant concern, necessitating a reactive approach. A long-term strategy of building soil and plant health reduces the need to use short-term cures.

SUMMARY

The overall strategies of ecologically sound crop and soil management focus on *prevention* of factors that might limit plant growth. These three strategies are to grow healthy plants with enhanced defense capabilities, stress pests, and enhance beneficial organisms. There are a variety of practices that contribute to these overall goals and have been discussed in this chapter as enhancing both aboveground habitat and soil habitat. There is some overlap, because cover crops, crop rotations, and tillage have effects both above and below ground. The various practices that improve and maintain soil habitats are discussed in detail in the following chapters of part 3.

As indicated in figure 8.4, in addition to the work of prevention (mainly accomplished before and during planting), there are routine management practices that are carried out during the season, and remedial or reactive approaches may need to be used if prevention practices are not enough to take care of some potential threat to the crop. However, just as with human and animal health, prevention is preferred to curing a problem after it develops. For this reason, the orientation of the remaining sections of the book are on practices that help prevent problems from developing that might limit the growth or quality of plants.

SOURCES

Borrero, C., J. Ordovs, M.I. Trillas, and M. Aviles. 2006. Tomato Fusarium wilt suppressiveness. The relationship between the organic plant growth media and their microbial communities as characterised by Biolog. *Soil Biology & Biochemistry* 38: 1631–1637.

Dixon, R. 2001. Natural products and plant disease resistance. *Nature*. 411: 843–847.

Gurr, G.M., S.D. Wratten, and M.A. Altieri, eds. 2004. *Ecological Engineering for Pest Management: Advances in Habitat Management for Arthropods.* Ithaca, NY: Comstock Publishing Association, Cornell University Press.

Magdoff, F. 2007. Ecological agriculture: Principles, practices, and constraints. *Renewable Agriculture and Food Systems* 22(2): 109–117.

Magdoff, F., and R. Weil. 2004. Soil organic matter management strategies. In *Soil Organic Matter in Sustainable Agriculture,* ed. F. Magdoff and R.R. Weil, pp. 45–65. Boca Raton, FL: CRC Press.

Park, S-W., E. Kaimoyo, D. Kumar, S. Mosher, and D.F. Klessig. 2007. Methyl salicylate is a critical mobile signal for plant systemic acquired resistance. *Science* 318: 313–318.

Rasmann, S., T.G. Kollner, J. Degenhardt, I. Hiltpold, S. Toepfer, U. Kuhlmann, J. Gershenzon, and T.C.J. Turlings. 2005. Recruitment of entomopathic nematodes by insect damaged maize roots. *Nature* 434: 732–737.

Sullivan, P. 2004. Sustainable management of soil-borne plant diseases. ATTRA, http://www.attra.org/attra-pub/PDF/soil-borne.pdf.

Vallad, G.E., and R.M. Goodman. 2004. Systemic acquired resistance and induced systemic resistance in conventional agriculture. *Crop Science* 44: 1920–1934.

Chapter 9

MANAGING FOR HIGH-QUALITY SOILS:
ORGANIC MATTER, SOIL PHYSICAL CONDITION, NUTRIENT AVAILABILITY

Because organic matter is lost from the soil through decay, washing, and leaching,
and because large amounts are required every year for crop production, the necessity of
maintaining the active organic-matter content of the soil, to say nothing of the desirability
of increasing it on many depleted soils, is a difficult problem.

—A.F. Gustafson, 1941

Increasing the quality of a soil—enhancing it as a habitat for plant roots and beneficial organisms—takes a lot of thought and action over many years. Of course, there are things that can be done right off—plant a cover crop this fall or just make a New Year's resolution not to work soils that really aren't ready in the spring (and then stick with it). Other changes take more time. You need to study carefully before drastically changing crop rotations, for example. How will the new crops be marketed, and are the necessary labor and machinery available?

All actions taken to improve soil health should contribute to one or more of the following: (a) growing healthy plants, (b) stressing pests, and (c) increasing beneficial organisms. First, various practices to build up and maintain high levels of soil organic matter are key. Second, developing and maintaining the best possible soil physical condition often require other types of practices, in addition to those that directly impact soil organic matter. Paying better attention to soil tilth and compaction is more important than ever, because of the use of very heavy field machinery. Last, although good organic matter management goes a long way toward providing good plant nutrition in an environmentally sound way, good nutrient management involves additional practices. In this chapter we'll focus on issues of organic matter management.

ORGANIC MATTER MANAGEMENT

As we discussed in chapter 3, there are no generally accepted guidelines as to how much organic matter should be in a particular soil. And it is difficult to be sure exactly why problems develop when organic matter is depleted in an individual field. However, even in the early 20th century, agricultural scientists proclaimed,

"Whatever the cause of soil unthriftiness, there is no dispute as to the remedial measures. Doctors may disagree as to what causes the disease, but agree as to the medicine. Crop rotation! The use of barnyard and green manuring! Humus maintenance! These are the fundamental needs" (Hills, Jones, and Cutler, 1908). A century later, these are still some of the major remedies available to us.

There seems to be a contradiction in our view of soil organic matter. On one hand, we want crop residues, dead microorganisms, and manures to decompose. If soil organic matter doesn't decompose, no nutrients are made available to plants, no glue to bind particles is manufactured, and no humus is produced to hold on to plant nutrients as water leaches through the soil. On the other hand, numerous problems develop when soil organic matter is significantly depleted through decomposition. This dilemma of wanting organic matter to decompose, but not wanting to lose too much, means that organic materials must be continually added to the soil. A supply of active organic matter must be maintained, so that soil organisms have sufficient food, and so that humus can continually accumulate. This does not mean that organic materials must be added to each field every year—although that happens to a greater or lesser degree if crop roots and aboveground residues remain. However, it does mean that a field cannot go without a significant quantity of organic residue additions for many years without paying the consequences.

Do you remember that plowing a soil is similar to opening up the air intake on a wood stove? What we really want in soil is a slow, steady burn of the organic matter. You get that in a wood stove by adding wood every so often and making sure the air intake is on a medium setting. In soil, you get a steady burn by adding organic residues regularly and by not disturbing the soil too often or too greatly.

There are four general strategies for organic matter management. First, use crop residues more effectively and find new sources of residues to add to soils. New residues can include those you grow on the farm, such as cover crops, or those available from various local sources. Second, try to use a number of different types of materials—crop residues, manures, composts, cover crops, leaves, etc. It is important to provide varied residue sources to help develop and maintain a diverse group of soil organisms. Third, although use of organic materials from off farm can be a good source for building soil organic matter and adding nutrients, some farmers overload their fields with excess nutrients by excess imports of organic materials. Crop residues (including cover crops) as well as on-farm-derived animal manures and composts help to supply organic materials and cycle nutrients without a buildup of excessive levels of nutrients. Fourth, implement practices that decrease the loss of organic matter from soils because of accelerated decomposition or erosion.

All practices that help to build organic matter levels either add more organic materials than in the past or decrease the rate of organic matter loss from soils. In addition, practices to build organic matter will usually enhance beneficial organisms and/or stress pests (table 9.1). Those practices that do both may be especially useful. Practices that reduce losses of organic matter either slow down the rate of decomposition or decrease the amount of erosion. Soil erosion must be controlled to keep organic matter–enriched topsoil in place. In addition, organic matter added to a soil must either match or exceed the rate of loss by decomposition. These additions can come from manures and composts brought from off the field, crop residues and mulches that remain following harvest, or cover crops. Reduced tillage lessens the rate of organic matter decomposition and also may result in less erosion. When reduced tillage increases crop growth and residues returned to soil, it is usually a result of better water infiltration and storage and less surface evaporation. It is not possible in this book to give specific management recommendations for

Table 9.1
Effects of Different Management Practices on Gains and Losses of Organic Matter, Beneficial Organisms, and Pests

Management Practice	Gains Increase	Losses Decrease	Enhance Beneficials (EB), Stress Pests (SP)
Add materials (manures, composts, other organic materials) from off the field	yes	no	EB, SP
Better utilize crop residue	yes	no	EB
Include high-residue-producing crops in rotation	yes	no	EB, SP
Include sod crops (grass/legume forages) in rotation	yes	yes	EB, SP
Grow cover crops	yes	yes	EB, SP
Reduce tillage intensity	yes/no*	yes	EB
Use conservation practices to reduce erosion	yes/no*	yes	EB

* Practice may increase crop yields, resulting in more residue.

all situations. In chapters 10 through 16, we will evaluate management options that enhance the soil environment and issues associated with their use. Most of these practices improve organic matter management, although they have many different types of effects on soils.

Using Organic Materials

Amounts of crop residues. Crop residues are usually the largest source of organic materials available to farmers. The amount of crop residue left after harvest varies depending on the crop. Soybeans, potatoes, lettuce, and corn silage leave little residue. Small grains, on the other hand, leave more residue, while sorghum and corn harvested for grain leave the most. A ton or more of crop residues per acre may sound like a lot of organic material being returned to the soil. However, keep in mind that after residues are decomposed by soil organisms, only about 10–20% of the original amount is converted into stable humus.

The amount of roots remaining after harvest also can range from very low to fairly high (table 9.2). In addition to the actual roots left at the end of the season, there are considerable amounts of sloughed-off root cells, as well as exudates from the roots during the season. This may actually increase the plant's belowground inputs of organic matter by another 50%. Probably the most effective way to increase soil organic matter is to grow crops

with large root systems. Compared to aboveground residues, the organic material from roots decomposes more slowly, contributes more to stable soil organic matter, and, of course, does not have to be incorporated into the soil to achieve deep distribution. When no-till is used, root residues, along with root exudates given off when they were alive, tend to promote formation and stabilization of aggregates—more so than surface-derived residue. One of the reasons that the many soils of the Midwest are so rich is that for thousands of years prairie plants with extensive and deep root systems grew there—annually contributing large quantities of organic matter deep into the soil.

Some farmers remove aboveground residues such as small grain straw from the field for use as animal

Table 9.2
Estimated Root Residue Produced by Crops

Crop	Estimated Root Residues (lbs/acre)
Native prairie	15,000–30,000
Italian ryegrass	2,600–4,500
Winter cereal	1,500–2,600
Red clover	2,200–2,600
Spring cereal	1,300–1,800
Corn	3,000–4,000
Soybeans	500–1,000
Cotton	500–900
Potatoes	300–600

Sources: Topp et al. (1995) and other sources.

ABOVEGROUND CROP RESIDUES

The amount of aboveground residue left in the field after harvest depends on the type of crop and its yield. The top table contains the amounts of residues found in California's highly productive, irrigated San Joaquin Valley. These residue amounts are higher than would be found on most farms, but the relative amounts for the various crops are interesting.

Crop Residues in the San Joaquin Valley (California)

CROP	TONS/ACRE
Corn (grain)	5
Broccoli	3
Cotton	2.5
Wheat (grain)	2.5
Sugarbeets	2
Safflower	1.5
Tomatoes	1.5
Lettuce	1
Corn (silage)	.5
Garlic	.5
Wheat (after baling)	.25
Onions	.25

Residues of Common Crops in the Midwest and Great Plains

CROP	TONS/ACRE
Corn (120 bu.)	3.5
Sorghum (80 bu.)	2.5
Wheat (35 bu.)	2
Soybeans (35 bu.)	less than 1

—FROM VARIOUS SOURCES

bedding or to make compost. Later, these residues return to contribute to soil fertility as manures or composts. Sometimes residues are removed from fields to be used by other farmers or to make another product. There is increasing interest in using crop residues as a feedstock for the production of biofuels. This activity could cause considerable harm to soil health if sufficient residues are not allowed to return to soils.

Burning of wheat, rice, and other crop residues in the field still occurs, although it is becoming less common in the United States as well as in other countries. Residue is usually burned to help control insects or diseases or to make next year's fieldwork easier. Residue burning may be so widespread in a given area that it causes a local air pollution problem. Burning also diminishes the amount of organic matter returned to the soil and the amount of protection against raindrop impact.

Sometimes important needs for crop residues and manures may prevent their use in maintaining or building soil organic matter. For example, straw may be removed from a grain field to serve as mulch in a strawberry field. These trade-offs of organic materials can sometimes cause a severe soil-fertility problem if allowed to continue for a long time. This issue is of much more widespread importance in developing countries, where resources are scarce. In those countries, crop residues and manures frequently serve as fuel for cooking or heating when gas, coal, oil, and wood are not available. In addition, straw may be used in making bricks or used as thatch for housing or to make fences. Although it is completely understandable that people in resource-poor regions use residues for such purposes, the negative effects of these uses on soil productivity can be substantial. An important way to increase agricultural productivity in developing countries is to find alternate sources for fuel and building materials to replace the crop residues and manures traditionally used.

Using residues as mulches. Crop residues or composts can be used as mulch on the soil surface. This

CROP RESIDUES: FUEL VS. SOIL ORGANIC MATTER

Partial removal of corn stover after harvest for use as biofuel.

There is currently a huge effort under way to more efficiently convert structural plant material (cellulose) into fuel. As we write this, it is not commercially feasible yet—but this may change in the future. One of the dangers for soil health is that if the conversion of plant structural material (not grain) to ethanol becomes commercially viable, there may be a temptation to use crop residues as an energy source, thus depriving the soil of needed organic inputs. For example, most aboveground corn residue needs to return to the soil to maintain the soil's quality. It is estimated that between 2 and 5 tons of corn residue are needed to maintain a soil's favorable properties. A long-term study in New York indicated that, at least for that particular soil, modest removal of cornstalks did not cause a deterioration of soil. However, we must be very cautious when considering removing crop residue as a routine practice. As the legendary soil scientist Hans Jenny put it in 1980, "I am arguing against indiscriminate conversion of biomass and organic wastes to fuels. The humus capital, which is substantial, deserves being maintained because good soils are a national asset."

If a perennial crop such as switchgrass is harvested to burn as an energy source or to convert into liquid fuel, at least soil organic matter may continue to increase because of the contributions of extensive root systems and the lack of tillage. On the other hand, large amounts of nitrogen fertilizer plus other energy-consuming inputs will reduce the conversion efficiency of switchgrass into liquid fuel.

occurs routinely in some reduced-tillage systems when high-residue-yielding crops are grown or when killed cover crops remain on the surface. In some small-scale vegetable and berry farming, mulching is done by applying straw from off site. Strawberries grown in the colder, northern parts of the country are routinely mulched with straw for protection from winter heaving. The straw is blown on in late fall and is then moved into the inter-rows in the spring, providing a surface mulch during the growing season.

Mulching has numerous benefits, including:

- enhanced water availability to crops due to better infiltration into the soil and less evaporation from the soil (approximately 1/3 of water loss in dryland irrigated agriculture is from evaporation from the soil, which can be greatly reduced by using a surface mulch)
- weed control
- less extreme changes in soil temperature
- reduced splashing of soil onto leaves and fruits and vegetables (making them look better as well as reducing diseases)
- reduced infestations of certain pests (Colorado potato beetles on potatoes and tomatoes are less severe when these crops are grown in a mulch system)

On the other hand, residue mulches in cold climates can delay soil warming in the spring, reduce early-season growth, and increase problems with slugs during wet periods. When it is important to get a rotation crop in early, you might consider using a low-residue crop like soybeans the previous year. Of course, one of the reasons for the use of plastic mulches (clear and black) for crops like tomatoes and melons is to help warm the soil.

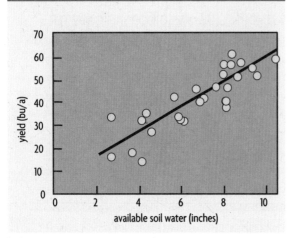

Figure 9.1. Relationship between winter wheat grain yield and soil water at wheat planting over six years. Modified from Nielsen et al. (2002).

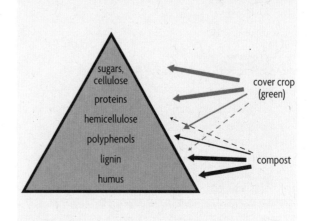

Figure 9.2. Different types of residues have varying effects on soils (thicker lines indicate more material, dashed lines indicate very small percentage). Modified from Oshins and Drinkwater (1999).

Residue management in arid and semiarid regions. In arid and semiarid regions water is usually the most common limitation to crop yields. For winter wheat in semiarid regions, for example, the available water at planting often foretells final yields (figure 9.1). Thus, in order to provide more available water for crops, we want to use practices that help store more water in soils and keep it from evaporating directly to the atmosphere. Standing residue allows more snow to be maintained in the field after being deposited, significantly increasing available soil water in spring—sunflower stalks used in this way can increase soil water by 4 to 5 inches. And a mulch during the growing season helps both to store water from irrigation or rainfall and to keep it from evaporating.

Effects of Residue Characteristics on Soil
Decomposition rates and effects on aggregation. Residues of various crops and manures have different properties and, therefore, have different effects on soil organic matter. Materials with low amounts of harder-to-degrade hemicellulose, polyphenols, and lignin, such as cover crops (especially legumes) when still very green

and soybean residue, decompose rapidly (figure 9.2) and have a shorter-term effect on soil organic matter levels than residues with high levels of these chemicals (for example, cornstalks and wheat straw). Manures, especially those that contain lots of bedding (high in hemicellulose, polyphenols, and lignin), decompose more slowly and tend to have more long-lasting effects on total soil organic matter than crop residues and manures without bedding. Also, cows—because they eat a diet containing lots of forages that are not completely decomposed during digestion—produce manure with longer-lasting effects on soils than nonruminants, such as chickens and hogs, that are fed exclusively a high-grain and low-fiber diet. Composts contribute little active organic matter to soils but add a lot of well-decomposed materials (figure 9.2).

In general, residues containing a lot of cellulose and other easy-to-decompose materials will have a greater effect on soil aggregation than compost, which has already undergone decomposition. Because aggregates are formed from by-products of decomposition by soil organisms, organic additions like manures, cover crops, and straw will usually enhance aggregation more than compost. (However, adding compost does improve soils in many ways, including increasing the water-holding capacity.)

Although it's important to have adequate amounts of organic matter in soil, that isn't enough. A variety of residues are needed to provide food to a diverse population of organisms, provide nutrients to plants, and furnish materials that promote aggregation. Residues low in hemicellulose and lignin usually have very high levels of plant nutrients. On the other hand, straw or sawdust (containing a lot of lignin) can be used to build up organic matter, but a severe nitrogen deficiency and an imbalance in soil microbial populations will occur unless a readily available source of nitrogen is added at the same time (see discussion of C:N ratios below). In addition, when insufficient N is present, less of the organic material added to soils actually ends up as humus.

C:N ratio of organic materials and nitrogen availability. The ratio of the amount of a residue's carbon to the amount of its nitrogen influences nutrient availability and the rate of decomposition. The ratio, usually referred to as the C:N ratio, may vary from around 15:1 for young plants, to between 50:1 and 80:1 for the old straw of crop plants, to over 100:1 for sawdust. For comparison, the C:N ratio of soil organic matter is usually in the range of about 10:1 to 12:1, and the C:N of soil microorganisms is around 7:1.

The C:N ratio of residues is really just another way of looking at the percentage of nitrogen (figure 9.3). A high C:N residue has a low percentage of nitrogen. Low C:N residues have relatively high percentages of nitrogen. Crop residues usually average 40% carbon, and this figure doesn't change much from plant to plant. On the other hand, nitrogen content varies greatly depending on the type of plant and its stage of growth.

If you want crops to grow immediately following the application of organic materials, care must be taken to make nitrogen available. Nitrogen availability from residues varies considerably. Some residues, such as fresh,

young, and very green plants, decompose rapidly in the soil and, in the process, may readily release plant nutrients. This could be compared to the effect of sugar eaten by humans, which results in a quick burst of energy. Some of the substances in older plants and in the woody portion of trees, such as lignin, decompose very slowly in soils. Materials such as sawdust and straw, mentioned above, contain little nitrogen. Well-composted organic residues also decompose slowly in the soil because they are fairly stable, having already undergone a significant amount of decomposition.

Mature plant stalks and sawdust that have C:N over 40:1 (table 9.3) may cause temporary problems for plants. Microorganisms using materials that contain 1% nitrogen (or less) need extra nitrogen for their growth and reproduction. They will take the needed nitrogen from the surrounding soil, diminishing the amount of nitrate and ammonium available for crop use. This reduction of soil nitrate and ammonium by microorganisms decomposing high C:N residues is called immobilization of nitrogen.

When microorganisms and plants compete for scarce nutrients, the microorganisms usually win, because

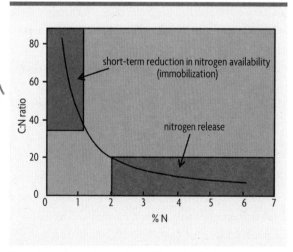

Figure 9.3. Nitrogen release and immobilization with changing nitrogen content. Based on data of Vigil and Kissel (1991).

Table 9.3
C:N Ratios of Selected Organic Materials

Material	C:N
Soil	10–12
Poultry manure	10
Clover and alfalfa (early)	13
Compost	15
Dairy manure (low bedding)	17
Alfalfa hay	20
Green rye	36
Corn stover	60
Wheat, oat, or rye straw	80
Oak leaves	90
Fresh sawdust	400
Newspaper	600

Note: Nitrogen is always 1 in the ratios.

they are so well distributed in the soil. Plant roots are in contact with only 1–2% of the soil volume, whereas microorganisms populate almost the entire soil. The length of time during which the nitrogen nutrition of plants is adversely affected by immobilization depends on the quantity of residues applied, their C:N ratio, and other factors influencing microorganisms, such as fertilization practices, soil temperature, and moisture conditions. If the C:N ratio of residues is in the teens or low 20s, corresponding to greater than 2% nitrogen, there is more nitrogen present than the microorganisms need for residue decomposition. When this happens, extra nitrogen becomes available to plants fairly quickly. Green manure crops and animal manures are in this group. Residues with C:N in the mid 20s to low 30s, corresponding to about 1–2% nitrogen, will not have much effect on short-term nitrogen immobilization or release.

Sewage sludge on your fields? In theory, using sewage sludge—commonly called biosolids—on agricultural land makes sense as a way to resolve problems related to people living in cities, far removed from the land that grows their food. However, there are some troublesome issues associated with agricultural use of sludges. By far, the most important problem is that they frequently contain contaminants from industry and from various products used around the home. Although many of these metal contaminants naturally occur at low levels in soils and plants, their high concentrations in some sludges create a potential hazard. The U.S. standards for toxic materials in sludges are much more lenient than those in some other industrialized countries and permit higher loading of potentially toxic metals. So, although you are allowed to use many sludges, you should carefully examine a sludge's contents before applying it to your land.

Another issue is that sludges are produced by varied processes and, therefore, have different properties. Most sludges are around neutral pH, but, when added to soils, cause some degree of acidification, as do most nitrogen fertilizers. Because many of the problem metals are more soluble under acidic conditions, the pH of soils receiving these materials should be monitored and maintained at around 6.8 or above. On the other hand, lime (calcium hydroxide and ground limestone used together) is added to some sludges to raise the pH and kill disease bacteria. The resulting "lime-stabilized" sludge has extremely high levels of calcium, relative to potassium and magnesium. This type of sludge should be used primarily as a liming source, and levels of magnesium and potassium in the soil carefully monitored to be sure they are present in reasonable amounts, compared with the high levels of added calcium.

The use of "clean" sludges—those containing low levels of metal and organic contaminants—for agronomic crops is certainly an acceptable practice. Sludges should not be applied to soils when growing crops for direct human consumption unless it can be demonstrated that, in addition to low levels of potentially toxic materials, organisms dangerous to humans are absent.

Application rates for organic materials. The amount of residue added to a soil is often determined by the cropping system. The crop residues can be left on the surface or incorporated by tillage. Different amounts of

94

C:N RATIO OF ACTIVE ORGANIC MATTER

As residues are decomposed by soil organisms, carbon is lost as CO_2, while nitrogen is mostly conserved. This causes the C:N ratio of decomposing residues to decrease. Although the ratio for most agricultural soils is in the range of 10:1 to 12:1, the different types of organic matter within a soil have different ratios. The larger particles of soil organic matter have higher C:N ratios, indicating that they are less decomposed than smaller fractions (see figure 9.4, right). Microscopic evidence also indicates that the larger fractions are less decomposed than the smaller particles.

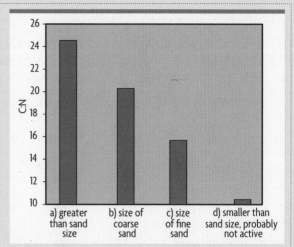

Figure 9.4. C:N ratio of different-size fractions of organic matter. From F. Magdoff, unpublished data, average for three soils.

residue will remain under different crops, rotations, or harvest practices. For example, 3 or more tons per acre of leaf, stalk, and cob residues remain in the field when corn is harvested for grain depending on yield. If the entire plant is harvested to make silage, there is little left except the roots.

When "imported" organic materials are brought to the field, you need to decide how much and when to apply them. In general, application rates of these residues will be based on their probable contribution to the nitrogen nutrition of plants. We don't want to apply too much available nitrogen because it will be wasted. Nitrate from excessive applications of organic sources of fertility may leach into groundwater just as easily as nitrate originating from purchased synthetic fertilizers. In addition, excess nitrate in plants may cause health problems for humans and animals.

Sometimes the fertility contribution of phosphorus may be the main factor governing application rates of organic material. Excess phosphorus entering lakes can cause an increase in the growth of algae and other aquatic weeds, decreasing water quality for drinking and recreation. In locations where this occurs, farmers must be careful to avoid loading the soil with too much phosphorus, from either commercial fertilizers or organic sources.

Effects of residue and manure accumulations. When any organic material is added to soil, it decomposes relatively rapidly at first. Later, when only resistant parts (for example, straw stems high in lignin) are left, the rate of decomposition decreases greatly. This means that although nutrient availability diminishes each year after adding a residue to the soil, there are still long-term benefits from adding organic materials. This can be expressed by using a "decay series." For example, 50, 15, 5, and 2% of the amount of nitrogen added in manure may be released in the first, second, third, and fourth years following addition to soils. In other words, crops in a regularly manured field get some nitrogen from manure that was applied in past years. So, if you are starting to manure a field, somewhat more manure will be needed in the first year than will be needed in years 2, 3, and 4 to supply the same total amount of nitrogen to a crop. After some years, you may need only half of the amount used to supply all the nitrogen needs in the first year. However, it is not uncommon to find farmers who are trying to build up high levels of organic matter actually overloading their soils with nutrients, with potential negative effects on crop quality and the environment. Instead of reducing the amount of off-farm residue with time, they use a standard amount annually. This may lead to excess amounts of nitrate, lessening the quality of many plants and harming groundwater, as well as excess amounts of phosphorus, a potential surface water pollution problem.

Organic Matter Management on Different Types of Farms

Animal-based farms. It is certainly easier to maintain soil organic matter in animal-based agricultural systems. Manure is a valuable by-product of having animals. Animals also can use sod-type grasses and legumes as pasture, hay, and haylage (hay stored under airtight conditions so that some fermentation occurs). It is easier to justify putting land into perennial forage crops for part of a rotation when there is an economic use for the crops. Animals need not be on the farm to have positive effects on soil fertility. A farmer may grow hay to sell to a neighbor and trade for some animal manure from the neighbor's farm, for example. Occasionally, formal agreements between dairy farmers and vegetable growers lead to cooperation on crop rotations and manure application.

Systems without animals. It is more challenging, although not impossible, to maintain or increase soil organic matter on non-livestock farms. It can be done by using reduced tillage, intensive use of cover crops, intercropping, living mulches, rotations that include crops with high amounts of residue left after harvest, and attention to other erosion-control practices. Organic residues, such as leaves or clean sewage sludges, can sometimes be obtained from nearby cities and towns. Straw or grass clippings used as mulch also add organic matter when they later become incorporated into the soil by plowing or by the activity of soil organisms. Some vegetable farmers use a "mow-and-blow" system in which crops are grown on strips for the purpose of chopping them and spraying the residues onto an adjacent strip. When you use off-farm organic materials such as composts and manures, soil should be tested regularly to ensure that it does not become overloaded with nutrients.

MAINTAINING ORGANIC MATTER IN SMALL GARDENS

There are a number of different ways that home gardeners can maintain soil organic matter. One of the easiest is using lawn grass clippings for mulch during the growing season. The mulch can then be worked into the soil or left on the surface to decompose until the next spring. Leaves can be raked up in the fall and applied to the garden. Cover crops can be used on small gardens. Of course, manures, composts, or mulch straw can also be purchased.

There are a growing number of small-scale market gardeners, many with insufficient land to rotate into a sod-type crop. They also may have crops in the ground late into the fall, making cover cropping a challenge. One possibility is to establish cover crops by overseeding after the last crop of the year is well established. Another source of organic materials—grass clippings— is probably in short supply compared with the needs of cropped areas but is still useful. It might also be possible to obtain leaves from a nearby town. These can either be directly applied and worked into the soil or be composted first. As with home gardeners, market gardeners can purchase manures, composts, and straw mulch, but they should get volume discounts on the amounts needed for an acre or two.

MAINTAINING SOIL BIODIVERSITY

The role of diversity is critical to maintaining a well-functioning and stable agriculture. Where many different types of organisms coexist, there are fewer disease, insect, and nematode problems. There is more competition for food and a greater possibility that many types of predators will be found. This means that no single pest organism will be able to reach a population high enough to cause a major decrease in crop yield. We can promote a diversity of plant species growing on the land by using cover crops, intercropping, and crop rotations. However, don't forget that diversity below the soil surface is as important as diversity above ground. Growing cover crops and using crop rotations help maintain the diversity below ground, but adding manures and composts and making sure that crop residues are returned to the soil are also critical for promoting soil organism diversity.

BESIDES ORGANIC MATTER MANAGEMENT

Although enhanced soil organic matter management practices go a long way to helping all aspects of soil health, other practices are needed to maintain an enhanced physical and chemical environment. Plants thrive in a physical environment that allows roots to actively explore a large area, gets all the oxygen and water needed, and maintains a healthy mix of organisms. Although the soil's physical environment is strongly influenced by organic matter, the practices and equipment used—from tillage to planting to cultivation to harvest—have a major impact. If a soil is too wet—whether it has poor internal drainage or receives too much water—some remedies are needed to grow high-yielding and healthy crops. Also, erosion—whether by wind or water—is an environmental hazard that needs to be kept as low as possible. Erosion is most likely when the surface of a soil is bare and doesn't contain sufficient medium- to large-size water-stable aggregates. Practices for management of soil physical properties are discussed in chapters 14 to 17.

Many of the practices that build up and maintain soil organic matter enrich the soil with nutrients or make it easier to manage nutrients in ways that satisfy crop needs and are also environmentally sound. For example, a legume cover crop increases a soil's active organic matter and reduces erosion, but it also adds nitrogen that can be used by the next crop. Cover crops and deep-rooted rotation crops help to cycle nitrate, potassium, calcium, and magnesium that might be lost to leaching below crop roots. Importing mulches or manures onto the farm also adds nutrients along with the organic materials. However, specific nutrient management practices are needed, such as testing manure and checking its nutrient content before applying additional nutrient sources. Other examples of nutrient management practices not directly related to organic matter management include applying nutrients timed to plant needs, liming acidic soils, and interpreting soil tests to decide on the appropriate amounts of nutrients to apply (see chapters 18 to 21). Development of farm nutrient management plans and watershed partnerships improves soil while also protecting the local environment. And as discussed above, it is possible to overload soils with nutrients by bringing large quantities of organic materials such as manures or composts from off the farm for routine annual applications.

SUMMARY

Improved soil organic matter management is at the heart of building better soils—creating a habitat below the ground that is suited to optimal root development and health. This means adding adequate annual quantities, tons per acre, of a variety of organic materials—crop residue, manure, composts, leaves, etc.—while not overloading the soil with nutrients from off the farm. It also means reducing the losses of soil organic matter as the result of excess tillage or erosion. But we're not just interested in the amount of organic matter in soil. Even if the organic matter content of the soil doesn't increase greatly—and it takes a while to find out whether it's increasing—better management will provide more active (particulate or "dead") organic matter that fuels the complex soil web of life, helps in formation of soil aggregates, and provides plant growth–stimulating chemicals, as well as reducing plant pest pressures. For a variety of reasons, it is easier to build and maintain higher levels of organic matter in animal-based systems than in those growing only crops. However, there are ways to improve organic matter management in any cropping system.

SOURCES

Barber, S.A. 1998. Chemistry of soil-nutrient interactions and future agricultural sustainability. *In Future Prospects for Soil Chemistry*, ed. P.M. Huang, D.L. Sparks, and S.A. Boyd. SSSA Special Publication No. 55. Madison, WI: Soil Science Society of America.

Brady, N.C., and R.R. Weil. 2008. *The Nature and Properties of Soils*, 14th ed. Upper Saddle River, NJ: Prentice Hall.

Cavigelli, M.A., S.R. Deming, L.K. Probyn, and R.R. Harwood, eds. 1998. *Michigan Field Crop Ecology: Managing Biological Processes for Productivity and Environmental Quality*. Extension Bulletin E-2646. East Lansing: Michigan State University.

Cooperband, L. 2002. *Building Soil Organic Matter with Organic Amendments*. Madison: University of Wisconsin, Center for Integrated Systems.

Hills, J.L., C.H. Jones, and C. Cutler. 1908. Soil deterioration and soil humus. *Vermont Agricultural Experiment Station Bulletin* 135: 142–177. Burlington: University of Vermont, College of Agriculture.

Jenny, H. 1980. Alcohol or humus? *Science* 209: 444.

Johnson, J. M-F., R.R. Allmaras, and D.C. Reicosky. 2006. Estimating source carbon from crop residues, roots and rhizo deposits using the National Grain-Yield Database. *Agronomy Journal* 98: 622–636.

Mitchell, J., T. Hartz, S. Pettygrove, D. Munk, D. May, F. Menezes, J. Diener, and T. O'Neill. 1999. Organic matter recycling varies with crops grown. *California Agriculture* 53(4): 37–40.

Moebius, B.N., H.M. van Es, J.O. Idowu, R.R. Schindelbeck, D.J. Clune, D.W. Wolfe, G.S. Abawi, J.E. Thies, B.K. Gugino, and R. Lucey. 2008. Long-term removal of maize residue for bioenergy: Will it affect soil quality? *Soil Science Society of America Journal* 72: 960–969.

Nielsen, D.C., M.F. Vigil, R.L. Anderson, R.A. Bowman, J.G. Benjamin, and A.D. Halvorson. 2002. Cropping system influence on planting water content and yield of winter wheat. *Agronomy Journal* 94: 962–967.

Oshins, C., and L. Drinkwater. 1999. *An Introduction to Soil Health*. A slide set previously available from the Northeast Region SARE.

Topp, G.C., K.C. Wires, D.A. Angers, M.R. Carter, J.L.B. Culley, D.A. Holmstrom, B.D. Kay, G.P. Lafond, D.R. Langille, R.A. McBride, G.T. Patterson, E. Perfect, V. Rasiah, A.V. Rodd, and K.T. Webb. 1995. Changes in soil structure. In *The Health of Our Soils: Toward Sustainable Agriculture in Canada*, ed. D.F. Acton and L.J. Gregorich. Center for Land and Biological Resources Research, Research Branch, Agriculture and Agri-Food Canada. Publication 1906/E. http://www.agr.gc.ca/nlwis-snite/index_e.cfm?s1=pub&s2=hs_ss&page=12.

Vigil, M.F., and D.E. Kissel. 1991. Equations for estimating the amount of nitrogen mineralized from crop residues. *Soil Science Society of America Journal* 55: 757–761.

Wilhelm, W.W., J.M.F. Johnson, D.L. Karlen, and D.T. Lightle. 2007. Corn stover to sustain soil organic carbon further constrains biomass supply. *Agronomy Journal* 99: 1665–1667.

BOB MUTH
GLOUCESTER COUNTY, NEW JERSEY

Farming 118 acres in what has recently become a bedroom community of Philadelphia, Bob Muth and his wife, Leda, raise a wide range of vegetables, small fruits, flowers, and hay, which are sold to wholesalers and through a 325-member CSA (community-supported agriculture).

Muth's operation is based on his passion for soil building. Since he took over running the family farm twenty-two years ago, Muth has spread thick layers of leaf mulch, provided for free by his local municipality, at the home farm, on rented fields, and, eventually, on additional purchased tracts of land. Mulching forms part of a rotation scheme that he devised early on and to which he has remained faithful: Only a fifth of his tillable acreage is planted in cash crops each year; the remaining area is put into pasture or cover crops. "When I started mulching and using this rotation, my [farmer] neighbors thought I was losing my marbles," he says. "The prevalent idea at the time was that you had to farm a lot of acreage as intensively as possible."

Muth's rotation—a high-value crop the first year, followed by a leaf application the second year, two to three years of a hay and sudex pasture, and ending with a year of a rye-vetch cover crop—really boosts the quality of his sandy soils. "With this strategy, I get all the positive indicators such as high CEC, organic matter, and nutrient levels, including enough N to grow good-quality crops without a lot of inputs," he says.

Muth tests the soil in his fields annually and carefully monitors changes in the data. "I like having hard numbers to back up what I'm observing in the field and to make good decisions as the years go by," he says. Such careful attention to detail has led him to reduce the thickness of leaf applications once fields have cycled

a few times through his rotation, in order to keep soil organic matter within an optimum range of 3.5–5%. "Anything higher than that, and I risk nutrient leaching," he notes.

Muth likes to use drip irrigation to reduce plant stress and disease and improve water use efficiency. "Water shortage is my biggest issue on the home farm, where I've got a well that pumps only 20–22 gallons a minute," he says. A residential development boom on the land surrounding his farm in recent years has drastically reduced the available groundwater. He says, "You have to be creative about breaking up your fields into zones in order to make water do what you need it to do."

Muth relies on a range of IPM (integrated pest management) techniques for pest and disease control. He scouts his fields daily and takes notes of his observations throughout each cropping cycle. "It's worth investing in a jeweler's loop," he advises, "because it's the pests that are most difficult to see—like the white flies, spider mites, and thrips—that will get you." He regularly plants trap-crop borders around his high-value crop fields, which enable him to monitor pest populations and determine when and how much to spray. For example, he suggests using red kale or mizuna as a trap crop to prevent tarnished plant bug damage on savoy cabbage.

"You have to figure out what [pests] require in their life cycles and disrupt them," he says. After several years of observation, "you begin to recognize if you've got a crop for which you haven't figured out a good control strategy."

Muth likes to encourage beneficial insect populations by leaving flowering strips of cover crops unmowed on the borders of his crop fields. He has found that interplanting cover crops—adding buckwheat and dill to vetch, for example—significantly extends bloom time, thus fostering multiple generations of beneficial insects.

In high tunnels, where he grows berries and flowers, he controls aphids and spider mites by releasing predatory mites. He selected a special film to cover the tunnels that enhances light diffusion, reduces condensate drip from the ceiling and purlins, and helps prevent overheated conditions, ensuring an overall superior growing environment.

"There are so many things you can do to help yourself," he says. He has learned how to prevent early-season pythium rot by waiting to plant crops until a preceding rye-vetch cover is fully broken down and

As an added bonus, he says that by diffusing more light into the plant canopy, the mulch boosts the color intensity (and marketability) of his produce.

the soil warms up. He keeps pythium—which also likes hot and wet conditions—in check later in the season by planting crops out on highly reflective metallic plastic mulch, under which soil temperatures are lower relative to those that occur under other colors of plastic mulch. The shiny mulch also repels aphids and thrips, Muth notes. As an added bonus, he says that by diffusing more light into the plant canopy, the mulch boosts the color intensity (and marketability) of his produce.

Overall, instead of adhering to a strict spray schedule, which "may control one critter but make things worse if you also kill your beneficials in the process," Muth suggests "layering together" different types of controls, such as improving soil quality, putting up bat houses, creating insectaries of flowering covers, using sprays judiciously, and letting pest and disease management strategies evolve as time goes by.

Muth's decisions to "go with a good soil building program" and IPM methods have smoothed his gradual transition of acreage into certified organic production. "When I started getting into organics, people told me, 'Bob, you better be careful or you're going to end up with buggy stuff that's full of disease that people don't want.' But I haven't seen any of that," he says. "I haven't been overwhelmed; in general, pests and disease levels on my farm amount to no more than a minor annoyance."

Encouraged by his success and customer demand, Muth is applying his expertise to figuring out how to grow more "difficult" crops organically. For example, when area specialists said that growing organic super sweet corn in New Jersey would be impossible, he could not resist the challenge. "We decided to start our corn plugs in the greenhouse," he says, noting that "the people at Rutgers thought this was revolutionary." He transplants corn plugs out after ten or eleven days (to prevent plugs from becoming pot-bound, which reduces ear length) onto plastic mulch and keeps row covers over the plants until they are 12 to 18 inches tall. Such strategies effectively foil corn earworm and corn borers, Muth says. "You can grow corn early, scout it closely, and with spot use of approved sprays for organic production, get three weeks of absolutely clean, fantastic-quality organic corn in July." His customers are thrilled and are willing to pay him a premium price for the fruits of his discovery. Muth says he hopes to crack the mystery of how to produce high-quality organic peaches next.

With so many new techniques emerging, and consumers increasingly interested in buying locally and organically produced food, Muth says this is "an exciting time to be in agriculture." "If you're savvy, you can farm a small piece of land and make a good living."

"I wish I was twenty-one again," he says, "because I'd do it all over again. It's a pleasure to get out there and get to work."

—UPDATED BY AMY KREMEN

Chapter 10

COVER CROPS

Where no kind of manure is to be had, I think the cultivation of lupines will be found

the readiest and best substitute. If they are sown about the middle of September in a poor soil,

and then plowed in, they will answer as well as the best manure.

—COLUMELLA, 1ST CENTURY, ROME

Cover crops have been used to improve soil and the yield of subsequent crops since antiquity. Chinese manuscripts indicate that the use of green manures is probably more than 3,000 years old. Green manures were also commonly used in ancient Greece and Rome. Today, there is a renewed interest in cover crops, and they are becoming important parts of many farmers' cropping systems.

Three different terms are used to describe crops grown specifically to help maintain soil fertility and productivity instead of for harvesting: *green manures*, *cover crops*, and *catch crops*. The terms are sometimes used interchangeably and are best thought of from the grower's perspective. A green manure crop is usually grown to help maintain soil organic matter and increase nitrogen availability. A cover crop is grown mainly to prevent soil erosion by covering the ground with living vegetation and living roots that hold on to the soil. This,

of course, is related to managing soil organic matter, because the topsoil lost during erosion contains the most organic matter of any soil layer. A catch crop is grown to retrieve available nutrients still in the soil following an economic crop and prevents nutrient leaching over the winter.

Sometimes which term to use is confusing. We usually have more than one goal when we plant these crops during or after our main crop, and plants grown for one of these purposes may also accomplish the other two goals. The question of which term to use is not really important, so in our discussion below, the term *cover crop* will be used.

Cover crops are usually killed on the surface or incorporated into the soil before they mature. (This is the origin of the term *green manure*.) Since annual cover crop residues are usually low in lignin content and high in nitrogen, they decompose rapidly in the soil.

Photo by Tim McCabe

101

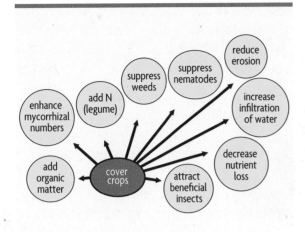

Figure 10.1. Cover crops have multiple benefits.

BENEFITS OF COVER CROPS

Cover crops provide multiple potential benefits to soil health and the following crops, while also helping maintain cleaner surface and groundwater (figure 10.1). They prevent erosion, improve soil physical and biological properties, supply nutrients to the following crop, suppress weeds, improve soil water availability, and break pest cycles. Some cover crops are able to break into compacted soil layers, making it easier for the following crop's roots to more fully develop. The actual benefits from a cover crop depend on the species and productivity of the crop you grow and how long it's left to grow before the soil is prepared for the next crop.

Organic matter. Grass cover crops are more likely than legumes to increase soil organic matter. The more residue you return to the soil, the better the effect on soil organic matter. The amount of residue produced by the cover crop may be very small, as little as half a ton of dry matter per acre. This adds some active organic matter, but because most of it decomposes rapidly after the crop is killed, there is no measurable effect on the total amount of organic matter present. On the other hand, good production of hairy vetch or crimson clover cover crops may yield from 1 1/2 to more than 4 tons of dry weight per acre. If a crop like winter rye is grown to maturity, it can produce 3 to 5 tons of residue.

A five-year experiment with clover in California showed that cover crops increased organic matter in the top 2 inches from 1.3% to 2.6% and in the 2- to 6-inch layer from 1% to 1.2%. Some researchers have found that cover crops do not seem to increase soil organic matter. Low-growing cover crops that don't produce much organic matter may not be able to counter the depleting effects of some management practices, such as intensive tillage. Even if they don't significantly increase organic matter levels, cover crops help prevent erosion and add at least some residues that are readily used by soil organisms.

Cover crops help maintain high populations of mycorrhizal fungi spores during the fallow period between main crops. The fungus also associates with almost all cover crops, which helps maintain or improve inoculation of the next crop. (As discussed in chapter 4, mycorrhizal fungi help promote the health of many crop plants in a variety of ways and also improve soil aggregation.) Cover crop pollen and nectar can be important food sources for predatory mites and parasitic wasps, both important for biological control of insect pests. A cover crop also provides a good habitat for spiders, and these general insect feeders help decrease pest populations. Use of cover crops in the Southeast has reduced the incidence of thrips, bollworm, budworm, aphids, fall armyworm, beet armyworm, and white flies. Living cover crop plants and their residues also increase water infiltration into soil, thus compensating for the water that cover crops use.

SELECTION OF COVER CROPS

Before growing cover crops, you need to ask yourself some questions:

- What type of crop should I plant?
- When and how should I plant the crop?
- When should the crop be killed or incorporated into the soil?

When you select a cover crop, you should consider the soil conditions, climate, and what you want to accomplish by answering these questions:

- Is the main purpose to add available nitrogen to the soil, or to scavenge nutrients and prevent loss from the system? (Legumes add N; other cover crops take up available soil N.)
- Do you want your cover crop to provide large amounts of organic residue?
- Do you plan to use the cover crop as a surface mulch, or incorporate it into the soil?
- Is erosion control in the late fall and early spring your primary objective?
- Is the soil very acidic and infertile, with low availability of nutrients?
- Does the soil have a compaction problem? (Some species, such as sudan grass, sweet clover, and forage radish, are especially good for alleviating compaction.)
- Is weed suppression your main goal? (Some species establish rapidly and vigorously, while some also chemically inhibit weed seed germination.)
- Which species are best for your climate? (Some species are more winter-hardy than others.)
- Will the climate and water-holding properties of your soil cause a cover crop to use so much water that it harms the following crop?
- Are root diseases or plant-parasitic nematodes problems that you need to address? (Winter [cereal] rye, for example, has been found to suppress a number of nematodes in various cropping systems.)

In most cases, there are multiple objectives and multiple choices for cover crops.

TYPES OF COVER CROPS

Many types of plants can be used as cover crops. Legumes and grasses (including cereals) are the most extensively used, but there is increasing interest in brassicas (such as rape, mustard, and forage radish) and continued interest in others, such as buckwheat. Some of the most important cover crops are discussed below.

Legumes

Leguminous crops are often very good cover crops. Summer annual legumes, usually grown only during the summer, include soybeans, peas, and beans. Winter annual legumes that are normally planted in the fall and counted on to overwinter include Austrian winter field peas, crimson clover, hairy vetch, and subterranean clover. Some, like crimson clover and field peas, can overwinter only in regions with mild frost. Berseem clover will overwinter only in hardiness zones 8 and above. Hairy vetch is able to withstand fairly severe winter weather. Biennials and perennials include red clover, white clover, sweet clover, and alfalfa. Crops usually used as winter annuals can sometimes be grown as summer annuals in cold, short-season regions. Also, summer annuals that are easily damaged by frost, such as cowpeas, can be grown as a winter annual in the deep southern United States.

One of the main reasons for selecting legumes as cover crops is their ability to fix nitrogen from the atmosphere and add it to the soil. Legumes that produce a substantial amount of growth, such as hairy vetch and crimson clover, may supply over 100 pounds of nitrogen per acre to the next crop. Legumes such as field peas, bigflower vetch, and red clover usually supply only 30 to 80 pounds of available nitrogen. Legumes also provide other benefits, including attracting beneficial insects, helping control erosion, and adding organic matter to soils.

Inoculation. If you grow a legume as a cover crop, don't forget to inoculate seeds with the correct nitrogen-fixing bacteria. Different types of rhizobial bacteria are specific to certain crops. There are different strains for alfalfa, clovers, soybeans, beans, peas, vetch, and cowpeas. Unless you've recently grown a legume from the same general group you are currently planting, inoculate the seeds with the appropriate commercial rhizobial inoculant before planting. The addition of water or milk to the seed-inoculant mix helps the bacteria stick to the seeds. Plant right away, so the bacteria don't dry out. Inoculants are readily available only if they are commonly used in your region. It's best to check with your seed supplier a few months before you need the inoculant, so it can be specially ordered if necessary. Keep in mind that the "garden inoculant" sold in many garden stores may not contain the specific bacteria you need; so be sure to find the right one for the crop you are growing and keep it refrigerated until used.

Winter Annual Legumes

Crimson clover is considered one of the best cover crops for the southeastern United States. Where adapted, it grows in the fall and winter and matures more rapidly than most other legumes. It also contributes a relatively large amount of nitrogen to the following crop. Because it is not very winter-hardy, crimson clover is not usually a good choice for the regions where significant frost occurs. In northern regions, crimson clover can be grown as a summer annual, but that prevents an economic crop from growing during that field season. Varieties like Chief, Dixie, and Kentucky Select are somewhat winter hardy if established early enough before winter. Crimson clover does not grow well on high-pH (calcareous) or poorly drained soils.

Field peas are grown in colder climates as a summer annual and as a winter annual over large sections of the South and California. They have taken the place of fallow in some dryland, small-grain production systems. Also called Austrian winter peas and Canadian field peas, they tend to establish quickly and grow rapidly in cool moist climates, producing a significant amount of residue—2 1/2 tons or more of dry matter. They fix plentiful amounts of nitrogen, from 100 to 150 or more pounds per acre.

Hairy vetch is winter-hardy enough to grow well in areas that experience hard freezing. Where adapted, hairy vetch produces a large amount of vegetation and fixes a significant amount of nitrogen, contributing 100 pounds of nitrogen per acre or more to the next crop. Hairy vetch residues decompose rapidly and release nitrogen more quickly than most other cover crops. This can be an advantage when a rapidly growing, high-nitrogen-demand crop follows hairy vetch. Hairy vetch will do better on sandy soils than many other green manures, but it needs good soil potassium levels to be most productive.

Subterranean clover is a warm-climate winter annual that, in many situations, can complete its life cycle before a summer crop is planted. When used this way, it doesn't need to be suppressed or killed and does not compete with the summer crop. If left undisturbed, it will naturally reseed itself from the pods that mature below ground. Because it grows low to the ground and does not tolerate much shading, it is not a good choice to interplant with summer annual row crops.

Summer Annual Legumes

Berseem clover is an annual crop that is grown as a summer annual in colder climates. It establishes easily and rapidly and develops a dense cover, making it a good choice for weed suppression. It's also drought tolerant and regrows rapidly when mowed or grazed. It can be grown in the mild climates during the winter. Some newer varieties have done very well in California, with Multicut outyielding Bigbee.

Cowpeas are native to Central Africa and do well in hot climates. The cowpea is, however, severely damaged by even a mild frost. It is deep rooted and is able to do well under droughty conditions. It usually does better on low-fertility soils than crimson clover.

Soybeans, usually grown as an economic crop for their oil- and protein-rich seeds, also can serve as a summer cover crop if allowed to grow until flowering. They require a fertile soil for best growth. As with cowpeas, soybeans are easily damaged by frost. If grown to

Figure 10.2. Velvet bean grown on hillsides in Central America. Left: growing vines; middle: maturing pods; right: mulched under corn crop. Left and middle photos by Ray Bryant.

maturity and harvested for seed, they do not add much in the way of lasting residues or nitrogen.

Velvet bean (mucuna) is widely adopted in tropical climates. It is an annual climbing vine that grows aggressively to several feet high and suppresses weeds well (figure 10.2). In a velvet bean–corn sequence, the cover crop provides a thick mulch layer and reseeds itself after the corn crop. The beans themselves are sometimes used for a coffee substitute and can also be eaten after long boiling. A study in West Africa showed that velvet bean can provide nitrogen benefits for two successive corn crops.

Similar tropical cover crops include *Canavalia, Crotalaria, Tephrosia,* all of which can be used as mulches after maturing.

Biennial and Perennial Legumes

Alfalfa is a good choice for well-drained soils that are near neutral in pH and high in fertility. The good soil conditions required for the best growth of alfalfa make it a poor choice for problem situations. Where adapted, it is usually grown in a rotation for a number of years (see chapter 11). Alfalfa is commonly interseeded with small grains, such as oats, wheat, and barley, and it grows after the grain is harvested. The alfalfa variety Nitro can be used as an annual cover crop because it is not very winter-hardy and usually winterkills under northern conditions. Nitro continues to fix nitrogen later into the fall than winter-hardy varieties. However, it does not

reliably winterkill every year, and the small amounts of extra fall growth and nitrogen fixation may not be worth the extra cost of the seed compared with perennial varieties.

Crown vetch is adapted only to well-drained soils, but it can be grown under lower fertility conditions than alfalfa. It has been used successfully for roadbank stabilization and is able to provide permanent groundcover. Crown vetch has been tried as an interseeded "living mulch," with only limited success at providing nitrogen to corn. However, it is relatively easy to suppress crown vetch with herbicides to reduce its competition with corn. Crown vetch establishes very slowly, so it should be used only for perennial cover.

Red clover is vigorous, shade tolerant, winter-hardy, and can be established relatively easily. It is commonly interseeded with small grains. Because it starts growing slowly, the competition between it and the small grain is not usually great. Red clover also successfully interseeds with corn in the Northeast.

Sweet clover (yellow blossom) is a reasonably winter-hardy, vigorous-growing crop with an ability to get its roots into compacted subsoils. It is able to withstand high temperatures and droughty conditions better than many other cover crops. Sweet clover requires a soil pH near neutrality and a high calcium level; it does poorly in wet, clayey soils. As long as the pH is high, sweet clover is able to grow well on low-fertility soils. It is sometimes grown for a full year or more, since it flowers and completes its life cycle in the second year. When used as a green manure crop, it is incorporated into the soil before full bloom.

White clover does not produce as much growth as many of the other legumes and is also less tolerant of droughty situations. (New Zealand types of white clover are more drought tolerant than the more commonly used Dutch white clover.) However, because it does not grow very tall and is able to tolerate shading better than many other legumes, it may be useful in orchard-floor covers or as a living mulch. It is also a common component of intensively managed pastures.

Grasses

Commonly used grass cover crops include the annual cereals (rye, wheat, barley, oats), annual or perennial forage grasses such as ryegrass, and warm-season grasses such as sorghum–sudan grass. Nonlegume cover crops, which are mainly grass species, are very useful for scavenging nutrients—especially N—left over from a previous crop. They tend to have extensive root systems, and some establish rapidly and can greatly reduce erosion. In addition, they can produce large amounts of residue and, therefore, can help add organic matter to the soil. They also can help suppress weed germination and growth.

Figure 10.3. Winter rye, which grows rapidly in the early spring.

A problem common to all the grasses is that if you grow the crop to maturity for the maximum amount of residue, you reduce the amount of available nitrogen for the next crop. This is because of the high C:N ratio, or low percentage of nitrogen, in grasses near maturity. The problem can be avoided by killing the grass early or by adding extra nitrogen in the form of fertilizer or manure. Another way to help with this problem is to supply extra nitrogen by seeding a legume-grass mix.

Winter rye, also called cereal or grain rye, is very winter-hardy and easy to establish. Its ability to germinate quickly, together with its winter-hardiness, means that it can be planted later in the fall than most other species, even in cold climates. Decomposing residue of winter rye has been shown to have an allelopathic effect, which means that it can chemically suppress germination of weed seeds. It grows quickly in the fall and also grows readily in the spring (figure 10.3). It is often the cover crop of choice as a catch crop and also works well with a roll-crimp mulch system—in which the cover crop is suppressed by rolling and crimping at the same time and crops are seeded or transplanted through the mulch (see figure 16.7, p. 180).

Oats are not winter-hardy. Summer or fall seedings will winterkill under most cold-climate conditions. This provides a naturally killed mulch the following spring and may help with weed suppression. As a mixture with one of the clovers, oats provide some quick cover in the fall. Oat stems help trap snow and conserve moisture, even after the plants have been killed by frost. Black oat is very popular with farmers in South America, where it is mulched for no-till row crops.

Annual ryegrass (not related to winter rye) grows well in the fall if established early enough. It develops an extensive root system and therefore provides very effective erosion control while adding significant quantities of organic matter. It may winterkill in cold climates. Some caution is needed with annual ryegrass; because it is difficult to kill, it may become a problem weed in some situations.

Sudan grass and sorghum-sudan hybrids are fast-growing summer annuals that produce a lot of growth in a short time. Because of their vigorous nature, they are good at suppressing weeds. If they are interseeded with a low-growing crop, such as strawberries or many vegetables, you may need to delay seeding so the main crop will not be severely shaded. They have been reported to suppress plant-parasitic nematodes and possibly other organisms, as they produce highly toxic substances during decomposition in soil. Sudan grass is especially helpful for loosening compacted soil. It can also be used as a livestock forage and so can do double duty in a cropping system with one or more grazings and still provide many benefits of a cover crop.

Other Crops

Buckwheat is a summer annual that is easily killed by frost. It will grow better than many other cover crops on low-fertility soils. It also grows rapidly and completes its life cycle quickly, taking around six weeks from planting into a warm soil until the early flowering stage. Buckwheat can grow more than 2 feet tall in the month following planting. It competes well with weeds because it grows so fast and, therefore, is used to suppress weeds following an early spring vegetable crop. It has also been reported to suppress important root pathogens, including Thielaviopsis and Rhizoctonia species. It is possible to grow more than one crop of buckwheat per year in many regions. Its seeds do not disperse widely, but it can reseed itself and become a weed. Mow or till it before seeds develop to prevent reseeding.

Brassicas used as cover crops include mustard, rapeseed, and forage radish. They are increasingly used as winter or rotational cover crops in vegetable and specialty crop production, such as potatoes and tree fruits. Rape (canola) grows well under the moist and cool conditions of late fall, when other kinds of plants are going dormant for winter. Rape is killed by harsh winter conditions but

is grown as a winter crop in the middle and southern sections of the U.S. Forage radish has gained a lot of interest because of its fast growth in late summer and fall, which allows significant uptake of nutrients. It develops a large taproot—1–2 inches in diameter and a foot or more deep—that can break through compacted layers, allowing deeper rooting by the next crop (figure 10.4). Forage radish will winterkill and decompose by spring, but it leaves the soil in friable condition and improves rainfall infiltration and storage. It also eases root penetration and development by the following crop.

Rape and other brassica crops may function as biofumigants, suppressing soil pests, especially root pathogens and plant-parasitic nematodes. Row crop farmers are increasingly interested in these properties. Don't expect brassicas to eliminate your pest problems, however. They are a good tool and an excellent rotation crop, but pest management results are inconsistent. More research is needed to further clarify the variables affecting the release and toxicity of the chemical compounds involved. Because members of this family do not develop mycorrhizal fungi associations, they will not promote mycorrhizae in the following crop.

COVER CROP MANAGEMENT

There are numerous management issues to consider when using cover crops. Once you decide what your major goals are for using cover crops, select one or more to try out. Consider using combinations of species. You also need to decide where cover crops best fit in your system—planted following the main crop, intercropped during part or all of the growing of the main crop, or grown for an entire growing season in order to build up the soil. The goal, while not always possible to attain, should be to have something growing in your fields (even if dormant during the winter) all the time. Other management issues include when and how to kill or suppress the cover crop, and how to reduce the possibility of interference with your main crops either by using too

a) Root of forage radish.

b) Root holes (bio-drilling) and root remains in spring following fall forage radish. Black pen (see arrow) in hole for scale.

c) Horizontal cracks with rye (left) and vertical cracks with forage radish (right).

Figure 10.4. Brassica cover crop roots. Photos by Ray Weil.

much water in dry climates or by becoming a weed in subsequent crops.

Mixtures of Cover Crops

Although most farmers use single species of cover crops in their fields, mixtures of different cover crops offer combined benefits. The most common mixture is a grass and legume, such as winter rye and hairy vetch, oats and red clover, or field peas and a small grain. Other mixtures might include a legume or small grain with forage radish or even just different small grains mixed together. Mixed stands usually do a better job of suppressing weeds than a single species. Growing legumes with grasses helps compensate for the decreases in nitrogen availability for the following crop when grasses are allowed to mature. In the mid-Atlantic region, the winter rye–hairy vetch mixture has been shown to provide another advantage for managing nitrogen: When

a lot of nitrate is left in the soil at the end of the season, the rye is stimulated (reducing leaching losses). When little nitrogen is available, the vetch competes better with the rye, fixing more nitrogen for the next crop.

A crop that grows erect, such as winter rye, may provide support for hairy vetch and enable it to grow better. Mowing close to the ground kills vetch supported by rye easier than vetch alone. This may allow mowing instead of herbicide use, in no-till production systems.

Planting

If you want to accumulate a lot of organic matter, it's best to grow a cover crop for the whole growing season (see figure 10.5a), which means no income-generating crop will be grown that year. This may be useful with very infertile or eroded soils. It also may help vegetable production systems when there is no manure available and where a market for hay crops justifies a longer rotation.

Planting after economic crop harvest. Most farmers sow cover crops after the economic crop has been harvested (figure 10.5b). In this case, as with the system shown in figure 10.5a, there is no competition

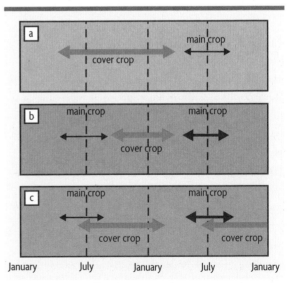

Figure 10.5. Three ways to time cover crop growth for use with a summer crop.

COVER CROP SELECTION AND PLANT PARASITIC NEMATODES

If nematodes become a problem in your crops (common in many vegetables such as lettuce, carrots, onions, and potatoes, as well as some agronomic crops), carefully select cover crops to help limit the damage. For example, the root-knot nematode (*M. hapla*) is a pest of many vegetable crops, as well as alfalfa, soybeans, and clover, but all the grain crops—corn, as well as small grains—are nonhosts. Growing grains as cover crops helps reduce nematode numbers. If the infestation is very bad, consider two full seasons with grain crops before returning to susceptible crops. The root-lesion nematode (*P. penetrans*) is more of a challenge because most crops, including almost all grains, can be hosts for this organism. Whatever you do, don't plant a legume cover crop such as hairy vetch if you have an infestation of root-lesion nematode—it will actually stimulate nematode numbers. However, sudan grass, sorghum-sudan crosses, and ryegrass, as well as pearl millet (a grain crop from Africa, grown in the U.S. mainly as a warm-season forage crop) have been reported to decrease nematode numbers dramatically. Some varieties appear better for this purpose than others. The suppressive activity of such cover crops is due to their poor host status to the lesion nematode, general stimulation of microbial antagonists, and the release of toxic products during decomposition. Forage millet; sudan grass; and brassicas such as mustard, rapeseed, oilseed radish, and flax all provide some biofumigation effect because, when they decompose after incorporation, they produce compounds that are toxic to nematodes. Marigolds can secrete compounds from their roots that are toxic to nematodes.

between the cover crop and the main crop. The seeds can be no-till drilled instead of broadcast, resulting in better cover crop stands. We recommend against the use of tillage prior to cover crop seeding, as it negates most of the benefits of the cover crop. In milder climates, you can usually plant cover crops after harvesting the main crop. In colder areas, there may not be enough time to establish a cover crop between harvest and winter. Even if you are able to get it established, there will be little growth in the fall to provide soil protection or nutrient uptake. The choice of a cover crop to fit between main summer crops (figure 10.5b) is severely limited in northern climates by the short growing season and severe cold. Winter rye is probably the most reliable cover crop for those conditions. In most situations, there are a range of establishment options.

Cover crops are also established following grain harvest in late spring (figure 10.6a). With some early-maturing vegetable crops, especially in warmer regions, it is also possible to establish cover crops in late spring or early summer (figure 10.6b). Cover crops also fit into an early vegetable–winter grain rotation sequence (figure 10.6c).

Interseeding. The third management strategy is to interseed cover crops during the growth of the main

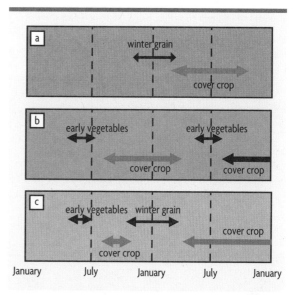

Figure 10.6. Timing cover crop growth for winter grain, early vegetable, and vegetable-grain systems.

crop. Cover crops are commonly interseeded at planting in winter grain cropping systems or frost-seeded in early spring. Seeding cover crops during the growth of economic crops (figure 10.5c) is especially helpful for the establishment of cover crops in areas with a short growing season. Delaying the cover crop seeding until the main crop is off to a good start means that the commercial crop will be able to grow well despite the competition. Good establishment of cover crops requires moisture and, for small-seeded crops, some covering of the seed by soil or crop residues. Winter rye is able to establish well without seed covering, as long as sufficient moisture is present (figure 10.7). Farmers using this system usually broadcast seed during or just after the last cultivation of a row crop. Aerial seeding, "highboy" tractors, or detasseling machines are used to broadcast green manure seed after a main crop is already fairly tall. When growing is on a smaller scale, seed is broadcast with the use of a hand-crank spin seeder.

Intercrops and living mulches. Growing a cover crop between the rows of a main crop has been practiced for a long time. It has been called a living mulch, an intercrop, polyculture (if more than one crop will be harvested), and an orchard-floor cover.

Figure 10.7. Winter rye interseeded with maturing soybeans.

Intercropping has many benefits. Compared with bare soil, a ground cover provides erosion control, better conditions for using equipment during harvesting, higher water-infiltration capacity, and an increase in soil organic matter. In addition, if the cover crop is a legume, a significant buildup of nitrogen may be available to crops in future years. Another benefit is the attraction of beneficial insects, such as predatory mites, to flowering plants. Less insect damage has been noted under polyculture than under monoculture.

Growing other plants near the main crop also poses potential dangers. The intercrop may harbor insect pests, such as the tarnished plant bug. Most of the management decisions for using intercrops are connected with minimizing competition with the main crop. Intercrops, if they grow too tall, can compete with the main crop for light, or may physically interfere with the main crop's growth or harvest. Intercrops may compete for water and nutrients. Using intercrops is not recommended if rainfall is barely adequate for the main crop and supplemental irrigation isn't available. One way to decrease competition is to delay seeding the intercrop until the main crop is well established. This is sometimes done in commercial fruit orchards. Soil-improving intercrops established by delayed planting into annual main crops are usually referred to as cover crops. Herbicides, mowing, and partial rototilling are used to suppress the cover crop and give an advantage to the main crop. Another way to lessen competition from the cover is to plant the main crop in a relatively wide cover-free strip (figure 10.8). This provides more distance between the main crop and the intercrop rows.

Cover Crop Termination

No matter when you establish cover crops, they are usually killed before or during soil preparation for the next economic crop. This is usually done by mowing (most annuals are killed that way) once they've flowered, plowing into the soil, using herbicides, rolling and

Figure 10.8. A wide cover-free strip and living mulch, which is also used for traffic.

crimping in the same operation, or naturally by winter injury. In many cases it is a good idea to leave a week or two between the time a cover crop is tilled in or killed and the time a main crop is planted. Studies have found that a sudex cover crop is especially allelopathic and that tomatoes, broccoli, and lettuce should not be planted until six to eight weeks to allow for thorough leaching of residue. This allows some decomposition to occur and may lessen problems of nitrogen immobilization and allelopathic effects, as well as avoiding increased seed decay and damping-off diseases (especially under wet conditions) and problems with cutworm and wireworm. It also may allow for the establishment of a better seed-bed for small-seeded crops, such as some of the vegetables. Establishing a good seedbed for crops with small seeds may be difficult, because of the lumpiness caused by the fresh residues. Good suppression of vetch in a no-till system has been obtained with the use of a modified rolling stalk chopper. Farmers are also experiencing good cover crop suppression using a crimper-roller that goes ahead of the tractor, allowing the possibility of no-till planting a main crop at the same time as suppressing the cover crop (see figure 16.7, p. 180). Although not

recommended for most direct-seeded vegetable crops, this works well for many agronomic crops.

Management Cautions

Cover crops can cause serious problems if not managed carefully. They can deplete soil moisture; they can become weeds; and—when used as an intercrop—they can compete with the cash crop for water, light, and nutrients.

In drier areas and on droughty soils, such as sands, late killing of a winter cover crop may result in moisture deficiency for the main summer crop. In that situation, the cover crop should be killed before too much water is removed from the soil. However, in warm, humid climates where no-till methods are practiced, allowing the cover crop to grow longer means more residue and better water conservation for the main crop. Cover crop mulch may more than compensate for the extra water removed from the soil during the later period of green manure growth. In addition, in very humid regions or on wet soils, the ability of an actively growing cover crop to "pump" water out of the soil by transpiration may be an advantage (see figure 15.8, p. 168). Letting the cover crop grow as long as possible results in more rapid soil drying and allows for earlier planting of the main crop.

Some cover crops can become unwanted weeds in succeeding crops. Cover crops are sometimes allowed to flower to provide pollen to bees or other beneficial insects. However, if the plants actually set seed, the cover crop may reseed unintentionally. Cover crops that may become a weed problem include buckwheat, ryegrass, crown vetch, and hairy vetch. On the other hand, natural reseeding of subclover, crimson clover, or velvet bean might be beneficial in some situations.

Finally, thick-mulched cover crops make good habitat for soil organisms—and also for some undesirable species. Animals like rats, mice, and snakes (in warm climates) may be found under the mulch, and caution is recommended when manual fieldwork is performed.

SOURCES

Abawi, G.S., and T.L. Widmer. 2000. Impact of soil health management practices on soilborne pathogens, nematodes and root diseases of vegetable crops. *Applied Soil Ecology* 15: 37–47.

Allison, F.E. 1973. *Soil Organic Matter and Its Role in Crop Production*. Amsterdam: Elsevier Scientific Publishing. In his discussion of organic matter replenishment and green manures (pp. 450–451), Allison cites a number of researchers who indicate that there is little or no effect of green manures on total organic matter, even though the supply of active (rapidly decomposing) organic matter increases.

Björkman, T., R. Bellinder, R. Hahn, and J. Shail, Jr. 2008. *Buckwheat Cover Crop Handbook*. Geneva, NY: Cornell University. http://www.nysaes.cornell.edu/hort/faculty/bjorkman/covercrops/pdfs/bwbrochure.pdf.

Cornell University. *Cover Crops for Vegetable Growers*. http://www.nysaes.cornell.edu/hort/faculty/bjorkman/covercrops/why.html.

Hargrove, W.L., ed. 1991. *Cover Crops for Clean Water*. Ankeny, IA: Soil and Water Conservation Society.

MacRae, R.J., and G.R. Mehuys. 1985. The effect of green manuring on the physical properties of temperate-area soils. *Advances in Soil Science* 3: 71–94.

Miller, P.R., W.L. Graves, W.A. Williams, and B.A. Madson. 1989. *Cover Crops for California Agriculture*. Leaflet 21471. Davis: University of California, Division of Agriculture and Natural Resources. This is the reference for the experiment with clover in California.

Pieters, A.J. 1927. *Green Manuring Principles and Practices*. New York: John Wiley.

Power, J.F., ed. 1987. *The Role of Legumes in Conservation Tillage Systems*. Ankeny, IA: Soil Conservation Society of America.

Sarrantonio, M. 1997. *Northeast Cover Crop Handbook*. Soil Health Series. Kutztown, PA: Rodale Institute.

Smith, M.S., W.W. Frye, and J.J. Varco. 1987. Legume winter cover crops. *Advances in Soil Science* 7: 95–139.

Sogbedji, J.M., H.M. van Es, and K.M. Agbeko. 2006. Cover cropping and nutrient management strategies for maize production in western Africa. *Agronomy Journal* 98: 883–889.

Summers, C.G., J.P. Mitchell, T.S. Prather, and J.J. Stapleton. Sudex cover crops can kill and stunt subsequent tomato, lettuce, and broccoli transplants through allelopathy. *California Agriculture* 63(2): 35-40.

Sustainable Agriculture Network. 2007. *Managing Cover Crops Profitably*, 3rd ed. Handbook Series, No. 9. Beltsville, MD: USDA Sustainable Agriculture Network. www.sare.org. An excellent source for practical information about cover crops.

Weil, R., and A. Kremen. 2007. Thinking across and beyond disciplines to make cover crops pay. *Journal of the Science of Food and Agriculture* 87: 551–557.

Widmer, T.L., and G.S. Abawi. 2000. Mechanism of suppression of *Meloidogyne hapla* and its damage by a green manure of sudan grass. *Plant Disease* 84: 562–568.

PETER KENAGY
ALBANY, OREGON

Peter Kenagy's rotation provides regular windows of opportunity to grow cover crops, which he has used for twenty years to build soil and control weeds on his farm. Kenagy raises processing vegetables, small grains, cover crop seed, and native grass forbs and seeds on 320 tillable and 130 riparian acres in Oregon's fertile Willamette Valley.

The period following green beans, which are in the ground just seventy days and come off in July or August, is a perfect time, Kenagy says, to plant a summer cover crop like sudan grass, which will grow up to 5 feet tall before winter-killing with the first frost. The thick grass mulch continues to provide a good ground cover when he plants corn into it in the spring. Sometimes he plants sudan grass as a bridge crop between beans and a fall-planted grass crop.

Maintaining weed-free fields is especially crucial for Kenagy's intensive production of native grass forbs and seeds, which are destined for wetlands mitigation and other restoration projects.

"I have a huge gap between one crop and the next," says Kenagy. "I have to control weeds during that period, which is just one of a number of things a cover crop does so well." Maintaining weed-free fields is especially crucial for Kenagy's intensive production of native grass forbs and seeds, which are destined for wetlands mitigation and other restoration projects.

Kenagy also uses cover crops to capture excess nutrients and silt and prevent them from flowing into the adjacent Willamette River during perennial flooding episodes on his low-lying fields. "The more cover crop vegetation you have there, the more silt you catch," he says. Besides sudan grass, he often relies on fall-planted oats—he uses the variety "Saia," planted at 30 pounds an acre—to produce abundant aboveground biomass.

He has experimented with many different covers, modifying his use of cover crops to fit changes in his cash crop rotation. In addition, practical concerns or experiences inform his choices of which cover crops to use. For example, he no longer plants dwarf essex rape because it could cause unwanted cross-pollination with other brassicas. He favors using oats rather than triticale because he's found the former are more readily and cheaply available and cause fewer disease problems when followed by a wheat crop.

Though Kenagy typically plants common vetch to fix nitrogen, he's searching for another legume that will provide solid cover and boost N levels in the late summer before fall planting of grass crops.

Phaecelia, which overwinters in the Willamette Valley, has become one of Kenagy's preferred covers in recent years. He plants this small-seeded cover crop at a rate of 2 to 4 pounds per acre. He says, "You don't have to plant the seed too deep, and with a little moisture, [phaecelia] grows like gangbusters" and is highly effective at suppressing weeds. "It's easy to kill, pretty much using any method you want. Its biggest attribute is that it breaks down really fast. Barely any effort is required to get rid of it."

"One of the most abusive things farmers do to the soil is till it, and most
do it repeatedly," Kenagy says. "Strip till does less abuse to the soil, and keeping the
residue on top is a much more natural way for it to be handled."

Reducing the effort required to manage any crop is a hallmark feature of Kenagy's operation. "I plan my rotation by looking at what I'm coming out of and figure out the easiest thing to rotate in, so that I don't have to do so much," he says. " I don't want to be stuck trying to till wheat stubble in the fall." Through his careful choice and timing of specific crops, Kenagy is able to till less, save money on fuel, and improve soil quality.

"Part of what's driving this is logistics," he says, describing a field of perennial ryegrass that he recently left to break down in the field for a year after it was killed with an herbicide. "The [ryegrass] crowns left good cover while they rotted; this was a good alternative to plowing the residue in right away," he says, noting that as a result "there will be less kick-up of sod bunnies into my [mechanical] bean picker."

Kenagy's commitment to building good soil goes beyond planting cover crops. Whenever possible, he uses no-till methods to plant and manage his cash and cover crops. For certain crops, such as sweet corn, he uses strip-tillage to cut through vegetative residue, which disturbs just 6 inches of soil—a mere one-fifth of the soil surface that is typically plowed with conventional tillage. (For information about strip tillage, see chapter 16.)

"One of the most abusive things farmers do to the soil is till it, and most do it repeatedly," Kenagy says. "Strip till does less abuse to the soil, and keeping the residue on top is a much more natural way for it to be handled," as it is thus mimicking a more natural system. Grassland and forests, he points out, undergo perpetual cycles of accumulating new residue and undergoing decomposition by soil fauna.

"As a society, we've made much too big a footprint on the land," Kenagy once told the *Oregon Statesman Journal*. "I think it's time to make it smaller."

—UPDATED BY AMY KREMEN

Chapter 11

CROP ROTATIONS

. . . with methods of farming in which grasses form an important part of the rotation, especially those that leave a large residue of roots and culms, the decline of the productive power is much slower than when crops like wheat, cotton, or potatoes, which leave little residue on the soil, are grown continuously.

—HENRY SNYDER, 1896

There are very good reasons to rotate crops. Rotating crops usually means fewer problems with insects, parasitic nematodes, weeds, and diseases caused by plant pathogens. Rotations that include nonhost plants are effective for controlling insects like corn rootworm, nematodes like soybean cyst nematode, and diseases like root rot of field peas. When specific soil diseases are present, the length of time between growing the same or similar crop may vary from relatively short (one to two years for leaf blight of onions) to fairly long (seven years for clubroot of radish or turnip). Also, the rotation should contain some crops that are nonhosts or actually suppress the disease. Root growth may be adversely affected when continuously cropping to any single crop (see figure 11.1). This means that the crops may be less efficient in using soil nutrients and added fertilizers. In addition, rotations that include legumes may supply significant amounts of nitrogen to succeeding crops. A

legume harvested for seed, such as soybeans, provides little N for the following crop. On the other hand, a multiyear legume sod such as alfalfa may well supply all the nitrogen needed by the following crop. Growing

CROP AND VARIETAL MIXTURES

Not only do rotations help in many ways, but growing mixtures of different crops and even different varieties (cultivars) of a given crop sometimes offers real advantages. For example, faba (fava) bean helps corn to get phosphorus on low P soils by acidifying the area around its roots. Also, when some varieties of a species are prized for a certain quality, such as taste, but are susceptible to a particular pest, growing a number of rows of the susceptible variety alternating with rows of resistant varieties tends to lessen the severity of the pest damage.

Photo courtesy the Rodale Institute

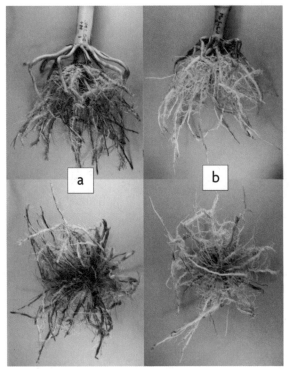

Figure 11.1. Corn roots: (a) continuous corn with mineral fertilizer, (b) corn following alfalfa with dairy manure compost. Photos by Walter Goldstein (Michael Fields Institute).

sod-type forage grasses, legumes, and grass-legume mixes as part of the rotation also increases soil organic matter. When you alternate two crops, such as corn and soybeans, you have a very simple rotation. More complex rotations require three or more crops and a five- to ten-year (or more) cycle to complete.

Rotations are an important part of any sustainable agricultural system. Yields of crops grown in rotations are typically 10% higher than those of crops grown in monoculture in normal growing seasons, and as much as 25% higher in droughty growing seasons. When you grow a grain or vegetable crop following a forage legume, the extra supply of nitrogen certainly helps. However, yields of crops grown in rotation are often higher than those of crops grown in monoculture, even when both are supplied with plentiful amounts

of nitrogen. Research in Iowa found that even using 240 pounds of N per acre when growing corn after corn, yields were not as good as corn grown following alfalfa with little or no N applied. In addition, following a nonlegume crop with another nonlegume produces higher yields than a monoculture using recommended fertilizer rates. For example, when you grow corn following grass hay, or cotton following corn, you get higher yields than when corn or cotton is grown year after year. This yield benefit from rotations is sometimes called a *rotation effect*. Another important benefit of rotations is that growing a variety of crops in a given year spreads out labor needs and reduces risk caused by unexpected climate or market conditions. Other benefits may occur when perennial forages (hay-type crops) are included in the rotation, including decreased soil erosion and nutrient loss.

ROTATIONS AND SOIL ORGANIC MATTER LEVELS

You might think you're doing pretty well if soil organic matter remains the same under a particular cropping system. However, if you are working soils with depleted organic matter, you need to build up levels to counter the effects of previous practices. Maintaining an inadequate level of organic matter won't do.

The types of crops you grow, their yields, the amount of roots produced, the portion of the crop harvested, and how you manage crop residues will all affect soil organic matter. Soil fertility itself influences the amount of organic residues returned, because more fertile soils grow higher-yielding crops, with more residues.

The decrease in organic matter levels when row crops are planted on a virgin forest or prairie soil is very rapid for the first five to ten years, but, eventually, a plateau or equilibrium is reached. After that, soil organic matter levels remain stable, as long as production practices aren't changed. An example of what can occur during twenty-five years of continuously grown corn is given in figure 11.2. Soil organic matter levels increase

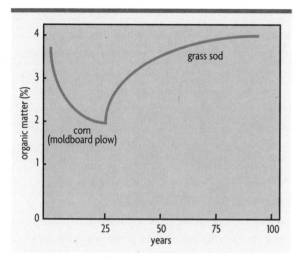

Figure 11.2. Organic matter changes in the plow layer during long-term cultivation followed by hay crop establishment.

when the cropping system is changed from a cultivated crop to a grass or mixed grass–legume sod. However, the increase is usually much slower than the decrease that occurred under continuous tillage.

A long-term cropping experiment in Missouri compared continuous corn to continuous sod and various rotations. More than 9 inches of topsoil was lost during sixty years of continuous corn. The amount of soil lost each year from the continuous corn plots was equivalent to 21 tons per acre. After sixty years, soil under continuous corn had only 44% as much topsoil as that under continuous timothy sod. A six-year rotation consisting of corn, oats, wheat, clover, and two years of timothy resulted in about 70% as much topsoil as found in the timothy soil, a much better result than with continuous corn. Differences in erosion and organic matter decomposition resulted in soil organic matter levels of 2.2% for the unfertilized timothy and 1.2% for the continuous corn plots.

In an experiment in eastern Canada, continuous corn led to annual increases in organic matter of about 100 pounds per acre, while two years of corn followed by two years of alfalfa increased organic matter by about 500 pounds per acre per year and four years of alfalfa increased organic matter by 800 pounds per acre per year. (Keep in mind that these amounts are small compared to the amounts of organic matter in most soils—3% organic matter represents about 60,000 pounds per acre to a depth of 6 inches.)

Two things happen when perennial forages are part of the rotation and remain in place for some years during a rotation. First, the rate of decomposition of soil organic matter decreases, because the soil is not continually being disturbed. (This also happens when using no-till planting, even for nonsod-type crops, such as corn.) Second, grass and legume sods develop extensive root systems, part of which will naturally die each year, adding new organic matter to the soil. Crops with extensive root systems stimulate high levels of soil biological activity and soil aggregation. The roots of a healthy grass or legume-grass sod return more organic matter to the soil than roots of most other crops. Older roots of grasses die, even during the growing season, and provide sources of fresh, active organic matter. Rotations that included three years of perennial forage crops have been found to produce a very high-quality soil in the corn and soybean belt of the Midwest.

We are not only interested in total soil organic matter—we want a wide variety of different types of organisms living in the soil. We also want to have a good amount of active organic matter and high levels of well-decomposed soil organic matter, or humus, in the soil. Although most experiments have compared soil organic matter changes under different cropping systems, few experiments have looked at the effects of rotations on soil ecology. The more residues your crops leave in the field, the greater the populations of soil microorganisms. Experiments in a semiarid region in Oregon found that the total amount of microorganisms in a two-year wheat-fallow system was only about 25% of the amount found under pasture. Conventional moldboard plow tillage systems are known to decrease the populations of earthworms, as well as other soil organisms. More complex rotations increase soil biological diversity. Including perennial forages in the rotation enhances this effect.

RESIDUE AVAILABILITY

As pointed out in chapters 3 and 9, more residues are left in the field after some crops than others. High residue-producing crops—especially those with extensive root systems—should be incorporated into rotations whenever possible. There is considerable interest in the possible future use of crop residue for a variety of purposes, such as for biofuel production. However, farmers should keep in mind that frequent removal of significant quantities of residue from their fields—and there may be more pressure to remove them if production of biofuels from crop residue becomes economically viable—can have a very negative effect on the soil's health.

SPECIES RICHNESS AND ACTIVE ROOTING PERIODS

In addition to the quantity of residues remaining following harvest, a variety of types of residues is also important. The goal should be a minimum of three different species in a rotation, more if possible. The percent of

Table 11.1
Comparison of Rotations:
Percent of Time Active Roots Are Present and Number of Species

Rotation	Years	Active Rooting Period (%)	Number of Species
Corn-soybeans	2	32	2
Dry beans–winter wheat	2	57	2
Dry beans–winter wheat/cover	2	92	3
Dry beans–winter wheat–corn	3	72	3
Corn–dry beans–winter wheat/cover	3	76	4
Sugar beets–beans–wheat/cover–corn	4	65	5

Source: Cavigelli et al. (1998).

the time that living roots are present during a rotation is also important. The period that active roots are present varies considerably, ranging from 32% of the time for a corn-soybeans rotation to 57% for a beans-wheat rotation to 76% for a three-year beans-wheat-corn rotation (table 11.1). As mentioned above, when soils are covered with living vegetation for a longer period of time, there tends to be decreased erosion as well as a decreased loss of nitrate and less groundwater contamination.

ROTATIONS AND WATER QUALITY

When annual crops are grown and planted in the spring, there is a considerable amount of time when the soil is not occupied by living plants. This means that for a large portion of the year there are no living plants to take up nutrients, especially nitrate, that can leach out of the soil. This is especially a problem in the Midwest, where many soils have tile drainage, which accentuates the discharge of high-nitrate water into streams and rivers. In addition to not taking up nutrients, the lack of growing plants means that the soils are wetter and more apt to produce runoff and erosion as well as leaching. Thus, rotations that include perennial forages and winter grains help maintain or enhance the quality of both ground and surface waters. And, while intensive use of cover crops helps water quality in a similar way, cover crops should not be viewed as a substitute for a good rotation of economic crops.

FARM LABOR AND ECONOMICS

Before discussing appropriate rotations, let's consider some of the possible effects on farm labor and finances. If you grow only one or two row crops, you must work incredibly long hours during planting and harvesting seasons, and not as much at other times. Including forage hay crops and early harvested crops along with those that are traditionally harvested in the fall would allow you to spread your labor over the growing season, making the farm more easy to manage by family labor alone.

CROP ROTATIONS AND PLANT DISEASES

Carefully selected rotations, especially when alternating between grains and broadleaf plants, can greatly assist control of plant diseases and nematodes. Sometimes a one-year break is sufficient for disease control, while for other diseases a number of years of growing a nonhost crop is needed to sufficiently reduce inoculum levels. Inclusion of pulse crops in a rotation seems to stimulate beneficial organisms and reduce the severity of cereal root diseases. Severity of common root rot of wheat and barley is reduced by a multiyear break of growing broadleaf plants. Rotations can be relatively easy to develop for control of diseases and nematodes that have a fairly narrow host range. However, some diseases or nematodes have a wider host range, and more care is needed in developing or changing rotations if these are present. In addition, some diseases enter the field on contaminated seed, while others, like wheat leaf rust, can travel with the wind for long distances. Other tactics, aside from rotations, are needed to deal with such diseases.

—KRUPINSKY ET AL. (2002).

In addition, when you grow a more diversified group of crops, you are less affected by price fluctuations of one or two crops. This may provide more year-round income and year-to-year financial stability.

Although there are many possible benefits of rotations, there are also some costs or complicating factors. It is critically important to carefully consider the farm's labor and management capacity when exploring diversification opportunities. You may need more equipment to grow a number of different crops. There may be conflicts between labor needs for different crops; cultivation and side-dressing nitrogen fertilizer for corn might occur at the same time as harvesting hay in some locations. In addition, some tasks, such as harvesting dry hay (mowing, tedding when needed, baling, and storing) can require quite a bit of labor that may not always be available. Finally, the more diversified the farm, the less chance for time to relax.

GENERAL PRINCIPLES

Try to consider the following principles when you're thinking about a new rotation:

1. Follow a legume forage crop, such as clover or alfalfa, with a high-nitrogen-demanding crop, such as corn, to take advantage of the nitrogen supply.

2. Grow less of nitrogen-demanding crops, such as oats, barley, and wheat, in the second or third year after a legume sod.

3. Grow the same annual crop for only one year, if possible, to decrease the likelihood of insects, diseases, and nematodes becoming a problem. (Note: For many years, the western corn rootworm was effectively controlled by alternating between corn and soybeans. Recently, populations of the rootworm with a longer resting period have developed in isolated regions in the Midwest, and they are able to survive the very simple two-year rotation.)

4. Don't follow a crop with a closely related species, since insect, disease, and nematode problems are frequently shared by members of closely related crops.

5. If specific nematodes are known problems, consider planting nonhost plants (such as grain crops for root-knot nematode) for a few years to decrease populations before planting a very susceptible crop such as carrots or lettuce. High populations of plant parasitic nematodes will also affect the choice of cover crops (see chapter 10 for a discussion of cover crops).

6. Use crop sequences that promote healthier crops. Some crops seem to do well following a particular crop (for example, cabbage family crops following onions, or potatoes following corn). Other crop sequences may have adverse effects, as when potatoes

have more scab following peas or oats.

7. Use crop sequences that aid in controlling weeds. Small grains compete strongly against weeds and may inhibit germination of weed seeds, row crops permit midseason cultivation, and sod crops that are mowed regularly or intensively grazed help control annual weeds.

8. Use longer periods of perennial crops, such as a forage legume, on sloping land and on highly erosive soils. Using sound conservation practices, such as no-till planting, extensive cover cropping, or strip cropping (a practice that combines the benefits of rotations and erosion control), may lessen the need to follow this guideline.

9. Try to grow a deep-rooted crop, such as alfalfa, safflower, or sunflower, as part of the rotation. These crops scavenge the subsoil for nutrients and water, and channels left from decayed roots can promote water infiltration.

10. Grow some crops that will leave a significant amount of residue, like sorghum or corn harvested for grain, to help maintain organic matter levels.

11. When growing a wide mix of crops—as is done on many direct-marketing vegetable farms—try grouping into blocks according to plant family, timing of crops (all early-season crops together, for example), type of crop (root vs. fruit vs. leaf), or cultural practices (irrigated, plastic mulch used).

12. In regions with limited rainfall, the amount of water used by a crop may be a critically important issue— usually one of the most important issues. Without plentiful irrigation, growing high-water-use crops such as hay, as well as sunflower and safflower, may not leave sufficient moisture in the soil for the next crop in the rotation.

13. Be flexible enough to adapt to annual climate and crop price variations, as well as development of soil pathogens and plant parasitic nematodes. For example, dryland rotations have been introduced in

the Great Plains to replace the wheat-fallow system, resulting in better use of water and less soil erosion. (It is estimated that less than 25% of the rainfall that falls during the fourteen-month fallow period in the Central High Plains is made available to a following crop of winter wheat.) (See box "Flexible Cropping Systems" and table 11.2, p. 121, for discussion and information on flexible, or dynamic, cropping systems.) As discussed above (see point 5), reconsider your crop sequence and cover crop use if nematodes become a problem.

ROTATION EXAMPLES

It's impossible to recommend specific rotations for a wide variety of situations. Every farm has its own unique combination of soil and climate and of human, animal, and machine resources. The economic conditions and needs are also different on each farm. You may get useful ideas by considering a number of rotations with historical or current importance.

A five- to seven-year rotation was common in the mixed livestock-crop farms of the northern Midwest and the Northeast during the first half of the 20th century. An example of this rotation is the following:

> *Year 1.* Corn
> *Year 2.* Oats (mixed legume–grass hay seeded)
> *Years 3, 4, and 5.* Mixed grass–legume hay
> *Years 6 and 7.* Pasture

The most nitrogen-demanding crop, corn, followed the pasture, and grain was harvested only two of every five to seven years. A less nitrogen-demanding crop, oats, was planted in the second year as a "nurse crop" when the grass-legume hay was seeded. The grain was harvested as animal feed, and oat straw was harvested to be used as cattle bedding; both eventually were returned to the soil as animal manure. This rotation maintained soil organic matter in many situations, or at least didn't

FLEXIBLE CROPPING SYSTEMS

As discussed in point 13 under "General Principles," it may be best for many farmers to adapt more "dynamic" crop sequences rather than strictly adhere to a particular sequence. Many things change from year to year, including prices paid for crops, pest pressures, and climate. And many farmers do deviate from plans and change what they plant in a particular field—for example, in a wetter than normal field a dry spring opens the opportunity for a vegetable farmer to plant an early-season crop, thus potentially enhancing the diversity of crops grown in that field. However, this issue is especially important for dryland farmers in water-limiting regions such as the Great Plains. In dryland agriculture low water availability is usually the greatest limitation to crop growth. In such regions, where much of the water needed for a crop is stored in the soil at planting time, growing of two heavy water users in a row may work out well if rainfall was plentiful the first year. However, if rainfall has been low, following a heavy-water-using crop (such as sunflowers or corn) with one that needs less water (such as dry pea or lentil) means that water stored in the soil may be enough, along with rainfall during the growing season, to result in a reasonable yield.

Table 11.2
Comparison of Monoculture, Fixed-Sequence Rotations, and Dynamic Cropping Systems

	Monoculture	Fixed-Sequence Rotations	Dynamic Cropping Systems
Numbers and types of crops	Single crop	Multiple crops; number depends on regionally adapted species, economics, farmer knowledge, infrastructure.	Multiple crops; number depends on regionally adapted species, economics, farmer knowledge, and infrastructure.
Crop diversity	N/A	Diversity depends on length of fixed sequence.	Diversity high due to annual variation in growing conditions and marketing opportunities, as well as changes in producer goals.
Crop-sequencing flexibility	N/A	None, although fixed-sequence cropping systems that incorporate opportunity crops increase flexibility.	High. All crops, in essence, are opportunity crops.
Biological and ecological knowledge	Basic knowledge of agronomy	Some knowledge of crop interactions is necessary.	Extended knowledge of complex, multiyear crop and crop-environment interactions.
Management complexity	Generally low, though variable depending on crop type	Complexity variable depending on length of fixed sequence and diversity of crops grown.	Complexity inherently high due to annual variation in growing conditions, markets, and producer goals.

Source: Modified from Hanson et al. (2007).

cause it to decrease too much. On prairie soils, with their very high original contents of organic matter, levels still probably decreased with this rotation.

In the corn belt region of the Midwest, a change in rotations occurred as pesticides and fertilizers became readily available and animals were fed in large feedlots instead of on crop-producing farms. Once the mixed livestock farms became grain-crop farms or crop-hog farms, there was little reason to grow sod crops. In addition, government commodity price support programs unintentionally encouraged farmers to narrow production to just two feed grains. The two-year corn-soybean rotation is better than monoculture, but it has a number of problems, including erosion, groundwater pollution with nitrates and herbicides, depletion of soil organic matter, and in some situations increased insect problems. Research indicates that with high yields of corn grain there may be sufficient residues to maintain organic matter. With soybeans, residues are minimal.

The Thompson mixed crop-livestock (hogs and beef)

farm in Iowa practices an alternative five-year corn belt rotation similar to the first rotation we described—corn/soybeans/corn/oats (mixed/grass hay seeded)/hay. For fields that are convenient for pasturing beef cows, the Thompson eight-year rotation is as follows:

Year 1. Corn
Year 2. Oats (mixed/grass hay seeded)
Years 3 to 8. Pasture

Organic matter is maintained through a combination of practices that include the use of manures and municipal sewage sludge, green manure crops (oats and rye following soybeans and hairy vetch between corn and soybeans), crop residues, and sod crops. These practices have resulted in a porous soil that has significantly lower erosion, higher organic matter content, and more earthworms than neighbors' fields

A four-year rotation researched in Virginia used mainly no-till practices as follows:

Year 1. Corn, winter wheat no-till planted into corn stubble
Year 2. Winter wheat grazed by cattle after harvest, foxtail millet no-till planted into wheat stubble and hayed or grazed, alfalfa no-till planted in fall
Year 3. Alfalfa harvested and/or grazed
Year 4. Alfalfa harvested and/or grazed as usual until fall, then heavily stocked with animals to weaken it so that corn can be planted the next year

This rotation follows many of the principles discussed earlier in this chapter. It was designed by researchers, extension specialists, and farmers and is similar to the older rotation described earlier. A few differences exist: This rotation is shorter; alfalfa is used instead of clover or clover-grass mixtures; and there is a special effort to minimize pesticide use under no-till practices. Weed-control problems occurred when going

from alfalfa (fourth year) back to corn. This caused the investigators to use fall tillage followed by a cover crop mixture of winter rye and hairy vetch. Some success was achieved suppressing the cover crop in the spring by just rolling over it with a disk harrow and planting corn through the surface residues with a modified no-till planter. The heavy cover crop residues on the surface provided excellent weed control for the corn.

Traditional wheat-cropping patterns for the semiarid regions of the Great Plains and the Northwest commonly include a fallow year to allow storage of water and more mineralization of nitrogen from organic matter for use by the next wheat crop. However, the wheat-fallow system has several problems. Because no crop residues are returned during the fallow year, soil organic matter decreases unless manure or other organic materials are provided from off the field. Water infiltrating below the root zone during the fallow year moves salts through the soil to the low parts of fields. Shallow groundwater can come to the surface in these low spots and create "saline seeps," where yields will be decreased. Increased soil erosion, caused by either wind or water, commonly occurs during fallow years, and organic matter decreases (at a rate of about 2% per year, in one experiment). In this wheat monoculture system, the buildup of grassy weed populations, such as jointed goat grass and downy brome, also indicates that crop diversification is essential.

Farmers in these regions who are trying to develop more sustainable cropping systems should consider using a number of species, including deeper-rooted crops, in a more diversified rotation. This would increase the amount of residues returned to the soil, reduce tillage, and lessen or eliminate the fallow period. (See box "Flexible Cropping Systems.")

A four-year wheat-corn-millet-fallow rotation under evaluation in Colorado was found to be better than the traditional wheat-fallow system. Wheat yields have been higher in this rotation than wheat grown in monoculture. The extra residues from the corn and millet also

CROP ROTATION ON ORGANIC FARMS

Crop rotation is always a good idea, but on organic farms a sound crop rotation is essential. Options for rescuing crops from disease are limited on organic farms, making disease prevention through good crop rotation more important. Similarly, weed management requires a multiyear approach. Since nutrients for organic crop production come largely through release from organic matter in soil, manure, compost, and cover crops, a crop rotation that maintains regular organic matter inputs and large amounts of active soil organic matter is critical.

To obtain the benefits of a diverse crop rotation and take advantage of specialty markets, organic farmers usually grow a high diversity of crops. Thus, organic field crop producers commonly grow five to ten crop species, and fresh market vegetable growers may grow thirty or more. However, because of the large variation in acreage among crops and frequent changes in the crop mix due to weather and shifting market demands, planning crop rotations on highly diversified farms is difficult. Therefore, many organic farmers do not follow any regular rotation plan, but instead place crops on individual fields (or parts of fields) based on the cropping history of the location and its physical and biological characteristics (e.g., drainage, recent organic matter inputs, weed pressure). Skilled organic growers usually have next year's cash crops and any intervening cover crops in mind as they make their placement decisions but find that planning further ahead is usually pointless because longer-term plans are so frequently derailed.

Although precise long-term rotation plans can rarely be followed on farms growing a diverse mix of crops, some experienced organic farmers follow a general repeating scheme in which particular crops are placed by the ad hoc approach described above. For example, some vegetable operations plant cash crops every other year and grow a succession of cover crops in alternate years. Many field crop producers alternate some sequence of corn, soybeans, and small grains with several years of hay on a regular basis, and some vegetable growers similarly alternate a few years in vegetables with two to three years in hay. These rest periods in hay or cover crops build soil structure, allow time for soilborne diseases and weed seeds to die off, and provide nitrogen for subsequent heavy-feeding crops. Some vegetable growers alternate groups of plant families in a relatively regular sequence, but this generally requires growing cover crops on part of the field in years when groups that require less acreage appear in the sequence. Within all of these generalized rotation schemes, the particular crop occupying a specific location is chosen by the ad hoc process described above. Organizing the choices with a general rotation scheme greatly simplifies the decision-making process.

Dividing the farm into many small, permanently located management units also greatly facilitates effective ad hoc placement of crops onto fields each year. By this means, a precise cropping history of every part of each field is easy to maintain. Moreover, problem spots and particularly productive locations can be easily located for planting with appropriate crops.

—CHARLES MOHLER, CORNELL UNIVERSITY

are helping to increase soil organic matter. Many producers are including sunflower, a deep-rooting crop, in a wheat-corn-sunflower-fallow rotation. Sunflower is also being evaluated in Oregon as part of a wheat cropping sequence.

Vegetable farmers who grow a large selection of crops find it best to rotate in large blocks, each containing crops from the same families or having similar production schedules or cultural practices. Many farmers are now using cover crops to help "grow their own nitrogen," utilize extra nitrogen that might be there at the end of the season, and add organic matter to the soil. A four- to five-year vegetable rotation might be as follows:

Year 1. Sweet corn followed by a hairy vetch/winter rye cover crop

Year 2. Pumpkins, winter squash, summer squash followed by a rye or oats cover crop

Year 3. Tomatoes, potatoes, peppers followed by a vetch/rye cover crop

Year 4. Crucifers, greens, legumes, carrots, onions, and miscellaneous vegetables followed by a rye cover crop

Year 5. (If land is available) oats and red clover or buckwheat followed by a vetch/rye cover crop

Another rotation for vegetable growers uses a two- to three-year alfalfa sod as part of a six- to eight-year cycle. In this case, the crops following the alfalfa are high-nitrogen-demanding crops, such as corn or squash, followed by cabbage or tomatoes, and, in the last two years, crops needing a fine seedbed, such as lettuce, onions, or carrots. Annual weeds in this rotation are controlled by the harvesting of alfalfa a number of times each year. Perennial weed populations can be decreased by cultivation during the row-crop phase of the rotation.

Most vegetable farmers do not have enough land—or the markets—to have a multiyear hay crop on a significant portion of their land. Aggressive use of cover crops will help to maintain organic matter in this situation. Manures, composts, or other sources of organic materials, such as leaves, should also be applied every year or two to help maintain soil organic matter.

Cotton alternating with peanut is a common simple rotation in the Southeast coastal region. The soils in this area tend to be sandy, low in fertility and water-holding capacity, and have a subsoil compact layer. As with the corn-soybean alternation of the Midwest, a more complex system is very desirable from many viewpoints.

A rotation including a perennial forage, for at least a few years, may provide many advantages to the cotton-peanut system. Research with two years of Bahia grass in a cotton-peanut system indicates greater cotton root growth, more soil organic matter and earthworms, and better water infiltration and storage.

SUMMARY

There are literally dozens of rotations that might work well on a particular farm. The specific selection depends on the climate and soils, the expertise of the farmer, whether there are livestock on the farm or nearby, equipment and labor availability, family quality-of-life considerations, and financial reality (potential price minus the cost of production). (However, vegetable farmers will sometimes include low-return crops in their rotations because customers expect to find them in the mix at a farm stand or farmers' market.) From an ecological view, longer and more complex rotations are preferred over shorter ones. It also makes a lot of sense, once equipment is in place, to stay flexible instead of having a rotation set in stone. If you're ready to adjust to rapid market changes, changes in labor availability, crop pest outbreaks, or unusual weather patterns, you'll be in a stronger position economically, while still maintaining a complex rotation.

SOURCES

Anderson, S.H., C.J. Gantzer, and J.R. Brown. 1990. Soil physical properties after 100 years of continuous cultivation. *Journal of Soil and Water Conservation* 45: 117–121.

Baldock, J.O., and R.B. Musgrave. 1980. Manure and mineral fertilizer effects in continuous and rotational crop sequences in central New York. *Agronomy Journal* 72: 511–518.

Barber, S.A. 1979. Corn residue management and soil organic matter. *Agronomy Journal* 71: 625–627.

Cavigelli, M.A., S.R. Deming, L.K. Probyn, and R.R. Harwood, eds. 1998. *Michigan Field Crop Ecology: Managing Biological Processes for Productivity and Environmental Quality.* Extension Bulletin E-2646. East Lansing: Michigan State University.

Coleman, E. 1989. *The New Organic Grower.* Chelsea, VT: Chelsea Green. See this reference for the vegetable rotation.

Francis, C.A., and M.D. Clegg. 1990. Crop rotations in sustainable production systems. In *Sustainable Agricultural Systems*, ed. C.A. Edwards, R. Lal, P. Madden, R.H. Miller, and G. House. Ankeny, IA: Soil and Water Conservation Society.

Hanson, J.D., M.A. Liebig, S.D. Merrill, D.L. Tanaka, J.M. Krupinsky, and D.E. Stott. 2007. Dynamic cropping systems: Increasing adaptability amid an uncertain future. *Agronomy Journal* 99: 939–943.

Gantzer, C.J., S.H. Anderson, A.L. Thompson, and J.R. Brown. 1991. Evaluation of soil loss after 100 years of soil and crop management. *Agronomy Journal* 83: 74–77. This source describes the long-term cropping experiment in Missouri.

Grubinger, V.P. 1999. *Sustainable Vegetable Production: From Start-Up to Market*. Ithaca, NY: Natural Resource and Agricultural Engineering Service.

Havlin, J.L., D.E. Kissel, L.D. Maddux, M.M. Claassen, and J.H. Long. 1990. Crop rotation and tillage effects on soil organic carbon and nitrogen. *Soil Science Society of America Journal* 54: 448–452.

Karlen, D.L., E.G. Hurley, S.S. Andrews, C.A. Cambardella, D.W. Meek, M.D. Duffy, and A.P. Mallarino. 2006. Crop rotation effects on soil quality at three northern corn/soybean belt locations. *Agronomy Journal* 98: 484–495.

Katsvairo, T.W., D.L. Wright, J.J. Marois, D.L. Hartzog, K.B. Balkcom, P.P. Wiatrak, and J.R. Rich. 2007. Cotton roots, earthworms, and infiltration characteristics in sod–peanut–cotton cropping systems. *Agronomy Journal* 99: 390–398.

Krupinsky, M.J., K.L. Bailey, M.P. McMullen, B.D. Gossen, and T.K. Turkington. 2002. Managing plant disease risk in diversified cropping systems. *Agronomy Journal* 94: 198–209.

Luna, J.M., V.G. Allen, W.L. Daniels, J.F. Fontenot, P.G. Sullivan, C.A. Lamb, N.D. Stone, D.V. Vaughan, E.S. Hagood, and D.B. Taylor. 1991. Low-input crop and livestock systems in the southeastern United States. In *Sustainable Agriculture Research and Education in the Field*, pp. 183–205. Proceedings of a conference, April 3–4, 1990, Board on Agriculture, National Research Council. Washington, DC: National Academy Press. This is the reference for the rotation experiment in Virginia.

Mallarino, A.P., and E. Ortiz-Torres. 2006. A long-term look at crop rotation effects on corn yield and response to nitrogen fertilization. In *2006 Integrated Crop Management Conference*, Iowa State University, pp. 209–217.

Merrill, S.D., D.L. Tanaka, J.M. Krupinsky, M.A. Liebig, and J.D. Hanson. 2007. Soil water depletion and recharge under ten crop species and applications to the principles of dynamic cropping systems. *Agronomy Journal* 99: 931–938.

Meyer-Aurich, A., A. Weersink, K. Janovicek, and B. Deen. 2006. Cost efficient rotation and tillage options to sequester carbon and mitigate GHG emissions from agriculture in eastern Canada. *Agriculture, Ecosystems and Environment* 117: 119–127.

Mohler, C.L., and S.E. Johnson. 2009. *Crop Rotation on Organic Farms: A Planning Manual*. No. 177. Ithaca, NY: Natural Resource, Agriculture, and Engineering Service.

National Research Council. 1989. *Alternative Agriculture*. Washington, DC: National Academy Press. This is the reference for the rotation used on the Thompson farm.

Peterson, G.A., and D.G. Westfall. 1990. Sustainable dryland agroecosystems. In *Conservation Tillage: Proceedings of the Great Plains Conservation Tillage System Symposium*, August 21–23, 1990, Bismark, ND. Great Plains Agricultural Council Bulletin No. 131. See this reference for the wheat-corn-millet-fallow rotation under evaluation in Colorado.

Rasmussen, P.E., H.P. Collins, and R.W. Smiley. 1989. *Long-Term Management Effects on Soil Productivity and Crop Yield in Semi-Arid Regions of Eastern Oregon*. Pendleton, OR: USDA Agricultural Research Service and Oregon State University Agricultural Experiment Station, Columbia Basin Agricultural Research Center. This describes the Oregon study of sunflowers as part of a wheat cropping sequence.

Werner, M.R., and D.L. Dindal. 1990. Effects of conversion to organic agricultural practices on soil biota. *American Journal of Alternative Agriculture* 5(1): 24–32.

ALEX AND BETSY HITT
GRAHAM, NORTH CAROLINA

Alex and Betsy Hitt were forced to reevaluate their farm fertility program in 1990 when a nearby horse stable that had provided them with manure went out of business. The Hitts, who raise 80 to 90 varieties of vegetables and 160 varieties of cut flowers on their 5-acre farm, have created elaborate rotations involving cover crops to supply organic matter and nitrogen, lessen erosion, and crowd out weeds. "We made a conscious decision in our rotation design to always use cover crops," Alex Hitt says. "We have to—it's the primary source for all of our fertility. If we can, we'll have two covers on the same piece of ground in the same year."

Alex and Betsy designed their initial rotation scheme to include all their farmed acreage, using the guiding principle of separating botanical families to break disease and insect cycles. They intentionally incorporated as many variables as possible into that rotation (cool- and warm-season crops, vegetables and flowers, heavy and light feeders, deep- and shallow-rooted plants, etc.). Later, as they came to rely more on cover crops for organic matter maintenance, the Hitts tweaked their rotation to maximize cover crop growth periods. "We always lean towards [cover] crops that will grow us the most biomass and fix the most nitrogen," says Alex. "These . . . usually . . . mature later and are harder to turn under and decompose." Other criteria include ease of establishment, seed cost and availability, and adaptability to their climate.

The payoffs from the Hitts' commitment to their rotation are clear. Their farm stays essentially free of soilborne diseases and pests, which they attribute to

"so much competition and diversity" in the soil. They see little or no erosion, despite farming some fields that have as much as a 5% slope. Furthermore, they have discovered that their covers smother and crowd out weeds, and the timing and spacing variations within their rotation have improved weed control. "We either have a different crop [from season to season] or we're planting it differently, so we don't get the same weeds the same time every year," Alex says. "When we went to a longer rotation and changed the timing, we noticed it quickly."

Over time, the Hitts' rotation scheme has evolved in

Their farm stays essentially free of soilborne diseases and pests, which they attribute to "so much competition and diversity" in the soil. They see little or no erosion, despite farming some fields that have as much as a 5% slope.

tandem with their production methods. Four different rotations are now used to maintain or boost soil quality in specific parts of their operation (see chart, p. 128). For example, their main field is in a five-year rotation plan, while the addition of six movable 16-by-48-foot hoop houses used for season extension led to the creation of a special twelve-year rotation. Areas under large-scale multi-bay high tunnels, as well as fields with flood-prone or heavy soils, have their own three-year rotations.

The Hitts use a consistent approach to managing cover crops in all of their rotations, regardless of rotation length. "We have essentially arrived at two winter and two summer combinations of cover crops," each of which always includes a legume and a grass, Alex explains. Typically, they plant rye and hairy vetch or sorghum sudan grass and cowpeas prior to late-planted spring crops, no-tilled summer cash crops, and fall-planted cover crops. Oats and crimson clover or pearl millet and soybeans precede early-spring-planted crops and fall-planted cash crops. The Hitts alter these combinations if needed to prevent disease buildup. They sometimes "fine-tune" their rotation by inserting an extra planting of a wheat, barley, or triticale cover crop prior to a first tomato planting.

The Hitts are interested in expanding no-till planting on their farm and trying out cover crops, such as rape and forage radish, that can easily be turned under in spring—because these are followed by an early-spring-seeded rye and hairy vetch cover that is rolled down to create a mulch layer under their no-till summer-planted crops. "I am still working on getting the right coulter/row openers for [no-till] seeding of certain flowers like zinnias and also sweet corn," Alex says.

The Hitts' flowers, fresh leafy greens, heirloom tomatoes, hot and sweet peppers, leeks, and other vegetables are popular with area chefs and at farmers' markets in nearby Chapel Hill. Their main challenges, Alex says, are twofold: to choose which cover crops should precede and follow their diverse set of cash crops, and to determine optimal spacing and timing for their cash crops. "If cash crops go in and out basically at the same time, this makes it easier to choose a cover crop and its following cash or cover crop," he says. "This also makes irrigation, cultivation, and other jobs more efficient." Standardizing bed widths and lengths and the spacing used for transplants and direct-seeded crops has made their cash crop management "essentially automatic when it comes to

planting, cultivating, irrigating, trellising, etc. There is no need to reset equipment or have different lengths of row covers if all the beds are the same."

The Hitts are making the most of their efficiency gains. In recent years, although they've scaled their production down from 5 to 3 acres, they are realizing greater profits by continually refining and diversifying a lucrative set of cash crops. In recognition of their innovation and success, Alex and Betsy received the prestigious Patrick Madden Award for Sustainable Agriculture from USDA's Sustainable Agriculture Research and Education (SARE) program in 2006.

The Hitts are convinced that the complexity built into their rotations has led to a reduction, rather than an increase, in their workload. Alex—who has found time over the years to volunteer for SARE committees—estimates that about ten days of work are required to manage the cover crops within his rotations each year. A week is used in the fall to seed, prepare, and hill 3 acres. In the spring, covers are mowed weekly as needed, and beds are turned under or rolled prior to planting. Once cash crops are harvested, rotational units are mowed, disked, and seeded with a summer cover crop, all in the same day. After eight weeks, this summer cover is mowed down and disked in preparation for another cash or cover crop planting.

The Hitts believe such time is well spent. "There are a billion benefits from cover crops," Alex says. "We have really active soil—we can see it by the good crops we grow, and by the problems we don't have. The whole [farm] is really in balance, and the rotation and cover crops have a lot to do with that."

—UPDATED BY AMY KREMEN

Key: O-CC = oats with crimson clover. R-HV = rye with hairy vetch. SG-CP = sudan grass with cowpeas. M-SB = millet with soybeans. FP = fall planted.

Main field rotation: 5 years

Year 1. O-CC → spring lettuce followed by summer flowers → R-HV.

Year 2. Peppers (half no-till into rye/hairy vetch) → O-CC.

Year 3. Half hardy flowers/1st summer flowers → SG-CP → O-CC.

Year 4. Spring vegetables followed by summer flowers → overwintered flowers (no cover crop).

Year 5. Overwintered flowers → SG-CP → O-CC.

Rotation for 16-by-48-foot sliding tunnels: 12 years

Year 1. O-CC → tunnel moves over → tomatoes → fall-planted hardy vegetables → tunnel moves off.

Year 2. FP hardy vegetables → M-SB lettuce and late-winter-planted vegetables.

Year 3. Overwintered bulb crops → late-summer lettuce → late-winter-planted vegetables.

Year 4. Late-winter-planted vegetables → tunnel moves off → M-SB → O-CC.

Year 5. O-CC → tunnel moves over → melons, cucumbers → FP hardy vegetables → tunnel moves off.

Year 6. FP hardy vegetables → M-SB → overwintered bulb crops planted → tunnel moves over.

Year 7. Overwintered bulb crops → late-summer lettuce and late-winter-planted vegetables.

Year 8. Late-winter-planted vegetables → tunnel moves off → M-SB → O-CC.

Year 9. O-CC → tunnel moves over → tomatoes → FP hardy vegetables → tunnel moves off.

Year 10. FP hardy vegetables → M-SB → overwintered bulb crops planted → tunnel moves over.

Year 11. Overwintered bulb crops → late-summer lettuce and late-winter-planted vegetables.

Year 12. Late-winter-planted vegetables → tunnel moves off → M-SB → O-CC.

Rotation for heavy and flood-prone soils: 3 years

Year 1. Winter squash into no-till into rye/hairy vetch residue → O-CC.

Year 2. Sweet corn (part no-till) → R-HV

Year 3. Mixed vegetables and flowers, grown using no-till if possible → R-HV.

Rotation for multi-bay tunnels: 3 years

Year 1. Tomatoes half no-till into rye w/ hairy vetch residue → O-CC.

Year 2. Mixed early and mid-season flowers → R-HV.

Year 3. SG-CP → half wheat w/ crimson clover, half rye w/ hairy vetch (prior to tomatoes).

Chapter 12

ANIMAL MANURES
FOR INCREASING ORGANIC MATTER AND SUPPLYING NUTRIENTS

The quickest way to rebuild a poor soil is to practice dairy farming, growing forage crops, buying . . .
grain rich in protein, handling the manure properly, and returning it to the soil promptly.

—J. L. HILLS, C. H. JONES, AND C. CUTLER, 1908

Once cheap fertilizers became widely available after World War II, many farmers, extension agents, and scientists looked down their noses at manure. People thought more about how to get rid of manure than how to put it to good use. In fact, some scientists tried to find out the absolute maximum amount of manure that could be applied to an acre without reducing crop yields. Some farmers who didn't want to spread manure actually piled it next to a stream and hoped that next spring's flood waters would wash it away. We now know that manure, like money, is better spread around than concentrated in a few places. The economic contribution of farm manures can be considerable. On a national basis, the manure from 100 million cattle, 60 million hogs, and 9 billion chickens contains about 23 million tons of nitrogen. At a value of 50 cents per pound, that works out to a value of about $25 billion for just the N contained in animal manures. The value of the nutrients in manure from a 100-cow dairy farm may exceed $20,000 per

year; manure from a 100-sow farrow-to-finish operation is worth about $16,000; and manure from a 20,000-bird broiler operation is worth about $6,000. The other benefits to soil organic matter buildup, such as enhanced soil structure and better diversity and activity of soil organisms, may double the value of the manure. If you're not getting the full fertility benefit from manures on your farm, you may be wasting money.

Animal manures can have very different properties, depending on the animal species, feed, bedding, handling, and manure-storage practices. The amounts of nutrients in the manure that become available to crops also depend on what time of year the manure is applied and how quickly it is worked into the soil. In addition, the influence of manure on soil organic matter and plant growth is influenced by soil type. In other words, it's impossible to give blanket manure application recommendations. They need to be tailored for every situation.

We'll start the discussion with dairy cow manure but

Photo by Edwin Remsburg

will also offer information about the handling, characteristics, and uses of some other animal manures.

MANURE HANDLING SYSTEMS
Solid versus Liquid

The type of barn on the farmstead frequently determines how manure is handled on a dairy farm. Dairy-cow manure containing a fair amount of bedding, usually around 20% dry matter or higher, is spread as a solid. This is most common on farms where cows are kept in individual stanchions or tie-stalls. Liquid manure-handling systems are common where animals are kept in a "free stall" barn and minimal bedding is added to the manure. Liquid manure is usually in the range of from 2% to 12% dry matter (88% or more water), with the lower dry matter if water is flushed from alleys and passed through a liquid-solid separator or large amounts of runoff enter the storage lagoon. Manures with characteristics between solid and liquid, with dry matter between 12% and 20%, are usually referred to as semisolid.

Composting manures is becoming an increasingly popular option for farmers. By composting manure, you help stabilize nutrients (although considerable ammonium is usually lost in the process), have a smaller amount of material to spread, and have a more pleasant material to spread—a big plus if neighbors have complained about manure odors. Although it's easier to compost manure that has been handled as a solid, it does take a lot of bedding to get fresh manure to a 20% solid level. Some farmers are separating the solids from liquid manure and then irrigating with the liquid and composting the solids. Some are separating solids following digestion for methane production and burning the gas to produce electricity or heat. Separating the liquid allows for direct composting of the solids without any added materials. It also allows for easier transport of the solid portion of the manure for sale or to apply to remote fields. For a more detailed discussion of composting, see chapter 13.

Some dairy farmers have built what are called "compost barns." No, the barns don't compost, but they are set up similar to a free-stall barn, where bedding and manure just build up over the winter and the pack is cleaned out in the fall or spring. However, with composting barns, the manure is stirred or turned twice daily with a modified cultivator on a skid steer loader or small tractor to a depth of 8 to 10 inches; sometimes ceiling fans are used to help aerate and dry the pack during each milking. Some farmers add a little new bedding each day, some do it weekly, and others do it every two to five weeks. In the spring and fall some or all of the bedding can be removed and spread directly or built into a traditional compost pile for finishing. Although farmers using this system tend to be satisfied with it, there is a concern about the continued availability of wood shavings and sawdust for bedding. More recently, vermicomposting has been introduced as a way to process dairy manure. In this case, worms digest the manure, and the castings provide a high-quality soil amendment.

Manure from hogs can also be handled in different ways. Farmers raising hogs on a relatively small scale sometimes use hoop houses, frequently placed in fields, with bedding on the floor. The manure mixed with bedding can be spread as a solid manure or composted first. The larger, more industrial-scale farmers mainly use little to no bedding with slatted floors over the manure pit and keep the animals clean by frequently washing the floors. The liquid manure is held in ponds for spreading, mostly in the spring before crops are planted and in the fall after crops have been harvested. Poultry manure is handled with bedding (especially for broiler production) or little to no bedding (industrial-scale egg production).

Storage of Manure

Researchers have been investigating how best to handle, store, and treat manure to reduce the problems that come with year-round manure spreading. Storage

Table 12.1
Typical Manure Characteristics

	Dairy Cow	Beef Cow	Chicken	Hog
DRY MATTER CONTENT (%)				
Solid	26	23	55	9
Liquid (fresh, diluted)	7	8	17	6
TOTAL NUTRIENT CONTENT (APPROXIMATE)				
Nitrogen				
pounds/ton	10	14	25	10
pounds/1,000 gallons	25	39	70	28
Phosphate, as P_2O_5				
pounds/ton	6	9	25	6
pounds/1,000 gallons	9	25	70	9
Potash, as K_2O				
pounds/ton	7	11	12	9
pounds/1,000 gallons	20	31	33	34
Approximate amounts of solid and liquid manure to supply 100 pounds N for a given species of animal*				
solid manure (tons)	10	7	4	10
liquid manure (gallons)	4000	2500	1500	3600

*Provides similar amounts of nutrients.
Source: Modified from various sources.

allows the farmer the opportunity to apply manure when it's best for the crop and during appropriate weather conditions. This reduces nutrient loss from the manure, caused by water runoff from the field. However, significant losses of nutrients from stored manure also may occur. One study found that during the year dairy manure stored in uncovered piles lost 3% of the solids, 10% of the nitrogen, 3% of the phosphorus, and 20% of the potassium. Covered piles or well-contained bottom-loading liquid systems, which tend to form a crust on the surface, do a better job of conserving the nutrients and solids than unprotected piles. Poultry manure, with its high amount of ammonium, may lose 50% of its nitrogen during storage as ammonia gas volatilizes, unless precautions are taken to conserve nitrogen. Regardless of storage method, it is important to understand how potential losses occur in order to select a storage method and location that minimize environmental impact.

CHEMICAL CHARACTERISTICS OF MANURES

A high percentage of the nutrients in feeds passes right through animals and ends up in their manure. Depending on the ration and animal type, over 70% of the nitrogen, 60% of the phosphorus, and 80% of the potassium fed may pass through the animal as manure. These nutrients are available for recycling on cropland. In addition to the nitrogen, phosphorus, and potassium contributions given in table 12.1, manures contain significant amounts of other nutrients, such as calcium, magnesium, and sulfur. For example, in regions that tend to lack the micronutrient zinc, there is rarely any crop deficiency found on soils receiving regular manure applications.

The values given in table 12.1 must be viewed with some caution, because the characteristics of manures from even the same type of animal may vary considerably from one farm to another. Differences in feeds, mineral supplements, bedding materials, and storage systems make manure analyses quite variable. Yet as long as feeding, bedding, and storage practices remain relatively stable on a given farm, manure nutrient characteristics will tend to be similar from year to year. However, year-to-year differences in rainfall can affect stored manure through more or less dilution.

The major difference among all the manures is that poultry manure is significantly higher in nitrogen and phosphorus than the other manure types. This is partly due to the difference in feeds given poultry versus other farm animals. The relatively high percentage of dry matter in poultry manure is also partly responsible for the higher analyses of certain nutrients when expressed on a wet ton basis.

It is possible to take the guesswork out of estimating manure characteristics; most soil-testing laboratories will also analyze manure. Manure analysis should become a routine part of the soil fertility management program on animal-based farms. This is of critical

importance for routine manure use. For example, while the average liquid dairy manure is around 25 pounds of N per 1,000 gallons, there are manures that might be 10 pounds N or less OR 40 pounds N or more per 1,000 gallons. Recent research efforts have focused on more efficient use of nutrients in dairy cows, and N and P intake can often be reduced by up to 25% without losses in productivity. This helps reduce nutrient surpluses on farms using only needed P.

EFFECTS OF MANURING ON SOILS
Effects on Organic Matter

When considering the influence of any residue or organic material on soil organic matter, the key question is how much solids are returned to the soil. Equal amounts of different types of manures will have different effects on soil organic matter levels. Dairy and beef manures contain undigested parts of forages and may have significant quantities of bedding. They therefore have a high amount of complex substances, such as lignin, that do not decompose readily in soils. Using this type of manure results in a much greater long-term influence on soil organic matter than does a poultry or swine manure without bedding. More solids are commonly applied to soil with solid-manure-handling systems than with liquid systems, because greater amounts of bedding are usually included. A number of trends in dairy farming mean that manures may have less organic material than in the past. One is the use of sand as bedding material in free-stall barns, much of which is recovered and reused. The other is the separation of solids and liquids with the sale of solids or the use of digested solids as bedding. Under both situations much less organic solids are returned to fields. On the other hand, the bedded pack (or compost barn) does produce a manure that is high in organic solid content.

When conventional tillage is used to grow a crop such as corn silage, whose entire aboveground portion is harvested, research indicates that an annual application of 20 to 30 tons of the solid type of dairy manure per acre is needed to maintain soil organic matter (table 12.2). As discussed above, a nitrogen-demanding crop, such as corn, may be able to use all of the nitrogen in 20 to 30 tons of manure. If more residues are returned to the soil by just harvesting grain, lower rates of manure application will be sufficient to maintain or build up soil organic matter.

An example of how a manure addition might balance annual loss is given in figure 12.1. One Holstein "cow year" worth of manure is about 20 tons. Although 20 tons of anything is a lot, when considering dairy manure, it translates into a much smaller amount of solids. If the approximately 5,200 pounds of solid material in the 20 tons is applied over the surface of one acre and mixed with the 2 million pounds of soil present to a 6-inch depth, it would raise the soil organic matter by about 0.3%. However, much of the manure will decompose during the year, so the net effect on soil organic matter will be even less. Let's assume that 75% of the solid matter decomposes during the first year, and the carbon ends up as atmospheric CO_2. At the beginning of the following year, only 25% of the original 5,200 pounds, or 1,300 pounds of organic matter, is added to the soil. The net effect is an increase in soil organic matter of 0.065% (the calculation is [1,300/2,000,000] x 100). Although this does not seem like much added organic matter, if a soil had 2.17% organic matter and 3% of that was decomposed annually during cropping, the loss would be 0.065% per year, and the manure addition would just balance that loss. Manures with lower amounts of bedding, although helping maintain organic matter and adding to the active ("dead") portion, will not have as great an effect as manures containing a lot of bedding material.

USING MANURES

Manures, like other organic residues that decompose easily and rapidly release nutrients, are usually applied to soils in quantities judged to supply sufficient nitrogen

The Influence of Manure on Many Soil Properties

The application of manures causes many soil changes—biological, chemical, and physical. A few of these types of changes are indicated in table 12.2, which contains the results of a long-term experiment in Vermont with continuous corn silage on a clay soil. Manure counteracted many of the negative effects of a monoculture cropping system in which few residues are returned to the soil. Soil receiving 20 tons of dairy manure annually (wet weight, including bedding—equivalent to approximately 8,000 pounds of solids) maintained organic matter and CEC levels and close to the original pH (although acid-forming nitrogen fertilizers also were used). Manures, such as from dairy and poultry, have liming effects and actually counteract acidification. (Note: If instead of the solid manure, liquid had been used to supply N and other nutrients for the crop, there would not have been anywhere near as large a beneficial effect on soil organic matter, CEC, and pore space.)

High rates of manure addition caused a buildup of both phosphorus and potassium to high levels. Soil in plots receiving manures were better aggregated and less dense and, therefore, had greater amounts of pore space than fields receiving no manure.

Table 12.2
Effects of 11 Years of Manure Additions on Soil Properties

	Original Level	Application Rate (tons/acre/year)			
		none	10 tons	20 tons	30 tons
Organic matter	5.2	4.3	4.8	5.2	5.5
CEC (me/100g)	19.8	15.8	17.0	17.8	18.9
pH	6.4	6.0	6.2	6.3	6.4
P (ppm)*	4.0	6.0	7.0	14.0	17.0
K (ppm)*	129.0	121.0	159.0	191.0	232.0
Total pore space (%)	ND	44.0	45.0	47.0	50.0

* P and K levels with 20 and 30 tons of manure applied annually are much higher than crop needs (see table 21.3A, p. 249).
Note: ND = not determined.
Sources: Magdoff and Amadon (1980); Magdoff and Villamil (1977).

for the crop being grown in the current year. It might be better for building and maintaining soil organic matter to apply manure at higher rates, but doing so may cause undesirable nitrate accumulation in leafy crops and excess nitrate leaching to groundwater. High nitrate levels in leafy vegetable crops are undesirable in terms of human health, and the leaves of many plants with high N seem more attractive to insects. In addition, salt damage to crop plants can occur from high manure

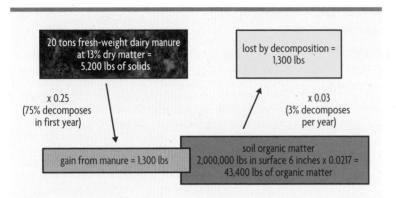

Figure 12.1. Example of dairy manure addition just balancing soil organic matter losses.

application rates, especially when there is insufficient leaching by rainfall or irrigation. Very high amounts of added manures, over a period of years, also lead to high soil phosphorus levels (table 12.2). It is a waste of money and resources to add unneeded nutrients to the soil, nutrients that will only be lost by leaching or runoff instead of contributing to crop nutrition.

Application Rates

A common per-acre rate of dairy-manure application is 10 to 30 tons fresh weight of solid, or 4,000 to 11,000 gallons of liquid, manure. These rates will supply approximately 50 to 150 pounds of available nitrogen (not total) per acre, assuming that the solid manure is not too high in straw or sawdust and actually ties up soil nitrogen for a while. If you are growing crops that don't need that much nitrogen, such as small grains, 10 to 15 tons (around 4,000 to 6,000 gallons) of solid manure should supply sufficient nitrogen per acre. For a crop that needs a lot of nitrogen, such as corn, 20 to 30 tons (around 8,000 to 12,000 gallons) per acre may be necessary to supply its nitrogen needs. Low rates of about 10 tons (around 4,000 gallons) per acre are also suggested for each of the multiple applications used on a grass hay crop. In total, grass hay crops need at least as much total nitrogen applied as does a corn crop. There has been some discussion about applying manures to

legumes. This practice has been discouraged because the legume uses the nitrogen from the manure, and much less nitrogen is fixed from the atmosphere. However, the practice makes sense on intensive animal farms where there can be excess nitrogen—although grasses may then be a better choice for manure application.

For the most nitrogen benefit to crops, manures should be incorporated into the soil in the spring immediately after spreading on the surface. About half of the total nitrogen in dairy manure comes from the urea in urine that quickly converts to ammonium (NH_4^+). This ammonium represents almost all of the readily available nitrogen present in dairy manure. As materials containing urea or ammonium dry on the soil surface, the ammonium is converted to ammonia gas (NH_3) and lost to the atmosphere. If dairy manure stays on the soil surface, about 25% of the nitrogen is lost after one day, and 45% is lost after four days—but that 45% of the total represents around 70% of the readily available nitrogen. This problem is significantly lessened if about half an inch of rainfall occurs shortly after manure application, leaching ammonium from the manure into the soil. Leaving manure on the soil surface is also a problem, because runoff waters may carry significant amounts of nutrients from the field. When this happens, crops don't benefit as much from the manure application, and surface waters become polluted. Some liquid manures— those with low solids content—penetrate the soil more deeply. When applied at normal rates, these manures will not be as prone to lose ammonia by surface drying. However, in humid regions, much of the ammonia-N from manure may be lost if it is incorporated in the fall when no crops are growing.

Other nutrients contained in manures, in addition to nitrogen, make important contributions to soil fertility. The availability of phosphorus and potassium in manures should be similar to that in commercial fertilizers. (However, some recommendation systems assume that only around 50% of the phosphorus and 90% of the potassium is available.) The phosphorus and potassium contributions contained in 20 tons of dairy manure are approximately equivalent to about 30 to 50 pounds of phosphate and 180 to 200 pounds of potash from fertilizers. The sulfur content as well as trace elements in manure, such as the zinc previously mentioned, also add to the fertility value of this resource.

Because one-half of the nitrogen and almost all of the phosphorus is in the solids, a higher proportion of these nutrients remain in sediments at the bottom when a liquid system is emptied without properly agitating the manure. Uniform agitation is recommended if the goal is to apply similar levels of solids and nutrients across target fields. A manure system that allows significant amounts of surface water penetration and then drainage, such as a manure stack of well-bedded dairy or beef cow manure, may lose a lot of potassium because it is so soluble. The 20% leaching loss of potassium from stacked dairy manure mentioned above occurred because potassium was mostly found in the liquid portion of the manure.

Timing of Applications

Manures are best applied to annual crops, such as corn, small grains, and vegetables, in one dose just before soil tillage (unless a high amount of bedding is used, which might tie up nitrogen for a while—see the discussion of C:N ratios in chapter 9). This allows for rapid incorporation by plow, chisel, harrow, disk, or aerator. Even with reduced tillage systems, application close to planting time is best, because the possibility of loss by runoff and erosion is reduced. It also is possible to inject liquid manures either just before the growing season starts or as a side-dressing to row crops. Fall manure applications on annual row crops, such as corn, may result in

considerable nitrogen loss, even if manure is incorporated. Losses of nitrogen from fall-applied manure in humid climates may be as much as 25% to 50%—resulting from conversion of ammonium to nitrate and then leaching and denitrification before nitrogen is available to next year's crop. It was determined in modeling studies that fall applications of liquid manure posed the greatest risk for nitrate leaching in a dairy system in New York.

Without any added nitrogen, perennial grass hay crops are constantly nitrogen deficient. Application of a moderate rate of manure—about 50–75 pounds worth of available nitrogen—in early spring and following each harvest is the best way to apply manure. Spring applications may be at higher rates, but wet soils in early spring may not allow manure application without causing significant compaction.

Although the best use of manure is to apply it near the time when the crop needs the nutrients, sometimes time and labor management or insufficient storage

Figure 12.2. Injection of liquid manure into shallow frozen soils, which eliminates compaction concerns and reduces spring application volumes. Photo by Eleanor Jacobs.

E. COLI 0157:H7

The bacteria strain known as E. coli 0157: H7 has caused numerous outbreaks of severe illness in people who ate contaminated meat and a few known outbreaks from eating vegetables—once when water used to wash lettuce was contaminated with animal manure and once from spinach grown near a cattle farm. This particular bacteria is a resident of cows' digestive systems. It does no harm to the cow, but—probably because of the customary practice of feeding low levels of antibiotics when raising cattle—it is resistant to a number of commonly used antibiotics for humans. This problem only reinforces the commonsense approach to manure use. When using manure that has not been thoroughly composted to grow crops for direct human consumption—especially leafy crops like lettuce that grow low to the ground and root crops such as carrots and potatoes—special care should be taken. Before planting your crop, avoid problems by planning a three-month period between incorporation and harvest. For short-season crops, this means that the manure should be incorporated long before planting. Although there has never been a confirmed instance of contamination of vegetables by E. coli 0157: H7 or other disease organisms from manure incorporated into the soil as a fertility amendment, being cautious and erring on the side of safety is well justified.

capacity causes farmers to apply it at other times. In the fall, manure can be applied to grasslands that don't flood or to tilled fields that will either be fall-plowed or planted to a winter cover crop. Although legal in most states, it is not a good practice to apply manures when the ground is frozen or covered with snow. The nutrient losses that can occur with runoff from winter-applied manure are both an economic loss to the farm and an environmental concern. Ideally, winter surface applications of manure would be done only on an emergency basis. However, research on frost tillage has shown that there are windows of opportunity for incorporating and injecting winter-applied manure during periods when the soil has a shallow frozen layer, 2 to 4 inches thick (see chapter 16). Farmers in cold climates may use those time periods to inject manure during the winter (figure 12.2), although the windows of opportunity may be limited.

POTENTIAL PROBLEMS

As we all know, too much of a good thing is not necessarily good. Excessive manure applications may cause plant-growth problems. It is especially important not to apply excess poultry manure, because the high soluble-salt content can harm plants.

Plant growth is sometimes retarded when high rates of fresh manure are applied to soil immediately before planting. This problem usually doesn't occur if the fresh manure decomposes for a few weeks in the soil and can be avoided by using a solid manure that has been stored for a year or more. Injection of liquid manure sometimes causes problems when used on poorly drained soils in wet years. The extra water applied and the extra use of oxygen by microorganisms may mean less aeration for plant roots, and loss of readily plant-available nitrate by denitrification may also be occurring.

When manures are applied regularly to a field to provide enough nitrogen for a crop like corn, phosphorus and potassium may build up to levels way in excess of crop needs (see table 12.2). When ammonium is properly conserved, the manure rate necessary to meet crop nitrogen requirement is substantially reduced. Correspondingly, phosphorus and potassium applications are moderated, reducing or eliminating the accumulation of these nutrients in soil.

When manure is applied based upon needed or allowed P additions, as required by some nutrient management plans, N-conserving management means that less fertilizer N will be needed. Erosion of phosphorus-

136

rich topsoils contributes sediments and phosphorus to streams and lakes, polluting surface waters. When very high phosphorus buildup occurs from the continual application of manure at rates to satisfy crop nitrogen needs, it may be wise to switch the application to other fields or to use strict soil conservation practices to trap sediments before they enter a stream. Including rotation crops, such as alfalfa—that do not need manure for N—allows a "draw-down" of phosphorus that accumulates from manure application to grains. (However, this may mean finding another location to apply manure. For a more detailed discussion of nitrogen and phosphorus management, see chapter 19.)

Farmers that purchase much of their animal feed may have too much manure to safely use all the nutrients on their own land. Although they don't usually realize it, they are importing large quantities of nutrients in the feed that remain on the farm as manures. If they apply all these nutrients on a small area of land, nitrogen and phosphorus pollution of groundwater and surface water is much more likely. It is a good idea to make arrangements with neighbors for use of the excess manure. Another option, if local outlets are available, is to compost the manure (see chapter 13) and sell the product to vegetable farmers, garden centers, landscapers, and directly to home gardeners.

Poultry and hogs are routinely fed metals such as copper and arsenic that appear to stimulate animal growth. However, most of the metals end up in the manure. In addition, dairy farmers using liquid manure systems commonly dump the used copper sulfate solutions that animals walk through to protect foot health into the manure pit. The copper content of average liquid dairy manures in Vermont increased about fivefold between 1992 and the early 2000s—from about 60 to over 300 ppm on a dry matter basis—as more farmers used copper sulfate footbaths for their animals and disposed of the waste in the liquid manure. Although there are few reports of metal toxicity to either plants or animals from the use of animal manures, if large quantities of high-metal-content manure are applied over the years, soil testing should be used to track the buildup.

Another potential issue is the finding that plants can take up antibiotics from manure applied to soil. About 70% of the antibiotics used in animal agriculture ends up in the manure. Although the amounts of antibiotics taken up by plants are small, this is an issue that may be of concern when using manures from concentrated animal production facilities that use considerable amounts of these substances.

SUMMARY

Animal manures can be very useful sources of amendments for building healthy soils. They are high in nutrients needed by plants and, depending on the species and the amount of bedding used, may help build and maintain soil organic matter levels. Because of the wide variability of the characteristics of manures, even from the same species—depending on feeding, bedding, and manure handling practices—it is important to analyze manures to more accurately judge the needed application rates. When using manures, it is important to keep in mind the potential limitations—pathogen contamination of crops for direct human consumption; accumulations of potentially toxic metals from high application of certain manures; and overloading the soil with N or P by applying rates that are in excess of needs, as demonstrated by soil test and known crop uptake.

SOURCES

Cimitile, M. 2009. Crops absorb livestock antibiotics, science shows. *Environmental Health News*. http://www.environmentalhealthnews.org/ehs/news/antibiotics-in-crops.

Elliott, L.F., and F.J. Stevenson, eds. 1977. *Soils for Management of Organic Wastes and Waste-waters*. Madison, WI: Soil Science Society of America.

Endres, M.I., and K.A. Janni. Undated. *Compost Bedded Pack Barns for Dairy Cows*. http://www.extension.umn.edu/dairy/Publications/CompostBarnSummaryArticle.pdf.

Harrison, E., J. Bonhotal, and M. Schwarz. 2008. *Using Manure Solids as Bedding*. Report prepared by the Cornell Waste Management Institute (Ithaca, NY) for the New York State Energy Research and Development Authority.

Madison, F., K. Kelling, J. Peterson, T. Daniel, G. Jackson, and L. Massie. 1986. *Guidelines for Applying Manure to Pasture and Cropland in Wisconsin*. Agricultural Bulletin A3392. Madison, WI.

Magdoff, F.R., and J.F. Amadon. 1980. Yield trends and soil chemical changes resulting from N and manure application to continuous corn. *Agronomy Journal* 72: 161–164. See this reference for dairy manure needed to maintain or increase organic matter and soil chemical changes under continuous cropping for silage corn.

Magdoff, F.R., J.F. Amadon, S.P. Goldberg, and G.D. Wells. 1977. Runoff from a low-cost manure storage facility. *Transactions of the American Society of Agricultural Engineers* 20: 658–660, 665. This is the reference for the nutrient loss that can occur from uncovered manure stacks.

Magdoff, F.R., and R.J. Villamil, Jr. 1977. *The Potential of Champlain Valley Clay Soils for Waste Disposal*. Proceedings of the Lake Champlain Environmental Conference, Chazy, NY, July 15, 1976.

Maryland State Soil Conservation Committee. Undated. *Manure Management Handbook: A Producer's Guide*. College Park, MD: Author.

Ontario Ministry of Agriculture and Food. 1994. *Livestock and Poultry Waste Management*. Best Management Practices Series. Available from the Ontario Federation of Agriculture, Toronto, Ontario, Canada.

Ontario Ministry of Agriculture and Food. 1997. *Nutrient Management*. Best Management Practices Series. Available from the Ontario Federation of Agriculture, Toronto, Ontario, Canada.

Pimentel, D., S. Williamson, C.E. Alexander, O. Gonzalez-Pagan, C. Kontak, and S.E. Mulkey. 2008. Reducing energy inputs in the US food system. *Human Ecology* 36: 459–471.

Soil Conservation Society of America. 1976. *Land Application of Waste Materials*. Ankeny, IA: Author.

van Es, H.M., A.T. DeGaetano, and D.S. Wilks. 1998. Space-time upscaling of plot-based research information: Frost tillage. *Nutrient Cycling in Agroecosystems* 50: 85–90.

DARRELL PARKS
MANHATTAN, KANSAS

Even if Darrell Parks didn't like working with hogs, he would still raise them on his 600-acre farm in the Flint Hills of Kansas, if only for the manure that makes up a key part of his soil fertility program. Each year, Parks's farm produces forty-five sows plus corn, milo, wheat, soybeans, and alfalfa.

Parks spot-treats his land with hog manure to help areas needing extra fertility. He likes how targeting problem areas with thicker applications of manure corrects soil micronutrient deficiencies. "I've been working to better utilize farm-produced manure and cover crops as well as a crop rotation and management system that will allow me to eliminate purchased fertilizer, herbicides, and insecticides," says Parks, who received a grant from USDA's Sustainable Agriculture Research and Education (SARE) program to hone his use of manure on cropland. He was successful in that endeavor, and his cropland has been certified organic since 1996.

Parks's crops are raised mainly in two rotations. In one rotation, alfalfa is grown for three years, followed by a year each of corn and soybeans before returning to alfalfa. In the other, he plants Austrian winter peas in the late fall following wheat harvest. The peas, incorporated in the spring, are followed with a cash crop of milo or soybeans prior to a fall- or spring-planted wheat crop.

To ensure a sufficient nutrient supply for his wheat crops, Parks typically treats his wheat fields with liquid manure at a rate of approximately 660 gallons per acre. He collects this manure in a concrete pit adjacent to a building where sows are housed for brief periods during breeding or when being sold. The liquid manure, for which he does not typically obtain a nutrient analysis, "catches a lot of rainfall and is fairly dilute—[essentially] high-powered water," he says. "I avoid wet conditions when spreading and try to hit the wheat in March or April during a dry period on a still day, before [the wheat] is too big."

Parks sometimes lets older sows out to pasture on some of his fields, where they spread their own manure. He cautions, however, against pasturing young pigs on alfalfa. "You'd think they'd balance their ration better," he says, "but they don't—they overeat."

For most of their lives, Parks's hogs are raised on half of a 10-acre field. He plants the remaining 5 acres to corn. Once the corn is harvested, he moves the hogs and their pens over to the "clean ground" of corn stubble. "Going back and forth like this seems to work well in keeping the worms down," he says. And he says that the 50–60 pounds of N per acre put down with the hogs' manure helps grow "some pretty good corn" in that field each year.

Parks notes that his tillage regime, on which he is dependent for weed control in his organic system, makes maintaining and improving his soil organic matter content especially challenging. That's why he remains committed to integrating the use of both animal and "green" manures on his farm.

In response to organic grain and fuel price spikes, he decided recently to reduce the number of hogs he raises from sixty to forty-five. Striving for economic sustainability, he is constantly weighing the pros and cons of becoming more self-sufficient by raising his own feed for the hogs versus taking advantage of the price premiums for organic grains.

"It's a hard decision," he says. "Right now, if I cut down on hogs, maybe it would be better economically. But if I get out [of raising hogs entirely], it's not easy to get back in."

For now, he is betting that over the longer term, he's better off keeping his hogs. "A lot of people don't like the idea of how pigs are raised" within a conventional operation, he says. "We're meeting [the demand of] a niche market in its infancy that is sure to grow."

—UPDATED BY AMY KREMEN

Chapter 13

MAKING AND USING COMPOSTS

The reason of our thus treating composts of various soils and substances,

is not only to dulcify, sweeten, and free them from the noxious qualities they otherwise retain. . . .

[Before composting, they are] apter to ingender vermin, weeds, and fungous . . . than to produce

wholsome [sic] plants, fruits and roots, fit for the table.

—J. EVELYN, 17TH CENTURY

Decomposition of organic materials takes place naturally in forests and fields all around us. Composting is the art and science of combining available organic wastes so that they decompose to form a uniform and stable finished product. Composts are excellent organic amendments for soils. Composting reduces bulk, stabilizes soluble nutrients, and hastens the formation of humus. Most organic materials, such as manures, crop residues, grass clippings, leaves, sawdust, and many kitchen wastes, can be composted.

The microorganisms that do much of the work of rapid composting perform well at elevated temperatures with plenty of oxygen and moisture. These compost-adapted organisms cover the entire range of warm, or mesophilic (up to 110°F), and hot, or thermophilic (from 110° up to 130°F and even higher), conditions. Temperatures above 160°F can develop in compost piles, helping kill off weed seeds and disease organisms, but this overheating usually slows down the process, since

it may cause extreme drying and triggers a die-off of all but the most heat-resistant organisms. At temperatures below 110°F, the more prolific mesophilic organisms take over and the rate of composting again slows down, especially as it drops toward ambient temperatures, a process known as "curing." The composting process is slowed by anything that inhibits good aeration or the maintenance of high enough temperatures and sufficient moisture.

Composting farm wastes and organic residues from off the farm has become a widespread practice.

TYPES OF COMPOSTING

Some people talk about "low-temperature" composting—including "sheet," worm (vermicomposting), and small-pile composting—and "high-temperature" composting. We like to use the term "composting" only when talking about the rapid decomposition that takes place at high temperatures.

141

EVEN BIRDS DO IT

The male brush turkey of Australia gathers leaves, small branches, moss, and other litter and builds a mound about 3 feet high and 5 feet across. It then digs holes into the mound repeatedly and refills them—helping to fragment and mix the debris. Finally, the pile is covered with a layer of sticks and twigs. The female lays her eggs in a hole dug into the pile, which heats up to close to 100°F around the eggs while the outside can be around 65°F. The heat of the composting process frees the birds from having to sit on the eggs to incubate them.

—R.S. SEYMOUR (1991)

Accepting and composting lawn and garden wastes provide some income for farmers near cities and towns. They may charge for accepting the wastes and for selling compost. Some farmers, especially those without animals or perennial forage crops that help increase organic matter, may want to utilize the compost as a source of organic matter for their own soils.

MAKING COMPOSTS
Moisture
The amount of moisture in a compost pile is important. If the materials mat and rainwater can't drain easily through the pile, it may not stay aerobic in a humid climatic zone. On the other hand, if composting is done inside a barn or under dry climatic conditions, the pile may not be moist enough to allow microorganisms to do their job. Moisture is lost during the active phase

---

A SAMPLE COMPOST RECIPE

Start with the following:

- grass clippings (77% moisture, 45% C, and 2.4% N)
- leaves (35% moisture, 50% C, and 0.75% N)
- food scraps (80 % moisture, 42% C, and 5.0% N)

The ratio of the materials needed to get 60% moisture and a C:N of 30:1 is: 100 lbs of grass, 130 lbs of leaves, and 80 lbs of food scraps.

—T. RICHARD (1996b)

---

of composting, so it may be necessary to add water to a pile. In fact, even in a humid region, it is a good idea to moisten the pile at first, if dry materials are used. However, if something like liquid manure is used to provide a high-nitrogen material, sufficient moisture will most likely be present to start the composting process. The ideal moisture content of composting material is about 40% to 60%, or about as damp as a wrung-out sponge. If the pile is too dry—35% or less—ammonia is lost as a gas, and beneficial organisms don't repopulate the compost after the temperature moderates. Very dry, dusty composts become populated by molds instead of the beneficial organisms we want.

Types of Starting Materials
The combined organic materials used should have lots of carbon and nitrogen available for the microorganisms to use. High-nitrogen materials, such as chicken manure, can be mixed with high-carbon materials like hay, straw, leaves, or sawdust. Compost piles are often built by alternating layers of these materials. Turning the pile mixes the materials. Manure mixed with sawdust or wood chips used for bedding can be composted as is. Composting occurs most easily if the average C:N ratio of the materials is about 25–40 parts carbon for every part nitrogen (see chapter 9 for a discussion of C:N ratios).

There are too many different types of materials that you might work with to give blanket recommendations about how much of each to mix to get the moisture content and the C:N into reasonable ranges so the process can get off to a good start. One example is given in the box "A Sample Compost Recipe" on p. 142.

Cornell University's website for composting issues (http://cwmi.css.cornell.edu/composting.htm) features formulas to help you estimate the proportions of the specific materials you might want to use in the compost pile. Sometimes it will work out that the pile may be too wet, too low in C:N (that means too high in nitrogen), or too high in C:N (low in nitrogen). To balance your pile, you may need to add other materials or change the ratios used. The problems can be remedied by adding dry sawdust or wood chips in the first two cases or nitrogen fertilizer in the third. If a pile is too dry, you can add water with a hose or sprinkler system.

One thing to keep in mind is that not all carbon is equally available for microorganisms. Lignin is not easily decomposed (we mentioned this when discussing soil organisms in chapter 4 and again in chapter 9, when we talked about the different effects that various residues have when applied to soil). Although some lignin is decomposed during composting—probably depending on factors such as the type of lignin and the moisture content—high amounts of carbon present as lignin may indicate that not all of the carbon will be available for rapid composting. When residues contain high amounts of lignin, it means that the effective C:N can be quite a bit lower than indicated by using total carbon in the calculation (table 13.1). For some materials, there is little

Figure 13.1. On-farm composting facility, in which tarps are used to control moisture and temperature. The piles in the background are curing.

difference between the C:N calculated with total carbon and calculated with only biodegradable carbon.

It's important to avoid using certain materials such as coal ash and especially wood chips from pressure-treated lumber. And it's a good idea to go easy using manure from pets or large quantities of fats, oils, or waxes. These types of materials may be difficult to compost or result in compost containing chemicals that can harm crops.

Wood chips or bark is sometimes used as a bulking agent to provide a "skeleton" for good aeration. These materials may be recycled by shaking the finished compost out of the bulking material, which can then be used for a few more composting cycles.

Pile Size

A compost pile or windrow (figure 13.1) is a large, natural convective structure—something like many

Table 13.1
Total vs. Biodegradable Carbon and Estimated C:N Ratios

Material	% Carbon	C:N	% Carbon	C:N	% Lignin	% Cell Wall	% Nitrogen
	(Total)		(Biodegradable)				
Newsprint	39	115	18	54	21	97	0.34
Wheat straw	51	88	34	58	23	95	0.58
Poultry manure	43	10	42	9	2	38	4.51
Maple wood chips	50	51	44	45	13	32	0.97

Source: T. Richard (1996a).

chimneys all next to each other. Oxygen moves into the pile as carbon dioxide, moisture, and heat rise from it. The materials need to fit together in a way that allows oxygen from the air to flow in freely. On the other hand, it is also important that not too much heat escape from the center of the pile. If small sizes of organic materials are used, a "bulking agent" may be needed to make sure that enough air can enter the pile. Sawdust, dry leaves, hay, and wood shavings are frequently used as bulking agents. Tree branches need to be "chipped" and hay chopped so that these ingredients don't mat and slow composting. Composting will take longer when large particles are used, especially those resistant to decay.

The pile needs to be large enough to retain much of the heat that develops during composting, but not so large and compacted that air can't easily flow in from the outside. Compost piles should be 3 to 5 feet tall and about 6 to 10 feet across the base after the ingredients have settled (see figure 13.2). (You might want it on the wide side in the winter, to help maintain warm temperatures, while gardeners can make compost in a 3-foot-tall by 3-foot-wide pile in the summer.) Easily condensed material should initially be piled higher than 5 feet. It is possible to have long windrows of composting materials, as long as they are not too tall or wide.

Turning the Pile

Turning the composting residues exposes all the materials to the high-temperature conditions at the center of the pile, and heat convection further exposes upper reaches of the pile (figure 13.3). Materials at the lower sides of the pile often barely compost. Turning the pile rearranges all the materials and creates a new center. If piles are gently turned every time the interior reaches and stabilizes for a few days at about 140°F, it is possible to complete the composting process within months, all other factors of moisture and aeration being optimal. On the other hand, if you turn the pile only occasionally, it

MINIMUM TURNING TECHNIQUE

Farm-quality composts can be produced by turning the pile only once or twice. You need to carefully construct the pile—building it up to reasonable dimensions, using and thoroughly mixing materials that give good porosity, and making sure the pile stays moist. A pile that is uniformly heating is getting sufficient air to decompose, and therefore may not need turning. As the heat declines, the pile may be getting too dense or not getting sufficient air, and it may need to be turned.

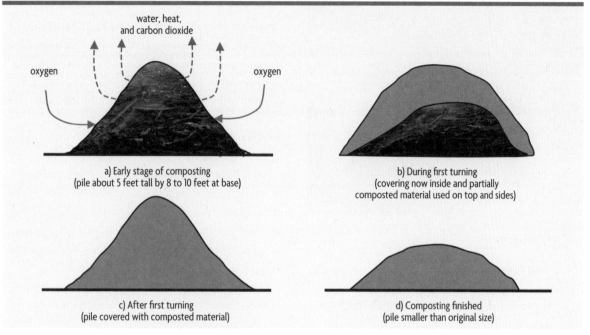

a) Early stage of composting
(pile about 5 feet tall by 8 to 10 feet at base)

b) During first turning
(covering now inside and partially
composted material used on top and sides)

c) After first turning
(pile covered with composted material)

d) Composting finished
(pile smaller than original size)

Figure 13.2. Compost pile dimensions and turning techniques.

may take a year or longer to complete, especially if it has settled down too densely. Equipment is now available to quickly turn long compost windrows at large-scale composting facilities (figure 13.3). Tractor-powered compost turners designed for composting on farms are also available, and some farmers use manure spreaders to remix and throw out piles.

Although turning compost frequently speeds up the process, too much turning may dry out the pile and cause more nitrogen and organic matter loss. If the pile is too dry, you might consider turning it on a rainy day to help moisten it. If the pile is very wet, you might want to turn it on a sunny day, or cover it with moisture protective material like chopped straw or compost fleece, a type of breathing cover that is now widely available. Very frequent turning may not be advantageous, because it can cause the physical breakdown of important structural materials that aid natural aeration. The right amount of turning depends on a variety of

factors, such as aeration, moisture, and temperature. Turn your compost pile to avoid cold, wet centers; break up clumps; and make the compost more uniform later in the process before use or marketing. Use caution turning in cold, windy weather if the pile is warm, for it may never reheat.

Figure 13.3. Turning a compost pile at a commercial facility. Photo by Alison Jack.

Figure 13.4. An example of a belowground composting pit, often used by small farmers in tropical countries.

The Curing Stage

Following high-temperature composting, the pile should be left to cure for about one to three months. Usually, this is done once pile temperatures cool to 105°F and high temperatures don't recur following turning. Curing is especially needed if the active (hot) process is short or poorly managed. There is a reduced need to turn the pile during curing because the phase of maximum decomposition is over and there is significantly less need for rapid oxygen entry into the pile's center when the decomposition rate is slow. (However, the pile may still need turning during the curing stage if it is very large or didn't really finish composting—determining when compost is finished is sometimes difficult, but if it reheats, it is not finished—or is soaked by rain.) Curing the pile furthers aerobic decomposition of resistant chemicals and larger particles. Common beneficial soil organisms populate the pile during curing, the pH becomes closer to neutral, ammonium is converted to nitrate, and soluble salts are leached out if the pile is outside and sufficient precipitation occurs. Be sure to maintain water content at the moisture-holding capacity (around 50% or less during curing) to ensure that active populations of beneficial organisms develop.

It is thought that the processes that occur during the early curing process give compost some of its disease-suppressing qualities. On the other hand, beneficial organisms require sources of food to sustain them. Thus, if composts are allowed to cure for too long—depleting all the available food sources—disease suppression qualities may decrease and eventually be lost.

OTHER COMPOSTING TECHNIQUES

High-temperature piles account for most composting in the U.S., but other methods are also used. Instead of making piles, small farmers in developing countries often dig pits for composting (figure 13.4), especially in dry and hot climates. The pits can be covered with soil material to prevent animals from getting into them, and they retain moisture in the compost material better.

Vermicomposting involves the use of earthworms—typically red worms—to perform the decomposition process. The method is, in a way, still mostly bacteria based, but the process occurs in the gut of the worm. The end product is worm casts, coated with mucus consisting of polysaccharides that make them into somewhat stable aggregates. The system requires bedding material—like newspaper strips, cardboard, hay, and similar materials—that mimics the decaying dried leaves that worms find in their natural habitat. The process is fast and efficient—worms can process half their weight in organic material in one day. The final product has an attractive feel and smell and is appealing to consumers.

Vermicomposting is often used to process kitchen scraps and can be done indoors in small bins. Recently, vermicomposting methods have been developed for large commercial operations. Two main approaches are used, using windrows or raised beds. With windrows, new materials are added on one side of the bed, and the other side is harvested for compost after about sixty days. With the raised-bed or container system—preferred for indoor operations in colder climates—the worms are fed at the top of the beds and the castings are removed at the bottom. Some vermicomposting operations are connected with livestock farms to process manure for export of excess nutrients off the farm as a value-added product.

USING COMPOSTS

Finished composts generally provide only low relative amounts of readily available nutrients. During composting, much of the nitrogen is converted into more stable

I don't make compost because it makes me feel good. I do it because composting is the only thing I've seen in farming that costs less, saves time, produces higher yields and saves me money.

—CAM TABB, WEST VIRGINIA BEEF AND CROP FARMER

organic forms, although potassium and phosphorus availability remains unchanged. However, it should be kept in mind that composts can vary significantly and some that have matured well may have high levels of nitrate. Even though most composts don't supply a large amount of available nitrogen per ton, they still supply fair amounts of other nutrients in available forms and greatly help the fertility of soil by increasing organic matter and by slowly releasing nutrients. Compost materials can be tested at selected commercial agricultural and environmental laboratories, which is especially important if certification is sought. Composts can be used on turf, in flower gardens, and for vegetable and agronomic crops. Composts can be spread and left on the surface or incorporated into the soil by plowing or rototilling. Composts also are used to grow greenhouse crops and form the basis of some potting soil mixes. Composts should not be applied annually at high rates. That is a recipe for overloading the soil with nutrients (see discussion in chapter 7).

DISEASE SUPPRESSION BY COMPOSTS

Research by Harry Hoitink and coworkers at Ohio State University shows that composts can suppress root and leaf diseases of plants. This suppression comes about because the plants are generally healthier (microorganisms produce plant hormones as well as chelates that make micronutrients more available) and, therefore, are better able to resist infection. Beneficial organisms compete with disease organisms for nutrients and either directly consume the disease-causing organisms or produce antibiotics that kill bacteria. Some organisms, such as springtails and mites, "actually search out pathogen propagules in soils and devour them," according to Hoitink. In addition, Hoitink found that potting mixes containing composts "rich in biodegradable organic matter support microorganisms that induce systemic resistance in plants. These plants have elevated levels of biochemical activity relative to disease control and are better prepared to defend themselves against diseases." This includes resistance to both root and leaf diseases.

Composts rich in available nitrogen may actually stimulate certain diseases, as was found for phytophthora root rot on soybeans, as well as fusarium wilts and fire blight on other crops. Applying these composts many months before cropping, allowing the salts to leach away, or blending them with low-nitrogen composts prior to application reduces the risk of stimulating diseases.

Composting can change certain organic materials used as surface mulches—such as bark mulches—from stimulating disease to suppressing disease.

PROTECTING DRINKING WATER SUPPLIES

Composting of manure is of special interest in watersheds that supply drinking water to cities, such as those that serve New York. The parasites *Giardia lamblia* (beaver fever) and *Cryptosporidium parvum* cause illness in humans and are shed through animal manure, especially young stock. These organisms are very resistant in the environment and are not killed by chlorination. Composting of manure, however, is an economical option that kills the pathogen and protects drinking water.

ADVANTAGES OF COMPOSTING

Composted material is less bulky than the original material, and easier and more pleasant to handle. During the composting process, carbon dioxide and water are lost to the atmosphere and the size of the pile decreases by 30–60%. In addition, many weed seeds and disease-causing organisms may be killed by the high temperatures in the pile. Unpleasant odors are eliminated. Flies, a common problem around manures and other organic wastes, are much less of a problem with composts. Composting reduces or eliminates the decline in nitrogen availability that commonly occurs when organic materials, such as sawdust or straw, are added directly to soil. Composting is also very useful for recycling kitchen wastes, leftover crop residues, weeds, and manures. Many types of local organic waste, such as apple pumice, lake weeds, leaves, and grass clippings, can be composted.

The reasons for composting and using composts need to be balanced by good practices such as locating the pile to minimize runoff and possible pollution of surface waters. Compost piles may produce odors when turned, so it's best to site piles away from where neighbors might get a more powerful whiff than they'd like. Composting in dry regions or under cover may produce composts that contain relatively high levels of salts, and you may need to apply them at lower rates to avoid damaging plants.

There is evidence that compost application lowers the incidence of plant root and leaf diseases, as mentioned. In addition, the chelates and the direct hormone-like chemicals present in compost stimulate the growth of healthy plants. Then there are the positive effects on soil physical properties that are derived from improving soil organic matter. These are some of the broad benefits to plant growth that are attributed to compost.

If you have a large amount of organic waste but not much land, composting may be very helpful and may create a valuable commercial product that improves farm profitability. Also, since making compost decreases the solubility of nutrients, composting may help lessen pollution in streams, lakes, and groundwater. On many poultry farms and on beef feedlots, where high animal populations on limited land may make manure application a potential environmental problem, composting may be the best method for handling the wastes. Composted material, with about half the bulk and weight of manure, and a higher commercial value, can be economically transported significant distances to locations where nutrients are needed. In addition, the high temperatures and biological activity during the composting process can help to decrease antibiotic levels in manures, which can be taken up by crops growing on manured land. Compost can also be stored easily, so it can be applied when soil and weather conditions are optimal.

Without denying the good reasons to compost, there are frequently very good reasons to just add organic materials directly to the soil, without composting. Compared with fresh residues, composts may not stimulate as much production of the sticky gums that help hold aggregates together. Also, some uncomposted materials have more nutrients readily available to feed plants than do composts. If your soil is very deficient in fertility, plants may need readily available nutrients from residues. Routine use of compost as a nitrogen source may cause high soil phosphorus levels to develop, because of the relatively low N:P ratio. Finally, more labor and energy usually are needed to compost residues than to simply apply the uncomposted residues directly.

SUMMARY

Composting organic residues before applying them to soil is a tried and true practice that can, if done correctly, eliminate plant disease organisms, weed seeds, and many (but not all) potentially noxious or undesirable chemicals. Compost provides extra water-holding capacity to a soil, provides a slow release of N, and may help to suppress a number of plant disease organisms as well as enhance the plant's ability to fight off diseases. Critical to good composting is to have (a) plentiful decomposable C- and N-containing materials, (b) good aeration, (c) moist conditions, and (d) enough size to allow high temperatures to develop. It is also necessary to turn the pile or windrow to ensure that all the organic materials have been exposed to the high temperatures. While these and other good reasons to make and use compost are important considerations, there are also good reasons to directly apply uncomposted organic residues to soil.

SOURCES

Cornell Waste Management Institute, http://cwmi.css.cornell.edu/.

Epstein, E. 1997. *The Science of Composting.* Lancaster, PA: Technomic Publishing Company.

Hoitink, H.A.J., D.Y. Han, A.G. Stone, M.S. Krause, W. Zhang, and W.A. Dick. 1997. Natural suppression. *American Nurseryman* (October 1): 90–97.

Martin, D.L., and G. Gershuny, eds. 1992. *The Rodale Book of Composting: Easy Methods for Every Gardener.* Emmaus, PA: Rodale Press.

Millner, P.D., C.E. Ringer, and J.L. Maas. 2004. Suppression of strawberry root disease with animal manure composts. *Compost Science and Utilization* 12: 298–307.

Natural Rendering: Composting Livestock Mortality and Butcher Waste. Cornell Waste Management Institute, http://compost. css.cornell.edu/naturalrenderingFS.pdf.

Richard, T. 1996a. The effect of lignin on biodegradability. http://compost.css.cornell.edu/calc/lignin.html.

Richard, T. 1996b. Solving the moisture and carbon-nitrogen equations simultaneously. http://compost.css.cornell.edu/calc/simultaneous.html.

Rothenberger, R.R., and P.L. Sell. Undated. *Making and Using Compost.* Extension Leaflet (File: Hort 72/76/20M). Columbia: University of Missouri.

Rynk, R., ed. 1992. *On Farm Composting.* NRAES-54. Ithaca, NY: Northeast Regional Agricultural Engineering Service.

Seymour, R.S. 1991. The brush turkey. *Scientific American* (December).

Staff of *Compost Science.* 1981. *Composting: Theory and Practice for City, Industry, and Farm.* Emmaus, PA: JG Press.

Weil, R.R., D.B. Friedman, J.B. Gruver, K.R. Islam, and M.A. Stine. Soil Quality Research at Maryland: An Integrated Approach to Assessment and Management. Paper presented at the 1998 ASA/CSSA/SSSA meetings, Baltimore. This is the source of the quote from Cam Tabb.

CAM TABB
KEARNEYSVILLE, WEST VIRGINIA

During back-to-back drought years in 2006 and 2007, West Virginia beef farmer Cam Tabb's crop yields exceeded the averages for his area. At times, neighbors have wondered whether Tabb enjoys some kind of miraculous microclimate, since he seems to make it through dry periods with seemingly little impact.

"I get blamed for getting more water than they got because the corn looks better," laughs Tabb, who raises 500 Angus beef cattle and grows small grains, hay, and corn for grain and silage, using no-till methods, on

Tabb's composting efforts, combined with annual soil tests and rotations, have done more than improve his soil and crop yields; in fact, composting has become one of the farm's most important sources of income.

1,900 acres near Charles Town, West Virginia. Tabb credits his strong yields to fifteen years of applying composted horse, dairy, and cattle manure to his fields. "I get a healthier plant with a better root system because my soil structure is better," he says. "So the rain that you do get really sinks in."

Tabb's composting efforts, combined with annual soil tests and rotations, have done more than improve his soil and crop yields; in fact, composting has become one of the farm's most important sources of income.

Tabb has come a long way since he used to pile manure on hard-packed ground and watch it ice over in the winter. "Before, I handled the manure as a waste, not a resource," he says. "I thought it had to smell bad to be any good. That was before I realized that I was smelling nitrogen being lost into the air as ammonia."

Inspired by a West Virginia University researcher's presentation on back yard composting, Tabb realized he needed to add a carbon source to his manure and turn the piles to encourage aeration. Once he began mixing in sawdust from horse stalls and turning the piles, he was on his way to becoming a master composter. Now, after years of fine-tuning his operation, he can talk about compost for hours.

He earns money taking in and hauling away a wide range of compostable materials from a faithful clientele—including several municipalities, area fish hatcheries, horse operators, and neighbors—that has developed simply through word of mouth. "People can pay me at half the cost it would take them to get their trash hauled away," he says. "We then process and sell the materials we take away."

The ingenuity of Tabb's composting operation lies in having found ways to make money several times off of these "waste" materials. For example, he chips scrap wood that he's been paid to haul from home construction sites and sells that material as bedding to horse operators. He rents containers to the horse owners to store used bedding, which he hauls back to his farm, composts, and sifts to create a high-grade compost product that he either sells or uses on his farm. He estimates that he composts at least 26,000 cubic yards of horse manure annually.

The fish wastes that Tabb receives from a federal fish hatching facility are composted with sawdust and horse manure. "This quickly creates a nice compost that contains 15–16 pounds N per ton, almost double the N content of our basic compost product," he says.

Tabb also rents out containers to contractors clearing land of trees and stumps. "When we get logs, we save them aside—they're better for [reselling as] firewood," he says. After the soil and rocks are removed from the scraps and split stumps, the wood is mulched and sold to nurseries. The stump dirt, which he describes as being "about 85% dirt and 15% compost" is sifted and screened, creating a topsoil product that he markets back to the contractors for landscaping purposes. "None of the topsoil we sell comes from our own farm," he says. "It is all from recycled materials that we have brought in."

While "crop response and the reduction of manure volume" are what initially got Tabb excited about composting, today he is particularly motivated by the major role that composting plays in ensuring his farm's economic sustainability. "It pays us to have a good [compost] supply on the farm," he says. "There are the longer-term benefits of increased organic matter and plant health, while with fertilizer prices [rising even higher] in 2008, [our] compost is worth more than it ever has been."

The water-retention and slow-nutrient-release qualities of his compost have boosted Tabb's yields in good growing years and buffered his operation during hard ones. One year, he recorded an 80-bushel corn yield advantage on an acre amended with his compost compared to an acre where no compost had been applied.

Tabb spreads between 10 and 12 tons of compost per acre to his crop fields, depending on soil test results, just once every three years. His compost—which supplies 9, 12, and 15 pounds of nitrogen, phosphorus, and potash per ton, respectively—provides, with the exception of nitrogen, sufficient nutrients for his grain and hay crops. The compost he spreads is never less than a year old. Over time, he has become more selective about where he spreads, focusing on fields with 2–3% organic matter content instead of those that have attained 5–7%.

Tabb's windrow piles of compost—"They're bigger than anything you've ever seen," he says—measure 100 feet long, 20–25 feet wide, and 15 feet high. The piles are set up at eight different locations on his farm, which reduces the number of tractor trips, cost, and risk of soil compaction while spreading.

He relies on experience and observation instead of adhering to strict rules while making compost. "Everyone around the farm knows what to look for in turning the piles," he says. Heat-loving fungi, stimulated into releasing spores once the pile heats up to temperatures above 140°F, form mushrooms as the pile cools down. "We wait until the temperature goes under 130°F, and turn the pile when we see the fragile mushrooms," he explains. He adds, "We never turn a pile that is going upwards in heat," so that piles will reach sufficient temperatures to kill pathogens and weed seeds. Turning, which Tabb does with a front-end loader, pays for itself by reducing the volume of the pile. Turning also stimulates more rapid and thorough decomposition of materials in the pile, inducing temperatures hot enough to kill weed seeds and diseases. Based on his experience, Tabb recommends maintaining a large ratio of old to fresh materials within compost piles. This ensures that the moisture released from fresh materials will be absorbed by drier, older materials, thus preventing leachate formation and speeding the piles' overall inoculation and decomposition rates.

Tabb is pleased by the long-term results of applying compost at his farm, where the soil has taken on a spongier feel and has become more abundant in earthworms. He also sees little to no runoff from his compost-treated fields. "Our land makes up a total small watershed, and our springs feed a federal fish hatchery. If there were any negative runoff in the water, it'd be ours, and we'd hear about it from the people downstream," he observes.

Impressed by his results, several of Tabb's neighbors have begun to make and spread their own "black gold" in recent years. "Almost any farmer would understand what I do," Tabb says. "I hadn't realized that I was a practicing environmentalist, but almost every farmer is. These days, you can't afford not to be."

—UPDATED BY AMY KREMEN

Chapter 14

REDUCING EROSION AND RUNOFF

So long! It's been good to know you.
This dusty old dust is a gettin' my home.
And I've got to be drifting along.

—WOODY GUTHRIE, 1940

The dust storms that hit the Great Plains of the U.S. during the 1930s were responsible for one of the great migrations in our history. As Woody Guthrie pointed out in his songs, soil erosion was so bad that people saw little alternative to abandoning their farms. They moved to other parts of the country in search of work. Although changed climatic conditions and agricultural practices improved the situation for a time, there was another period of accelerated wind and water erosion during the 1970s and 1980s. Also, in many other countries land degradation has forced families off the farm to urban areas or caused them to seek out new lands by developing natural areas like rainforests.

Erosion by wind and water has occurred since the beginning of time. Although we should expect some soil loss to occur on almost all soils, agriculture can greatly aggravate the problem. Erosion is the major hazard or limitation to the use of about half of all cropland in the United States. On much of that land, erosion is occurring fast enough to reduce future productivity. As we discussed earlier, erosion is also an organic-matter issue because it removes the richest soil layer, the topsoil. The soil removed from fields also has huge negative effects off the farm, as sediment accumulates in streams, rivers, reservoirs, and estuaries, or blowing dust reaches towns and cities. In fact, sediment remains the number one contaminant for most waters around the world, and it often also carries other contaminants like nutrients, pesticides, and other chemicals.

Climate and soil type are important factors affecting erosion. Intense or prolonged rainstorms are major causes of water erosion and landslides, while drought and strong winds are critical factors in wind erosion. Soil type is important because it influences the susceptibility to erosion as well as the amount that can occur without loss of productivity. In chapter 6 we discussed how some soils (especially silts) with poor aggregation are more susceptible than other soils, especially those

Photo courtesy Harold van Es

Figure 14.1. A waterway scoured into a gulley on a midwestern cornfield after erosive spring rains. Photo by Andrew Phillips.

Figure 14.2. Erosion on steep lands in Central America. Removal of the fine topsoil left mostly boulders behind. Sorghum plants show drought stress due to lack of rain and low water storage capacity in soil.

with good aggregation. This is reflected in the soil *erodibility* ratings, which soil conservationists use to plan control practices.

A small amount of erosion is acceptable, as long as new topsoil can be created as rapidly as soil is lost. The maximum amount of soil that can be lost to erosion each year, while maintaining reasonable productivity, is called the *soil loss tolerance,* or T value. For a deep soil with a rooting depth of greater than 5 feet, the T value is 5 tons per acre each year. Although this sounds like a large amount of soil loss, keep in mind that the weight of an acre of soil to 6 inches of depth is about 2 million pounds, or 1,000 tons. So 5 tons is equivalent to about .03 inch (less than 1 mm). If soil loss continued at that rate, at the end of 33 years about 1 inch would be lost. On deep soils with good management of organic matter,

the rate of topsoil creation can balance this loss. The soil loss tolerance amount is reduced for soils with less rooting depth. When it is less than 10 inches, the tolerable rate of soil loss is the same as losing 0.006 inch per year and is equivalent to 1 inch of loss in 167 years. Of course, on agricultural fields the soil loss is not evenly distributed over the field, and areas of water confluence experience greater losses (figure 14.1). Also, many conservationists would argue that any amount of erosion is unacceptable, as the off-site damage to water and air quality may still be considerable.

When soil loss is greater than the tolerance value, productivity suffers in the long run. Yearly losses of 10 or 15 tons or more per acre occur in many fields. In extreme cases, as with croplands on steep slopes in tropical climates, losses of five or ten times that much

EROSION: A SHORT-TERM MEMORY PROBLEM?

It's difficult to fully appreciate erosion's damage potential, because the most severe erosion occurs during rare weather events and climate anomalies. Wind erosion during the Dust Bowl days of the 1930s, which resulted from a decade of extremely dry years, was especially damaging. And about one-third of the water erosion damage that occurs in a particular field during a thirty-year period commonly results from a single extreme rainfall event. Like stock market crashes and earthquakes, catastrophic erosion events are rare, but the impacts are great. We must do our best to understand the risks, prevent complacency, and adequately protect our soils from extreme weather events.

may occur. For example, originally fertile soils on steep slopes in southern Honduras are now severely eroded (figure 14.2) after years of slash-and-burn agriculture.

Management practices are available to help reduce runoff and soil losses. For example, an Ohio experiment in which runoff from conventionally tilled and no-till continuous-corn fields was monitored showed that over a four-year period, runoff averaged about 7 inches of water each year for conventional tillage and less than 0.1 inch for the no-till planting system. Researchers in the state of Washington found that erosion on winter wheat fields was about 4 tons each year when a sod crop was included in the rotation, compared to about 15 tons when sod was not included.

ADDRESSING RUNOFF AND EROSION

Effective runoff and erosion control is possible without compromising crop productivity. However, it may require considerable investment or new management. The numerous methods of controlling soil and water can be grouped into two general approaches: structural measures and agronomic practices. Creating structures for reducing erosion generally involves engineering practices, in which an initial investment is made to build terraces, diversion ditches, drop structures, etc. Agronomic practices that reduce erosion focus on changes in soil and crop management, such as reduced tillage and cover cropping, and planting vegetation in critical areas. Appropriate conservation methods may vary among fields and farms, but recently there has been a clear trend away from structural measures in favor of agronomic practices. The primary reasons for this change are as follows:

- Management measures help control erosion, while also improving soil health and crop productivity.
- Significant advances have been made in farm machinery and methodologies for alternative soil and crop management.

- Structures generally focus on containing runoff and sediment once erosion has been initiated, whereas agronomic measures try to prevent erosion from occurring in the first place by decreasing runoff potential.
- Structures are often expensive to build and maintain.
- Most structures do not reduce tillage erosion.

The use of soil-building conservation management practices is preferred for long-term sustainability of crop production, and they are also the first choice for controlling runoff and erosion. Structural measures still have a place, but that is primarily to complement agronomic measures. Erosion reduction works by either decreasing the shear forces of water and wind or keeping soil in a condition in which it can't easily erode. Many conservation practices actually reduce erosion by using both approaches. In general, the following are good principles:

- Keep the soil covered; water and wind erosion occur almost exclusively when the soil is exposed.
- Use management practices that increase aggregation and infiltration.
- Do not loosen the soil unless it is well covered. Loose soil is more erodible than stable soil, like in no-till systems. Loosening may initially reduce runoff potential but this effect is generally short-lived, as the soil will settle. If loosening is required to reduce compaction, do it with tools that limit disturbance (e.g., zone builders or strip tillers). Soil disturbance is also the single cause of tillage erosion.
- Take a landscape-scale approach for additional control. Focus on areas with high risk, those where runoff water concentrates, and maximize the use of inexpensive biological approaches like grass seeding in waterways and filter strips.
- Focus on critical periods. For example, in temperate areas the soil is most susceptible after the winter fallow, and in semiarid regions it is most fragile after the dry period when heavy rains begin and there is little surface cover. In some regions, heavy rainfall is associated with hurricane or monsoon seasons.

155

Figure 14.3. Soybeans grown under no-till with corn residue.

Reduced Tillage

Transition to tillage systems that increase surface cover and reduce disturbance is probably the single most effective and economical approach to reducing erosion. Restricted and no-till regimes succeed in many cropping systems by providing better economic returns than conventional tillage, while also providing excellent runoff and erosion control. Maintaining residues on the soil surface (figure 14.3) and eliminating the problem of soil loosening by tillage greatly reduce dispersion of surface aggregates by raindrops and runoff waters. The effects of wind on surface soil are also greatly reduced by leaving crop stubble on untilled soil and anchoring the soil with roots. These measures facilitate infiltration of precipitation where it falls, thereby reducing runoff and increasing plant water availability.

In cases where tillage is necessary, reducing its intensity and leaving some residue on the surface minimizes the loss of soil organic matter and aggregation. Leaving a rougher soil surface by eliminating secondary tillage passes and packers that crush natural soil aggregates may significantly reduce runoff and erosion losses by preventing surface sealing after intense rain (see figure 6.9, p. 63). Reducing or eliminating tillage also diminishes tillage erosion and keeps soil from being moved downhill. The gradual losses of soil from upslope areas expose subsoil and may in many cases further aggravate runoff and erosion. We discuss tillage practices further in chapter 16.

Significance of Plant Residues and Competing Uses

Reduced-tillage and no-tillage practices result in less soil disturbance and leave significant quantities of crop residue on the surface. Surface residues are important because they intercept raindrops and can slow down water running over the surface. The amount of residue on the surface may be less than 5% for the moldboard plow, while continuous no-till planting may leave 90% or more of the surface covered by crop residues. Other reduced-tillage systems, such as chiseling and disking (as a primary tillage operation), typically leave more than 30% of the surface covered by crop residues. Research has shown that 100% soil cover virtually eliminates runoff and erosion on most agricultural lands. Even 30% soil cover reduces erosion by 70%.

As discussed in chapter 9, there are many competing uses for crop residues as fuel sources, as well as building materials. Unfortunately, permanent removal of large quantities of crop residues will have a detrimental effect on soil health and the soil's ability to withstand water and wind erosion.

Cover Crops

Cover crops result in decreased erosion and increased water infiltration in a number of ways. They add organic residues to the soil and help maintain soil aggregation and levels of organic matter. Cover crops frequently can be grown during seasons when the soil is especially susceptible to erosion, such as the winter and early spring in temperate climates, or early dry seasons in semiarid climates. Their roots help to bind soil and hold it in place. Because raindrops lose most of their energy when they hit leaves and drip to the ground, less soil crusting occurs. Cover crops are especially effective in reducing erosion if they are cut and mulched, rather than incorporated. Ideally, this is done when the cover crop has nearly matured (typically, milk stage)—that is, when it is somewhat lignified but seeds are not yet viable and C:N ratios are not so high as to cause nutrient immobilization. In recent years, new methods of cover cropping, mulching, and no-tillage crop production, often jointly referred to as conservation agriculture, have been worked out by innovative farmers in several regions of the world (figure 14.4; see also the farmer case study at the end of this chapter). In parts of temperate South America this practice has revolutionized farming with rapid and widespread adoption in recent years. It has been shown to virtually eliminate runoff and erosion and also appears to have great benefits for moisture conservation, nitrogen cycling, weed control, reduced fuel consumption, and time savings, which altogether can result in significant increases in farm profitability. See chapter 10 for more information on cover crops.

Perennial Rotation Crops

Grass and legume forage crops can help lessen erosion because they maintain a cover on most of the soil surface for the whole year. Their extensive root systems hold soil in place. When they are rotated with annual row crops, the increased soil quality will reduce erosion and runoff potential during that part of the crop cycle.

Benefits are greatest when such rotations are combined with reduced- and no-tillage practices for the annual crops. Perennial crops like alfalfa and grass are often rotated with row crops, and that rotation can be readily combined with the practice of strip cropping (figure 14.5). In such a system, strips of perennial sod crops and row crops are laid out across the slope, and erosion from the row crop is filtered out when the water reaches the sod strip. This conservation system is quite effective in fields with moderate erosion potential and on operations that use both row and sod crops (for example, dairy farms). Each crop may be grown for two to five years on a strip, which is then rotated into the other crop.

Permanent sod, often as pasture, is a good choice for steep soils or other soils that erode easily, although slumping and landslides may be a concern under extreme conditions.

Adding Organic Materials

Maintaining good soil organic matter levels helps keep topsoil in place. A soil with more organic matter usually has better soil aggregation and less surface crusting. These conditions ensure that more water is able to infiltrate the soil instead of running off the field, taking soil with it. When you build up organic matter, you help control erosion by making it easier for rainfall to

Figure 14.4. Field and close-up views of soybean grown in black oat cover crop mulch in South America. Photos by Rolf Derpsch.

Figure 14.5. Corn and alfalfa grown in rotation through alternating strips.

Figure 14.6. Equipment for manure injection with minimal soil disturbance.

enter the soil. Reduced tillage and the use of cover crops already help build organic matter levels, but regularly providing additional organic materials like compost and manure results in larger and more stable soil aggregates and stimulates earthworm activity.

The adoption rate for no-till practices is lower for livestock-based farms than for grain and fiber farms. Manures may need to be incorporated into the soil for best use of nitrogen, protection from runoff, and odor control. Also, the severe compaction resulting from the use of heavy manure spreaders on very moist soils may

need to be relieved by tillage. Direct injection of liquid organic materials in a zone-till or no-till system is a recent approach that allows for reduced soil disturbance and minimal concerns about manure runoff and odor problems (figure 14.6).

Other Practices and Structures for Soil Conservation

Soil-building management practices are the first approach to runoff and erosion control, but structural measures may still be appropriate. For example, *diversion ditches* are channels or swales that are constructed

Figure 14.7. Hillside ditch in Central America channeling runoff water to a waterway on the side of the slope (not visible). A narrow filter strip is located on the upslope edge to remove sediment.

Figure 14.8. Grassed waterway in a midwestern cornfield safely channels and filters runoff water. Photo courtesy of USDA-NRCS.

Figure 14.9. Edge-of-field filter strips control sediment losses to streams. Photo courtesy of USDA-NRCS.

across slopes to divert water across the slope to a waterway or pond (figure 14.7). Their primary purpose is to channel water from upslope areas away and prevent the downslope accumulation of runoff water that would then generate increased scouring and gullies.

Grassed waterways are field water channels that reduce scouring in areas where runoff water accumulates; they also help prevent surface water pollution by filtering sediments out of runoff (figure 14.8). They require only small areas to be taken out of production and are used extensively in the midwestern U.S. grain belt region, where long gentle slopes are common.

Terracing soil in hilly regions is an expensive and labor-intensive practice, but it is also one that results in a more gradual slope and reduced erosion. Well-constructed and maintained structures can last a long time. Most terraces have been built with significant cost-sharing from government soil conservation programs prior to the widespread adoption of no-tillage and cover cropping systems.

Tilling and planting along the contour is a simple practice that helps control erosion. When you work along the contour, instead of up- and downslope, wheel tracks and depressions caused by the plow, harrow, or planter will retain runoff water in small puddles and allow it to slowly infiltrate. This approach is not very

effective when dealing with steep erodible lands, however, and also does not reduce tillage erosion.

There are a number of other practices that do little to reduce runoff and erosion or build soil health but can decrease channel erosion and sediment losses. *Filter strips* remove sediment and nutrients before runoff water enters ditches and streams (figure 14.9). *Sediment control basins* have been constructed in many agricultural regions to allow sediment to settle before stream water is further discharged; they are often used in areas where conventional soil management systems still generate a lot of erosion (figure 14.10).

Wind erosion is reduced by most of the same practices that control water erosion by keeping the soil covered and increasing aggregation: reduced tillage or

Figure 14.10. Top: A sediment control basin in a Central European landscape where conventional tillage is widely used. Bottom: Sediment regularly fills the basin and needs to be dredged.

Figure 14.11. Field shelterbelt reduces wind erosion and evaporative demand and increases landscape biodiversity.

Figure 14.12. An experiment with wide-spaced poplar trees planted in a New Zealand pasture to reduce landslide risk.

no-till, cover cropping, and perennial rotation crops. In addition, practices that increase roughness of the soil surface diminish the effects of wind erosion. The rougher surface increases turbulent air movement near the land surface and reduces the wind's shear and ability to sweep soil material into the air. Therefore, if fields are tilled and cover crops are not used, it makes sense to leave soil subject to wind erosion in a rough-tilled state when crops aren't growing. Also, *tree shelterbelts* planted at regular distances perpendicular to the main wind direction act as windbreaks and help reduce evaporative demand from dry winds (figure 14.11). They have recently received new attention as ecological corridors in agricultural landscapes that help increase landscape biodiversity.

Finally, a few words about landslides. They are difficult to control, and unstable steep slopes are best left in forest cover. A compromise solution is the use of wide-spaced trees that allow for some soil stabilization by roots but leave enough sunlight for a pasture or crops (figure 14.12). In some cases, horizontal drains are installed in critical zones to allow dewatering and prevent supersaturation during prolonged rains, but these are generally expensive to install.

SOURCES

American Society of Agricultural Engineers. 1985. *Erosion and Soil Productivity.* Proceedings of the national symposium on erosion and soil productivity, December 10–11, 1984, New Orleans. American Society of Agricultural Engineers Publication 8-85. St. Joseph, MI: Author.

Edwards, W.M. 1992. Soil structure: Processes and management. In *Soil Management for Sustainability*, ed. R. Lal and F.J. Pierce, pp. 7–14. Ankeny, IA: Soil and Water Conservation Society. This is the reference for the Ohio experiment on the monitoring of runoff.

Lal, R., and F.J. Pierce, eds. 1991. *Soil Management for Sustainability.* Ankeny, IA: Soil and Water Conservation Society.

Ontario Ministry of Agriculture, Food, and Rural Affairs. 1997. *Soil Management.* Best Management Practices Series. Available from the Ontario Federation of Agriculture, Toronto, Ontario, Canada.

Reganold, J.P., L.F. Elliott, and Y.L. Unger. 1987. Long-term effects of organic and conventional farming on soil erosion. *Nature* 330: 370–372. This is the reference for the Washington State study of erosion.

Smith, P.R., and M.A. Smith. 1998. Strip intercropping corn and alfalfa. *Journal of Production Agriculture* 10: 345–353.

Soil and Water Conservation Society. 1991. *Crop Residue Management for Conservation.* Proceedings of national conference, August 8–9, Lexington, KY. Ankeny, IA: Author.

United States Department of Agriculture. 1989. *The Second RCA Appraisal: Soil Water, and Related Resources on Nonfederal Land in the United States, Analysis of Conditions and Trends.* Washington, DC: Government Printing Office.

Chapter 15

PREVENTING AND LESSENING COMPACTION

A lasting injury is done by ploughing land too wet.

—S.L. DANA, 1842

We've already discussed the benefits of cover crops, rotations, reduced tillage, and organic matter additions for improving soil structure. However, these practices still may not prevent compacted soils unless specific steps are taken to reduce the impact of heavy loads from field equipment and inappropriately timed field operations. The causes of compaction were discussed in chapter 6, and in this chapter we'll discuss strategies to prevent and lessen soil compaction. The first step is to decide whether compaction is a problem and which type is affecting your soils. The symptoms, as well as remedies and preventive measures, are summarized in table 15.1, p. 162.

CRUSTING AND SURFACE SEALING

Crusting and surface sealing may be seen at the soil surface after heavy rains in the early growing season, especially with clean-tilled soil, and in the fall and spring after a summer crop (figure 15.1). Keep in mind that crusting and surface sealing may not happen every year, especially if heavy rains do not occur before the

plant canopy forms to protect the soil from direct raindrop impact. Certain soil types, such as sandy loams and silt loams, are particularly susceptible to crusting. Their aggregates usually aren't very stable, and, once broken down, the small particles fill in the pore space between the larger particles, making very dense crusts.

Figure 15.1. Rainfall energy destroys weak soil aggregates and creates a surface seal that increases runoff potential. Photo is of soil in the wheat-growing Palouse region of Washington State. When it dries, the seal turns into a hard crust that prevents seedling emergence.

Table 15.1
Types of Compaction and Their Remedies

Compaction Type	Indications	Remedies/Prevention
Surface crusting	Breakdown of surface aggregates and sealing of surface Poor seedling emergence Accelerated runoff and erosion	Reduce tillage intensity. Leave residues on surface. Add organic matter. Grow cover crops.
Plow layer	Deep wheel tracks Prolonged saturation or standing water Poor root growth Hard to dig and resistant to penetrometer Cloddy after tillage	Plow with moldboard or chisel plow, but reduce secondary tillage. Do primary tillage before winter (if no erosion danger exists). Use zone builders. Increase organic matter additions. Use cover crops or rotation crops that can break up compact soils. Use better load distribution. Use controlled traffic. Don't travel on soils that are wet. Improve soil drainage.
Subsoil	Roots can't penetrate subsoil Resistant to penetrometer at greater depths	Don't travel on soils that are wet. Improve soil drainage. Till deeply with a subsoiler or zone builder. Use cover crops or rotation crops that penetrate compact subsoils. Use better load distribution. Use controlled traffic. Don't use wheels in open furrows.

The impact of surface crusting is most damaging when heavy rains occur between planting and seedling emergence. The hard surface crust may delay seedling emergence and growth until the crust mellows with the next rains. If such follow-up showers do not occur, the crop may be set back considerably. Crusting and sealing of the soil surface also reduce water infiltration capacity. This reduction in infiltration increases runoff and erosion and lessens the amount of available water for crops.

Reducing Surface Crusting

Crusting is a symptom of the breakdown of soil structure that develops especially with intensively and clean-tilled soils. As a short-term solution, farmers sometimes use tools such as rotary hoes to break up the crust. The best long-term approach is to reduce tillage intensity, use tillage and cover cropping systems that leave residue or mulch on the surface, and improve aggregate stability with organic matter additions. Even residue covers as low as 30% will greatly reduce crusting and provide important pathways for water entry. A good heavy-duty conservation planter—with rugged coulter blades for in-row soil loosening, tine wheels to remove surface residue from the row, and accurate seed placement—can be a highly effective implement because it can successfully establish crops without intensive tillage (see chapter 16). Reducing tillage and maintaining significant amounts of surface residues not only prevent crusting, but also rebuild the soil by increasing organic matter and aggregation. Soils with very low aggregate stability—especially those high in sodium—may sometimes benefit from surface applications of gypsum (calcium sulfate). The added calcium and the effect of the greater salt concentration in the soil water as the gypsum dissolves promotes aggregation.

PLOW LAYER AND SUBSOIL COMPACTION

Deep wheel tracks, extended periods of saturation, or even standing water following a rain or irrigation may indicate plow layer compaction. Compacted plow layers also tend to be extremely cloddy when tilled (figure 15.2). A field penetrometer, which we will discuss in greater detail in chapter 22, is an excellent tool to assess soil compaction. A simple shovel can be used to visually evaluate soil structure and rooting, and digging can

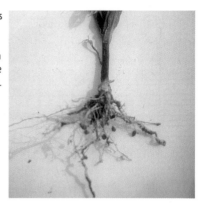

Figure 15.3. Corn roots from a compacted plow layer are thick, show crooked growth patterns, and lack fine laterals and root hairs.

provide good insights on the quality of the soil. This is best done when the crop is in an early stage of development but after the rooting system has had a chance to get established. If you find a dense rooting system with many fine roots that protrude well into the subsoil, you probably do not have a compaction problem. Well-structured soil shows good aggregation, is easy to dig, and will fall apart into granules when you throw a shovelful of soil on the ground. Compare the difference between soil and roots in wheel tracks and nearby areas to observe compaction effects on soil structure and plant growth behavior.

Roots in a compacted plow layer are usually stubby and have few root hairs (figure 15.3). The roots often follow crooked paths as they try to find zones of weakness in the soil. Rooting density below the plow layer is a good indicator for subsoil compaction. Roots are almost completely absent from the subsoil below severe plow pans and often move horizontally above the pan (see figure 6.6, p. 61). Keep in mind, however, that shallow-rooted crops, such as spinach and some grasses, may not necessarily experience problems from subsoil compaction.

Compaction may also be recognized by observing crop growth. A poorly structured plow layer will settle into a dense mass after heavy rains, leaving few large pores for air exchange. If soil wetness persists, anaerobic conditions may occur, causing reduced growth and denitrification (exhibited by leaf yellowing), especially

Figure 15.2. Large soil clods after tillage are indicative of compaction and poor aggregation.

CROPS THAT ARE HARD ON SOILS

Some crops are particularly hard on soils:

- Root and tuber crops like potatoes require intensive tillage and return low rates of residue to the soil.
- Silage corn and soybeans return low rates of residue.
- Many vegetable crops require a timely harvest, so field traffic occurs even when the soils are too wet.

Special care is needed to counter the negative effects of such crops. Counter measures may include selecting soil-improving crops to fill out the rotation, extensive use of cover crops, using controlled traffic, and adding extra organic materials such as manures and composts. In an eleven-year experiment in Vermont with continuous corn silage on a clay soil, we found that applications of dairy manure were critical to maintaining good soil structure. Applications of 0, 10, 20, and 30 tons (wet weight) of dairy manure per acre each year of the experiment resulted in pore spaces of 44, 45, 47, and 50% of the soil volume, respectively.

In many cases, soil compaction is combined with poor sanitary practices and lack of rotations, creating a dependency on heavy chemical inputs.

Preventing or Lessening Plow Layer Compaction

Preventing or reducing soil compaction generally requires a comprehensive, long-term approach to addressing soil health issues and rarely gives immediate results. Compaction on any particular field may have multiple causes, and the solutions are often dependent on the soil type, climate, and cropping system. Let's go over some general principles of how to solve these problems.

Proper use of tillage. Tillage can either cause or lessen problems with soil compaction. Repeated intensive tillage reduces soil aggregation and compacts the soil over the long term, causes erosion and loss of topsoil, and may bring about the formation of plow pans. On the other hand, tillage can relieve compaction by loosening the soil and creating pathways for air and water movement and root growth. This relief, however, as effective as it may be, is temporary and may need to be repeated in the following growing seasons if poor soil management and traffic patterns are continued.

Farmers frequently use more intense tillage to offset the problems of cloddiness associated with compaction of the plow layer. The solution to these problems is not necessarily to stop tillage altogether. Compacted soils frequently become "addicted" to tillage, and going "cold turkey" by converting to no-till management may result in failure. Practices that perform some soil loosening with minor disturbance at the soil surface may help in the transition from a tilled to an untilled management system. Aerators (figure 15.4) provide some shallow compaction relief in dense surface layers but do minimal tillage damage and are especially useful when aeration is of concern. They are also used to incorporate manure with minimal tillage damage. Strip tillage (6 to 8 inches deep) employs narrow shanks that disturb the soil only where future plant rows will be located (figure 15.4). It is

in areas that are imperfectly drained. In addition, these soils may "hard set" if heavy rains are followed by a drying period. Crops in their early growth stages are very susceptible to these problems (because roots are still shallow), and the plants commonly go through a noticeable period of stunted growth on compacted soils.

Reduced growth caused by compaction affects the crop's ability to fight or compete with pathogens, insects, and weeds. These pest problems may become more apparent, therefore, simply because the crop is weakened. For example, during wet periods dense soils that are poorly aerated are more susceptible to infestations of fungal root diseases such as *Fusarium, Pythium, Rhizoctonia, Thieviopsis* and plant-parasitic nematodes such as northern root-knot. These problems can be identified by observing washed roots. Healthy roots are light colored, while diseased roots are black or show lesions.

Figure 15.4. Tools that provide compaction relief with minimal soil disturbance: aerator (left) and strip tiller (right). Right photo by Bob Schindelbeck.

especially effective for promoting root proliferation.

Another approach may be to combine organic matter additions (compost, manure, etc.) with reduced tillage intensity (for example, chisel plows with straight points, or chisel plows specifically designed for high-residue conditions) and a planter that ensures good seed placement with minimal secondary tillage. Such a soil management system builds organic matter over the long term.

Deep tillage (subsoiling) is a method to alleviate compaction below the 6- to 8-inch depths of normal tillage and is often done with heavy-duty rippers (figure 15.5) and large tractors. Subsoiling is often erroneously seen as a cure for all types of soil compaction, but it does relatively little to address plow layer compaction. Subsoiling is a rather costly and energy-consuming practice that is difficult to justify for use on a regular basis. Practices such as zone building also loosen the soil below the plow layer, but zone builders have narrow shanks that disturb the soil less and leave crop residues on the surface (figure 15.5).

Deep tillage may be beneficial on soils that have developed a plow pan. Simply shattering this pan allows for deeper root exploration. To be effective, deep tillage needs to be performed when the entire depth of tillage is sufficiently dry and in the friable state. The practice tends to be more effective on coarse-textured soils (sands, gravels), as crops on those soils respond better to deeper rooting. In fine-textured soils, the entire subsoil often has high strength values, so the effects of deep tillage are less beneficial. In some cases it may even

Lessening and preventing soil compaction are important to improving soil health. The specific approaches should meet the following criteria:

• They should be selected based on where the compaction problem occurs (subsoil, plow layer, or surface).

• They must fit the soil and cropping system and their physical and economic realities.

• They should be influenced by other management choices, such as tillage system and use of organic matter amendments.

Figure 15.5. Left: Subsoiler shank provides deep compaction relief (wings at the tip provide lateral shattering). Right: Zone building provides compaction relief and better rooting with minimal surface disturbance. Right photo by George Abawi.

be harmful for those soils, especially if the deep tillage was performed when the subsoil was wet and caused smearing, which may generate drainage problems. After performing deep tillage, it is important to prevent future re-compaction of the soil by keeping heavy loads off the field and not tilling the soil when inappropriate soil moisture conditions exist.

Better attention to working and traveling on the soil. Compaction of the plow layer or subsoil is often the result of working or traveling on a field when the soil is too wet (figure 15.6). Avoiding this may require equipment modifications and different timing of field operations. The first step is to evaluate all traffic and practices that occur on a field during the year and determine which operations are likely to be most

damaging. The main criteria should be:

- the soil moisture conditions when the traffic occurs; and
- the relative compaction effects of various types of field traffic (mainly defined by equipment weight and load distribution).

For example, with a late-planted crop, soil moisture conditions during tillage and planting may be generally dry, and minimal compaction damage occurs. Likewise, mid-season cultivations usually do little damage, because conditions are usually dry and the equipment tends to be light. However, if the crop is harvested under wet conditions, heavy harvesting equipment and uncontrolled traffic by trucks that transport the crop off the field will do considerable compaction damage. In

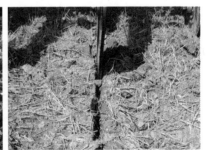

Figure 15.6. Compaction and smearing from wet (plastic) soil conditions: wheel traffic (left), plowing (middle), and zone building leaving open and smeared slot (right).

Figure 15.7. Reduction of soil compaction by increased distribution of equipment loads. Left: Tracks on a tractor. Middle: Dual wheels on a tractor that also increase traction. Right: Multiple axles and flotation tires on a liquid manure spreader

this scenario, emphasis should be placed on improving the harvesting operations. In another scenario, a high-plasticity clay loam soil is often spring-plowed when still too wet. Much of the compaction damage may occur at that time, and alternative approaches to tillage and timing should be a priority.

Better load distribution. Improving the design of field equipment may help reduce compaction problems by better distributing vehicle loads. The best example of distributing loads is through the use of tracks (figure 15.7), which greatly reduce the potential for subsoil compaction. But beware! Tracked vehicles may provide a temptation to traffic the land when the soil is still too wet. Tracked vehicles have better flotation and traction, but they can still cause compaction damage, especially through smearing under the tracks. Plow layer compaction may also be reduced by lowering the inflation pressure of tires. A rule of thumb: Cutting tire inflation pressure in half doubles the size of the tire footprint to carry an equivalent equipment load and cuts the contact pressure on the soil in half.

The use of multiple axles reduces the load carried by the tires. Even though the soil receives more tire passes by having a larger number of tires, the resulting compaction is significantly reduced. Using large, wide tires with low inflation pressures also helps reduce potential soil compaction by distributing the equipment load over a larger soil surface area. Use of dual wheels similarly reduces compaction by increasing the footprint, although this load distribution is less effective for reducing subsoil compaction, because the pressure cones from neighboring tires (see figure 6.10, p. 64) merge at shallow depths. Dual wheels are very effective at increasing traction but, again, pose a danger because of the temptation (and ability) to do fieldwork under relatively wet conditions. Duals are not recommended on tractors for performing seeding and planting operations because of the larger footprint (see also discussion on controlled traffic below).

Improved soil drainage. Fields that do not drain in a timely manner often have more severe compaction problems. Wet conditions persist in these fields, and traffic or tillage operations often have to be performed when the soil is too wet. Improving drainage may go a long way toward preventing and reducing compaction problems on poorly drained soils. Subsurface (tile) drainage improves timeliness of field operations, helps dry the subsoil, and, thereby, reduces compaction in deeper layers. On heavy clay soils where the need for close drain spacing is very expensive, surface shaping and mole drains are effective methods. Drainage is discussed in more detail in chapter 17.

Clay soils often pose an additional challenge with respect to drainage and compaction, because they remain in the plastic state for extended periods after drying from wet conditions. Once the upper inch of the

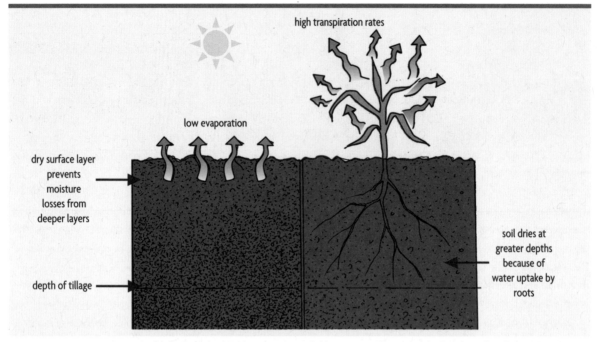

high transpiration rates

low evaporation

dry surface layer
prevents
moisture
losses from
deeper layers

depth of tillage

soil dries at
greater depths
because of
water uptake by
roots

Figure 15.8. Cover crops enhance the drying of a clay soil. Without cover crops (left), evaporation losses are low after the surface dries. With cover crops (right), water is removed from deeper in the soil, because of root uptake and transpiration from plant leaves, resulting in better tillage and traffic conditions.

soil surface dries out, it becomes a barrier that greatly reduces further evaporation losses. This is often referred to as *self-mulching*. This barrier keeps the soil below in a plastic state, preventing it from being worked or trafficked without causing excessive smearing and compaction damage. For this reason, farmers often fall-till clay soils. A better approach, however, might be to use cover crops to dry the soil in the spring. When a crop like winter rye grows rapidly in the spring, the roots effectively pump water from layers below the soil surface and allow the soil to transition from the plastic to the friable state (figure 15.8). Because these soils have high moisture-holding capacity, there is normally little concern about cover crops depleting water for the following crop.

Cover and rotation crops. Cover and rotation crops can significantly reduce soil compaction. The choice of crop should be defined by the climate, cropping system, nutrient needs, and the type of soil compaction.

Perennial crops commonly have active root growth early in the growing season and can reach into the compacted layers when they are still wet and relatively soft. Grasses generally have shallow, dense, fibrous root systems that have a very beneficial effect, alleviating compaction in the surface layer, but these shallow-rooting crops don't help ameliorate subsoil compaction. Crops with deep taproots, such as alfalfa, have fewer roots at the surface, but the taproots can penetrate into a compacted subsoil. As described and shown in chapter 10, forage radish roots can penetrate deeply and form vertical "drill" holes in the soil (see figure 10.4, p. 108). In many cases, a combination of cover crops with shallow and deep rooting systems is preferred (figure 15.9). Ideally, such crops are part of the rotational cropping system, which is typically used on ruminant livestock farms.

The relative benefits of incorporating or mulching a cover or rotation crop are site specific. Incorporation through tillage loosens the soil, which may be beneficial if the soil has been heavily trafficked. This would be the case with a sod crop that was actively managed for forage production, sometimes with traffic under relatively wet conditions. Incorporation through tillage also encourages rapid nitrogen mineralization. Compared to plowing down a sod crop, cutting and mulching in a no-till or zone-till system reduces nutrient availability and does not loosen the soil. But a heavy protective mat at the soil surface provides some weed control and better water infiltration and retention. Some farmers have been successful with cut-and-mulch systems involving aggressive, tall cover or rotation crops, such as rye and sudan grass.

Addition of organic materials. Regular additions of animal manure, compost, or sewage sludge benefit the surface soil layer to which these materials are applied by providing a source of organic matter and glues for aggregation. The long-term benefits of applying

Figure 15.9. A combination of deep alfalfa roots and shallow, dense grass roots helps address compaction at different depths.

these materials relative to soil compaction may be very favorable, but in many cases the application procedure itself is a major cause of compaction. Livestock-based farms in humid regions usually apply manure using heavy spreaders (often with poor load distribution) on wet or marginally dry soils, resulting in severe compaction of both the surface layer and the subsoil. In general, the addition of organic materials should be done with care to obtain the biological and chemical benefits, while not aggravating compaction problems.

Controlled traffic and permanent beds. One of the most promising practices for reducing soil compaction is the use of controlled traffic lanes in which all field operations are limited to the same lanes, thereby preventing compaction in all other areas. The primary benefit of controlled traffic is the lack of compaction for most of the field at the expense of limited areas that receive all the compaction. Because the degree of soil compaction doesn't necessarily worsen with each equipment pass (most of the compaction occurs with the heaviest loading and does not greatly increase beyond it), damage in the traffic lanes is not much more severe than that occurring on the whole field in a system with uncontrolled traffic. Controlled traffic lanes may actually have an advantage in that the consolidated soil is able to bear greater loads, thereby better facilitating field traffic. Compaction also can be reduced significantly by maximizing traffic of farm trucks along the field boundaries and using planned access roads, rather than allowing them to randomly travel over the field.

Controlled traffic systems require adjustment of field equipment to ensure that all wheels travel in the same lanes; they also require some discipline from equipment operators. For example, planter and combine widths need to be compatible (although not necessarily the same), and wheel spacing may need to be expanded (figure 15.10). A controlled traffic system is most easily adopted with row crops in zone, ridge, or no-till systems (not requiring full-field tillage; see chapter 16), because

Figure 15.10. A tractor with wide wheel spacing to fit a controlled traffic system.

crop rows and traffic lanes remain recognizable year after year. Ridge tillage, in fact, dictates controlled traffic, as wheels should not cross the ridges. Zone- and no-till do not necessarily require controlled traffic, but they greatly benefit from it, because the soil is not regularly loosened by aggressive tillage.

Adoption of controlled traffic has been rapidly expanded in recent years with the availability of RTK (real-time kinematic) satellite navigation systems.

With these advanced global positioning systems, a single reference station on the farm provides the real-time corrections to less than 1 inch level of accuracy, which facilitates precision steering of field equipment. Controlled traffic lanes can therefore be laid out with unprecedented accuracy, and water (for example, drip irrigation) and nutrients can be applied at precise distances from the crop (figure 15.11).

A permanent (raised) bed system is a variation on controlling traffic in which soil shaping is additionally applied to improve the physical conditions in the beds (figure 15.11, right). Beds do not receive traffic after they've been formed. This bed system is especially attractive where traffic on wet soil is difficult to avoid (for example, with certain fresh-market vegetable crops) and where it is useful to install equipment, such as irrigation lines, for multiple years.

SUMMARY

Compaction frequently goes unrecognized by farmers, but it can result in decreased yields. There are a number of ways to avoid the development of compacted soil, the most important of which is keeping equipment off wet soil (when it's in a plastic state). Draining wet soils,

Figure 15.11. Controlled traffic farming with precision satellite navigation. Left: Twelve-row corn-soybean strips with traffic lanes between the fourth and fifth row from the strip edge (Iowa; note that both current- and previous-year harvested crop rows are still visible). Right: Zucchini on mulched raised beds with drip irrigation (Queensland, Australia).

using controlled traffic lanes, and using permanent beds (that are never driven on) are ways to avoid compaction. Also, reduced tillage and larger organic matter additions make the surface less susceptible to the breakdown of aggregates and to crust formation—as does maintaining a surface mulch and routine use of cover crops. Reducing compaction once it occurs involves using cover crops that are able to break into subsurface compact layers and using equipment such as subsoilers and zone builders to break up compact subsoil.

SOURCES

Gugino, B.K., Idowu, O.J., Schindelbeck, R.R., van Es, H.M., Wolfe, D.W., Thies, J.E., et al. 2007. *Cornell Soil Health Assessment Training Manual* (Version 1.2). Geneva, NY: Cornell University.

Kok, H., R.K. Taylor, R.E. Lamond, and S. Kessen. 1996. *Soil Compaction: Problems and Solutions.* Cooperative Extension Service Publication AF 115. Manhattan: Kansas State University.

Moebius, B.N., H.M. van Es, J.O. Idowu, R.R. Schindelbeck, D.J. Clune, D.W. Wolfe, G.S. Abawi, J.E. Thies, B.K. Gugino, and R. Lucey. 2008. Long-term removal of maize residue for bioenergy: Will it affect soil quality? *Soil Science Society of America Journal* 72: 960–969.

Ontario Ministry of Agriculture, Food, and Rural Affairs. 1997. *Soil Management.* Best Management Practices Series. Available from the Ontario Federation of Agriculture, Toronto, Ontario, Canada.

Chapter 16

REDUCING TILLAGE

. . . the crying need is for a soil surface similar to that which we find in nature . . .
[and] the way to attain it is to use an implement that is incapable of burying the trash it encounters;
in other words, any implement except the plow.

—E.H. FAULKNER, 1943

Although tillage is an ancient practice, the question of which tillage system is most appropriate for any particular field or farm is still difficult to answer. Before we discuss different tillage systems, let's consider why people started tilling ground. Tillage was first practiced by farmers who grew small-grain crops, such as wheat, rye, and barley, primarily in western Asia (the Fertile Crescent), Europe, and northern Africa. Tillage was primarily practiced because it created a fine seedbed, thereby greatly improving germination. It also gave the crop a head-start before a new flush of weeds, and stimulated mineralization of organic nitrogen to forms that plants could use. The soil was presumably loosened by a simple ard (scratch plow) in several directions to create fine aggregates and a smooth seedbed. The loosened soil also tended to provide a more favorable rooting environment, facilitating seedling survival and plant growth. Animal traction was employed to accomplish this arduous task. At the end of the growing season, the

entire crop was harvested, because the straw also had considerable economic value for animal bedding, roofing thatch, brick making, and fuel. Sometimes, fields were burned after crop harvest to remove remaining crop residues and to control pests. Although this cropping system lasted for centuries, it resulted in excessive erosion, especially in the Mediterranean region, where it caused extensive soil degradation. Eventually deserts spread as the climate became drier.

Ancient agricultural systems in the Americas did not use intensive full-field tillage for grain production, as they did not have oxen or horses to perform the arduous tillage work. Instead, the early Americans used mostly direct seeding with planting sticks, or manual hoes that created small mounds (hilling). These practices were well adapted to the staple crops of corn and beans, which have large seeds and require lower plant densities than the cereal crops of the Old World. Several seeds were placed in each small hill, which was spaced several feet apart

173

JETHRO TULL AND TILLAGE: A MIXED LEGACY AND AN IMPORTANT LESSON

Jethro Tull (1674–1741) was an early English agricultural experimentalist whose book *The New Horse Hoeing Husbandry: An Essay on the Principles of Tillage and Vegetation* was published in 1731. It was the first textbook on the subject and set the standard for soil and crop management for the next century (it is now available online as part of core historical digital archives; see "Sources" at the end of the chapter). In a way, Tull's publication was a predecessor to this book, as it discussed manure, rotations, roots, weed control, legumes, tillage, ridges, and seeding.

Tull noticed that traditional broadcast sowing methods for cereal crops provided low germination rates and made weed control difficult. He designed a drill with a rotating grooved cylinder (now referred to as a coulter) that directed seeds to a furrow and subsequently covered them to provide good seed-soil contact. Such row seeding also allowed for mechanical cultivation of weeds, hence the title of the book. This was a historically significant invention, as seed drills and planters are now key components of conservation agriculture and building soils. But the concept of growing crops in rows is attributed to the Chinese, who used it as early as the 6th century B.C.E.

Tull believed that intensive tillage was needed not only for good seed-soil contact but also for plant nutrition, which he believed was provided by small soil particles. He grew wheat for thirteen consecutive years without adding manure; he basically accomplished this by mining the soil of nutrients that were released from repeated soil pulverization. He therefore promoted intensive tillage, which we now know has long-term negative consequences. Perhaps this was an important lesson for farmers and agronomists: Practices that may appear beneficial in the short term may turn out detrimental over long time periods.

from the next one. In temperate or wet regions the hills were elevated to provide a temperature and moisture advantage to the crop. In contrast with the cereal-based systems (wheat, rye, barley, rice) of growing only one crop in a monoculture, these fields often included the intercropping of two or three plant species growing at the same time, like the corn, bean, and squash of the Three Sisters system in North America. This hilling system was

TECHNOLOGIES THAT HAVE LESSENED THE NEED FOR TILLAGE...

- herbicides
- new zone and strip tillage tools that provide targeted decompaction
- new planters and transplanters
- new methods for cover crop management

generally less prone to erosion than whole-field tillage, but climate and soil conditions on steep slopes still frequently caused considerable soil degradation.

A third ancient tillage system was practiced as part of the rice-growing cultures in southern and eastern Asia. There, paddies are tilled to control weeds and puddle the soil to create a dense layer that limits downward losses of water through the soil. The puddling process occurs when the soil is worked while wet—in the plastic or liquid consistency state; see chapter 6—and is specifically aimed at destroying soil aggregates. This system was designed to benefit rice plants, which thrive under flooded conditions, especially relative to competing weeds. There is little soil erosion, because paddy rice must be grown either on flat or terraced lands, and runoff is controlled as part of the process of growing the crop. Recent research efforts have focused on less puddling and ponding to conserve soil health and water.

Figure 16.1. Rolled-rye cover crop being prepared for row-crop planting. Photo by Anu Rangarajan.

Full-field tillage systems became more widespread because they are better adapted to mechanized agriculture, and in time some of the traditional hill crops like corn became row crops. The moldboard plow was invented by the Chinese 2,500 years ago but was redesigned into a more effective tool in England in the 1700s. It provided weed control by fully turning under crop residues, growing weeds, and weed seeds. Its benefits were compelling at first; it allowed for a more stable food supply and also facilitated the breaking of new lands in the Americas. The development of increasingly powerful tractors made tillage an easier task (some say a recreational activity) and resulted in more intensive soil disturbance, ultimately contributing to the degradation of soils.

New technologies have lessened the need for tillage. The development of herbicides reduced the need for soil plowing as a weed control method. New planters achieve better seed placement, even without preparing a seedbed beforehand. Amendments, such as fertilizers and liquid manures, can be directly injected or band-applied. Now there are even vegetable transplanters that provide good soil-root contact in no-till systems. Although herbicides often are used to kill cover crops before planting the main crop, farmers and researchers have found

that they can obtain good cover crop control through well-timed mowing or rolling (figures 16.1, 16.7)—greatly reducing the amount of herbicide needed. If there is sufficient cover crop biomass, the mat acts as an effective barrier to weeds and provides nearly complete control.

Increased mechanization, intensive tillage, and erosion have degraded many agricultural soils to such an extent that people think tillage is required to provide temporary relief from compaction. As aggregates are destroyed, crusting and compaction create a soil "addicted" to tillage. Except perhaps for organic production systems, in which tillage is often needed because herbicides aren't used, a crop produced with limited or no tillage can generate better economic returns than one produced with conventional tillage systems. Managing soil in the right way to make reduced tillage systems successful, however, remains a challenge.

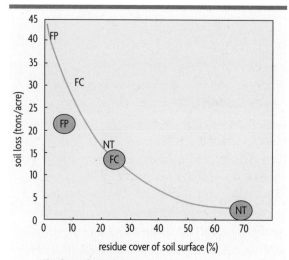

This figure shows that:
• surface residue reduces erosion,
• reduced tillage (chisel and no-till) leaves more residue and results in less erosion than plowing, and
• corn (circled) returns more residue than soybeans.

Figure 16.2. Soil erosion dramatically decreases with increasing surface cover. *Note:* FP = fall plow, FC = fall chisel, NT = no-till; circles = corn, no circles = soybeans. Modified from *Manuring* (1979).

Table 16.1
Tillage System Benefits and Limitations

Tillage System	Benefits	Limitations
Full-Field Tillage		
Moldboard plow	Allows easy incorporation of fertilizers and amendments. Buries surface weed seeds. Allows soil to dry out fast. Temporarily reduces compaction.	Leaves soil bare. Destroys natural aggregation and enhances organic matter loss. Commonly leads to surface crusting and accelerated erosion. Causes plow pans. Requires high energy use.
Chisel plow	Same as above, but leaves some surface residues.	Same as above, but less aggressively destroys soil structure; leads to less erosion, less crusting, no plow pans; requires less energy use.
Disk harrow	Same as above.	Same as above.
Restricted Tillage		
No-till	Leaves little soil disturbance. Requires few trips over field. Requires low energy use. Provides the most surface residue cover and erosion protection.	Makes it more difficult to incorporate fertilizers and amendments. Makes wet soils dry and warm up slowly in spring. Can't alleviate compaction.
Zone-till	Same as above.	Same as above, but compaction is alleviated.
Ridge-till	Allows easy incorporation of fertilizers and amendments. Provides some weed control as ridges are built. Allows seed zone on ridge to dry and warm more quickly.	Is hard to use with sod-type or narrow-row crop in rotation. Requires wheel spacing to be adjusted to travel between ridges.

TILLAGE SYSTEMS

Tillage systems are often classified by the amount of surface residue left on the soil surface. Conservation tillage systems leave more than 30% of the soil surface covered with crop residue. This amount of surface residue cover is considered to be at a level where erosion is significantly reduced (see figure 16.2). Of course, this residue cover partially depends on the amount and quality of residue left after harvest, which may vary greatly among crops and harvest method (corn harvested for grain or silage is one example). Although residue cover greatly influences erosion potential, it also is affected by factors such as surface roughness and soil loosening.

Another distinction of tillage systems is whether they are full-field systems or restricted systems. The benefits and limitations of various tillage systems are compared in table 16.1.

Conventional Tillage

A full-field system manages the soil uniformly across the entire field surface. Such conventional tillage systems typically involve a primary pass with a heavy tillage tool to loosen the soil and incorporate materials at the surface (fertilizers, amendments, weeds, etc.), followed by one or more secondary passes to create a suitable seedbed. Primary tillage tools are generally moldboard plows (see figure 16.3, left), chisels (figure 16.3, right), and heavy disks (figure 16.4, left), while secondary tillage is accomplished with finishing disks (figure 16.4, right), tine or tooth harrows, rollers, packers, drags, etc. These tillage systems create a uniform and often finely aggregated seedbed over the entire surface of the field. Such systems appear to perform well because they create near ideal conditions for seed germination and crop establishment.

But moldboard plowing is also energy intensive, leaves very little residue on the surface, and often requires multiple secondary tillage passes. It tends to create dense pans below the depth of plowing (typically 6 to 8 inches deep). However, moldboard plowing has traditionally been a reliable practice and almost always results in reasonable crop growth. Chisel implements generally provide results similar to those of the moldboard plow but require less energy and leave significantly more residue on the surface. Chisels also allow for more flexibility in the depth of tillage, generally from 5 to 12 inches, with some tools specifically designed to go deeper.

Disk plows come in a heavy version, as a primary tillage tool that usually goes 6 to 8 inches deep, or a lighter one that performs shallower tillage and leaves residue on the surface. Disks also create concerns with developing tillage pans at their bottoms. They are sometimes used as both primary and secondary tillage tools through repeated passes that increasingly pulverize the soil. This limits the upfront investment in tillage tools but is not sustainable in the long run.

Although full-field tillage systems have their disadvantages, they can help overcome certain problems, such as compaction and high weed pressures. Organic farmers often use moldboard plowing as a necessity to provide adequate weed control and facilitate nitrogen release from incorporated legumes. Livestock-based farms often use a plow to incorporate manure and to help make rotation transitions from sod crops to row crops.

Besides incorporating surface residue, full-field tillage systems with intensive secondary tillage crush the natural soil aggregates. The pulverized soil does not take heavy rainfall well. The lack of surface residue causes sealing at the surface, which generates runoff and erosion and creates hard crusts after drying. Intensively tilled soil will also settle after moderate to heavy rainfall and may "hardset" upon drying, thereby restricting root growth.

Full-field tillage systems can be improved by using tools, such as chisels (figure 16.3, right), that leave some residue on the surface. Reducing secondary tillage also

Figure 16.3. Left: Moldboard plowing inverts a sod and leaves no surface protection. Right: Chisel plow shanks till soil and leave some residue cover.

Figure 16.4. Left: A heavy disk (disk plow) can be used for primary and secondary tillage (photo by Mark Brooks). Right: A finishing disk.

helps decrease negative aspects of full-field tillage. Compacted soils tend to till up cloddy, and intensive harrowing and packing are then seen as necessary to create a good seedbed. This additional tillage creates a vicious cycle of further soil degradation and intensive tillage. Secondary tillage often can be reduced through the use of modern conservation planters, which create a finely aggregated zone around the seed without requiring the entire soil width to be pulverized. A good planter is perhaps the most important secondary tillage tool, because it helps overcome poor soil-seed contact without destroying surface aggregates over the entire field. A fringe benefit of reduced secondary tillage is that rougher soil often has much higher water infiltration rates and reduces problems with settling and hardsetting after rains. Weed seed germination is also generally reduced, but pre-emergence herbicides tend to be less effective than with smooth seedbeds. Reducing secondary tillage may, therefore, require greater emphasis on post-emergence weed control.

In more intensive horticultural systems, powered tillage tools, which are actively rotated by the tractor power takeoff system, are often used (figure 16.5). Rotary tillers (rotovators, rototillers) do intensive soil mixing that is damaging to soil in the long term. They should be considered only if the soil also regularly

Figure 16.5. Powered tillage tools used with horticultural crops: rotary tiller (left), and spader (right).

Figure 16.6. Left: A no-till seed drill requires no tillage or seedbed preparation for narrow-seeded crops or cover crops. Right: The cross-slot opener used in no-tillage planters. The disk slices soil, the inverted T blade allows seed and fertilizer placement on opposite ends of disk, and the packer wheels (right side) close and firm the seedbed.

receives organic materials like cover crop residue, compost, or manure. A spader is also an actively rotated tillage tool, but the small spades, similar to the garden tools, handle soil more gently and leave more residue or organic additions at the surface.

Restricted Tillage Systems

These systems are based on the idea that tillage can be limited to the area around the plant and does not have to disturb the entire field. Several tillage systems—no-till, zone- or strip-till, and ridge-till—fit this concept.

No-till system. The no-till system loosens the soil only in a very narrow and shallow area immediately around the seed zone. This localized disturbance is typically accomplished with a conservation planter (for row crops) or seed drill (for narrow-seeded crops; figure 16.6). This system represents the most extreme change from conventional tillage and is most effective in preventing soil erosion and building organic matter.

No-till systems have been used successfully on many soils in different climates. The surface residue protects against erosion (figure 14.3, p. 156) and increases biological activity by protecting the soil from temperature and heat extremes. Surface residues also reduce water evaporation, which—combined with deeper rooting—reduces the susceptibility to drought. This tillage system is especially well adapted to coarse-textured soils (sands and gravels) and well-drained soils, as these tend to be softer and less susceptible to compaction. No-till systems sometimes have initial lower yields than conventional

---

BEFORE CONVERTING TO NO-TILL

An Ohio farmer asked one of the authors of this book what could be done about a compacted, low-organic-matter, and low-fertility field that had been converted to no-till a few years before. Clearly, the soil's organic matter and nutrient levels should have been increased and the compaction alleviated before the change. Once you're committed to no-till, you've lost the opportunity to easily and rapidly change the soil's fertility or physical properties. The recommendation is the same as for someone establishing a perennial crop like an orchard or vineyard. Build up the soil and remedy compaction problems before converting to no-till. It's going to be much harder to do later on.

179

Table 16.2
The Effect of 32 Years of Plow and No Tillage under
Corn Production on Selected Soil Health Indicators

Soil Health Indicator	Plow-Tillage	No-Tillage
Physical		
Aggregate stability (%)	22	50
*Bulk density (g/cm3)	1.39	1.32
*Penetration resistance (psi)	140	156
Permeability (mm/hr)	2.1	2.4
Plant-available water capacity (%)	29.1	35.7
Infiltration capacity (mm/hr)	1.58	1.63
Chemical		
Early-season nitrate-N (lbs/ac)	13	20
Phosphorus (lbs/ac)	20	21
Potassium (lbs/ac)	88	95
Magnesium (lbs/ac)	310	414
Calcium (lbs/ac)	7,172	7,152
*pH	8.0	7.8
Biological		
Organic matter (%)	4.0	5.4
Cellulose decomposition rate (%/week)	3.0	8.9
Potentially mineralizable nitrogen (μg/g/week)	1.5	1.7
Easily extractable glomalin (mg/g soil)	1.2	1.7
Total glomalin (mg/g soil)	4.3	6.6

Note: Higher values indicate better health, except for those listed with an asterisk, for which lower values are better.
Source: Moebius et al. (2008).

Organic No Till?

Researchers at the Rodale Institute in Pennsylvania have developed innovative cover crop management equipment that facilitates growing row crops in a no-till system. An annual or winter annual cover crop is rolled down with a specially designed, front-mounted, heavy roller-crimper, resulting in a weed-suppressing mat through which it is possible to plant or drill seeds (figure 16.7) or set transplants. For this system to work best sufficient time must be allowed for the cover crop to grow large before rolling-crimping, so that the mulch can do a good job of suppressing weeds. Cover crops must have gone through the early stages of reproduction in order for the roller-crimper to kill them, but not be fully matured to avoid viable seeds that could become weeds in the following crop. Since timing of any farm operation is critical, careful attention to the details of these biologically based systems is needed for them to be successful.

Figure 16.7. Roller-crimper creates a weed-suppressing cover-crop mat through which it is possible to plant seeds or transplants. Here cotton is being planted behind rye that has been traveled over by the roller-crimper. Photo by Jeff Mitchell.

tillage systems. One of the reasons for this is the lower availability of N in the early years of no-till. Knowing this allows you to compensate by adding increased N (legumes, manures, fertilizers) during the transition years. It takes a few years for no-tilled soils to improve, after which they typically out-yield conventionally tilled soils. The transition can be challenging because a radical move from conventional to no tillage can create failures if the soil was previously degraded and compacted. It is best to first build degraded soils with organic matter

management and use intermediate tillage methods, as described in the next sections.

With the absence of tillage, seed placement, compaction prevention, and weed control become more critical. No-till planters and drills (figure 16.6) are advanced pieces of engineering that need to be rugged and adaptable to different soil conditions yet be able to place a seed precisely at a specified depth. The technology has come a long way since Jethro Tull's early seeders, especially in the past decades when no-till seeders have been

Figure 16.8. Left: A zone-tillage tool with hilling disks and rolling basket to create a zone of loosened soil. Right: Strip tillage also results in a narrow tilled zone that leaves most of the soil surface undisturbed. Photos by Robert Schindelbeck.

continually improved.

The quality of no-tilled soil improves over time, as seen in table 16.2, which compares physical, chemical, and biological soil health indicators after thirty-two years of plow and no tillage in a New York experiment. The beneficial effects of no tillage are quite consistent for physical indicators, especially with aggregate stability. Biological indicators are similarly more favorable for no tillage, and organic matter content is 35% higher than with plow tillage. The effects are less apparent for chemical properties, except the pH is slightly more favorable for no-till, and the early-season nitrate concentration is 50% higher. Other experiments have also demonstrated that long-term reduced tillage increases nitrogen availability from organic matter, which may result in significant fertilizer savings.

Zone, strip, and ridge tillage. Zone-, strip-, and ridge-tillage systems are adapted to wide-row crops with 30-inch spacing or more. Their approach is to disturb the soil in a narrow strip along the plant row and leave most of the soil surface undisturbed. Zone tillage involves the use of a zone builder (figure 16.8, left), which creates a loosened band that extends into the subsoil (12 to 16 inches). This "vertical tillage" approach promotes deeper root growth and water movement. This is followed by a row crop planter with multiple fluted coulters mounted on the front (figure 16.9). The planter creates a fine seedbed approximately 6 inches wide by 4 inches deep and uses trash wheels to move residue away from the row. Zone tillage provides soil quality improvements similar to those of no tillage, but it is more energy intensive. It is generally preferred over strict no-tillage systems on soils that have compaction problems (for example, fields that receive liquid manure or where crops are harvested when the soil is susceptible to compaction) and in humid and cold climates, where removal of residue from the row is desirable for soil drying and warm-up.

Figure 16.9. Zone-till planter: (a) coulters (cut up residues and break up soil in seed zone); (b) fertilizer disk openers (place granular starter fertilizer in a band next to the seed); (c) spider (trash) wheels (move residue away from the row); (d) seed placement unit; (e) press wheels (create firm seedbed); and (f) wheel used for transporting the planter.

Figure 16.10. Ridge tillage involves row planting on ridges (left), which are rebuilt with a weed cultivation/ridging operation during the growing season (right).

Strip tillage (figure 16.8, right) uses a similar approach, but the tillage shanks are shallower (typically to 8 inches), thereby reducing energy consumption. In temperate climates, zone building and strip tillage are often performed in the fall before spring row crop planting to allow for soil settling. Some farmers inject fertilizers with the tillage operations, thereby reducing the number of passes on the field.

The zone planter (figure 16.9) can also be used as a single-pass system when deeper disturbance is not needed.

Ridge tillage (figure 16.10) combines limited tillage with a ridging operation and requires controlled traffic. This system is particularly attractive for cold and wet soils, because the ridges offer seedlings a warmer and better-drained environment. The ridging operation can be combined with mechanical weed control and allows for band application of herbicides. Ridge tillage often decreases the cost of chemical weed control, allowing for about a two-thirds reduction in herbicide use. In vegetable systems, raised beds—basically wide ridges that also provide better drainage and warmer temperatures—are often used.

WHICH TILLAGE SYSTEM FOR YOUR FARM?

The correct choice of tillage system depends on climate, soils, cropping systems, and the farm's production objectives. Some general guidelines are provided in the following paragraphs.

Conventional grain and vegetable farms have great flexibility for adopting reduced tillage systems, because they are less constrained by repeated manure applications (needed on livestock farms) or mechanical weed or rotation crop management (needed on organic farms). In the long run, limited disturbance and residue cover improve soil health, reduce erosion, and boost yields. A negative aspect of these systems is the transition period, as discussed above, and changes in weed spectrum from annual to perennial plants. This may require different timing and methods of weed control. Combining reduced tillage with the use of cover crops frequently helps reduce weed problems. Weed pressures typically decrease significantly after a few years, especially if perennials are under control. Mulched cover crops, as well as newly designed mechanical cultivators, help provide effective weed control in high-residue systems. Some innovative farmers use no-till combined with a

FROST TILLAGE!

Readers from temperate regions may have heard of frost seeding legumes into a pasture, hayfield, or winter wheat crop in very early spring, but perhaps not of tilling a frozen soil. It seems a strange concept, but some farmers are using frost tillage as a way to be timely and reduce unintended tillage damage. It can be done after frost has first entered the soil, but before it has penetrated more than 4 inches. Water moves upward to the freezing front and the soil underneath dries. This frozen state makes the soil tillable as long as the frost layer is not too thick. Compaction is reduced because equipment is supported by the frozen layer. The resulting rough surface is favorable for water infiltration and runoff prevention. Some livestock farmers like frost tillage as a way to incorporate or inject manure in the winter without concerns for compaction from heavy equipment.

heavy cover crop, which is mowed or rolled to create a thick cover mulch (figure 16.7).

Farmers need to be aware of potential soil compaction problems with reduced tillage. If a strict no-till system is adopted on a compacted soil, especially on medium- or fine-textured soils, serious yield reductions may occur. As discussed in chapter 6, dense soils have a relatively narrow water range in which plant roots can grow well, compared to their ability to grow in uncompacted soil. When a compact soil is completely dry, roots have a difficult time making their way through the soil, and when a compact soil is wet, roots tend to have less air. Crops growing on compacted soils are more susceptible to inadequate aeration during wet periods and to restricted root growth and drought stress during drier periods. Compaction, therefore, reduces plant growth and makes crops more susceptible to pest pressures.

In poorly structured soils, tools like zone builders, strip tillers, and zone-till planters provide compaction relief in the row while maintaining an undisturbed soil surface. Over time, soil structure improves, unless recompaction occurs from other field operations. Crops grown on fields that do not drain in a timely manner tend to benefit greatly from ridging or bedding, because the sensitive seedling root zone remains aerobic during wet periods. These systems also use controlled traffic lanes, which greatly reduce compaction problems,

although matching wheel spacing and tire widths for planting and harvesting equipment is sometimes a challenging task, as we discussed in chapter 15.

For organic farms, as with traditional farms before agrichemicals were available, reduced tillage is challenging, and full-field tillage may be necessary for mechanical weed control and incorporation of manures and composts. After all, the two greatest challenges of organic crop production are weeds and nitrogen. Organic farming on lands prone to erosion may, therefore, involve trade-offs. Erosion can be reduced by using rotations with perennial crops, gentler tillage methods like spaders and ridgers, and modern planters that establish good crop stands without excessive secondary tillage. Soil structure may be easier to maintain on organic farms, because they use organic inputs heavily.

Livestock-based farms face special challenges related to applying manure or compost to the soil. Some type of incorporation usually is needed to avoid large losses of nitrogen by volatilization, and losses of phosphorus and pathogens in runoff. Transitions from sod to row crops are also usually easier with some tillage. Such farms can still use manure injection tools with zone and strip tillage, thereby providing compaction relief while minimizing soil disturbance. As with organic farms, livestock operations apply a lot of manure and compost and naturally have higher soil health.

Rotating Tillage Systems

A tillage program does not need to be rigid. Fields that are zone-, strip-, or no-tilled may occasionally need a full-field tillage pass to provide compaction relief or to incorporate amendments like lime. But this should be done on a very limited basis. Although a flexible tillage program offers a number of benefits, aggressive tillage with a moldboard plow and harrows can readily destroy the favorable soil structure built up by years of no-till management.

Timing of Field Operations

The success of a tillage system depends on many factors. For example, reduced tillage systems, especially in the early transition years, may require more attention to nitrogen management (often higher rates are needed initially, lower rates eventually), as well as weed, insect, and disease control. Also, the performance of tillage systems may be affected by the timing of field operations. If tillage or planting is done when the soil is too wet (when its water content is above the plastic limit), cloddiness and poor seed placement may result in poor stands. Also, a zone building operation done in plastic soil results in smeared surfaces and an open slot that does not allow for good seed-soil contact. A "ball test" (chapter 6) helps ensure that field conditions are right and is especially important when performing deeper tillage. Tillage is also not recommended when the soil is too dry, because it may be too hard, clods may be very large, and excess dust may be created, especially on compacted soils. Ideal tillage conditions generally occur when soils are at field-capacity water content (after a few days of free drainage and evaporation), except for fine-textured clays, which need more drying (see chapter 15).

Because soil compaction may affect the success of reduced tillage, a whole-system approach to soil management is needed. For example, no-till systems that involve harvesting operations with heavy equipment will succeed only if traffic can be restricted to dry conditions or fixed lanes within the field. Even zone-tillage methods will work better if fixed lanes are used for heavy harvest equipment.

SUMMARY

Reducing the intensity of tillage can help improve the soil in many ways. Maintaining more residue on the surface reduces runoff and erosion, while the reduction in soil disturbance allows for earthworm holes and old root channels to rapidly conduct water from intense rainstorms into the soil. There are many choices of reduced tillage systems, and equipment is available to help farmers succeed. Using cover crops along with reduced tillage has been found to be a winning combination, providing surface cover rapidly and helping to control weeds.

SOURCES

Cornell Recommendations for Integrated Field Crop Production. 2000. Ithaca, NY: Cornell Cooperative Extension.

Manuring. 1979. Cooperative Extension Service Publication AY-222. West Lafayette, IN: Purdue University.

Moebius, B.N., H.M. van Es, J.O. Idowu, R.R. Schindelbeck, D.J. Clune, D.W. Wolfe, G.S. Abawi, J.E. Thies, B.K. Gugino, and R. Lucey. 2008. Long-term removal of maize residue for bioenergy: Will it affect soil quality? *Soil Science Society of America Journal* 72: 960–969.

Ontario Ministry of Agriculture, Food, and Rural Affairs. 1997. *No-till: Making it Work.* Available from the Ontario Federation of Agriculture, Toronto, Ontario, Canada.

Rodale Institute. *No-Till Revolution.* http://rodaleinstitute.org/no-till_revolution.

Tull, J. 1733. *The Horse-Hoeing Husbandry: Or an Essay on the Principles of Tillage and Vegetation.* Printed by A. Rhames, for R. Gunne, G. Risk, G. Ewing, W. Smith, & Smith and Bruce, Booksellers. Available online through Core Historical Literature of Agriculture, Albert R. Mann Library, Cornell University. http://chla.library.cornell.edu.

van Es, H.M., A.T. DeGaetano, and D.S. Wilks. 1998. Upscaling plot-based research information: Frost tillage. *Nutrient Cycling in Agroecosystems* 50: 85–90.

STEVE GROFF
LANCASTER COUNTY, PENNSYLVANIA

Steve Groff raises vegetables, grains, and cover crop seeds on his 215-acre farm in Lancaster County, Pennsylvania, but his soil shows none of the degradation that can occur with intensive cropping. Mixing cash crops such as corn, alfalfa, soybeans, and tomatoes with cover crops in a unique no-till system, Groff has kept portions of his farm untouched by a plow for more than two decades.

"No-till is a practical answer to concerns about erosion, soil quality, and soil health," says Groff, who won a national no-till award in 1999. "I want to leave the soil in better condition than I found it."

Groff confronted a rolling landscape pocked by gullies when he began farming with his father after graduating from high school. They regularly used herbicides and insecticides, tilled annually or semiannually, and rarely used cover crops. Like other farmers in Lancaster County, they ignored the effects of tillage on a sloped landscape, which causes an average of 9 tons of soil per acre to wash into the Chesapeake Bay every year.

Tired of watching 2-foot-deep crevices form on the hillsides after every heavy rain, Groff began experimenting with no-till to protect and improve the soil. "We used to have to fill in ditches to get machinery in to harvest," Groff says. "I didn't think that was right."

Groff stresses, however, that switching to no-till alone isn't enough. He has created a new system, reliant on cover crops, rotations, *and* no-till, to improve the soil. He's convinced such methods contribute to better yields of healthy crops, especially during weather extremes.

He pioneered what he likes to call the "Permanent Cover" cropping system when the Pennsylvania chapter of the Soil and Water Conservation Society bought a no-till transplanter that could plant vegetable seedlings into slots cut into cover crop residue. Groff was one of the first farmers to try it. The slots are just big enough for the young plants and do not disturb the soil on either side. The result: Groff can prolong the erosion-slowing benefits of cover crops. He now owns two no-till

Groff stresses, however, that switching to no-till alone isn't enough. He has created a new system, reliant on cover crops, rotations, and no-till, to improve the soil. He's convinced such methods contribute to better yields of healthy crops, especially during weather extremes.

planters—one for planting tomatoes, the other for corn and pumpkins—customized with parts and implements from several different equipment companies.

Groff's no-till system relies on a selection of cover crops and residues that blanket the soil virtually all year. "The amount of acreage I devote to different cover crops every year is really subjective," he says, noting that he constantly modifies his cropping plans based on field observations, weather conditions, timing considerations, and other factors. In the fall, he uses a no-till seeder to drill a combination of rye and hairy vetch (at seeding rates of 30 and 25 pounds per acre, respectively). He likes the pairing because their root structures grow in different patterns, and the vegetation left behind after killing leaves different residues on the soil surface.

Introduced to forage radish through University of Maryland cover crop research trials hosted at his farm, Groff was so impressed by what he saw that he decided to integrate it into his cover crop combinations. His typical rotations include planting forage radish and oats or forage radish and crimson clover mixtures before sweet corn, and a forage radish–rye–vetch mixture before pumpkins.

Several attributes make forage radish a practical choice for no-till farmers. For example, its taproots can alleviate compaction problems—so much so that Groff now prefers using radishes instead of his deep ripper to loosen soil in his driveways. Complete dieback following hard frost, impressive weed suppression into spring, and relatively rapid nutrient cycling add to forage radish's appeal.

Upon discovering a few years ago that forage radish cover crop seed was not available locally, Groff decided to grow his own and sell the surplus to other farmers. He has increased his seed production every year in response to the "substantial growing interest" of conventional farmers in cover cropping. He now fills seed orders from farmers across the U.S.

In the spring, Groff uses a rolling stalk-chopper—modified from Midwest machines that chop cornstalks after harvest—to kill overwintering covers. He typically sprays glyphosate at low levels (1/2 pint, or $1 per acre) before rolling to ensure a more complete kill. The chopper flattens and crimps the cover crop, providing a thick mulch. Once it's flat, he makes a pass with the no-till planter or transplanter.

The system creates a very real side benefit in reduced insect pest pressure. Once an annual problem, Colorado potato beetle damage has all but disappeared from Groff's tomatoes. Since he began planting into the mulch, he has greatly reduced the spraying of pesticides. The thick mat also prevents splashing of soil during rain, a primary cause of early blight on tomatoes. "We have slashed our pesticide and fertilizer bill nearly in half, compared to a conventional tillage system," Groff says. "At the same time, we're building valuable topsoil and not sacrificing yields."

"No-till is not a miracle, but it works for me," he says. "It's good for my bottom line, I'm saving soil, and I'm reducing pesticides and increasing profits." He emphasizes that benefits from no-till management have developed gradually, along with his experience in handling each field. Knowing when to stay off wet fields and choosing the right crop and cover crop rotations, he says, can help farmers new to no-till avoid potential compaction and fertility problems. "My soils have developed a stability that lets me get away with things that I couldn't do earlier," he says. "You earn the right to be out there as your soil gets more stable. Basically, the rules of the game change as the game is played."

Groff is convinced his crops are better than those produced in soils managed conventionally, especially during weather extremes. His soils foster high levels of earthworm and other biological activity deep in the soil. He promotes his system at annual summer field days that draw huge crowds of farmers and through his informative website, www.cedarmeadowfarm.com.

—UPDATED BY AMY KREMEN

Chapter 17

MANAGING WATER: IRRIGATION AND DRAINAGE

Worldwide, over two billion acres of virgin land have been plowed and brought into agricultural use since 1860. Until the last decades of the twentieth century, clearing new land compensated for loss of agricultural land. In the 1980s the total amount of land under cultivation began declining for the first time since farming reached the land between the Tigris and the Euphrates.

—DAVID MONTGOMERY, 2007

Deficits and excesses of water are the most significant yield-limiting factors to crop production worldwide. It is estimated that more than half of the global food supply depends on some type of water management. In fact, the first major civilizations and population centers emerged when farmers started to control water, resulting in more consistent yields and stable food supplies. Examples include Mesopotamia—literally the "land between the rivers" (the Tigris and Euphrates), the lower Nile Valley, and China. High yields in drained and irrigated areas allowed for the development of trade specialization, because no longer did everyone need to provide their own food supply. This led to important innovations like markets, writing, and the wheel. Moreover, new water management schemes forced societies to get organized, work together on irrigation and drainage schemes, and develop laws on water allocations. But water management

failures were also responsible for the collapse of societies. Notably, the salinization of irrigated lands in Mesopotamia and filling up of ditches with sediments—cleaned out by enslaved Israelites among others—resulted in lost land fertility and an inability to sustain large centrally governed civilizations.

Today, many of the most productive agricultural areas depend on some type of water management. In the United States, average crop yields of irrigated farms are greater than the corresponding yields of dryland farms by 118% for wheat and 30% for corn. At a global scale, irrigation is used on 18% of the cultivated areas, but those lands account for 40% of the world's food production. The great majority of agricultural lands in the western U.S. and other dry climates around the world would not be productive without irrigation water, and the majority of the U.S. horticultural crop

Photo by Judy Brossy

Table 17.1
Approximate Amounts of Water Needed for Food Production

Product	Gallons of Water per Pound
Wheat	150
Rice	300
Corn	50
Potatoes	19
Soybeans	275
Beef	1,800
Pork	700
Poultry	300
Eggs	550
Milk	100
Cheese	600

Source: FAO.

acreage—especially in California—is entirely dependent on elaborate irrigation infrastructures. Even in humid regions most high-value crops are grown with irrigation during dry spells to insure crop quality and steady supplies for market outlets, in part because the soils have become less drought resistant from intensive use.

To address excess water problems, the best fields in the U.S. corn belt have had drainage systems installed, which made those soils even more productive than they were naturally. Drainage of wet fields allows for a longer growing season because farmers can get onto those

fields earlier in the spring and harvest later in the fall without causing extreme compaction.

The benefits of irrigation and drainage are thus obvious. They are critical to food security as well as to the agricultural intensification needed to protect natural areas. Concerns with climate change, which is resulting in greater occurrences of deficits and excesses of precipitation, will increase pressure for more irrigation and drainage. But they also exact a price on the environment. Drainage systems provide hydrological shortcuts and are responsible for increased chemical losses to water resources. Some irrigation systems have resulted in drastic changes in river and estuarine ecosystems, as well as land degradation through salinization and sodium buildup, and have been sources of international conflict. In the case of the Aral Sea—formerly the fourth largest inland freshwater body in the world—the diversion of rivers to use for irrigated cotton farming in the former USSR resulted in a 50% decrease in the area of the sea. It also became severely contaminated with drainage water from agricultural fields.

IRRIGATION

There are several different types of irrigation systems, depending on water source, size of the system, and water application method. Three main water sources exist: surface water, groundwater, and recycled

---

FIRST CONSIDER SOIL IMPROVEMENT

Healthy soils with good and stable aggregation, enhanced organic matter levels, and limited or no compaction go a long way toward "drought proofing" your farm. In addition, reduced tillage with residues on the surface also helps to enhance water infiltration and reduce evaporation losses from the soil. Cover crops, while using water for their growth, can act as a water-conserving surface mulch once they are suppressed. But, of course, water is needed to grow crops—from 19 gallons to hundreds or more gallons of water for each pound of plant or animal product (table 17.1). And if it doesn't rain for a few weeks, crops on even the best soils will start to show drought stress. Even in humid regions there can be stretches of dry weather that cause stress and reduce crop yield or quality. Irrigation, therefore, is an essential part of growing crops in many regions of the world. But the healthier the soil you have, the less irrigation water that will be needed because natural rainfall will be used more efficiently.

Figure 17.1. A farm pond (left) is used as a water source for a traveling overhead sprinkler system (right) on a vegetable farm.

wastewater. Irrigation systems run from small on-farm arrangements—using a local water supply—to vast regional schemes that involve thousands of farms and are controlled by governmental authorities. Water application methods include conventional flood, or furrow, irrigation—which depends on gravity flow—and pumped water for sprinkler and drip irrigation systems.

Surface Water Sources

Streams, rivers, and lakes have traditionally been the main source of irrigation supplies. Historical efforts involved the diversion of river waters and then the development of storage ponds. Small-scale systems—like those used by the Anazasi in the southwestern U.S. and the Nabateans in what is now Jordan—involved cisterns that were filled by small stream diversions.

Small-scale irrigation systems nowadays tend to pump water directly out of streams or farm ponds (figure 17.1). These water sources are generally sufficient for cases in which supplemental irrigation is used—in humid regions where rainfall and snowmelt supply most of the crop water needs but limited amounts of additional water may be needed for good yields or high-quality crops. Such systems, generally managed by a single farm, have limited environmental impacts. Most states require permits for such water diversions to ensure against excessive impacts on local water resources.

Large-scale irrigation schemes have been developed around the world with strong involvement of state and federal governments. The U.S. government invested $3 billion to create the intricate Central Valley project in California that has provided a hundredfold

Figure 17.2. The Ataturk Dam, part of the GAP project in Turkey, diverts water from the Euphrates River (left). The main canal (middle) conveys water to the Harran Plain for distribution to individual fields (right).

Figure 17.3. Left: Satellite image of southwest Kansas, showing crop circles from center-pivot irrigation systems. Photo by NASA. Right: Groundwater-fed center-pivot system on a pasture.

return on investment. The Imperial Irrigation District, located in the dry desert of Southern California, was developed in the 1940s with the diversion of water from the Colorado River. Even today, large-scale irrigation systems, like the GAP project in southeastern Turkey (figure 17.2), are being initiated. Such projects often drive major economic development efforts in the region and function as a major source for national or international food or fiber production. On the other hand, large dams also frequently have detrimental effects of displacing people and flooding productive cropland or important wetlands.

Groundwater

When good aquifers are present, groundwater is a relatively inexpensive source of irrigation water. A significant advantage is that it can be pumped locally and does not require large government-sponsored investments in dams and canals. It also has less impact on regional hydrology and ecosystems, although pumping water from deep aquifers requires energy. Center-pivot overhead sprinklers (figure 17.3, right) are often used, and individual systems, irrigating from 120 to 500 acres, typically draw from their own well. A good source of groundwater is critical for the success of such systems, and low salt levels are especially critical to prevent the buildup of soil salinity. Most of the western U.S. Great Plains—much of it part of the former Dust Bowl

area—uses center-pivot irrigation systems supported by the large (174,000-square-mile) Ogallala aquifer, which is a relatively shallow and accessible water source (figure 17.3, left). It is, however, being used faster than it is recharging from rainfall—clearly an unsustainable practice. Deeper wells that require more energy—plus, more expensive energy—to pump water will make this mining of water an increasingly questionable practice.

Recycled Wastewater

In recent years, water scarcity has forced governments and farmers to look for alternative sources of irrigation water. Since agricultural water does not require the

Figure 17.4. Recycled wastewater from the City of Adelaide, Australia, is pumped into an irrigation pond for a vegetable farm. Wastewater-conveying pipes are painted purple to distinguish them from freshwater conduits.

same quality as drinking water, recycled wastewater is a good alternative. It is being used in regions where (1) densely populated areas generate significant quantities of wastewater and are close to irrigation districts, and (2) surface or groundwater sources are very limited or need to be transported over long distances. Several irrigation districts in the U.S. are working with municipalities to provide safe recycled wastewater, although some concerns still exist about long-term effects. Other nations with advanced agriculture and critical water shortages—notably Israel and Australia—have also implemented wastewater recycling systems for irrigation purposes (figure 17.4).

Irrigation Methods

Flood, or furrow, irrigation is the historical approach and remains widely used around the world. It basically involves the simple flooding of a field for a limited amount of time, allowing the water to infiltrate. If the field has been shaped into ridges and furrows, the water is applied through the furrows and infiltrates down and laterally into the ridges (figure 17.5). Such systems mainly use gravity flow and require nearly flat fields. These systems are by far the cheapest to install and use, but their water application rates are very

> ### MAIN TYPES OF IRRIGATION
> - Flood, or furrow, irrigation
> - Sprinkler irrigation
> - Drip, or trickle, irrigation
> - Manual irrigation

inexact and typically uneven. Also, these systems are most associated with salinization concerns, as they can easily raise groundwater tables. Flood irrigation is also used in rice production systems in which dikes are used to keep the water ponded.

Sprinkler irrigation systems apply water through pressurized sprinkler heads and require conduits (pipes) and pumps. Common systems include stationary sprinklers on risers (figure 17.6) and traveling overhead sprinklers (center-pivot and lateral; figures 17.3 and 17.1). These systems allow for more precise water application rates than flooding systems and more efficient water use. But they require larger up-front investments, and the pumps use energy. Large, traveling gun sprayers can efficiently apply water to large areas and are also used to apply liquid manure.

Localized irrigation—especially useful for tree crops—can often be accomplished using small sprinklers

Figure 17.5. Furrow irrigation is generally inexpensive but also inefficient with respect to water use. Photo by USDA-ERS.

Figure 17.6. Portable sprinkler irrigation system commonly used with horticultural crops.

Figure 17.7. Small (micro) sprinklers allow for localized water application at low cost. Photo by Thomas Scherer.

(figure 17.7) that are connected using small-diameter "spaghetti tubing" and relatively small pumps, making the system comparatively inexpensive.

Drip, or trickle, irrigation systems also use flexible or spaghetti tubing combined with small emitters. They are mostly used in bedded or tree crops using a line source with many regularly spaced emitters or applied directly near the plant through a point-source emitter (figure 17.8). The main advantage of drip irrigation is the parsimonious use of water and the high level of control.

Drip irrigation systems are relatively inexpensive, can be installed easily, use low pressure, and have low energy consumption. In small-scale systems like market gardens, pressure may be applied through a gravity hydraulic head from a water container on the small platform. Subsurface drip irrigation systems, in which the lines and emitters are semipermanently buried to allow field operations, are now also coming into use. Such systems require attention to the placement of the tubing and emitters; they need to be close to the plant roots, as lateral water flow from the trickle line through the soil is limited.

Manual irrigation involves watering cans, buckets, garden hoses, inverted soda bottles, etc. Although it doesn't fit with large-scale agriculture, it is still widely used in gardens and small-scale agriculture in underdeveloped countries.

Fertigation is an efficient method to apply fertilizer to plants through pumped systems like sprinkler and drip irrigation. The fertilizer source is mixed with the irrigation water to provide low doses of liquid fertilizer that are readily absorbed by the crop. This also allows for "spoon feeding" of fertilizer to the crop through multiple small applications, which would otherwise be a logistical challenge.

Figure 17.8. Drip irrigation of bean plants. Lateral movement of water to reach plant roots may be limited with drip systems (left), unless each crop row has its own drip line or the spacing between rows is decreased by using narrow twin rows (right). Note: The apparent leaf discoloration is due to a low sun angle.

Figure 17.9. Over-irrigation can raise groundwater tables (visible at bottom of pit, left). Surface evaporation of water traveling upward through soil capillaries (very small channels) from the shallow groundwater causes salt accumulation (right).

Environmental Concerns and Management Practices

Irrigation has numerous advantages, but significant concerns exist as well. The main threat to soil health in dry regions is the accumulation of salts—and in some cases also sodium. As salt accumulation increases in the soil, crops have more difficulty getting the water that's there. When sodium accumulates, aggregates break down and soils become dense and impossible to work (chapter 6). Over the centuries, many irrigated areas have been abandoned due to salt accumulation, and it is still a major threat in several areas in the U.S. and elsewhere (figure 17.9). Salinization is the result of the evaporation of irrigation water, which leaves salts behind. It is especially prevalent with flood irrigation systems, which tend to over-apply water and can raise saline groundwater tables. Once the water table gets close to the surface, capillary water movement transports soil water to the surface, where it evaporates and leaves salts behind. When improperly managed, this can render soils unproductive within a matter of years. Salt accumulation can also occur with other irrigation practices—even with drip systems, especially when the climate is so dry that leaching of salts does not occur through natural precipitation.

The removal of salts is difficult, especially when lower soil horizons are also saline. Irrigation systems in arid regions should be designed to *supply* water and also to *remove* water—implying that irrigation should be combined with drainage. This may seem paradoxical, but salts need to be removed by application of additional water to dissolve the salts, leach them out of the soil, and subsequently remove the leachate through drains or ditches, where the drain water may still create concerns for downstream areas due to its high salt content. One of the long-term success stories of irrigated agriculture— the lower Nile Valley—provided irrigation during the river's flood stage in the fall and natural drainage after it subsided to lower levels in the winter and spring. In

CONCERNS WITH IRRIGATION

- accumulation of salts and/or sodium in the soil
- energy use
- increased potential for nutrient and pesticide loss
- water use diverted from natural systems
- displacement of people by large dams and possible flooding of productive cropland, wetlands, or archaeological sites
- competing users: urban areas and downstream communities

some cases, deep-rooted trees are used to lower regional water tables, which is the approach used in the highly salinized plains of the Murray Darling Basin in south-eastern Australia. Several large-scale irrigation projects around the world were designed only for the water supply component, and funds were not allocated for drainage systems, ultimately causing salinization.

The removal of sodium can be accomplished by exchange with calcium on the soil exchange complex, which is typically done through the application of gypsum. In general, salinity and sodicity are best prevented through good water management. (See chapter 20 for discussion of reclaiming saline and sodic soils.)

Salt accumulation is generally not an issue in humid regions, but over-irrigation raises concerns about nutrient and pesticide leaching losses in these areas. High

application rates and amounts can push nitrates and pesticides past the root zone and increase groundwater contamination. Soil saturation from high application rates can also generate denitrification losses.

A bigger issue with irrigation, especially at regional and global scales, is the high water consumption levels and competing interests. Agriculture consumes approximately 70% of the global water withdrawals. Humans use less than a gallon of water per day for direct consumption, but about 150 gallons are needed to produce a pound of wheat and 1,800 gallons are needed for a pound of beef (table 17.1, p. 188). According to the U.S. Geological Survey, 68% of high-quality groundwater withdrawals in the U.S. are used for irrigation. Is this sustainable? The famous Ogallala aquifer mostly holds "ancient" water that accumulated during previous wetter climates. As mentioned above, withdrawals are currently larger than the recharge rates, and this limited resource is therefore slowly being mined.

Several large irrigation systems affect international relations. The high withdrawal rates from the Colorado River diminish it to a trickle by the time it reaches the U.S.-Mexico border and the estuary in the Gulf of California. Similarly, Turkey's decision to promote agricultural development through the diversion of Euphrates waters has created tensions with the downstream countries, Syria and Iraq.

Irrigation Management at the Farm Level

Sustainable irrigation management and prevention of salt and sodium accumulation require solid planning, appropriate equipment, and monitoring. A first step is to build the soil so it optimizes water use by the crop. As we discussed in chapters 5 and 6, soils that are low in organic matter and high in sodium have low infiltration capacities due to surface sealing and crusting from low aggregate stability. Overhead irrigation systems often apply water as "hard rain," creating further problems with surface sealing and crusting.

GOOD IRRIGATION MANAGEMENT

- Build soil to be more resistant to crusting and drought by increasing organic matter contents, aggregation, and rooting volume.
- Use water conservatively: Consider deficit irrigation scheduling.
- Monitor soil, plant, and weather for precise estimation of irrigation needs.
- Use precise water application rates; do not over-irrigate.
- Use water storage systems to accumulate rainfall when feasible.
- Use good-quality recycled wastewater when available.
- Reduce tillage and leave surface residues.
- Use mulches to reduce surface evaporation.
- Integrate water and fertilizer management to reduce losses.
- Prevent salt or sodium accumulation: Leach salt through drainage, and reduce sodium contents through gypsum application.

Healthy soils have more water supply capacity than soils that are compacted and depleted of organic matter. It is estimated that for every 1% loss in organic matter content in the surface foot, soil can hold 16,500 gallons less of plant-available water per acre. Additionally, surface compaction creates lower root health and density, and hard subsoils limit rooting volume. These processes are captured by the concept of the *optimum water range*—which we discussed in chapter 6—where the combination of compaction and lower plant-available water retention capacity limits the soil water range for healthy plant growth. Such soils therefore have less efficient crop water use and require additional applications of irrigation water. In fact, it is believed that many farms in humid climates have started to use supplemental irrigation because their soils have become compacted and depleted of organic matter. As we discussed before, poor soil management is often compensated for by increased inputs.

Reducing tillage, adding organic amendments, preventing compaction, and using perennial crops in rotations can increase water storage. A long-term experiment showed that reducing tillage and using crop rotations increased plant-available water capacity in the surface horizon by up to 34% (table 17.2). When adding organic matter, consider stable sources that are mostly composed of "very dead" materials such as composts. They are more persistent in soil and are a primary contributor to soil water retention. But don't forget fresh residues (the "dead") that help form new and stable aggregates. Increasing rooting depth greatly increases plant water availability by extending the volume of soil available for roots to explore. When distinct plow pans are present, ripping through them makes subsoil water accessible to roots. Practices like zone tillage increase rooting depth and also result in long-term increases in organic matter and water storage capacity.

These practices have the most significant impact in humid regions where supplemental irrigation is used to reduce drought stress during dry periods between

Table 17.2
Plant-Available Water Capacity in Long-Term Tillage and Rotation Experiments in New York

Tillage Experiments	Plant-Available Water Capacity (%)		
	Plow till	No till	% increase
Silt loam—33 years	24.4	28.5	17%
Silt loam—13 years	14.9	19.9	34%
Clay loam—13 years	16.0	20.2	26%
Rotation Experiment	Continuous corn	Corn after grass	% increase
Loamy sand—12 years	14.5	15.4	6%
Sandy clay—12 years	17.5	21.3	22%

Source: Moebius et al. (2008).

rainfall events. Building a healthier soil will reduce irrigation needs and conserve water, because increased plant water availability extends the time until the onset of drought stress and greatly reduces the probability of stress. For example, let's assume that a degraded soil with a plow pan (A) can provide adequate water to a crop for 8 days without irrigation, and a healthy soil with deep rooting (B) allows for 12 days. A 12-day continuous drought, however, is much less likely. Based on climate data for the northeastern U.S., the probability of such an event in the month of July is 1 in 100 (1%), while the probability for an 8-day dry period is 1 in 20 (5%). The crops growing on soil A would run out of water and suffer stress in July in 5% of years, while the crops on soil B would be stressed in only 1% of years. A healthy soil would reduce or eliminate the need for irrigation in many cases.

Increasing surface cover—especially with heavy mulch—significantly reduces evaporation from the soil surface. Cover crops can increase soil organic matter and provide surface mulch, but caution should be used with cover crops, because when growing, they can consume considerable amounts of water that may be needed to leach salts or supply the cash crop.

Conservative water use prevents many of the problems that we discussed above. This can be

195

Figure 17.10. Tensiometers used for soil moisture sensing in irrigation management. Photo courtesy of the Irrometer Company.

Figure 17.11. No-till irrigated vegetables grown on beds with cover crop mulch. Drip irrigation lines are placed at 1–2 inches depth in the beds (not visible).

accomplished by monitoring the soil, the plant, or weather indicators and applying water only when needed. Soil sensors—like tensiometers (figure 17.10), moisture blocks, and new TDR or capacitance probes—can evaluate soil moisture conditions. When the soil moisture levels become critical, irrigation systems can be turned on and water applications can be made to meet the crop's needs without excess. The crop itself can also be monitored, as water stress results in increased leaf temperatures that can be detected with thermal or near infrared imaging.

Another approach involves the use of weather information—from either government weather services or small on-farm weather stations—to estimate the balance between natural rainfall and evapotranspiration. Electronic equipment is available for continuous measuring of weather indicators, and they can be read from a distance using wireless or phone communication. Computer technology and site-specific water and fertilizer application equipment—now available with large modern sprinkler systems—allow farmers to tailor irrigation to acre-scale localized water and fertilizer needs. Researchers have also demonstrated that deficit irrigation—water applications that are less than 100%

of evapotranspiration—can provide equal yields with reduced water consumption and promote greater reliance on stored soil water. Deficit irrigation is used purposely with grapevines that need limited water stress to enrich quality-enhancing constituents like anthocyanins.

Many of these practices can be effectively combined. For example, a vegetable grower in Australia uses beds with controlled traffic (figure 17.11). A sorghum-sudan cover crop is planted during the wet season and mulched down after maturing, leaving a dense mulch. Subsurface trickle irrigation is installed in the beds and stays in place for five or more years (in contrast, annual removal and reinstallation are necessary with tilled systems). No tillage is performed, and vegetable crops are planted using highly accurate GPS technology to ensure that they are within a couple of inches from the drip emitters.

DRAINAGE

Soils that are naturally poorly drained and have inadequate aeration are generally high in organic matter content. But poor drainage makes them unsuitable for growing most crops other than a few water-loving plants like rice and cranberries. When such soils are artificially drained, they become very productive, as the high

Figure 17.12. The Wouda pumping station was built to drain large areas in Friesland, Netherlands, and is the largest steam pumping station ever built. It is now on the World Heritage List.

agriculture. Excess water was removed by windmill power, and later by steam- and oil-powered pumping stations (figure 17.12). Today, new drainage efforts are primarily accomplished with subsurface corrugated PVC tubes that are installed with laser-guided systems (figure 17.13). In the United States land drainage efforts have been significantly reduced as a result of wetland protection legislation, and large-scale government-sponsored projects are no longer initiated. But at the farm level, recent adoption of yield monitors on crop combines has quantified the economic benefits of drainage on existing cropland, and additional drainage lines are being installed at an accelerated pace in many of the very productive lands in the U.S. corn belt and elsewhere.

organic matter content provides all the good qualities we discussed in earlier chapters. Over the centuries, humans have converted swamps into productive agricultural land by digging ditches and canals, subsequently also combined with pumping systems to remove the water from low-lying areas. Aztec cities were supported in part by food from *chinampas*, which are canals dug in shallow lakes with the rich mud used to build raised beds. Large areas of Holland were drained with ditches to create pasture and hay land to support dairy-based

Benefits of Drainage

Drainage results in the lowering of water tables by removal of water through ditches or tubes (figure 17.14). The main benefit is the creation of a deeper soil volume that is adequately aerated for growth of common crop plants. If crops are grown that can tolerate shallow rooting conditions—like grasses for pastures or hay—the water table can still be maintained relatively close to the surface or drainage lines can be spaced far apart, thereby reducing installation and maintenance costs, especially

Figure 17.13. Left: Drainage ditch removes excess water and lowers water table. Right: Installation of perforated corrugated PVC drain lines using a laser-guided trencher.

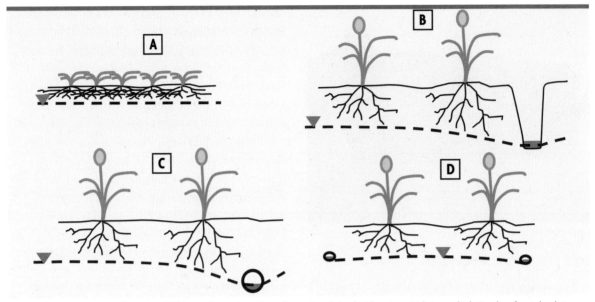

Figure 17.14. Drainage systems lower water tables and increase rooting volume. A: undrained with pasture; B: drainage ditch; C: subsurface tube drain (tile); and D: mole drain. Water table is indicated by dashed line with inverted triangle.

in low-lying areas that require pumping. Most commercial crops, like corn, alfalfa, and soybeans, require a deeper aerated zone, and subsurface drain lines need to be installed 3 to 4 feet deep and spaced from 20 to 80 feet apart, depending on soil characteristics.

Drainage increases the timeliness of field operations and reduces the potential for compaction damage. Farmers in humid regions have limited numbers of dry days for spring and fall fieldwork, and inadequate drainage then prevents field operations prior to the next rainfall. With drainage, field operations can commence within several days after rain. As we discussed in chapters 6 and 15, most compaction occurs when soils are wet and in the plastic state, and drainage helps soils transition into the friable state more quickly during drying periods—except for soils with high plasticity, like most clays. Runoff potential is also reduced by subsurface drainage, because compaction is reduced and soil water content is decreased by removal of excess water. This allows the soil to absorb more water through infiltration.

Installing drains in poorly drained soils therefore has agronomic and environmental benefits because it reduces compaction and loss of soil structure. This also addresses other concerns with inadequate drainage, like high nitrogen losses through denitrification. A large fraction of denitrification losses can occur as nitrous oxide, which is a potent greenhouse gas. As a general principle, croplands that are regularly saturated during the growing season should either be drained, or revert to pasture or natural vegetation.

Types of Drainage Systems

Ditching was used to drain lands for many centuries, but most agricultural fields are now drained through perforated corrugated PVC tubing that is installed in trenches and backfilled (figure 17.13, right). They are still often referred to as drain "tile," which dates back to the practice of installing clay pipes during the 1800s and early 1900s. Subsurface drain pipes are preferred in a modern agricultural setting, as ditches interfere with field

Is Drainage Really Needed?

Croplands with shallow or perched water tables benefit from drainage. But prolonged water ponding on the soil surface is not necessarily an indication of a shallow water table. Inadequate drainage can also result from poor soil structure (figure 17.15). Intensive use, loss of organic matter, and compaction make a soil drain poorly in wet climates. It may be concluded that the installation of drainage lines will solve this problem. Although this may help reduce further compaction, the correct management strategy is to build soil health and increase its permeability.

Figure 17.15. A soil with apparent drainage problems that are the result of poor soil structure.

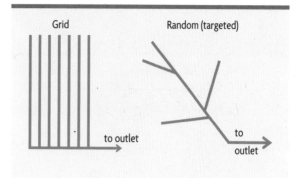

Figure 17.16. Grid and random (targeted) patterns for subsurface drain lines.

feet, while in sandy soil drain pipes may be installed at 100-foot spacing, which is considerably less expensive. Installing conventional drains in heavy clay soils is often too expensive due to the need for close drain spacing. But alternatives can be used. *Mole* drains are developed by pulling a tillage-type implement with a large bullet through soil in the plastic state at approximately 2 feet of depth (figure 17.17). The implement cracks the drier surface soil to create water pathways. The bullet creates a drain hole, and an expander smears the sides to give it more stability. Such drains are typically effective for several years, after which the process needs to be repeated. Like PVC drains, mole drains discharge into ditches at the edge of fields.

Clay soils may also require *surface drainage,* which involves shaping the land to allow water to discharge over the soil surface to the edge of fields, where it can enter a grass waterway (figure 17.18). Soil shaping is also

operations and take land out of production. A drainage system still needs ditches at the field edges to convey the water away from the field, to wetlands, streams, or rivers (figure 17.13, left).

If the entire field requires drainage, the subsurface pipes may be installed in *grids* with mostly parallel lines (figure 17.16). This is common for flat terrains. On undulating lands, drain lines are generally installed in swales and other low-lying areas where water accumulates. This is generally referred to as *random* drainage (although a better term is *targeted* drainage). *Interceptor* drains may be installed at the bottom of slopes to remove excess water from upslope areas.

Fine-textured soils are less permeable than coarse-textured ones and require closer drain spacing to be effective. A common drain spacing for a fine loam is 50

COMMON TYPES OF DRAINAGE PRACTICES USED IN AGRICULTURE

- Ditches
- Subsurface drain lines (tile)
- Mole drains
- Surface drains
- Raised beds and ridges

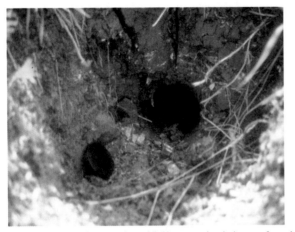 

Figure 17.17. A mole drain in a clay soil (left) is created with the use of a mole plow (right).

used to smooth out localized depressions where water would otherwise accumulate and remain ponded for extended periods of time.

A very modest system of drainage involves the use of *ridges* and *raised beds*, especially on fine-textured soils. This involves limited surface shaping, in which the crop rows are slightly raised relative to the inter-rows. This may provide a young seedling with enough aeration to survive through a period of excessive rainfall. These systems may also include reduced tillage—ridge tillage involves minimal soil disturbance—as well as controlled traffic to reduce compaction (chapters 15 and 16).

Figure 17.18. Surface drainage on clay soils in Ontario, Canada. Excess water travels over the surface to a grass waterway.

Concerns with Drainage

The extensive drainage of lands has created concerns, and many countries are now strictly controlling new drainage efforts. In the U.S., the 1985 Food Security Act contains the so-called Swampbuster Provision, which strongly discourages conversion of wetlands to cropland and has since been strengthened. The primary justification for such laws was the loss of wetland habitats and landscape hydrological buffers.

Wetlands are among the richest natural habitats due to the ample supplies of organic sources of food, and they are critical to migrating waterfowl that require food and habitat away from land predators. These wetlands also play important roles in buffering the hydrology of watersheds. During wet periods and snowmelt they fill with runoff water from surrounding areas, and during dry periods they receive groundwater that resurfaces in a lower landscape position. The retention of this water in swamps reduces the potential for flooding in downstream areas and allows nutrients to be cycled into aquatic plants and stored as organic material. When the swamps are drained, these nutrients are released by the oxidation of the organic materials and are mostly lost through the drainage system into watersheds. The extensive drainage of glacially derived pothole swamps

Figure 17.19. Subsurface drain line discharges into an edge-of-field ditch, diverting groundwater to surface waters.

in the north central and northeastern U.S. and Canada has contributed to significant increases in flooding and losses of nutrients into watersheds.

Drainage systems also increase the potential for losses of nutrients, pesticides, and other contaminants by providing a hydrologic shortcut for percolating waters. While under natural conditions water would be retained in the soil and slowly seep to groundwater, it is captured by drainage systems and diverted into ditches, canals, streams, lakes, and estuaries (figure 17.19). This is especially a problem because medium- and fine-

textured soils generally allow for very rapid movement of surface-applied chemicals to subsurface drain lines (figure 17.20). Unlike sands, which can effectively filter percolating water, fine-textured soils contain structural cracks and large (macro) pores down to the depth of a drain line. Generally, we would consider these to be favorable, because they facilitate water percolation and aeration. However, when application of fertilizers, pesticides, or liquid manure is followed by significant precipitation—especially intense rainfall that causes short-term surface ponding—these contaminants can enter the large pores and rapidly (sometimes within one hour) move to the drain lines. Bypassing the soil matrix and not filtered or adsorbed by soil particles, these contaminants can enter drains and surface waters at high concentrations (figure 17.21). Management practices can be implemented to reduce the potential for such losses (see the box "To Reduce Rapid Chemical and Manure Leaching to Drain Lines," next page).

Artificial drainage of the soil profile also reduces the amount of water stored in the soil and the amount of water available for a crop. Farmers who want to drain water out of the soil in case of excess rain but would like to retain it in case of drought play a game with the weather. *Controlled drainage* allows for some flexibility

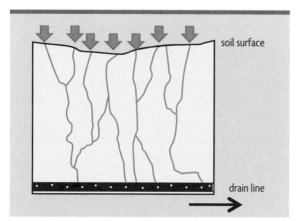

Figure 17.20. Continuous large (macro) pores may cause rapid movement of contaminants from the soil surface to drain lines, bypassing the soil matrix.

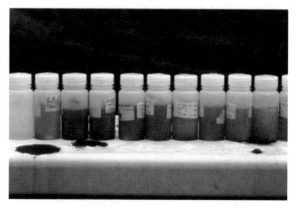

Figure 17.21. Water samples taken from a subsurface drain line when heavy rainfall followed liquid manure application. From left, water samples represent 15-minute sampling intervals from the onset of drain discharge. Photo by Larry Geohring.

TO REDUCE RAPID CHEMICAL AND MANURE LEACHING TO DRAIN LINES

- Build soils with a crumb structure that readily absorbs rainfall and reduces the potential for surface ponding.
- Avoid applications on wet soils (with or without artificial drainage) or prior to heavy rainfall.
- Inject or incorporate applied materials. Even modest incorporation reduces flow that bypasses the mass of the soil.

and involves retention of water in the soil system through the use of weirs in the ditches at the sides of fields. In effect, this keeps the water table at a higher level than the depth of the drains, but the weir can be lowered in case the soil profile needs to be drained. Controlled drainage is also recommended during winter fallows to slow down oxidations of organic matter in muck (organic) soils and reduce nitrate leaching in sandy soils.

SUMMARY

Irrigation and drainage allow for high yields in areas that otherwise have shortages or excesses of water. There is no doubt that we need such water management practices to secure a food supply for a growing population and provide the high yields needed to arrest the conversion of natural lands into agriculture. Some of the most productive lands use drainage and/or irrigation, and the ability to control water regimes provides great advantages. Yet there is a larger context: These practices exact a price on the environment by diverting water from its natural course and increasing the potential for soil and water contamination. Good management

practices can be used to reduce the impacts of altered water regimes. Building healthy soils is an important component of making soil and water management more sustainable by reducing the need for irrigation and drainage. In addition, other practices that promote more judicious use of water and chemical inputs help reduce environmental impacts.

SOURCES

Geohring, L.D., O.V. McHugh, M.T. Walter, et al. 2001. Phosphorus transport into subsurface drains by macropores after manure applications: Implications for best manure management practices. *Soil Science* 166: 896–909.

Geohring, L.D., and H.M. van Es. 1994. Soil hydrology and liquid manure applications. In *Liquid Manure Application Systems: Design, Management, and Environmental Assessment.* Publication no. 79. Ithaca, NY: Natural Resource, Agricultural, and Engineering Service.

Hudson, B.E. 1994. Soil organic matter and available water capacity. *Journal of Soil and Water Conservation* 49: 189–194.

McKay, M., and D.S. Wilks. 1995. *Atlas of Short-Duration Precipitation Extremes for the Northeastern United States and Southeastern Canada.* Northeast Regional Climate Center Research Publication RR 95-1, 26 pp. Also accessible at http://www.nrcc.cornell.edu/pptext/.

Moebius, B.N., H.M. van Es, J.O. Idowu, R.R. Schindelbeck, D.J. Clune, D.W. Wolfe, G.S. Abawi, J.E. Thies, B.K. Gugino, and R. Lucey. 2008. Long-term removal of maize residue for bioenergy: Will it affect soil quality? *Soil Science Society of America Journal* 72: 960–969.

Montgomery, D. 2007. *Dirt: The Erosion of Civilizations.* Berkeley: University of California Press.

Siebert, S., P. Döll, J. Hoogeveen, J-M. Faures, K. Frenken, and S. Feick. 2005. Development and validation of the global map of irrigation areas. *Hydrology and Earth System Sciences* 9: 535–547.

Sullivan, P. 2002. *Drought resistant soil.* Agronomy Technical Note. Appropriate Technology Transfer for Rural Areas. Fayetteville, AR: National Center for Appropriate Technology.

van Es, H.M., T.S. Steenhuis, L.D. Geohring, J. Vermeulen, and J. Boll. 1991. Movement of surface-applied and soil-embodied chemicals to drainage lines in a well-structured soil. In *Preferential Flow*, ed. T.J. Gish and A. Shirmohammadi, pp. 59–67. St. Joseph, MI: American Society of Agricultural Engineering.

Chapter 18

NUTRIENT MANAGEMENT: AN INTRODUCTION

The purchase of plant food is an important matter, but the use of a [fertilizer] is not a cure-all, nor will it prove an adequate substitute for proper soil handling.

—J.L. HILLS, C.H. JONES, AND C. CUTLER, 1908

Of the eighteen elements needed by plants, only three—nitrogen (N), phosphorus (P), and potassium (K)—are commonly deficient in soils. Deficiencies of other nutrients, such as magnesium (Mg), sulfur (S), zinc (Zn), boron (B), and manganese (Mn), certainly occur, but they are not as widespread. Deficiencies of sulfur, magnesium, and some micronutrients may be more common in regions with highly weathered minerals, such as the southeastern states, or those with high rainfall, such as portions of the Pacific Northwest. On higher-pH calcareous soils, especially in drier regions, keep an eye out for deficiencies of iron, zinc, copper, and manganese. In contrast, in locations with relatively young soil that contains minerals that haven't been weathered much by nature—such as glaciated areas with moderate to low rainfall like the Dakotas—K deficiencies are less common.

Environmental concerns have resulted in more emphasis on better management of N and P over the past few decades. While these nutrients are critical to soil fertility management, they also cause widespread environmental problems. Poor soil and crop management; overuse of fertilizers; misuse of manures, sewage sludges (biosolids), and composts; and high animal numbers on limited land area have contributed to surface and groundwater pollution in many regions of the U.S. Because both N and P are used in large quantities and their overuse has potential environmental implications, we'll discuss them together in chapter 19. Other nutrients, cation exchange, soil acidity (low pH) and liming, and arid and semiarid region problems with sodium, alkalinity (high pH), and excess salts are covered in chapter 20.

THE BOTTOM LINE: NUTRIENTS AND PLANT HEALTH, PESTS, PROFITS, AND THE ENVIRONMENT

Management practices are all related. The key is to visualize them all as whole-farm management, leading you to the goals of better crop growth and better

Photo by Dennis Nolan

BUILDING SOILS FOR BETTER CROPS: SUSTAINABLE SOIL MANAGEMENT

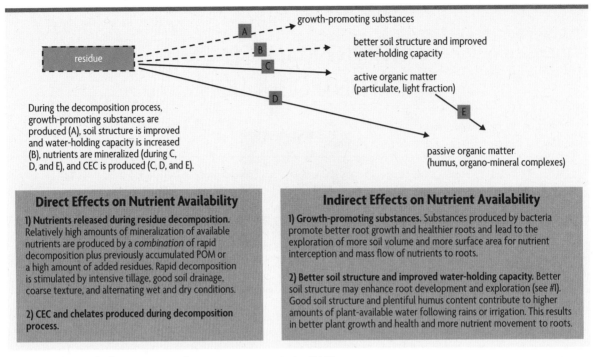

growth-promoting substances

better soil structure and improved
water-holding capacity

active organic matter
(particulate, light fraction)

residue

During the decomposition process,
growth-promoting substances are
produced (A), soil structure is improved
and water-holding capacity is increased
(B), nutrients are mineralized (during C,
D, and E), and CEC is produced (C, D, and E).

passive organic matter
(humus, organo-mineral complexes)

Direct Effects on Nutrient Availability

1) **Nutrients released during residue decomposition.**
Relatively high amounts of mineralization of available
nutrients are produced by a *combination* of rapid
decomposition plus previously accumulated POM or
a high amount of added residues. Rapid decomposition
is stimulated by intensive tillage, good soil drainage,
coarse texture, and alternating wet and dry conditions.

2) **CEC and chelates produced during decomposition
process.**

Indirect Effects on Nutrient Availability

1) **Growth-promoting substances.** Substances produced by bacteria
promote better root growth and healthier roots and lead to the
exploration of more soil volume and more surface area for nutrient
interception and mass flow of nutrients to roots.

2) **Better soil structure and improved water-holding capacity.** Better
soil structure may enhance root development and exploration (see #1).
Good soil structure and plentiful humus content contribute to higher
amounts of plant-available water following rains or irrigation. This results
in better plant growth and health and more nutrient movement to roots.

Figure 18.1. Influence of soil organic matter and its management on nutrient availability.

environmental quality. If a soil has good tilth, no
subsurface compaction, good drainage, adequate water,
and a good supply of organic matter, plants should be
healthy and have large root systems. This enables plants
to efficiently take up nutrients and water from the soil
and to use those nutrients to produce higher yields.

Doing a good job of managing nutrients on the farm
and in individual fields is critical to general plant health
and management of plant pests. Too much available N in
the early part of the growing season allows small-seeded
weeds, with few nutrient reserves, to get well established.
This early jump start may then enable them to out-
compete crop plants later on. Crops do not grow properly
if nutrients aren't present at the right time of the season
in sufficient quantities and in reasonable balance to one
another. Plants may be stunted if nutrient levels are low,
or they may grow too much foliage and not enough fruit
if N is too plentiful relative to other nutrients. Plants that
are under nutrient stress or growing abnormally—for

example, in the presence of too low or too high N levels—
are not able to emit as much of the natural chemicals that
signal beneficial insects when insect pests feed on leaves
or fruit. Low K levels aggravate stalk rot of corn. On the
other hand, pod rot of peanuts is associated with excess K
within the fruiting zone of peanuts (the top 2 to 3 inches
of soil). Blossom-end rot of tomatoes is related to low calcium levels, often made worse by droughty, or irregular
rainfall or irrigation, conditions.

When plants either don't grow well or are more
susceptible to pests, that affects the economic return.
Yield and crop quality usually are reduced, lowering the amount of money received. There also may be
added costs to control pests that take advantage of poor
nutrient management. In addition, when nutrients are
applied beyond plant needs, it's like throwing money
away. And when N and P are lost from the soil by leaching to groundwater or running into surface water, entire
communities may suffer from poor water quality.

ORGANIC MATTER AND NUTRIENT AVAILABILITY

The best single overall strategy for nutrient management is to enhance the levels of organic matter in soils (figure 18.1). This is especially true of N and P. Soil organic matter, together with any freshly applied residues, are well-known sources of N for plants. Mineralization of P and sulfur from organic matter is also an important source of these nutrients. As discussed earlier, organic matter helps hold on to positively charged potassium (K^+), calcium (Ca^{++}), and magnesium (Mg^{++}) ions. It also provides natural chelates that maintain micronutrients such as zinc, copper, and manganese in forms that plants can use. In addition, the improved soil tilth and the growth-promoting substances produced during organic matter decomposition help the plant develop a more extensive root system, allowing it to obtain nutrients from a larger volume of soil.

IMPROVING NUTRIENT CYCLING ON THE FARM

For economic and environmental reasons, it makes sense for plants to more efficiently utilize nutrient cycling on the farm. Goals should include a reduction in long-distance nutrient flows, as well as promoting "true" on-farm cycling, in which nutrients return in the form of crop residue or manure to the fields from which they came. There are a number of strategies to help farmers reach the goal of better nutrient cycling:

- **Reduce unintended losses** by promoting water infiltration and better root health through enhanced management of soil organic matter and physical properties. Ways organic matter can be built up and maintained include increased additions of a variety of sources of organic matter, plus methods for reducing losses via tillage and conservation practices. In addition, apply only the amount of irrigation water needed to refill the root zone. Applying more irrigation water than needed can cause both runoff and leaching losses of nutrients. (In arid climates occasional extra water applications will be needed to leach accumulating

THE ABCS OF NUTRIENT MANAGEMENT

a. Build up and maintain high soil organic matter levels.

b. Test manures and credit their nutrient content before applying fertilizers or other amendments.

c. Incorporate manures into the soil quickly, if possible, to reduce N volatilization and potential loss of nutrients in runoff.

d. Test soils regularly to determine the nutrient status and whether or not manures, fertilizers, or lime is needed.

e. Balance nutrient inflows and removals to maintain optimal levels and allow a little "drawdown" if nutrient levels get too high.

f. Enhance soil structure and reduce field runoff by minimizing soil compaction damage.

g. Use forage legumes or legume cover crops to provide N to following crops and develop good soil tilth.

h. Use cover crops to tie up nutrients in the off season, enhance soil structure, reduce runoff and erosion, and provide microbes with fresh organic matter.

i. Maintain soil pH in the optimal range for the most sensitive crops in your rotation.

j. When P and K are very deficient, broadcast some of the fertilizer to increase the general soil fertility level, and band apply some as well.

k. To get the most efficient use of a fertilizer when P and K levels are in the medium range, consider band application at planting, especially in cool climates.

salts from the irrigation below the root zone.)

- **Enhance nutrient uptake efficiency** by carefully using fertilizers and amendments, as well as irrigation practices. Better placement and synchronizing application with plant growth both improve efficiency of fertilizer nutrients. Sometimes changing planting dates or switching to a new crop creates a

Essential Nutrients for Plants

Element	Common Available Form	Source
Needed in large amounts		
Carbon	CO_2	atmosphere
Oxygen	O_2, H_2O	atmosphere and soil pores
Hydrogen	H_2O	water in soil pores
Nitrogen	NO_3^-, NH_4^+	soil
Phosphorus	$H_2PO_4^-$, HPO_4^{-2}	soil
Potassium	K^+	soil
Calcium	Ca^{+2}	soil
Magnesium	Mg^{+2}	soil
Sulfur	SO_4^{-2}	soil
Needed in small amounts		
Iron	Fe^{+2}, Fe^{+3}	soil
Manganese	Mn^{+2}	soil
Copper	Cu^+, Cu^{+2}	soil
Zinc	Zn^{+2}	soil
Boron	H_3BO_3	soil
Molybdenum	MoO_4^{-2}	soil
Chlorine	Cl^-	soil
Cobalt	Co^{+2}	soil
Nickel	Ni^{+2}	soil

Notes:
1. Sodium (Na) is considered an essential element for some plants.
2. Although selenium (Se) is not considered an essential element for plants, it is essential for animals and so the Se content of plants is important for animal nutrition. On the other hand, plants growing on high-Se soils (such as locoweed, asters, and saltbushes) accumulate enough Se to become toxic to grazing animals.
3. Silica (Si) is considered essential for the normal growth and health of rice.

better match between the timing of nutrient availability and crop needs.

• ***Tap local nutrient sources*** by seeking local sources of organic materials, such as leaves or grass clippings from towns, aquatic weeds harvested from lakes, produce waste from markets and restaurants, food processing wastes, and clean sewage sludges (see discussion on sewage sludge in chapter 9). Although some of these do not contribute to true nutrient

cycles, the removal of agriculturally usable nutrients from the "waste stream" makes sense and helps develop more environmentally sound nutrient flows.

• ***Promote consumption of locally produced foods*** by supporting local markets as well as returning local food wastes to farmland. When people purchase locally produced foods, there are more possibilities for true nutrient cycling to occur. Some community-supported agriculture (CSA) farms, where subscriptions for produce are paid before the start of the growing season, encourage their members to return produce waste to the farm for composting, completing a true cycle.

• ***Reduce exports of nutrients in farm products*** by adding animal enterprises to crop farms. The best way to reduce nutrient exports per acre, as well as to make more use of forage legumes in rotations, is to add an animal (especially a ruminant) enterprise to a crop farm. Compared with selling crops, feeding crops to animals and exporting animal products result in far fewer nutrients leaving the farm. (Keep in mind that, on the other hand, raising animals with mainly purchased feed overloads a farm with nutrients.)

• ***Bring animal densities in line with the land base of the farm.*** This can be accomplished by renting or purchasing more land—to grow a higher percentage of animal feeds and for manure application—or by limiting animal numbers.

NUTRIENT MANAGEMENT GOALS
• Satisfy crop nutrient requirements for yield and quality.
• Minimize pest pressure caused by excess N fertilizer or deficiency of nutrients.
• Minimize the environmental and economic costs of supplying nutrients.
• Use local sources of nutrients whenever possible.
• Get full nutrient value from fertility sources.
—MODIFIED FROM OMAFRA (1997)

> ## STRATEGIES FOR IMPROVING NUTRIENT CYCLES
> - Reduce unintended losses.
> - Enhance nutrient uptake efficiency.
> - Tap local nutrient sources.
> - Promote consumption of locally produced foods.
> - Reduce exports of nutrients in farm products.
> - Bring animal densities in line with the land base of the farm.
> - Develop local partnerships to balance flows among different types of farms.

- ***Develop local partnerships to balance flows among different types of farms.*** As pointed out in chapter 9 when we discussed organic matter management, sometimes neighboring farmers cooperate with both nutrient management and crop rotations. This is especially beneficial when a livestock farmer has too many animals and imports a high percentage of feed and a neighboring vegetable or grain farm has a need for nutrients and an inadequate land base for allowing a rotation that includes a forage legume. By cooperating on nutrient management and rotations, both farms win, sometimes in ways that were not anticipated (see "Win-Win Cooperation" box). Encouragement and coordination from an extension agent may help neighboring farmers work out cooperative agreements. It is more of a challenge as the distances become greater.

Some livestock farms that are overloaded with nutrients are finding that composting is an attractive alternative way to handle manure. During the composting process, volume and weight are greatly reduced (see chapter 13), resulting in less material to transport. Organic farmers are always on the lookout for reasonably priced animal manures and composts. The landscape industry also uses a fair amount of compost. Local or regional compost exchanges can help remove nutrients from overburdened animal operations and place them on nutrient-deficient soils.

USING FERTILIZERS AND AMENDMENTS

There are four main questions when applying nutrients:
- How much is needed?
- What source(s) should be used?
- When should the fertilizer or amendment be applied?
- How should the fertilizer or amendment be applied?

Chapter 21 details the use of soil tests to help you decide how much fertilizer or organic nutrient sources to apply. Here we will go over how to approach the other three issues.

Nutrient Sources: Commercial Fertilizers vs. Organic Materials

There are numerous fertilizers and amendments that are normally used in agriculture (some are listed in table 18.1). Fertilizers such as urea, triple superphosphate, and muriate of potash (potassium chloride) are convenient to store and use. They are also easy to blend

> ## WIN-WIN COOPERATION
> Cooperation between Maine potato farmers and their dairy farm neighbors has led to better soil and crop quality for both types of farms. As potato farmer John Dorman explains, after cooperating with a dairy farm on rotations and manure management, soil health "has really changed more in a few years than I'd have thought possible." Dairy farmer Bob Fogler feels that the cooperation with the potato farmer allowed his family to expand the dairy herd. He notes, "We see fewer pests and better-quality corn. Our forage quality has improved. It's hard to put a value on it, but forage quality means more milk."
>
> —FROM *HOARD'S DAIRYMAN*, APRIL 10, 1999

Table 18.1
Composition of Various Common Amendments and Commercial Fertilizers (%)

	N	P₂O₅	K₂O	Ca	Mg	S	Cl
N Materials							
Anhydrous ammonia	82						
Aqua ammonia	20						
Ammonium nitrate	34						
Ammonium sulfate	21					24	
Calcium nitrate	16			19	1		
Urea	46						
UAN solutions (urea + ammonium nitrate)	28–32						
P and N+P Materials							
Superphosphate (ordinary)		20		20		12	
Triple superphosphate		46		14		1	
Diammonium phosphate (DAP)	18	46					
Monoammonium phosphate (MAP)	11–13	48–52					
K Materials							
Potassium chloride (muriate of potash)			60				47
Potassium–magnesium sulfate ("sul-po-mag")			22		11	23	2
Potassium sulfate			50		1	18	2
Other Materials							
Gypsum				23		18	
Limestone, calcitic				25–40	0.5–3		
Limestone, dolomitic				19–22	6–13		1
Magnesium sulfate				2	11	14	
Potassium nitrate	13		44				
Sulfur						30–99	
Wood ashes		2	6	23	2		

to meet nutrient needs in specific fields and provide predictable effects. Their behavior in soils and the ready availability of the nutrients are well established. The timing, rate, and uniformity of nutrient application are easy to control when using commercial fertilizers. However, there also are drawbacks to using commercial fertilizers. All of the commonly used N materials (those containing urea, ammonia, and ammonium) are acid forming, and their use in humid regions, where native lime has been weathered out, requires more frequent lime additions. The production of nitrogen fertilizers is also very energy intensive—it's estimated that N fertilizers account for 25% to 30% of the energy that goes into growing a corn crop. Also, the high nutrient solubility can result in salt damage to seedlings when excess fertilizer is applied close to seeds or plants. Because nutrients in commercial fertilizers are readily available, under some circumstances more may leach to groundwater than when using organic nutrient sources when both are used properly. For example, high rainfall events on a sandy soil soon after ammonium nitrate fertilizer application will probably cause more nitrate loss than if compost had been applied. (On the other hand, high rainfall events on a recently plowed-down alfalfa

DO ORGANIC NUTRIENT SOURCES REDUCE ENVIRONMENTAL IMPACTS? IT DEPENDS!

It is commonly assumed that the use of organic nutrient sources always results in lower environmental impacts. This is generally true, but only if good management practices are followed. For example, in temperate climates a plowed alfalfa sod releases a lot of organic nitrogen that can easily meet all the needs of the following corn crop. But if the plowing is done too early—for example, in the early fall—much of the organic N is mineralized in the following months when the soil is still warm and then lost through leaching or denitrification over the winter and spring. A study in Sweden compared conventional and organic crop production and found similar nitrate leaching losses. Organic sources like manure may create a problem with nutrient runoff if left on the surface, or with leaching when applied in the fall. So, even when using organic nutrient sources, good agronomic management and careful consideration of environmental impacts are essential.

field may also result in significant nitrate leaching below the zone that roots can reach.) Sediments lost by erosion from fields fertilized with commercial fertilizers probably will contain more available nutrients than those from fields fertilized with organic sources, resulting in more severe water pollution. Of course, soils overloaded with either inorganic or organic sources of nutrients can be large sources of pollution. The key to wisely using either commercial fertilizers or organic sources is not applying more nutrients than the crop can use and applying in ways that minimize losses to the environment.

Organic sources of nutrients have many other good qualities, too. Compared to commercial fertilizers that only "feed the plants," organic materials also "feed the soil." They are also sources of soil organic matter, providing food for soil organisms that aid in forming aggregates and humus. Organic sources can provide a more slow-release source of fertility, and the N availability is frequently more evenly matched to the needs of growing plants. Sources like manures or crop residues commonly contain all the needed nutrients, including the micronutrients, but they may not be present in the proper proportion for a particular soil and crop; thus, routine soil testing is important. Poultry manure, for example, has about the same levels of N and P, but plants take up three to five times more N than P. During the composting process a lot of N is commonly lost, making the compost much richer in P relative to N. Thus, applying a large

quantity of compost to a soil might supply a crop's N needs but serve to enrich the soil in unneeded P, creating a greater pollution potential.

One of the drawbacks to organic materials is the variable amounts and uncertain timing of nutrient release for plants to use. The value of manure as a nutrient source depends on the type of animal, its diet, and how the manure is handled. For cover crops, the N contribution depends on the species, the amount of growth in the spring, and the weather. Also, manures typically

ORGANIC FARMING VS. ORGANIC NUTRIENT SOURCES

We've used the term "organic sources" of nutrients to refer to nutrients contained in crop residues, manures, and composts. These types of materials are used by all farmers—"conventional" and "organic." Both also use limestone and a few other materials. However, most of the commercial fertilizers listed in table 18.1 are not allowed in organic production. In place of sources such as urea, anhydrous ammonia, diammonium phosphate, concentrated superphosphate, and muriate of potash, organic farmers use products that come directly from minerals, such as greensand, granite dust, and rock phosphate. Other organic products come from parts of organisms, such as bone meal, fish meal, soybean meal, and bloodmeal (see table 18.2).

are bulky and may contain a high percentage of water—so considerable work is needed to apply them per unit of nutrients. The timing of nutrient release is uncertain, because it depends both on the type of organic materials used and on the action of soil organisms. Their activities change with temperature and rainfall. Finally, the relative nutrient concentrations for a particular manure used may not match soil needs. For example, manures may contain high amounts of both N and P when your soil already has high P levels.

Selection of Commercial Fertilizer Sources

It is recommended to include organic fertilizer sources as part of a nutrient management program to sustain soil health, but on many farms additional commercial fertilizers are still needed to achieve good yields. On the global scale, until better practices (use of cover crops, better rotations, decreased tillage, and integrating animal and plant agriculture, etc.) are used on farms, commercial fertilizers are still needed to meet the demands of our growing population. There are numerous forms of commercial fertilizers, many given in table 18.1. When you buy fertilizers in large quantities, you usually choose the cheapest source. When you buy bulk blended fertilizer, you usually don't know what sources were used unless you ask. All you know is that it's a 10-20-20 or a 20-10-10 (both referring to the percent of available N, P_2O_5, and K_2O) or another blend. However, below are a number of examples of situations in which you might not want to apply the cheapest source:

- Although the cheapest N form is anhydrous ammonia, the problems with injecting it into a soil with many large stones or the losses that might occur if you inject it into very moist clay may call for other N sources to be used instead.
- If both N and P are needed, diammonium phosphate (DAP) is a good choice because it has approximately the same cost and P content as concentrated superphosphate and also contains 18% N.

Table 18.2
Products Used by Organic Growers to Supply Nutrients

	%N	%P_2O_5	%K_2O
Alfalfa pellets	2.7	0.5	2.8
Blood meal	13.0	2.0	—
Bone meal	3.0	20.0	0.5
Cocoa shells	1.0	1.0	3.0
Colloidal phosphate	—	18.0	—
Compost	1.0	0.4	3.0
Cottonseed meal	6.0	2.0	2.0
Fish scraps, dried & ground	9.0	7.0	—
Granite dust	—	—	5.0
Greensand	—	—	7.0
Hoof & horn meal	11.0	2.0	—
Linseed meal	5.0	2.0	1.0
Rock phosphate	—	30.0	—
Seaweed, ground	1.0	0.2	2.0
Soybean meal	6.0	1.4	4.0
Tankage	6.5	14.5	—

Notes:
1. Values of P_2O_5 and K_2O represent total nutrients present. For fertilizers listed in table 18.1, the numbers are the amount that are readily available.
2. Organic growers also use potassium–magnesium sulfate ("sul-po-mag" or "K-mag"), wood ashes, limestone, and gypsum (listed in table 18.1). Although some use only manure that has been composted, others will use aged manures (see chapter 12). There are also a number of commercial organic products with a variety of trade names.
Source: R. Parnes (1990).

- Although muriate of potash (potassium chloride) is the cheapest K source, it may not be the best choice under certain circumstances. If you also need magnesium and don't need to lime the field, potassium–magnesium sulfate would be a better choice.

Method and Timing of Application

The timing of fertilizer application is frequently related to the application method chosen, so in this section we'll go over both practices together.

Broadcast application, in which fertilizer is evenly distributed over the whole field and then usually incorporated during tillage, is best used to increase the nutrient level of the bulk of the soil. It is especially useful to build P and K when they are very deficient. Broadcasting with incorporation is usually done in the fall or in spring just before tillage. Broadcasting on top of a growing crop, called *topdressing*, is commonly used to apply N, especially to crops that occupy the entire soil surface, such as wheat or a grass hay crop. (Amendments used in large quantities, like lime and gypsum, are also broadcast prior to incorporation into the soil.)

There are various methods of applying localized placement of fertilizer. *Banding* small amounts of fertilizer to the side and below the seed at planting is a common application method. It is especially useful for row crops grown in cool soil conditions—early in the season, for example—on soils with high amounts of sur-face residues, with no-till management, or on wet soils that are slow to warm in the spring. It is also useful for soils that test low to medium (or even higher) in P and K. Band placement of fertilizer near the seed at planting,

usually called *starter fertilizer*, may be a good idea even in warmer climates when planting early. It still might be cool enough to slow root growth and release of nutrients from organic matter. Including N as part of the starter fertilizer appears to help roots use fertilizer P more efficiently, perhaps because N stimulates root growth. Starter fertilizer for soils very low in fertility frequently contains other nutrients, such as sulfur, zinc, boron, or manganese.

Splitting N applications is a good management practice—especially on sandy soils, where nitrate is easily lost by leaching, or on heavy loams and clays, where it can be lost by denitrification. Some N is applied before planting or in the band as starter fertilizer, and the rest is applied as a *sidedress* or topdress during the growing season. Although unusual, sometimes split applications of K are recommended for very sandy soils with low organic matter, especially if there has been enough rainfall to cause K to leach into the subsoil. Unfortunately, relying on sidedressing N can increase the risk of reduced yields

CROP VALUE, FERTILIZER COSTS, AND FERTILIZER RATES

The cost of N fertilizer is directly tied to energy costs, because so much energy is used for its manufacture and transport. The costs of other fertilizers are less sensitive to fluctuating energy prices but have been increasing, nevertheless. Use of fertilizers has increased worldwide, and dwindling global reserves combined with the increase in fuel and other input costs to manufac-ture them have recently led to large price increases.

Most agronomic crops grown on large acreages are worth around $400 to $1,000 per acre, and the fertilizer used may repre-sent 30% to 40% of out-of-pocket growing costs. So, if you use 100 pounds of N you don't need, that's perhaps around $65/acre and may represent 10% or more of your gross income. Some years ago, one of the authors of this book worked with two brothers who operated a dairy farm in northern Vermont that had high soil test levels of N, P, and K. Despite his recommenda-tion that no fertilizer was needed, the normal practice was followed, and N, P, and K fertilizer worth $70 per acre (in 1980s prices) was applied to their 200 acres of corn. The yields on 40-foot-wide, no-fertilizer strips that they left in each field were the same as where fertilizer had been applied, so the $14,000 they spent for fertilizer was wasted.

When growing fruit or vegetable crops—worth thousands of dollars per acre—fertilizers represent about 1% of the value of the crop and 2% of the costs. But when growing specialty crops (medicinal herbs, certain organic vegetables for direct market-ing) worth over $10,000 per acre, the cost of fertilizer is dwarfed by other costs, such as hand labor. A waste of $65/acre in unneeded nutrients for these crops would cause a minimal economic penalty—assuming you maintain a reasonable balance between nutrients—but there may also be environmental reasons against applying too much fertilizer.

FERTILIZER GRADE: OXIDE VS. ELEMENTAL FORMS?

When talking or reading about fertilizer P or K, the oxide form is usually assumed. This is used in all recommendations and when you buy fertilizer. The terms "phosphate" (P_2O_5) and "potash" (K_2O) have been used for so long to refer to phosphorus and potassium in fertilizers, it is likely that they will be with us indefinitely—even if they are confusing. When you apply 100 pounds of potash per acre, you actually apply 100 pounds of K_2O—the equivalent of 83 pounds of elemental potassium. Of course, you're really using not K_2O but rather something like muriate of potash (KCl). A similar thing is true of phosphate—100 pounds of P_2O_5 per acre is the same as 44 pounds of P—and you're really using fertilizers like concentrated superphosphate (that contains a form of calcium phosphate) or ammonium phosphate. However, in your day-to-day dealing with fertilizers you need to think in terms of nitrogen, phosphate, and potash and don't worry about the actual amount of elemental P or K you purchase or apply.

if the weather is too wet to apply the fertilizer (and you haven't put on enough preplant or as starter) or too dry following an application for the fertilizer to come into contact with roots. Then the fertilizer stays on the surface instead of washing into the root zone.

Once the soil nutrient status is optimal, try to balance farm nutrient inflows and outflows. When nutrient levels, especially P, are in the high or very high range, stop application and try to maintain or "draw down" soil test levels. It usually takes years of cropping without adding P to lower soil test P appreciably.

Tillage and Fertility Management: To Incorporate or Not?

With systems that provide some tillage, such as moldboard plow and harrow, disk harrow alone, chisel plow, zone-till, and ridge-till, it is possible to incorporate fertilizers and amendments. However, when using no-till production systems, it is not possible to mix materials into the soil to uniformly raise the fertility level in that portion of the soil where roots are especially active.

The advantages of incorporating fertilizers and amendments are numerous. Significant quantities of ammonia may be lost by volatilization when the most commonly used solid N fertilizer, urea, is left on the soil surface. Also, nutrients remaining on the surface after application are much more likely to be lost in runoff during rain events. Although the amount of runoff is usually lower with reduced tillage systems than with conventional tillage, the concentration of nutrients in the runoff may be quite a bit higher.

If you are thinking about changing from conventional tillage to no-till or other forms of reduced tillage, you might consider incorporating needed lime, phosphate, and potash, as well as manures and other organic residues, before making the switch. It's the last chance to easily change the fertility of the top 8 or 9 inches of soil.

SOURCES

Mikkelsen, R., and T.K. Hartz. 2008. Nitrogen sources for organic crop production. *Better Crops* 92(4): 16–19.

OMAFRA (Ontario Ministry of Agriculture, Food, and Rural Affairs). 1997. *Nutrient Management.* Best Management Practices Series. Available from the Ontario Federation of Agriculture, Toronto, Ontario, Canada.

Parnes, R. 1990. *Fertile Soil: A Grower's Guide to Organic and Inorganic Fertilizers.* Davis, CA: agAccess.

Torstensson, G., H. Aronsson, and L. Bergstrom. 2006. Nutrient use efficiencies and leaching of organic and conventional cropping systems in Sweden. *Agronomy Journal* 98: 603–615.

van Es, H.M., K.J. Czymmek, and Q.M. Ketterings. 2002. Management effects on N leaching and guidelines for an N leaching index in New York. *Journal of Soil and Water Conservation* 57(6): 499–504.

SOIL TESTS

Soil tests, one of the key nutrient management tools, are discussed in detail in chapter 21.

Chapter 19

MANAGEMENT OF NITROGEN AND PHOSPHORUS

. . . an economical use of fertilizers requires that they merely supplement the natural supply in the soil, and that the latter should furnish the larger part of the soil material used by the crop.

—T.L. LYON AND E.O. FIPPIN, 1909

Both nitrogen and phosphorus are needed by plants in large amounts, and both can cause environmental harm when present in excess. They are discussed together in this chapter because we don't want to do a good job of managing one and, at the same time, do a poor job with the other. Nitrogen losses are a serious economic concern for farmers; if not managed properly, a large fraction (as much as half in some cases) of applied N fertilizer can be lost instead of used by crops. Environmental concerns with N include the leaching of soil nitrate to groundwater; excess N in runoff; and losses of nitrous oxide, a potent greenhouse gas. For P, the main concerns are losses to freshwater bodies.

High-nitrate groundwater is a health hazard to infants and young animals because it decreases the blood's ability to transport oxygen. In addition, nitrate stimulates the growth of algae and aquatic plants just as it stimulates the growth of agricultural plants. The growth of plants in many brackish estuaries and salt-water environments is believed to be limited by a lack

of N. So, when nitrate leaches through soil, or runs off the surface and is discharged into streams, eventually reaching water bodies like the Gulf of Mexico or the Chesapeake Bay, undesirable microorganisms flourish. In addition, the algal blooms that result from excess N and P cloud water, blocking sunlight to important underwater grasses that are home to numerous species of young fish, crabs, and other bottom dwellers. The greatest concern, however, is the dieback of the algae and other aquatic plants. These plants settle on the bottom of the affected estuaries, and their decomposition consumes dissolved oxygen in the water. The result is an extended area of very low oxygen concentrations in which fish and other aquatic animals cannot live. This is a serious concern in many estuaries around the world.

Denitrification is a microbial process that occurs primarily in surface layers when soils are saturated with water. Soil bacteria convert nitrate to both nitrous oxide (N_2O) and N_2. While N_2 (two atoms of nitrogen bonded together) is the most abundant gas in the atmosphere

Photo by Dennis Nolan

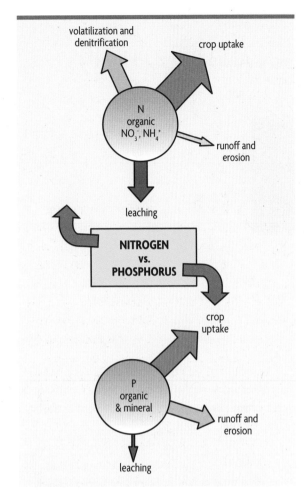

Figure 19.1. Different pathways for nitrogen and phosphorus losses from soils (relative amounts indicated by width of arrows). Based on an unpublished diagram by D. Beegle, Penn State University.

damages the environment when excess amounts are added to a lake from human activities (agriculture, rural home septic tanks, or urban sewage and street runoff). This increases algae growth (eutrophication), making fishing, swimming, and boating unpleasant or difficult. When excess aquatic organisms die, decomposition removes oxygen from water and leads to fish kills.

All farms should work to have the best N and P management possible—for economic as well as environmental reasons. This is especially important near bodies of water that are susceptible to accelerated weed or algae growth. However, don't forget that nutrients from farms in the Midwest are contributing to problems in the Gulf of Mexico—over 1,000 miles away.

There are major differences between the way N and P behave in soils (figure 19.1, table 19.1). Both N and P can, of course, be supplied in applied fertilizers. But aside from legumes that can produce their own N because of the bacteria living in root nodules, crop plants get their N from decomposing organic matter. On the other hand, plants get their P from both organic matter and soil minerals. Nitrate, the primary form in which plants absorb nitrogen from the soil, is very mobile in soils, while P movement in soils is very limited.

Most unintentional N loss from soils occurs when nitrate leaches or is converted into gases by the process of denitrification, or when surface ammonium is volatilized. Large amounts of nitrate may leach from sandy soils, while denitrification is generally more significant in heavy loams and clays. On the other hand, most unintended P loss from soils is carried away in runoff or sediments eroded from fields, construction sites, and other exposed soil (see figure 19.1 for a comparison between relative pathways for N and P losses). Phosphorus leaching is a concern in fields that are artificially drained. With many years of excessive manure or compost application, soils saturated with P (often sands with low P sorption capacity) can start leaking P with the percolating water and discharge it through drain lines or ditches.

and not of environmental concern, each molecule of N_2O gas—largely generated by denitrification, with some contribution from nitrification—has approximately 300 times more global warming impact than a molecule of carbon dioxide.

Phosphorus losses from farms are generally small in relation to the amounts present in soils. However, small quantities of P loss have great impacts on water quality because P is the nutrient that appears to limit the growth of freshwater aquatic weeds and algae. Phosphorus

> **PROBLEMS USING EXCESS N FERTILIZER**
>
> There are quite a few reasons you should not apply more N than needed by crops. N fertilizers are now quite expensive, and many farmers are being more judicious than when N was relatively cheap. However, there are other problems associated with using more N than needed: (1) ground and surface water become polluted with nitrates; (2) more N_2O (a potent greenhouse gas and source of ozone depletion) is produced during denitrification in soil; (3) a lot of energy is consumed in producing N, so wasting N is the same as wasting energy; (4) using higher N than needed is associated with acceleration of decomposition and loss of soil organic matter; and (5) very high rates of N are frequently associated with high levels of insect damage.

Also, liquid manure can move through preferential flow paths (wormholes, root holes, cracks, etc., especially in clay soils) directly to subsurface drain lines and contaminate water in ditches, which is then discharged into streams and lakes (see also chapter 17).

Except when coming from highly manured fields, P losses—mainly as dissolved P in the runoff waters—from healthy grasslands are usually quite low, because both runoff water and sediment loss are very low. Biological N fixation carried on in the roots of legumes and by some free-living bacteria actually adds new N to soil, but there is no equivalent reaction for P or any other nutrient.

Improving N and P management can help reduce reliance on commercial fertilizers. A more ecologically based system—with good rotations, reduced tillage, and more active organic matter—should provide a large proportion of crop N and P needs. Better soil structure and attention to use of appropriate cover crops can lessen loss of N and P by reducing leaching, denitrification, and/or runoff. Reducing the loss of these nutrients is an economic benefit to the farm and, at the same time, an environmental benefit to society. The greater N availability may be thought of as a fringe benefit of a farm with an ecologically based cropping system.

In addition, the manufacture, transportation, and application of N fertilizers are very energy intensive. Of all the energy used to produce corn (including the manufacture and operation of field equipment), the manufacture and application of N fertilizer represents close

to 30%. Although energy was relatively inexpensive for many years, its cost has fluctuated greatly in recent years, as has the cost of fertilizers, and is expected to be relatively high for the foreseeable future. So relying more on biological fixation of N and efficient cycling in soils reduces depletion of a nonrenewable resource and may save you money as well. Although P fertilizers are less energy consuming to produce, a reduction in their use helps preserve this nonrenewable resource—the world's P mines are expected to run out in the next fifty to one hundred years.

Table 19.1
Comparing Soil N and P

Nitrogen	Phosphorus
Nitrogen becomes available from decomposing soil organic matter.	Phosphorus becomes available from decomposing soil organic matter and minerals.
N is mostly available to plants as nitrate (NO_3^-)—a form that is very mobile in soils	P is available mainly as dissolved phosphate in soil water—but little is present in solution even in fertile soils, and it is not mobile.
Nitrate can be easily lost in large quantities by leaching to groundwater or by conversion to gases (N_2, N_2O).	P is mainly lost from soils by runoff and erosion. However, liquid manure application on well-structured soils and those with tile drainage has resulted in P loss to drainage water.
Nitrogen can be added to soils by biological N fixation (legumes).	No equivalent reaction can add new P to soil, although many bacteria and some fungi help make P more available to plants.

MANAGEMENT OF N AND P

Nitrogen and phosphorus behave very differently in soils, but many of the management strategies are actually the same or very similar. They include the following:

1. Take all nutrient sources into account.
   - Estimate nutrient availability from all sources.
   - Use soil tests to assess available nutrients.
   - Use manure and compost tests to determine nutrient contributions.
   - Consider nutrients in decomposing crop residues (for N only).
2. Reduce losses and enhance uptake.
   - Use nutrient sources more efficiently.
   - Use localized placement of fertilizers whenever possible.
   - Split fertilizer application if leaching or denitrification losses are a potential problem (for N only).
   - Apply nutrients when leaching or runoff threats are minimal.
   - Reduce tillage.
   - Use cover crops.
   - Include perennial forage crops in rotation.
3. Balance farm imports and exports once crop needs are being met.

Estimating Nutrient Availability

Good N and P management practices take into account the large amount of plant-available nutrients that come from the soil, especially soil organic matter and any additional organic sources like manure, compost, or a rotation or cover crop. Fertilizer should be used only to supplement the soil's supply in order to provide full plant nutrition (figure 19.2). Organic farmers try to meet all demands through these soil sources, as additional organic fertilizers are generally very expensive. On crop-livestock farms these soil organic N and P sources are typically sufficient to meet the crop's demand, but not always.

Since most plant-available P in soils is relatively strongly adsorbed by organic matter and clay minerals, estimating P availability is routinely done by soil tests. The amount of P extracted by chemical soil solutions can be compared with results from crop response experiments and can provide good estimates of the likelihood of a response to P fertilizer additions, which we discuss in chapter 21.

Estimating N fertilizer needs is more complex, and soil tests generally cannot provide all the answers. The primary reason is that the amounts of plant-available N—mostly nitrate—can fluctuate rapidly as organic matter is mineralized and N is lost through leaching or denitrification. These processes are greatly dependent on soil organic matter contents, additional N contributions from organic amendments, and weather-related factors like soil temperature (higher temps increase N mineralization) and soil wetness (saturated soils cause large denitrification losses, especially when soils are warm). Mineral forms of N begin to accumulate in soil

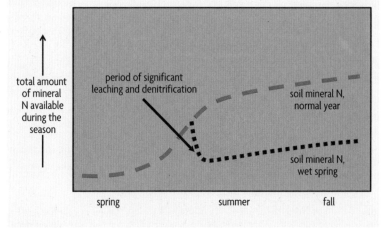

Figure 19.2. Available N in soil depends on recent weather. After increasing for a period, mineral N decreases during a wet spring because leaching and denitrification losses are greater than N being converted to mineral forms. More mineral N is available for plants when the spring is drier.

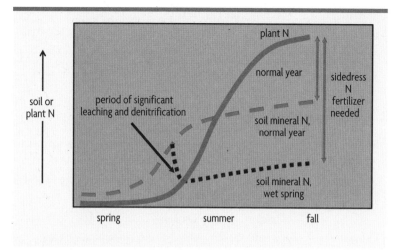

Figure 19.3. Need for supplemental N fertilizer depends on early-season weather. *Note:* The amount of mineral N in soil will actually decrease (not shown) as plants begin to grow rapidly and take up large quantities of N faster than new N is converted to mineral forms. Soil N shown in figure 19.2 and here is the total amount made available by the soil during the growing season.

in the spring but may be lost by leaching and denitrification during a very wet period (figure 19.2). When corn germinates in the spring, it takes a while until it begins to grow rapidly and take up a lot of N (figure 19.3). Weather affects the required amount of supplemental N in two primary ways. In years with unusually wet weather in the spring, an extra amount of sidedress N may be needed to compensate for relatively high mineral N loss from soil (figure 19.3). However, in dry years—especially drought spells during the critical pollination period—corn yield will be reduced, and the N uptake and needed N fertilizer are therefore lower (not shown in figure 19.3). However, you really don't know at normal sidedress time whether there will be a drought during pollination, so there is no way to adjust for that. The actual amount of required N depends on the complex and dynamic interplay of crop growth patterns with weather events, which is difficult to predict. In fact, optimum N fertilizer rates for corn without organic amendments in the U.S. corn belt may vary from as little as 0 pounds per acre in one year to as much as 250 pounds

per acre in another year. Those are the extremes, but, nevertheless, it is a great challenge to determine the optimum economic N rate.

Fixed and Adaptive Methods for Estimating Crop N Needs

Several general approaches are used to estimate crop N needs, and they can be grouped into fixed and weather-adaptive approaches. *Fixed approaches* assume that the N fertilizer needs do not vary from one season to another based on weather conditions but may vary because of the previous crop. They are useful for planning purposes and work well in dryer climates, but they are very imprecise in a humid climate.

The mass-balance approach, a fixed approach, is the most commonly used method for estimating N fertilizer recommendations. It is generally based on a yield goal and associated N uptake, minus credits given for non-fertilizer N sources such as mineralized N from soil organic matter, preceding crops, and organic amendments. However, recent studies have shown that the relationship between yield and optimum N rate is very weak for humid regions. While higher yields do require more N, the weather pattern that produces higher yields means (1) that larger and healthier root systems can take up more N, and (2) that frequently the weather pattern stimulates the presence of higher levels of nitrate in the soil.

Several leading U.S. corn-producing states have adopted **the maximum return to N (MRTN) approach,** another fixed approach, which largely abandons the mass-balance method. It provides generalized recommendations based on extensive field trials, model-fitting, and economic analyses. It is only available for corn at this time. The rate with the largest average net return to the farmer over multiple years is the MRTN, and the recommendations vary with grain and fertilizer prices. Adjustments based on realistic yield expectation are sometimes encouraged. The MRTN recommendations are based on comprehensive field information, but owing to generalizing over large areas and for many seasons, it does not account for the soil and weather factors that affect N availability.

The *adaptive approaches,* described in the following paragraphs, attempt to take into account seasonal weather, soil type, and management effects and require some type of measurement or model estimate during the growing season.

The pre-sidedress nitrate test (PSNT) measures soil nitrate content in the surface layer of 0 to 12 inches and allows for adaptive sidedress or topdress N applications. It implicitly incorporates information on early-season weather conditions (figure 19.2) and is especially successful in identifying N-sufficient sites—those that do not need additional N fertilizer. It requires a special sampling effort during a short time window in late spring, and it is sensitive to timing and mineralization rates during the early spring. The PSNT is usually called the late spring nitrate test (LSNT) in the midwestern U.S.

The pre-plant nitrate test (PPNT) measures soil nitrate or soil nitrate plus ammonium in the soil (typically from 0 to 2 ft) early in the season to guide N fertilizer applications at planting. It is effectively used in dryer climates—like the U.S. Great Plains—where seasonal gains of inorganic forms of N are more predictable and losses are minimal. The PPNT cannot incorporate the seasonal weather effects, as the samples are analyzed prior to the growing season, which inherently limits its precision compared to the PSNT.

Recent advances in crop sensing using reflectance spectroscopy allow adaptive approaches based on seasonal weather and local soil variation. **Leaf chlorophyll meters or satellite, aerial, or tractor-mounted sensors** that measure light reflecting from leaves are used for assessing leaf or canopy N status,

which can then guide sidedress N applications. These methods generally require a reference strip of corn that has received high levels of N fertilizer. This approach has been proven effective for spring N topdressing in cereal production, especially of winter wheat, but so far there has been limited success using this with corn due to more complicated crop and soil N dynamics.

Environmental information systems and simulation models are now also being employed for N management, with successful applications for wheat and corn. This is an adaptive approach that takes advantage of increasingly sophisticated environmental databases—like radar-based high-resolution precipitation estimates—that can be used to provide input information for computer models. N mineralization and losses are simulated together with crop growth to estimate soil N contributions and fertilizer N needs.

Evaluation at the End of the Season

To evaluate the success of a fertility recommendation, farmers sometimes plant field strips with different N rates and compare yields at the end of the season. **The lower stalk nitrate test** is also sometimes used to assess, after the growing season, whether corn N rates were approximately right or too low or too high. These two methods are neither fixed nor adaptive approaches for the current year since evaluation is made at the end of the season, but they may help farmers make changes to their fertilizer application rates in following years. Adaptive management may therefore also include farmer-based experimentation and adjustment to local conditions.

PLANNING FOR N AND P MANAGEMENT

Although N and P behave very differently in soils, the general approaches to their management are similar (table 19.2). The following considerations are important for planning management strategies for N and P:

Credit nutrients in manures, decomposing

Table 19.2
Comparison of N and P Management Practices

Nitrogen	Phosphorus
Use fixed-rate approaches for planning purposes and adaptive approaches to achieve precision.	Test soil regularly (and follow recommendations).
Test manures and credit their N contribution.	Test manures and credit their P contribution.
Use legume forage crops in rotation and/or legume cover crops to fix N for following crops *and* properly credit legume N contribution to following crops.	No equivalent practice available.
Time N applications as close to crop uptake as possible.	Time P application to reduce runoff potential.
Reduce tillage in order to leave residues on the surface and decrease runoff and erosion.	Reduce tillage in order to leave residues on the surface and decrease runoff and erosion.
Use sod-type forage crops in rotation to reduce nitrate leaching and runoff.	Use sod-type forage crops in rotation to reduce the amount of runoff and erosion losses of P.
Use grass cover crops, such as winter rye, to capture soil nitrates left over following the economic crop.	Use grass cover crops, such as winter rye, to protect soil against erosion.
Make sure that excessive N is not coming onto the farm (biological N fixation + fertilizers + feeds).	After soil tests are in optimal range, balance farm P flow (don't import much more onto the farm than is being exported).

sods, and other organic residues. Before applying commercial fertilizers or other off-farm nutrient sources, you should properly credit the various on-farm sources of nutrients. In some cases, there is more than enough fertility in the on-farm sources to satisfy crop needs. If manure is applied before sampling soil, the contribution of much of the manure's P and all its potassium should be reflected in the soil test. The pre-sidedress nitrate test can estimate the N contribution of the manure (see chapter 21 for a description of N soil tests). The only way to really know the nutrient value of a particular manure is to have it tested before applying it to the soil. Many soil test labs will also analyze manures for their fertilizer value. (Without testing the manure or the soil following application, estimates can be made based on average manure values, such as those given in table 12.1, p. 131.) Because significant ammonia N losses can occur in as little as one or two days after manure application, the way to derive the full N benefit from manure is to incorporate it as soon as possible. Much of the manure N made available to the crop is in the ammonium form, and losses occur as some is

volatilized as ammonia gas when manures dry on the soil surface. A significant amount of the manure's N may also be lost when application is a long time before crop uptake occurs. About half of the N value of a fall manure application—even if incorporated—may be lost by the time of greatest crop need the following year.

Legumes, either as part of rotations or as cover crops, and well-managed grass sod crops can add N to the soil for use by the following crops (table 19.3). Nitrogen fertilizer decisions should take into account the amount of N contributed by manures, decomposing sods, and cover crops. If you correctly fill out the form that accompanies your soil sample, the recommendation you receive may take these sources into account. However, not all soil testing labs do take them into account; most do not even ask whether you've used a cover crop. If you can't find help deciding how to credit nutrients in organic sources, take a look at chapters 10 (cover crops), 11 (rotations), and 12 (animal manures). For an example of crediting the nutrient value of manure and cover crop, see the section "Making Adjustments to Fertilizer Application Rates," p. 250 in chapter 21.

Table 19.3
Examples of Nitrogen Credits for Previous Crops*

Previous Crop	N Credits (lbs/acre)
Corn and most other crops	0
Soybeans**	0–40*
Grass (low level of management)	40
Grass (intensively managed)	70
2-year stand red or white clover	70
3-year alfalfa stand (20–60% legume)	70
3-year alfalfa stand (>60% legume)	120
Hairy vetch cover crop (excellent growth)	110

*Less credit should be given for sandy soils with high amounts of leaching potential.
**Some labs give 30 or 40 pounds of N credit for soybeans, while others give no N credit. Credits can be higher in dry years (figure 19.2).

Relying on legumes to supply N to following crops. Nitrogen is the only nutrient of which you can "grow" your own supply. High-yielding legume cover crops, such as hairy vetch and crimson clover, can supply most, if not all, of the N needed by the following crop. Growing a legume as a forage crop (alfalfa, alfalfa/grass, clover, clover/grass) in rotation also can provide much, if not all, of the N for row crops. The N-related aspects of both cover crops and rotations with forages were discussed in chapters 10 and 11.

Animals on the farm or on nearby farms? If you have ruminant animals on your farm or on nearby farms for which you can grow forage crops (and perhaps use the manure on your farm), there are many possibilities for actually eliminating the need to use N fertilizers. A forage legume, such as alfalfa, red clover, or white clover, or a grass-legume mix can supply substantial N for the following crop. Frequently, nutrients are imported onto livestock-based farms as various feeds (usually grains and soybean meal mixes). This means that the manure from the animals will contain nutrients imported from outside the farm, and this reduces the need to purchase fertilizers.

No animals? Although land constraints don't usually allow it, some vegetable farmers grow a forage legume for one or more years as part of a rotation, even when they are not planning to sell the crop or feed it to animals. They do so to rest the soil and to enhance the soil's physical properties and nutrient status. Also, some cover crops, such as hairy vetch—grown off-season in the fall and early spring—can provide sufficient N for some of the high-demanding summer annuals. It's also possible to undersow sweet clover and then plow it under the next July to prepare for fall brassica crops.

Reducing N and P Losses

Use N and P fertilizers more efficiently. If you've worked to build and maintain soil organic matter, you should have plenty of active organic materials present. These readily decomposable small fragments provide N and P as they are decomposed, reducing the amount of fertilizer that's needed.

The timing and method of application of commercial fertilizers and manures affect the efficiency of use by crops and the amount of loss from soils—especially in humid climates. In general, it is best to apply fertilizers close to the time they are needed by plants. Losses of fertilizer and manure nutrients are also frequently reduced by soil incorporation with tillage.

If you're growing a crop for which a reliable in-season adaptive method is available, like the PSNT, spectroscopy, or a computer model, you can hold off applying most of the fertilizer until the test or model indicates a need. At that point, apply N as a sidedress or topdress. However, if you know that your soil is probably very N deficient (for example, a sandy soil low in organic matter), you may need to band-apply higher than normal levels of starter N at planting or broadcast some N before planting to supply sufficient N nutrition until the soil test indicates whether there is a need for more N (applied as a sidedress or topdress). For row crops in colder climates, about 15 to 20 pounds of starter N per acre (in a band at planting) is highly

NEW TECHNOLOGY FOR CORN NITROGEN FERTILIZATION

Corn is a tropical plant that is more efficient at utilizing N than most other crops—it produces more additional yield for each extra pound of N absorbed by the plant. But corn production systems as a whole have low efficiency of fertilizer N, typically less than 50%. Environmental N losses (leaching, denitrification, and runoff) are much higher for corn than for crops such as soybean and wheat, and especially when compared to alfalfa and grasses. This can be attributed to different crop growth cycles, fertilizer rates, fertilizer application schedules, timing of crop water and N uptake, and rooting depth. Intensive corn production areas have therefore become the focus of policy debates that address environmental concerns like groundwater contamination and low dissolved oxygen levels in estuaries.

Nitrogen management for corn is still mostly done without recognition of the effects of seasonal weather—particularly precipitation—that can cause high N losses through leaching and denitrification. The PSNT was the first approach that addressed these dynamic processes and therefore provided inherently more precise N fertilizer recommendations and eliminated a lot of unnecessary N applications. Still, many farmers like to apply additional "insurance fertilizer" because they want to be certain of an adequate N supply in wet years. But they may actually need it in only one out of four seasons. For those other years excess N application creates high environmental losses.

In addition to the PSNT, new technologies are emerging that allow us to more precisely manage N. Computer models and climate databases can be employed to adapt N recommendations by accounting for weather events and in-field soil variability. Also, crop reflectance of light, which is affected by the degree of N nutrition in the plant, can be measured using aerial and satellite images or tractor-mounted sensors and used to adjust sidedress N fertilizer rates on the go.

---

recommended. When organic farmers use fishmeal or seed meals to supply N to crops, they should plan on it becoming available over the season, with little available in the first weeks of decomposition.

Some of the N in surface-applied urea, the cheapest and most commonly used solid N fertilizer, is lost as a gas if it is not rapidly incorporated into the soil. If as little as a quarter inch of rain falls within a few days of surface urea application, N losses are usually less than 10%. However, losses may be 30% or more in some cases (a 50% loss may occur following surface application to a calcareous soil that is over pH 8). When urea is used for no-till systems, it can be placed below the surface. When fertilizer is broadcast as a topdress on grass or row crops, you might consider the economics of using ammonium nitrate. Although ammonium nitrate is more costly than urea per unit of N and not always readily available, its N is generally not lost as a gas when left on the surface. Anhydrous ammonia, the least expensive source of N fertilizer, causes large changes in soil pH in and around the injection band. The pH increases for a period of weeks, many organisms are killed, and organic matter is rendered more soluble. Eventually, the pH decreases, and the band is repopulated by soil organisms. However, significant N losses can occur when anhydrous is applied in a soil that is too dry or too wet. Even if stabilizers are used, anhydrous applied long before crop uptake significantly increases the amount of N that may be lost in humid regions.

If the soil is very deficient in P, P fertilizers are commonly incorporated to raise the general level of the nutrient. Incorporation is not possible with no-till systems, and, if the soil was initially very deficient, some P fertilizer should be incorporated before starting no-till. Nutrients accumulate near the surface of reduced tillage systems when fertilizers or manures are repeatedly surface-applied.

Reducing tillage usually leads to marked reductions of N and P loss in runoff and nitrate leaching loss to groundwater. However, there are two complicating factors that should be recognized:

- If intense storms occur soon after application of surface-applied urea or ammonium nitrate, N is more likely to be lost via leaching than if it had been incorporated. Much of the water will flow over the surface of no-till soils, picking up nitrate and urea, before entering wormholes and other channels. It then easily moves deep into the subsoil. It is best not to broadcast fertilizer and leave it on the surface with a no-till system.

- P accumulates on the surface of no-till soils (because there is no incorporation of broadcast fertilizers, manures, crop residues, or cover crops). Although there is less runoff, fewer sediments, and less total P lost with no-till, the concentration of dissolved P in the runoff may actually be higher than for conventionally tilled soils.

This is when band application may be preferred.

In soils with optimal P levels, some P fertilizer is still recommended, along with N application, for row crops in cool regions. (Potassium is also commonly recommended under these conditions.) Frequently, the soils are cold enough in the spring to slow down root development, P diffusion toward the root, and mineralization of P from organic matter, reducing P availability to seedlings. This is probably why it is a good idea to use some starter P in these regions—even if the soil is in the optimal P soil test range.

Use perennial forages (sod-forming crops) in rotations. As we've discussed a number of times, rotations that include a perennial forage crop help reduce runoff and erosion; build better soil tilth; break harmful weed, insect, and nematode cycles; and build soil organic matter. Decreasing the emphasis on row crops in a rotation and including perennial forages also help decrease leaching losses of nitrate. This happens for two main reasons:

1. There is less water leaching under a sod because it uses more water over the entire growing season than does an annual row crop (which has a bare soil in the spring and after harvest in the fall).

2. Nitrate concentrations under sod rarely reach anywhere near as high as those under row crops.

So, whether the rotation includes a grass, a legume, or a legume-grass mix, the amount of nitrate leaching to groundwater is usually reduced. (A critical step, however, is the conversion from sod to row crop. When a sod crop is plowed, a lot of N is mineralized. If this occurs many months before the row crop takes it up, high nitrate leaching and denitrification losses occur.) Using grass, legume, or grass-legume forages in the rotation also helps with P management because of the reduction of runoff and erosion and the effects on soil structure for the following crop.

Use cover crops to prevent nutrient losses. High levels of soil nitrate may be left at the end of the growing season if drought causes a poor crop year or if excess N fertilizer or manure has been applied. The potential for nitrate leaching and runoff can be reduced greatly if you sow a fast-growing cover crop like winter rye immediately after the main crop has been harvested. One option available to help manage N is to use a combination of a legume and grass. The combination of hairy vetch and winter rye works well in cooler temperate regions. When nitrate is scarce, the vetch does much better than the rye and a large amount of N is fixed for the next crop. On the other hand, the rye competes well with the vetch when nitrate is plentiful; less N is fixed (of course, less is needed); and much of the nitrate is tied up in the rye and stored for future use.

In general, having any cover crop on the soil during the off-season is helpful for P management. A cover crop that establishes quickly and helps protect the soil against erosion will help reduce P losses.

Reduce tillage. Because most P is lost from fields by erosion of sediments, environmentally sound P management should include reduced tillage systems. Leaving residues on the surface and maintaining stable soil aggregation and lots of large pores help water to infiltrate into soils. When runoff does occur, less sediment is carried along with it than if conventional plow-harrow tillage is used. Reduced tillage, by decreasing runoff and erosion, usually decreases both P and N losses from fields. Recent studies also showed that reduced tillage results in more effective N cycling. Although N fertilizer needs are generally slightly higher in early transition years, long-term no-tillage increases organic matter contents over conventional tillage and also, after some years, results in 30 to 50 pounds per acre more N mineralization, a significant economic benefit to the farm.

Working Toward Balancing Nutrient Imports and Exports

Nitrogen and phosphorus are lost from soils in many ways, including runoff that takes both N and P, leaching of nitrate (and in some situations P, as well), denitrification, and volatilization of ammonia from surface-applied urea and manures. Even if you take all precautions to reduce unnecessary losses, some loss of N and P will occur. While you can easily overdo it with fertilizers, use of more N and P than needed also occurs on many livestock farms that import a significant proportion of their feeds. If a forage legume, such as alfalfa, is an important part of the rotation, the combination of biological N fixation plus imported N in feeds may exceed the farm's needs. A reasonable goal for farms with a large net inflow of N and P would be to try to reduce imports of these nutrients on farms (including legume N), or increase exports, to a point closer to balance.

On crop farms, as well as livestock-based farms with low numbers of animals per acre, it's fairly easy to bring inflows and outflows into balance by properly crediting

N from the previous crop and N and P in manure. On the other hand, it is a more challenging problem when there are a large number of animals for a fixed land base and a large percentage of the feed must be imported. This happens frequently on factory-type animal production facilities, but it can also happen on smaller, family-sized farms. At some point, thought needs to be given to either expanding the farm's land base or exporting some of the manure to other farms. In the Netherlands, nutrient accumulation on livestock farms became a national problem and generated legislation that limits animal units on farms. One option is to compost the manure—which makes it easier to transport or sell and causes some N losses during the composting process—stabilizing the remaining N before application. On the other hand, the availability of P in manure is not greatly affected by composting. That's why using compost to supply a particular amount of "available" N usually results in applications of larger total amounts of P than plants need.

Using Organic Sources of Phosphorus and Potassium

Manures and other organic amendments are frequently applied to soils at rates estimated to satisfy N needs of crops. This commonly adds more P and potassium than the crop needs. After many years of continuous application of these sources to meet N needs, soil test levels for P and potassium may be in the very high (excessive) range. Although there are a number of ways to deal with this issue, all solutions require reduced applications of fertilizer P and P-containing organic amendments. If it's a farm-wide problem, some manure may need to be exported and N fertilizer or legumes relied on to provide N to grain crops. Sometimes, it's just a question of better distribution of manure around the various fields—getting to those fields far from the barn more regularly. Changing the rotation to include crops such as alfalfa, for which no manure N is needed, can help. However, if you're raising livestock on a limited land base, you should make arrangements to have the manure used on a neighboring farm or sell the manure to a composting facility.

Managing High-P Soils

High-P soils occur because of a history of either excessive applications of P fertilizers or—more commonly—application of lots of manure. This is a problem on livestock farms with limited land and where a medium to high percentage of feed is imported. The nutrients imported in feeds may greatly exceed the nutrients exported in animal products. In addition, where manures or composts are used at rates required to provide sufficient N to crops, more P than needed usually is added. It's probably a good idea to reduce the potential for P loss from all high-P soils. However, it is especially important to reduce the risk of environmental harm from those high-P soils that are also likely to produce significant runoff (because of steep slope, fine texture, poor structure, or poor drainage).

There are a number of practices that should be followed with high-P soils:

- First, deal with the "front end" and reduce animal P intake to the lowest levels needed. Not that long ago a survey found that the average dairy herd in the U.S. was fed about 25% more P than recommended by the standard authority (the National Research Council, or NRC). Using so much extra can cost dairy farmers thousands of dollars to feed a 100-cow herd supplemental P that the animals don't need and that ends up as a potential pollutant.

- Second, reduce or eliminate applications of extra P. For a livestock farm, this may mean obtaining the use of more land to grow crops and to spread manure over a larger land area. For a crop farm, this may mean using legume cover crops and forages in rotations to supply N without adding P. The cover crops and forage rotation crops are also helpful to build up and maintain good organic matter levels in the absence of importing manures or composts or other organic material from off the farm. The lack of imported organic sources of nutrients (to try to reduce P imports) means that a crop farmer will need more creative use of crop residues, rotations, and cover crops to maintain good organic matter levels. Also, don't use a high-P source to meet N demands. Compost has many benefits, but if used to provide N fertility, it will build up P over the long term.

- Third, reduce runoff and erosion to minimal levels. P is usually a problem only if it gets into surface waters. Anything that helps water infiltration or impedes water and sediments from leaving the field—reduced tillage, strip cropping along the contour, cover crops, grassed waterways, riparian buffer strips, etc.—decreases problems caused by high-P soils. (Note: Significant P losses in tile drainage water have been observed, especially from fields where large amounts of liquid manure are applied.)

- Fourth, continue to monitor soil P levels. Soil test P will slowly decrease over the years, once P imports, as fertilizers, organic amendments, or feeds, are reduced or eliminated. Soils should be tested every two or three years for other reasons, anyway. So just remember to keep track of soil test P to confirm that levels are decreasing.

Phosphorus accumulates especially rapidly in the surface of no-till soils that have received large applications of manure or fertilizer over the years. One management option in these cases is a one-time tillage of the soil to incorporate the high-P layer. If this is done, follow practices that don't result in building up surface soil P once again.

SUMMARY

Both N and P are needed by plants in large amounts, but when soils are too rich in these nutrients, they are environmental hazards. And although N and P behave differently in soils, most sound management practices for one are also sound for the other. Using soil tests (and for N on corn the end-of-season lower stalk nitrate test) and modern nutrient management planning that credits all sources, such as manures and decomposing sods, can help better manage these nutrients. Reduced tillage, cover crops, and rotation with sod crops decrease runoff and erosion and help in many other ways, including better N and P management.

SOURCES

Balkcom, K.S., A.M. Blackmer, D.J. Hansen, T.F. Morris, and A.P. Mallarino. 2003. Testing soils and cornstalks to evaluate nitrogen management on the watershed scale. *Journal of Environmental Quality* 32: 1015–1024.

Brady, N.C., and R.R. Weil. 2008. *The Nature and Properties of Soils*, 14th ed. Upper Saddle River, NJ: Prentice Hall.

Cassman, K.G., A. Dobermann, and D.T. Walters. 2002. Agroecosystems, nitrogen-use efficiency, and nitrogen management. *Ambio* 31: 132–140.

Jokela, B., F. Magdoff, R. Bartlett, S. Bosworth, and D. Ross. 1998. Nutrient Recommendations for *Field Crops in Vermont*. Burlington: University of Vermont, Extension Service.

Kay, B.D., A.A. Mahboubi, E.G. Beauchamps, and R.S. Dharmakeerthi. 2006. Integrating soil and weather data to describe variability in plant available nitrogen. *Soil Science Society of America Journal* 70: 1210–1221.

Laboski, C.A.M., J.E. Sawyer, D.T. Walters, L.G. Bundy, R.G. Hoeft, G.W. Randall, and T.W. Andraski. 2008. Evaluation of the Illinois Soil Nitrogen Test in the North Central region of the United States. *Agronomy Journal* 100: 1070–1076.

Magdoff, F.R. 1991. Understanding the Magdoff pre-sidedress nitrate soil test for corn. *Journal of Production Agriculture* 4: 297–305.

Melkonian, J., H.M. van Es, A.T. DeGaetano, J.M. Sogbedji, and L. Joseph. 2007. Application of dynamic simulation modeling for nitrogen management in maize. In *Managing Crop Nutrition for Weather,* ed. T. Bruulsema, pp. 14–22. Norcross, GA: International Plant Nutrition Institute Publication.

Mitsch, W.J., J.W. Day, J.W. Gilliam, P.M. Groffman, D.L. Hey, G.W. Randall, and N. Wang. 2001. Reducing nitrogen loading to the Gulf of Mexico from the Mississippi River basin: Strategies to counter a persistent ecological problem. *BioScience* 51: 373–388.

National Research Council. 1988. *Nutrient Requirements of Dairy Cattle,* 6th rev. ed. Washington, DC: National Academy Press.

Olness, A.E., D. Lopez, J. Cordes, C. Sweeney, and W.B. Voorhees. 1998. Predicting nitrogen fertilizer needs using soil and climatic data. In *Procedures of the 11th World Fertilizer Congress,* Gent, Belgium, Sept. 7–13, 1997, ed. A. Vermoesen, pp. 356–364. Gent, Belgium: International Centre of Fertilizers.

Sawyer, J., E. Nafziger, G. Randall, L. Bundy, G. Rehm, and B. Joern. 2006. *Concepts and Rationale for Regional Nitrogen Guidelines for Corn.* Iowa State University Extension Publication PM2015, 27 pp.

Sharpley, A.N. 1996. Myths about P. *Proceedings from the Animal Agriculture and the Environment North American Conference,* Dec. 11–13, Rochester, NY. Ithaca, NY: Northeast Region Agricultural Engineering Service.

van Alphen, B.J., and J.J. Stoorvogel. 2000. A methodology for precision nitrogen fertilization in high-input farming systems. *Precision Agriculture* 2: 319–332.

Vigil, M.F., and D.E. Kissel. 1991. Equations for estimating the amount of nitrogen mineralized from crop residues. *Soil Science Society of America Journal* 55: 757–761.

Wortmann, C., M. Helmers, A. Mallarino, C. Barden, D. Devlin, G. Pierzynski, J. Lory, R. Massey, J. Holz, and C. Shapiro. 2005. *Agricultural Phosphorus Management and Water Quality Protection in the Midwest.* Lincoln: University of Nebraska.

Chapter 20

OTHER FERTILITY ISSUES: NUTRIENTS, CEC, ACIDITY, AND ALKALINITY

The potential available nutrients in a soil, whether natural or added in manures or fertilizer, are only in part utilized by plants . . .

—T.L. LYON AND E.O. FIPPIN, 1909

OTHER NUTRIENTS

Although farmers understandably focus on nitrogen and phosphorus—because of the large quantities used and the potential for environmental problems—additional nutrient and soil chemical issues remain important. Overuse of other fertilizers and amendments seldom causes problems for the environment, but it may waste money and reduce yields. There are also animal health considerations. For example, excess potassium in feeds for dry cows (cows that are between lactations) results in metabolic problems, and low magnesium availability to dairy or beef cows in early lactation can cause grass tetany. As with most other issues we have discussed, focusing on the management practices that build up and maintain soil organic matter will help eliminate many problems or at least make them easier to manage.

Potassium (K) is one of the N-P-K "big three" primary nutrients needed in large amounts, but in humid regions it is frequently not present in sufficient quantities for optimum yields of crops. It's generally available to plants as a cation, and the soil's *cation exchange capacity* (CEC) is the main storehouse for this element for a given year's crop. Potassium availability to plants is sometimes decreased when a soil is limed to increase its pH by one or two units. The extra calcium, as well as the "pull" on potassium exerted by the new cation exchange sites (see the next section, "Cation Exchange Capacity Management"), contributes to lower potassium availability. Problems with low potassium levels are usually dealt with easily by applying muriate of potash (potassium chloride), potassium sulfate, or sul-po-mag or K-mag (potassium and magnesium sulfate). Manures also usually contain large quantities of potassium.

Magnesium deficiency is easily corrected if the soil is acidic by using a high-magnesium (dolomitic) limestone to raise the soil pH (see "Soil Acidity," p. 230). If K is also low and the soil does not need liming, sul-po-mag

Photo by Dennis Nolan

> The risk for sulfur deficiency varies with the soil type, the crops grown on the soil, the manure history, and the level of organic matter in the soil. A deficiency is more likely to occur on acidic, sandy soils; soils with low organic matter levels and high nitrogen inputs; and soils that are cold and dry in the spring, which condition decreases sulfur mineralization from soil organic matter. Manure is a significant supplier of sulfur, and manured fields are not likely to be S deficient; however, sulfur content in manure can vary.
>
> —S. PLACE ET AL. (2007)

is one of the best choices for correcting an Mg deficiency. For a soil that has sufficient K and is at a satisfactory pH, a straight Mg source such as magnesium sulfate (Epsom salts) would be a good choice.

Calcium deficiencies are generally associated with low pH soils and soils with low CECs. The best remedy is usually to lime and build up the soil's organic matter. However, some important crops, such as peanuts, potatoes, and apples, commonly need added calcium. Calcium additions also may be needed to help alleviate soil structure and nutrition problems of sodic soils (see "Remediation of Sodic (Alkali) and Saline Soils," p. 233). In general, if the soil does not have too much sodium, is properly limed, and has a reasonable amount of organic matter, there will be no advantage to adding a calcium source, such as gypsum. However, soils with very low aggregate stability may sometimes benefit from the extra salt concentration and calcium associated with surface gypsum applications. This is not a calcium nutrition effect but a stabilizing effect of the dissolving gypsum salt. Higher soil organic matter and surface residues should do as well as gypsum to alleviate this problem.

Sulfur deficiencies are common on soils with low organic matter. Some soil testing labs around the country offer a sulfur soil test. (Those of you who grow garlic should know that a good supply of sulfur is important for the full development of garlic's pungent flavor.) Much of the sulfur in soils occurs as organic matter, so building up and maintaining organic matter should result in sufficient sulfur nutrition for plants. Although reports of crop response to added sulfur in the Northeast are rare, it is thought that deficiencies of this element may become more common now that there is less sulfur air pollution, originating mainly in the Midwest. Some fertilizers used for other purposes, such as sul-po-mag and ammonium sulfate, contain sulfur. Calcium sulfate (gypsum) also can be applied to remedy low soil sulfur. The amounts used on sulfur-deficient soils are typically 20 to 25 pounds of sulfur per acre.

Zinc deficiencies occur with certain crops on soils low in organic matter and in sandy soils or soils with a pH at or above neutral. Zinc problems are sometimes noted on silage corn when manure hasn't been applied for a while. Zinc also can be deficient following topsoil removal from parts of fields as land is leveled for furrow irrigation. Cool and wet conditions may cause zinc to be deficient early in the season. Sometimes crops outgrow the problem as the soil warms up and organic sources become more available to plants. Applying about 10 pounds of zinc sulfate (which contains about 3 pounds of zinc) to soils is one method used to correct zinc deficiencies. If the deficiency is due to high pH, or if an orchard crop is zinc deficient, a foliar application is commonly used. If a soil test before planting an orchard reveals low zinc levels, zinc sulfate should be applied.

Boron deficiencies show up in alfalfa when it grows on eroded knolls where the topsoil and organic matter have been lost. Root crops seem to need higher soil boron levels than many other crops. Cole crops, apples, celery, and spinach are also sensitive to low boron levels. The most common fertilizer used to correct a boron deficiency is sodium tetraborate (about 15% boron). Borax (about 11% boron), a compound containing sodium borate, also can be used to correct boron deficiencies. On sandy soils low in organic matter, boron may be needed on a routine basis. Apply no more than 3 pounds of actual B (about 27 pounds of borax) per acre at any one time—it can be toxic to some plants at higher rates.

Manganese deficiency, usually associated with soybeans and cereals grown on high-pH soils and vegetables grown on muck soils, is corrected with the use of manganese sulfate (about 27% manganese). About 10 pounds of water-soluble manganese per acre should satisfy plant needs for a number of years. Up to 25 pounds per acre of manganese is recommended if the fertilizer is broadcast on a very deficient soil. Natural, as well as synthetic, chelates (at about 5% to 10% manganese) usually are applied as a foliar spray.

Iron deficiency occurs in blueberries when they are grown on moderate- to high-pH soils, especially a pH of over 6.5. Iron deficiency also sometimes occurs on soybeans, wheat, sorghum, and peanuts growing on soil with a pH greater than 7.5. Iron (ferrous) sulfate or chelated iron is used to correct iron deficiency. Both manganese and iron deficiencies are frequently corrected by using foliar application of inorganic salts.

Copper is another nutrient that is sometimes deficient in high-pH soils. It is also sometimes deficient in organic soils (soils with 10–20% or more organic matter). Some crops—for example, tomatoes, lettuce, beets, onions, and spinach—have a relatively high copper need. A number of copper sources, such as copper sulfate and copper chelates, can be used to correct a copper deficiency.

CATION EXCHANGE CAPACITY MANAGEMENT

The CEC in soils is due to well-humified ("very dead") organic matter and clay minerals. The total CEC in a soil is the sum of the CEC due to organic matter and due to clays. In fine-textured soils with medium- to high-CEC clays, much of the CEC may be due to clays. On the other hand, in sandy loams with little clay, or in some of the soils of the southeastern U.S. that contain clays with low CEC, organic matter may account for an overwhelming fraction of the total CEC.

There are two practical ways to increase the ability of soils to hold nutrient cations such as potassium, calcium, magnesium, and ammonium:

- Add organic matter by using the methods discussed in earlier chapters.
- If the soil is too acidic, use lime (see "pH Management," p. 231) to raise its pH to the high end of the range needed for the crops you grow.

One of the benefits of liming acid soils is increasing soil CEC. Here's why: As the pH increases, so does the CEC of organic matter as well as some clay minerals. As hydrogen (H^+) on humus is neutralized by liming, the site where it was attached now has a negative charge and can hold Ca^{++}, Mg^{++}, K^+, etc.

Many soil testing labs will run CEC if asked. However, there are a number of possible ways to do the test. Some labs determine what the CEC would be if the soil's pH was 7 or higher. They do this by adding the

---

ESTIMATING ORGANIC MATTER'S CONTRIBUTION TO A SOIL'S CEC

The CEC of a soil is usually expressed in terms of the number of milliequivalents (me) of negative charge per 100 grams of soil. (The actual number of charges represented by one me is about 6 followed by 20 zeros.) A useful rule of thumb for estimating the CEC due to organic matter is as follows: For every pH unit above pH 4.5, there is 1 me of CEC in 100 grams of soil for every percent of organic matter. (Don't forget that there will also be CEC due to clays.) SOM = soil organic matter.

Example 1: pH = 5.0 and 3% SOM → (5.0 − 4.5) x 3 = 1.5 me/100g

Example 2: pH = 6.0 and 3% SOM → (6.0 − 4.5) x 3 = 4.5 me/100g

Example 3: pH = 7.0 and 3% SOM → (7.0 − 4.5) x 3 = 7.5 me/100g

Example 4: pH = 7.0 and 4% SOM → (7.0 − 4.5) x 4 = 10.0 me/100g

---

SOIL ACIDITY

Background

- pH 7 is neutral.
- Soil with pH levels above 7 are alkaline; those of less than 7 are acidic.
- The lower the pH, the more acidic is the soil.
- Soils in humid regions tend to be acidic; those in semiarid and arid regions tend to be around neutral or alkaline.
- Acidification is a natural process.
- Most commercial nitrogen fertilizers are acid forming, but many manures are not.
- Crops have different pH needs—probably related to nutrient availability or susceptibility to aluminum toxicity at low pH.
- Organic acids on humus and aluminum on the CEC account for most of the acid in soils.

Management

- Use limestone to raise the soil pH (if magnesium is also low, use a high-magnesium—or dolomitic—lime).
- Mix lime thoroughly into the plow layer.
- Spread lime well in advance of sensitive crops if at all possible.
- If the lime requirement is high—some labs say greater than 2 tons; others say greater than 4 tons—consider splitting the application over two years.
- Reducing soil pH (making soil more acid) for acid-loving crops is done best with elemental sulfur (S).

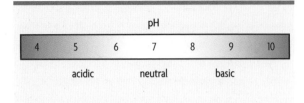

Figure 20.1. Soil pH and acid-base status.
Note: Soils at pH 7.5–8 frequently contain fine particles of lime (calcium carbonate). Soils above pH 8.5–9 usually have excess sodium (sodic, also called alkali, soils).

SOIL ACIDITY

Background

Many soils, especially in humid regions, were acidic before they were ever farmed. Leaching of bases from soils and the acids produced during organic matter decomposition combined to make these soils naturally acidic. As soils were brought into production and organic matter was decomposed (mineralized), more acids were formed. In addition, all the commonly used N fertilizers are acidic—needing from 4 to 7 pounds of agricultural limestone to neutralize the acid formed from each pound of N applied to soils.

Plants have evolved under specific environments, which in turn influence their needs as agricultural crops. For example, alfalfa originated in a semiarid region where soil pH was high; alfalfa requires a pH in the range of 6.5 to 6.8 or higher (see figure 20.1 for common soil pH levels). On the other hand, blueberries, which evolved under acidic conditions, require a low pH to provide needed iron (iron is more soluble at low pH). Other crops, such as peanuts, watermelons, and sweet potatoes, do best in moderately acid soils in the range of pH 5 to 6. Most other agricultural plants do best in the range of pH 6 to 7.5.

Several problems may cause poor growth of acid-sensitive plants in low pH soils. The following are three common ones:

- aluminum and manganese are more soluble and can be toxic to plants;

acidity that would be neutralized if the soil was limed to the current soil CEC. This is the CEC the soil *would* have at the higher pH but is not the soil's current CEC. For this reason, some labs total the major cations actually held on the CEC ($Ca^{++} + K^+ + Mg^{++}$) and call it *effective CEC*. It is more useful to know the effective CEC—the actual current CEC of the soil—than CEC determined at a higher pH.

- calcium, magnesium, potassium, phosphorus, or molybdenum (especially needed for nitrogen fixation by legumes) may be deficient; and
- decomposition of soil organic matter is slowed and causes decreased mineralization of nitrogen.

The problems caused by soil acidity are usually less severe, and the optimum pH is lower, if the soil is well supplied with organic matter. Organic matter helps to make aluminum less toxic, and, of course, humus increases the soil's CEC. Soil pH will not change as rapidly in soils that are high in organic matter. Soil acidification is a natural process that is accelerated by acids produced in soil by most nitrogen fertilizers. Soil organic matter slows down acidification and buffers the soil's pH because it holds the acid hydrogen tightly. Therefore, more acid is needed to decrease the pH by a given amount when a lot of organic matter is present. Of course, the reverse is also true—more lime is needed to raise the pH of high-organic-matter soils by a given amount (see "Soil Acidity" box, p. 230).

Limestone application helps create a more hospitable soil for acid-sensitive plants in many ways, such as the following:

- by neutralizing acids;
- by adding calcium in large quantities (because limestone is calcium carbonate, $CaCO_3$);
- by adding magnesium in large quantities if dolomitic limestone is used (containing carbonates of both calcium and magnesium);
- by making molybdenum and phosphorus more available;
- by helping to maintain added phosphorus in an available form;
- by enhancing bacterial activity, including the rhizobia that fix nitrogen in legumes; and
- by making aluminum and manganese less soluble.

Almost all the acid in acidic soils is held in reserve on the solids, with an extremely small amount active in the soil water. If all that we needed to neutralize was the acid in the soil water, a few handfuls of lime per acre would be enough to do the job, even in a very acid soil. However, tons of lime per acre are needed to raise the pH. The explanation for this is that almost all of the acid that must be neutralized in soils is reserve acidity associated with either organic matter or aluminum.

pH Management

Increasing the pH of acidic soils is usually accomplished by adding ground or crushed limestone. Three pieces of information are used to determine the amount of lime that's needed:

1. What is the soil pH? Knowing this and the needs of the crops you are growing will tell you whether lime is needed and what target pH you are shooting for. If the soil pH is much lower than the pH needs of the crop, you need to use lime. But the pH value doesn't tell you how much lime is needed.

2. What is the lime requirement needed to change the pH to the desired level? (The lime requirement is the amount of lime needed to neutralize the hydrogen, as well as the reactive aluminum, associated with organic matter.) A number of different tests used by soil testing laboratories estimate soil lime requirements. Most give the results in terms of tons per acre of agricultural grade limestone to reach the desired pH.

Soil testing labs usually use the information you provide about your cropping intentions and integrate the three issues (see the discussion under "pH Management," above, of the three pieces of information needed) when recommending limestone application rates. Laws govern the quality of limestone sold in each state. Soil testing labs give recommendations based on the use of ground limestone that meets the minimum state standard.

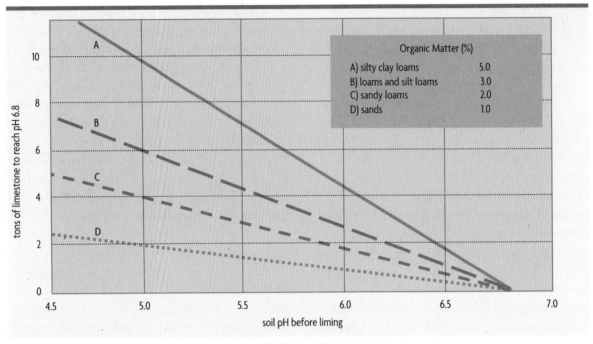

Figure 20.2. Examples of approximate lime needed to reach pH 6.8. Modified from Peech (1961).

3. Is the limestone you use very different from the one assumed in the soil test report? The fineness and the amount of carbonate present govern the effectiveness of limestone—how much it will raise the soil's pH. If the lime you will be using has an effective calcium carbonate equivalent that's very different from the one used as the base in the report, the amount applied may need to be adjusted upward (if the lime is very coarse or has a high level of impurities) or downward (if the lime is very fine, is high in magnesium, and contains few impurities).

Soils with more clay and more organic matter need more lime to change their pH (see figure 20.2). Although organic matter buffers the soil against pH decreases, it also buffers against pH increases when you are trying to raise the pH with limestone. Most states recommend a soil pH of around 6.8 only for the most sensitive crops, such as alfalfa, and of about 6.2 to 6.5 for many of the clovers. As pointed out above, most of the commonly grown crops do well in the range of pH 6.0 to 7.5.

There are other liming materials in addition to limestone. One commonly used in some parts of the U.S. is wood ash. Ash from a modern airtight wood-burning stove may have a fairly high calcium carbonate content (80% or higher). However, ash that is mainly black— indicating incompletely burned wood—may have as little as 40% effective calcium carbonate equivalent. Lime sludge from wastewater treatment plants and fly ash sources may be available in some locations. Normally, minor sources like these are not locally available in sufficient quantities to put much of a dent in the lime needs of a region. Because they might carry unwanted contaminants to the farm, be sure that any new by-product liming sources are field tested and thoroughly evaluated for metals before you use them.

"Overliming" injury. Sometimes problems are created when soils are limed, especially when a very acidic soil has been quickly raised to high pH levels. Decreased crop growth because of "overliming" injury is usually associated with a lowered availability of phosphorus, potassium, or boron, although zinc, copper, and manganese deficiencies can be produced by liming acidic sandy soils. If there is a long history of the use of triazine herbicides, such as atrazine, liming may release these chemicals and kill sensitive crops.

Need to lower the soil's pH? When growing plants that require a low pH, you may want to add acidity to the soil. This is probably only economically possible for blueberries and is most easily done with elemental sulfur (S), which is converted into an acid by soil microorganisms over a few months. For the examples in figure 20.2, the amount of S needed to drop the pH by one unit would be approximately 3/4 ton per acre for silty clay loams, 1/2 ton per acre for loams and silt loams, 600 pounds per acre for sandy loams, and 300 pounds per acre for sands. Sulfur should be applied the year before planting blueberries. Alum (aluminum sulfate) may also be used to acidify soils. About six times more alum than elemental sulfur is needed to achieve the same pH change. If your soil is calcareous—usually with a pH over 7.5 and naturally containing calcium carbonate—don't even try to decrease the pH. Acidifying material will have no lasting effect on the pH because it will be fully neutralized by the soil's lime.

REMEDIATION OF SODIC (ALKALI) AND SALINE SOILS

The origin and characteristics of saline and sodic soils were discussed at the end of chapter 6, p. 65. There are a number of ways to deal with saline soils that don't have shallow salty groundwater. One is to keep the soil continually moist. For example, if you use drip irrigation with low-salt water plus a surface mulch, the salt content will not get as high as it would if allowed to concentrate when the soil dries. Another way is to grow crops or varieties of crops that are more tolerant of soil salinity. Saline-tolerant plants include barley, Bermuda grass, oak, rosemary, and willow. However, the only way to get rid of the salt is to add sufficient water to wash it below the root zone. If the subsoil does not drain well, drainage tiles might need to be installed to get rid of the salty water leached from the soil. (However, this means that a high-salt water is being discharged into a ditch and may harm downstream water quality.) The amount of water needed to do this is related to the salt content of the irrigation water, expressed as electrical conductivity (ECw), and the salt content desired in the drainage water, expressed as electrical conductivity (ECdw). The amount of water needed can be calculated using the following equation:

Water needed = (amount of water needed to saturate soil) x (ECw/ECdw)

The amount of extra irrigation water needed to leach salts is also related to the sensitivity of the plants that you're growing. For example, sensitive crops like onions and strawberries may have twice the leaching requirement of moderately sensitive broccoli or tomatoes. Drip irrigation uses relatively low amounts of water, so lack of leaching may cause salt buildup even for moderately saline irrigation sources. This means that the leaching may need to occur during the growing season, but care is needed to prevent leaching of nitrate below the root zone.

For sodic soils, a calcium source is added—usually gypsum (calcium sulfate). The calcium replaces sodium held by the cation exchange capacity. The soil is then irrigated so that the sodium can be leached deep into the soil. Because the calcium in gypsum easily replaces the sodium on the CEC, the amount of gypsum needed can be estimated as follows: For every milliequivalent of sodium that needs to be replaced to 1 foot, about 2 tons of agricultural-grade gypsum is needed per acre. Adding gypsum to nonsodic soils doesn't help physical properties if the soil is properly limed, except for those soils that contain easily dispersible clay and are also low in organic matter.

SOURCES

Hanson, B.R., S.R. Grattan, and A. Fulton. 1993. *Agricultural Salinity and Drainage*. Publication 3375. Oakland: University of California, Division of Agriculture and Natural Resources.

Havlin, J.L., J.D. Beaton, S.L. Tisdale, and W.I. Nelson. 2005. *Soil Fertility and Fertilizers*. Upper Saddle River, NJ: Pearson/Prentice Hall.

Magdoff, F.R., and R.J. Bartlett. 1985. Soil pH buffering revisited. *Soil Science Society of America Journal* 49: 145–148.

Peech, M. 1961. *Lime Requirement vs. Soil pH Curves for Soils of New York State*. Mimeographed. Ithaca, NY: Cornell University Agronomy Department.

Pettygrove, G.S., S.R. Grattan, T.K. Hartz, L.E. Jackson, T.R. Lockhart, K.F. Schulbach, and R. Smith. 1998. *Production Guide: Nitrogen and Water Management for Coastal Cool-Season Vegetables*. Publication 21581. Oakland: University of California, Division of Agriculture and Natural Resources.

Place, S., T. Kilcer, Q. Ketterings, D. Cherney, and J. Cherney. 2007. *Sulfur for Field Crops*. Agronomy Fact Sheet Series no. 34. Ithaca, NY: Cornell University Cooperative Extension.

Rehm, G. 1994. *Soil Cation Ratios for Crop Production*. North Central Regional Extension Publication 533. St. Paul: University of Minnesota Extension Service.

Chapter 21

GETTING THE MOST
FROM ROUTINE SOIL TESTS

. . . the popular mind is still fixed on the idea that a fertilizer is the panacea.

—J.L. HILLS, C.H. JONES, AND C. CUTLER, 1908

Although fertilizers and other amendments purchased from off the farm are not a panacea to cure all soil problems, they play an important role in maintaining soil productivity. Soil testing is the farmer's best means for determining which amendments or fertilizers are needed and how much should be used.

The soil test report provides the soil's nutrient and pH levels and, in arid climates, the salt and sodium levels. Recommendations for application of nutrients and amendments accompany most reports. They are based on soil nutrient levels, past cropping, and manure management and should be a customized recommendation based on the crop you plan to grow.

Soil tests—and proper interpretation of results—are an important tool for developing a farm nutrient management program. However, deciding how much fertilizer to apply—or the total amount of nutrients needed from various sources—is part science, part philosophy, and part art. Understanding soil tests and how to interpret them can help farmers better customize the test's

recommendations. In this chapter, we'll go over sources of confusion about soil tests, discuss N and P soil tests, and then examine a number of soil tests to see how the information they provide can help you make decisions about fertilizer application.

TAKING SOIL SAMPLES

The usual time to take soil samples for general fertility evaluation is in the fall or the spring, before the growing season has begun. These samples are analyzed for pH and lime requirement as well as phosphorus, potassium, calcium, and magnesium. Some labs also routinely analyze for organic matter and other selected nutrients, such as boron, zinc, sulfur, and manganese. Whether you sample a particular field in the fall or in the early spring, stay consistent and repeat samples at approximately the same time of the year and use the same laboratory for analysis. As you will see below, this allows you to make better year-to-year comparisons.

Photo by Dena Leibman

GUIDELINES FOR TAKING SOIL SAMPLES

1. Don't wait until the last minute. The best time to sample for a general soil test is usually in the fall. Spring samples should be taken early enough to have the results in time to properly plan nutrient management for the crop season.

2. Take cores from at least fifteen to twenty spots randomly over the field to obtain a representative sample. One sample should not represent more than 10 to 20 acres.

3. Sample between rows. Avoid old fence rows, dead furrows, and other spots that are not representative of the whole field.

4. Take separate samples from problem areas if they can be treated separately.

5. Soils are not homogeneous—nutrient levels can vary widely with different crop histories or topographic settings. Sometimes different colors are a clue to different nutrient contents. Consider sampling some areas separately, even if yields are not noticeably different from the rest of the field.

6. In cultivated fields, sample to plow depth.

7. Take two samples from no-till fields: one to a 6-inch depth for lime and fertilizer recommendations, and one to a 2-inch depth to monitor surface acidity.

8. Sample permanent pastures to a 3- or 4-inch depth.

9. Collect the samples in a clean container.

10. Mix the core samplings, remove roots and stones, and allow mixed sample to air dry.

11. Fill the soil-test mailing container.

12. Complete the information sheet, giving all of the information requested. Remember, the recommendations are only as good as the information supplied.

13. Sample fields at least every three years and at the same season of the year each time. On higher-value crops annual soil tests will allow you to fine-tune nutrient management and may allow you to cut down on fertilizer use.

Note: For a discussion of how to sample to assess the extent of nutrient variability across a large field, see the section "Managing Field Nutrient Variability," p. 251.

—MODIFIED FROM *THE PENN STATE AGRONOMY GUIDE* (2007–2008)

ACCURACY OF RECOMMENDATIONS BASED ON SOIL TESTS

Soil tests and their recommendations, although a critical component of fertility management, are not 100% accurate. Soil tests are an important tool, but they need to be used by farmers and farm advisors along with other information to make the best decision regarding amounts of fertilizers or amendments to apply.

Soil tests are an estimate of a limited number of plant nutrients based on a small sample, which is supposed to represent many acres in a field. With soil testing, the answers aren't as certain as we might like them to be. A low-potassium soil test indicates that you will probably increase yield by adding the nutrient. However, adding fertilizer may not increase crop yields in a field with a low soil test level. The higher yields may be prevented because the soil test is not calibrated for that particular soil (and because the soil had sufficient potassium for the crop despite the low test level) or because of harm caused by poor drainage or compaction. Occasionally, using extra nutrients on a high-testing soil increases crop yields. Weather conditions may have made the nutrient less available than indicated by the soil test. So it's important to use common sense when interpreting soil test results.

SOURCES OF CONFUSION ABOUT SOIL TESTS

People may be easily confused about the details of soil tests, especially if they have seen results from more than one soil testing laboratory. There are a number of reasons for this, including the following:

- laboratories use a variety of procedures;
- labs report results differently; and
- different approaches are used to make recommendations based on soil test results.

Varied Lab Procedures

One of the complications with using soil tests to help determine nutrient needs is that testing labs across the country use a wide range of procedures. The main difference among labs is the solutions they use to extract the soil nutrients. Some use one solution for all nutrients, while others will use one solution to extract potassium, magnesium, and calcium; another for phosphorus; and yet another for micronutrients. The various extracting solutions have different chemical compositions, so the amount of a particular nutrient that lab A extracts may be different from the amount extracted by lab B. Labs frequently have a good reason for using a particular solution, however. For example, the Olsen test for phosphorus (see table 21.1, p. 242) is more accurate for high-pH soils in arid and semiarid regions than the various acid-extracting solutions commonly used in more humid regions. Whatever procedure the lab uses, soil test levels must be calibrated with the crop response to added nutrients. For example, do yields increase when you add phosphorus to a soil that tested low in P? In general, university and state labs in a given region use the same or similar procedures that have been calibrated for local soils and climate.

Reporting Soil Test Levels Differently

Different labs may report their results in different ways. Some use parts per million (10,000 ppm = 1%); some use pounds per acre (usually by using parts per two million, which is twice the ppm level); and some use an index (for example, all nutrients are expressed on a scale of 1 to 100). In addition, some labs report phosphorus and potassium in the elemental form, while others use the oxide forms, P_2O_5 and K_2O.

Most testing labs report results as both a number and a category such as *low, medium, optimum, high,* and *very high.* However, although most labs consider *high* to be above the amount needed (the optimum), some labs use *optimum* and *high* interchangeably. If the significance of the various categories is not clear on your report, be sure to ask. Labs should be able to furnish you with the probability of getting a response to added fertilizer for each soil test category.

Different Recommendation Systems

Even when labs use the same procedures, as is the case in most of the Midwest, different approaches to making recommendations lead to different amounts of recommended fertilizer. Three different systems are used to make fertilizer recommendations based on soil tests: (1) the sufficiency-level system; (2) the buildup and maintenance system, and (3) the basic cation saturation ratio system (only used for Ca, Mg, and K).

The *sufficiency-level system* suggests that there is a point, the sufficiency or critical soil test value, above which there is little likelihood of crop response to an added nutrient. Its goal is not to produce the highest yield every year, but rather to produce the highest average return over time from using fertilizers. Experiments that relate yield increases with added fertilizer to soil test level provide much of the evidence supporting this approach. As the soil test level increases from optimum (or medium) to high, yields without adding fertilizer are close to the maximum obtained by adding more fertilizer (figure 21.1). Of course, farmers should be aiming for the maximum *economic* yields, which are slightly below the highest *possible* yields, as indicated in figure 21.1.

The buildup and maintenance system calls for building up soils to high levels of fertility and then keeping

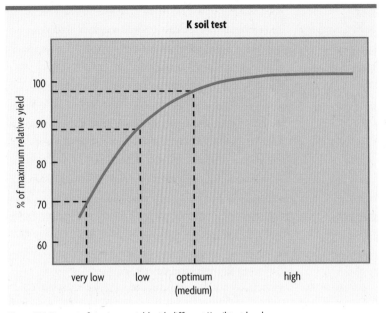

K soil test

% of maximum relative yield

100
90
80
70
60

very low   low   optimum (medium)   high

Figure 21.1. Percent of maximum yield with different K soil test levels.

them there by applying enough fertilizer to replace nutrients removed in harvested crops. This approach usually recommends more fertilizer than the sufficiency system. It is used mainly for phosphorus, potassium, and magnesium recommendations; it can also be used for calcium when high-value vegetables are being grown on low-CEC soils. However, there may be a justification for using the buildup and maintenance approach for phosphorus and potassium—in addition to using it for calcium—on high-value crops because: (1) the extra costs are such a small percent of total costs; and (2) when weather is sub-optimal (cool and damp, for example), this approach may occasionally produce a higher yield that would more than cover the extra expense of the fertilizer. If you use this approach, you should pay attention to levels of phosphorus; adding more P when levels are already optimum can pose an environmental risk.

The basic cation saturation ratio system (BCSR; also called the base ratio system), a method for estimating calcium, magnesium, and potassium needs, is based on the belief that crops yield best when calcium,

magnesium, and potassium—usually the dominant cations on the CEC—are in a particular balance. This system was developed out of work by Firman E. Bear in New Jersey and William A. Albrecht in Missouri and has become accepted by many farmers despite a lack of modern research supporting the system (see "The Basic Cation Saturation Ratio System," p. 251). Few university testing laboratories use this system, but a number of private labs use it because many "alternative" and organic farmers believe that it is valuable. This system calls for calcium to occupy about 60–80% of the CEC, magnesium to be 10–20%, and potassium 2–5%. This is based on the notion that if the percent saturation of the CEC is good, there will be enough of each of these nutrients to support optimum crop growth. When using the BCSR, it is important to recognize its practical as well as theoretical flaws. For one, even when the ratios of the nutrients are within the recommended crop guidelines, there may be such a low CEC (such as in a sandy soil that is very low in organic matter) that the amounts present are insufficient for crops. If the soil has a CEC of only 2 milliequivalents per 100 grams of soil, for example, it can have a "perfect" balance of Ca (70%), Mg (12.5%), and K (3.5%) but contain only 560 pounds Ca, 60 pounds of Mg, and 53 pounds of K per acre to a depth of 6 inches. Thus, while these elements are in a supposedly good ratio to one another, there isn't enough of any of them. The main problem with this soil is a low CEC; the remedy is to add a lot of organic matter over a period of years, and, if the pH is low, it should be limed.

The opposite situation also needs attention. When there is a high CEC and satisfactory pH for the crops being grown, even though there is plenty of a particular nutrient, the cation ratio system may call for adding more. This can be a problem with soils that are naturally moderately high in magnesium, because the recommendations may call for high amounts of calcium and potassium to be added when none are really needed—wasting the farmer's time and money.

Research indicates that plants do well over a broad range of cation ratios, as long as there are sufficient supplies of potassium, calcium, and magnesium. However, the ratios are sometimes out of balance. For example, when magnesium occupies more than 50% of the CEC in soils with low organic matter and low aggregate stability, using gypsum (calcium sulfate) may help restore aggregation because of the extra calcium as well as the higher level of dissolved salts. As mentioned previously, liming very acidic soils sometimes results in decreased potassium availability, and this would be apparent when using the cation ratio system. The sufficiency system would also call for adding potassium, because of the low potassium levels in these limed soils.

The sufficiency-level approach is used by most fertility recommendation systems for potassium, magnesium, and calcium, as well as phosphorus and nitrogen (where N tests are available). It generally calls for lower application rates for potassium, magnesium, and calcium and is more consistent with the scientific data than the cation ratio system. The cation ratio system can be used to reduce the chance of nutrient deficiencies, if interpreted with care and common sense—not ignoring the total amounts present and paying attention to the implications of a soil's pH. Using this system, however, will usually mean applying more nutrients than suggested by the sufficiency system—with a low probability of actually getting a higher yield or better crop quality.

Labs sometimes use a combination of these systems, something like a hybrid approach. Some laboratories that use the sufficiency system will have a target for magnesium but then suggest adding more if the potassium level is high. Others may suggest that higher

potassium levels are needed as the soil CEC increases. These are really hybrids of the sufficiency and cation ratio systems. At least one state university lab uses the sufficiency system for potassium and a cation ratio system for calcium and magnesium. Also, some labs assume that soils will not be tested annually. The recommendation that they give is, therefore, produced by the sufficiency system (what is needed for the crop) with a certain amount added for maintenance. This is done to be sure there is enough fertility in the following year.

Plant Tissue Tests

Soil tests are the most common means of assessing fertility needs of crops, but plant tissue tests are especially useful for nutrient management of perennial crops, such as apples, blueberries, citrus and peach orchards, and vineyards. For most annuals, including agronomic and vegetable crops, tissue testing, though not widely used, can help diagnose problems. The small sampling window available for most annuals and an inability to effectively fertilize them once they are well established,

---

To estimate the percentages of the various cations on the CEC, the amounts need to be expressed in terms of quantity of charge. Some labs give concentration by both weight (ppm) and charge (me/100g). If you want to convert from ppm to me/100g, you can do it as follows:

(Ca in ppm)/200 = Ca in me/100g
(Mg in ppm)/120 = Mg in me/100g
(K in ppm)/390 = K in me/100g

As discussed in chapter 20, adding up the amount of charge due to calcium, magnesium, and potassium gives a very good estimate of the CEC for most soils above pH 5.5.

except for N during early growth stages, limit the usefulness of tissue analysis for annual crops. However, leaf petiole nitrate tests are sometimes done on potato and sugar beets to help fine-tune in-season N fertilization. Petiole nitrate is also helpful for N management of cotton and for help managing irrigated vegetables, especially during the transition from vegetative to reproductive growth. With irrigated crops, particularly when the drip system is used, fertilizer can be effectively delivered to the rooting zone during crop growth.

What Should You Do?

After reading the discussion above you may be somewhat bewildered by the different procedures and ways of expressing results, as well as the different recommendation approaches. It is bewildering. Our general suggestions of how to deal with these complex issues are as follows:

1. Send your soil samples to a lab that uses tests evaluated for the soils and crops of your state or region. Continue using the same lab or another that uses the same system.

2. If you're growing low value-per-acre crops (wheat, corn, soybeans, etc.), be sure that the recommendation system used is based on the sufficiency approach. This system usually results in lower fertilizer rates and higher economic returns for low-value crops. (It is not easy to find out what system a lab uses. Be persistent, and you will get to a person who can answer your question.)

3. Dividing a sample in two and sending it to two labs may result in confusion. You will probably get different recommendations, and it won't be easy to figure out which is better for you, unless you are willing to do a comparison of the recommendations. In most cases you are better off staying with the same lab and learning how to fine-tune the recommendations for your farm. If you are willing to experiment, however, you can send duplicate samples to two different labs,

RECOMMENDATION SYSTEM COMPARISON

Most university testing laboratories use the sufficiency-level system, but some make potassium or magnesium recommendations by modifying the sufficiency system to take into account the portion of the CEC occupied by the nutrient. The buildup and maintenance system is used by some state university labs and many commercial labs. An extensive evaluation of different approaches to fertilizer recommendations for agronomic crops in Nebraska found that the sufficiency-level system resulted in using less fertilizer and gave higher economic returns than the buildup and maintenance system. Studies in Kentucky, Ohio, and Wisconsin have indicated that the sufficiency system is superior to both the buildup and maintenance and cation ratio systems.

with one going to your state-testing laboratory. In general, the recommendations from state labs call for less, but enough, fertilizer. If you are growing crops over a large acreage, set up a demonstration or experiment in one field by applying the fertilizer recommended by each lab over long strips and see if there is any yield difference. A yield monitor for grain crops would be very useful for this purpose. If you've never set up a field experiment before, you should ask your extension agent for help. You might also find SARE's brochure *How to Conduct Research on Your Farm or Ranch* of use (see "Sources" at the end of the chapter).

4. Keep a record of the soil tests for each field, so that you can track changes over the years (figure 21.2). If records show a buildup of nutrients to high levels, reduce nutrient applications. If you're drawing nutrient levels down too low, start applying fertilizers or off-farm organic nutrient sources. In some rotations, such as the corn–corn–four years of hay shown at

the bottom of figure 21.2, it makes sense to build up nutrient levels during the corn phase and draw them down during the hay phase.

SOIL TESTING FOR NITROGEN

Soil samples for nitrogen tests are usually taken at a different time and using a different method than samples for the other nutrients (which are typically sampled to plow depth in the fall or spring).

In the humid regions of the U.S. there was no reliable soil test for N availability before the mid-1980s. The nitrate test commonly used for corn in humid regions was developed during the 1980s in Vermont. It is usually called the pre-sidedress nitrate test (PSNT) but is also called the late spring nitrate test (LSNT) in parts of the Midwest. In this test a soil sample is taken to a depth of 1 foot when corn is between 6 inches and 1 foot tall. The original idea behind the test was to wait as long as possible before sampling, because soil and weather conditions in the early growing season may reduce or increase N availability for the crop later in the season. After the corn is 1 foot tall, it is difficult to get samples to a lab and back in time to apply any needed sidedress N fertilizer. The PSNT is now used on field corn, sweet corn, pumpkins, and cabbage. Although it is widely used, it is not very accurate in some situations, such as the sandy coastal plains soils of the Deep South.

Different approaches to using the PSNT work for different farms. In general, using the soil test allows a farmer to avoid adding excess amounts of "insurance fertilizer." Two contrasting examples follow:

- **For farms using rotations with legume forages and applying animal manures regularly (so there's a lot of active soil organic matter),** the best way to use the test is to apply only the amount of manure necessary to provide sufficient N to the plant. The PSNT will indicate whether the farmer needs to side-dress any additional N fertilizer. It will also indicate whether the farmer has

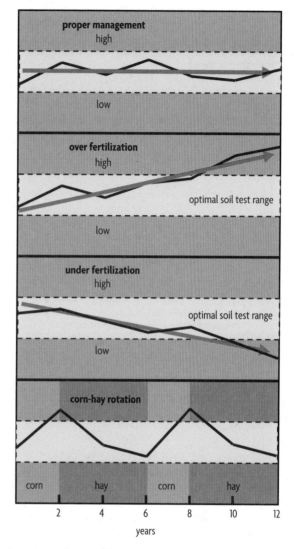

Figure 21.2. Soil test phosphorus and potassium trends under different fertility management regimes. Modified from *The Penn State Agronomy Guide* (2007–2008).

done a good job of estimating N availability from manures.

- **For farms growing cash grains without using legume cover crops,** it's best to apply a conservative amount of fertilizer N before planting and then use the test to see if more is needed. This is

Table 21.1
Phosphorus Soil Tests Used in Different Regions

Region	Soil Test Solutions Used for P
Arid and semiarid Midwest, West, and Northwest	Olsen AB-DTPA
Humid Midwest, mid-Atlantic, Southeast, and eastern Canada	Mehlich 3 Bray 1 (also called Bray P-1 or Bray-Kurtz P)
North Central and Midwest	Bray 1 (also called Bray P-1 or Bray-Kurtz P)
Southeast and mid-Atlantic	Mehlich 1
Northeast (New York and most of New England), some labs in Idaho and Washington	Morgan or modified Morgan Mehlich 3

Source: Modified from Allen, Johnson, and Unruh et al. (1994).

Table 21.2
Interpretation Ranges for Different P Soil Tests

	Low	Optimum	High	Very High
Olsen	0–7	7–15	15–21	>21
Morgan	0–4	4–7	7–20	>20
Bray 1 (Bray P-1)	0–15	15–24	24–31	>31
Mehlich 1	0–25	25–50		>50
Mehlich 3	0–15	15–31	24–31	>31
AB-DTPA (for irrigated crops)	0–7	8–11	12–15	>15

Note: Units are in parts per million phosphorus (ppm P), and ranges used for recommendations may vary from state to state.

especially important in regions where rainfall cannot always be relied upon to quickly bring fertilizer into contact with roots. The PSNT test provides a backup and allows the farmer to be more conservative with preplant applications, knowing that there is a way to make up any possible deficit.

Other Nitrogen Soil Tests

In humid regions there is no other widely used soil test for N availability. A few states in the upper Midwest offer a pre-plant nitrate test, which calls for sampling to 2 feet in the spring. For a number of years there was considerable interest in the Illinois Soil Nitrogen Test. The ISNT, which measures the amino-sugar portion of soil N, has unfortunately been found to be an unreliable predictor of whether the plant needs extra N.

In the drier parts of the country, a nitrate soil test that requires samples to 2 feet or more has been used with success since the 1960s. The deep-soil samples can be taken in the fall or early spring, before the growing season, because of low leaching and denitrification losses and low levels of active organic matter (so hardly any nitrate is mineralized from organic matter). Soil samples can be taken at the same time for analysis for other nutrients and pH.

SOIL TESTING FOR P

Soil test procedures for phosphorus are different than those for nitrogen. When testing for phosphorus, the soil is usually sampled to plow depth in the fall or in the early spring before tillage and the sample usually analyzed for phosphorus, potassium, sometimes other nutrients (such as calcium, magnesium, and micronutrients), and pH. The methods used to estimate available P vary from region to region and sometimes from state to state within a region (table 21.1). Although the relative test value for a given soil is usually similar according to different soil tests (for example, a high P-testing soil by one procedure is generally also high by another procedure), the actual numbers can be different (table 21.2).

The various soil tests for P take into account a large portion of the available P contained in recently applied manures and the amount that will become available from the soil minerals. However, if there is a large amount of active organic matter in your soils from crop residues or manure additions in previous years, there may well be more available P for plants than indicated by the soil test. (On the other hand, the PSNT reflects the amount of N that may become available from decomposing organic matter.)

TESTING SOILS FOR ORGANIC MATTER

A word of caution when comparing your soil test organic matter levels with those discussed in this book. If your laboratory reports organic matter as "weight loss" at high temperature, the numbers may be higher than if the lab uses the traditional wet chemistry method. A soil with 3% organic matter by wet chemistry might have a weight-loss value of between 4% and 5%. Most labs use a correction factor to approximate the value you would get by using the wet chemistry procedure. Although either method can be used to follow changes in your soil, when you compare soil organic matter of samples run in different laboratories, it's best to make sure the same method was used.

There is now a laboratory that will determine various forms of living organisms in your soil. Although it costs quite a bit more than traditional testing for nutrients or organic matter, you can find out the amount (weight) of fungi and bacteria in a soil, as well as obtaining an analysis for other organisms. (See the "Resources" section, p. 283, for laboratories that run tests in addition to basic soil fertility analysis.)

INTERPRETING SOIL TEST RESULTS

Below are five soil test examples, including discussion about what they tell us and the types of practices farmers should follow to satisfy plant nutrient needs on these soils. Suggestions are provided for conventional farmers and organic producers. These are just suggestions—there are other satisfactory ways to meet the needs of crops growing on the soils sampled. The soil tests were run by different procedures, to provide examples from around the U.S. Interpretations of a number of commonly used soil tests—relating test levels to general

> ### UNUSUAL SOIL TESTS
> From time to time we've come across unusual soil test results. A few examples and their typical causes are given below:
>
> - Very high phosphorus levels—High poultry or other manure application over many years.
>
> - Very high salt concentration in humid region—Recent application of large amounts of poultry manure, or location immediately adjacent to road where de-icing salt was used.
>
> - Very high pH and high calcium levels relative to potassium and magnesium—Large amounts of lime-stabilized sewage sludge used.
>
> - Very high calcium levels given the soil's texture and organic matter content—Use of an acid solution, such as the Morgan, Mehlich 1, or Mehlich 3, to extract soils containing free limestone, causing some of the lime to dissolve.
>
> - Soil pH >7 and very low P—Use of an acid such as Mehlich I or Mehlich 3 on an alkaline, calcareous soil; the soil neutralizes much of the acid, and so little P is extracted.

fertility categories—are given later in the chapter (see tables 21.3 and 21.4, pp. 249, 250). Many labs estimate the cation exchange capacity that would exist at pH 7 (or even higher). Because we feel that the soil's current CEC is of most interest (see chapter 20), the CEC is estimated by summing the exchangeable bases. The more acidic a soil, the greater the difference between its current CEC and the CEC it would have near pH 7.

Following the five soil tests below is a section on modifying recommendations for particular situations.

—SOIL TEST #1—
(New England)

Soil Test #1 Report Summary*

	MEASUREMENT	LBS/ACRE	PPM	Soil Test CATEGORY	Recommendation SUMMARY
Field name: North	P	4	2	low	50–70 lbs P$_2$O$_5$/acre
Sample date: September (PSNT sample taken the following June)	K	100	50	low	150–200 lbs K$_2$O/acre
	Mg	60	30	low	lime (see below)
Soil type: loamy sand	Ca	400	200	low	lime (see below)
Manure added: none	pH	5.4			2 tons dolomitic limestone/acre
Cropping history: mixed vegetables	CEC**	1.4 me/100g			
	OM	1%			add organic matter: compost, cover crops, animal manures
Crop to be grown: mixed vegetables					
	PSNT	5		low	side-dress 80–100 lbs N/acre

*Nutrients were extracted by modified Morgan's solution (see table 21.3A for interpretations).
**CEC by sum of bases. The estimated CEC would probably double if "exchange acidity" were determined and added to the sum of bases.
Note: ppm = parts per million; P = phosphorus; K = potassium; Mg = magnesium; Ca = calcium; OM = organic matter; me = milliequivalent; PSNT = pre-sidedress nitrate test; N = nitrogen.

What can we tell about soil #1 based on the soil test?

- It is too acidic for most agricultural crops, so lime is needed.
- Phosphorus is low, as are potassium, magnesium, and calcium. All should be applied.
- This low organic matter soil is probably also low in active organic matter (indicated by the low PSNT test, see table 21.4A) and will need an application of nitrogen. (The PSNT is done during the growth of the crop, so it is difficult to use manure to supply extra N needs indicated by the test.)
- The coarse texture of the soil is indicated by the combination of low organic matter and low CEC.

General recommendations:

1. Apply dolomitic limestone, if available, in the fall at about 2 tons per acre (and work it into the soil and establish a cover crop if possible). This will take care of the calcium and magnesium needs at the same time the soil's pH is increased. It will also help make soil phosphorus more available, as well as increasing the availability of any added phosphorus.
2. Because no manure is to be used after the test is taken, broadcast significant amounts of phosphate (P$_2$O$_5$—probably around 50 to 70 pounds per acre) and potash (K$_2$O—around 150 to 200 pounds per acre). Some phosphate and potash can also be applied in starter fertilizer (band-applied at planting). Usually, N is also included in starter fertilizer, so it might be reasonable to use about 300 pounds of a 10-10-10 fertilizer, which will apply 30 pounds of N, 30 pounds of phosphate, and 30 pounds of potash per acre. If that rate of starter is to be used, broadcast 400 pounds per acre of a 0-10-30 bulk blended fertilizer. The broadcast plus the starter will supply 30 pounds of N, 70 pounds of phosphate, and 150 pounds of potash per acre.
3. If only calcitic (low-magnesium) limestone is available, use sul-po-mag as the potassium source in the bulk blend to help supply magnesium.
4. Nitrogen should be side-dressed at around 80 to 100 (or more) pounds per acre for N-demanding crops such as corn or tomatoes. About 300 pounds of ammonium nitrate or 220 pounds of urea per acre will supply 100 pounds of N.
5. Use various medium- to long-term strategies to build up soil organic matter, including the use of cover crops and animal manures. Most of the nutrient needs of crops on this soil could have been met by using about 20 tons wet weight of solid cow manure per acre or its equivalent. It is best to apply it in the spring, before planting. If the manure had been applied, the PSNT test would probably have been quite a bit higher, perhaps around 25 ppm.

Recommendations for organic producers:

1. Use dolomitic limestone to increase the pH (as recommended for the conventional farmer, above). It will also help make soil phosphorus more available, as well as increasing the availability of any added phosphorus.
2. Apply 2 tons per acre of rock phosphate, or about 5 tons of poultry manure for phosphorus, or—better yet—a combination of 1 ton rock phosphate and 2 1/2 tons of poultry manure. If the high level of rock phosphate is applied, it should supply some phosphorus for a long time, perhaps a decade.
3. If poultry manure is used to raise the phosphorus level, add 2 tons of compost per acre to provide some longer-lasting nutrients and humus. If rock phosphate is used to supply phosphorus, use livestock manure and compost (to add N, potassium, magnesium, and some humus).
4. Establish a good rotation with soil-building crops and legume cover crops.
5. Use manure with care. Although the application of uncomposted manure is allowed by organic-certifying organizations, there are restrictions. For example, four months may be needed between application of uncomposted manure and either harvest of crops with edible portions in contact with soil or planting of crops that accumulate nitrate, such as leafy greens or beets. A three-month period may be needed between uncomposted manure application and harvest of other food crops.

—SOIL TEST #2—
(Pennsylvania and New York)
Soil Test #2 Report Summary*

	MEASUREMENT	LBS/ACRE	PPM	Soil Test CATEGORY	Recommendation SUMMARY
Field name: Smith upper	P	174	87	high	none
Sample date: November (no sample for PSNT will be taken)	K	360	180	high	none
	Mg	274	137	high	none
Soil type: silt loam	Ca	3,880	1,940	high	no lime needed
Manure added: none this year (some last year)	pH	7.2			
Cropping history: legume cover crops used routinely	CEC	11.7 me/100g			
Crop to be grown: corn	OM	3%			add organic matter: compost, cover crops, animal manures
	N	no soil test			little to no N needed

*Soil was sent to a commercial laboratory and extracted for P using the Bray-1 solution. This is probably the equivalent of over 20 ppm by using the Morgan or Olsen procedures. Other nutrients were extracted with pH 7 ammonium acetate (see table 21.3D).
Note: ppm = parts per million; P = phosphorus; K = potassium; Mg = magnesium; Ca = calcium; OM = organic matter; me = milliequivalent; PSNT = pre-sidedress nitrate test; N = nitrogen.

What can we tell about soil #2 based on the soil test?
- The high pH indicates that this soil does not need any lime.
- Phosphorus is high, as are potassium, magnesium, and calcium (see table 21.3D).
- The organic matter is very good for a silt loam.
- There was no test done for nitrogen, but this soil probably supplies a reasonable amount of N for crops, because the farmer uses legume cover crops and allows them to produce a large amount of dry matter.

General recommendations:
1. Continue building soil organic matter.
2. No phosphate, potash, or magnesium needs to be applied. The lab that ran this soil test recommended using 38 pounds of potash and 150 pounds of magnesium (MgO) per acre. However, with a high K level, 180 ppm (about 8% of the CEC) and a high Mg, 137 ppm (about 11% of the CEC), there is a very low likelihood of any increase in yield or crop quality from adding either element.
3. Nitrogen fertilizer is probably needed in only small to moderate amounts (if at all), but we need to know more about the details of the cropping system or run a nitrogen soil test to make a more accurate recommendation.

Recommendations for organic producers:
1. A good rotation with legumes and fall legume cover crops will provide nitrogen for other crops and prevent loss of soluble nutrients.

—SOIL TEST #3—
(Humid Midwest)

Soil Test #3 Report Summary*

Field info	MEASUREMENT	LBS/ACRE	PPM	Soil Test CATEGORY	Recommendation SUMMARY
Field name: #12	P	20	10	very low	30 lbs P_2O_5/acre
Sample date: December (no sample for PSNT will be taken)	K	58	29	very low	200 lbs K_2O/acre
Soil type: clay (somewhat poorly drained)	Mg	138	69	high	none
Manure added: none	Ca	8,168	4,084	high	none
Cropping history: continuous corn	pH	6.8			no lime needed
Crop to be grown: corn	CEC	21.1 me/100g			
	OM	4.3%			rotate to forage legume crop
	N	no N soil test			100–130 lbs N/acre

*All nutrient needs were determined using the Mehlich 3 solution (see table 21.3C).
Note: ppm = parts per million; P = phosphorus; K = potassium; Mg = magnesium; Ca = calcium; OM = organic matter; me = milliequivalent; PSNT = pre-sidedress nitrate test; N = nitrogen.

What can we tell about soil #3 based on the soil test?

- The high pH indicates that this soil does not need any lime.
- Phosphorus and potassium are low. [Note: 20 pounds of P per acre is low, according to the soil test used (Mehlich 3). If another test, such as Morgan's solution, was used, a result of 20 pounds of P per acre would be considered a high result.]
- The organic matter is relatively high. However, considering that this is a somewhat poorly drained clay, it probably should be even higher.
- About half of the CEC is probably due to the organic matter and the rest probably due to the clay.
- Low potassium indicates that this soil has probably not received high levels of manures recently.
- There was no test done for nitrogen, but given the field's history of continuous corn and little manure, there is probably a need for nitrogen. A low amount of active organic matter that could have supplied nitrogen for crops is indicated by the history (the lack of rotation to perennial legume forages and lack of manure use) and the moderate percent of organic matter (considering that it is a clay soil).

General recommendations:

1. This field should probably be rotated to a perennial forage crop.
2. Phosphorus and potassium are needed—probably around 30 pounds of phosphate and 200 or more pounds of potash applied broadcast, preplant, if a forage crop is to be grown. If corn will be grown again, all of the phosphate and 30 to 40 pounds of the potash can be applied as starter fertilizer at planting. Although magnesium, at about 3% of the effective CEC, would be considered low by relying exclusively on a basic cation saturation ratio system recommendation, there is little likelihood of an increase in crop yield or quality by adding magnesium.

3. Nitrogen fertilizer is probably needed in large amounts (100 to 130 pounds/acre) for high N-demanding crops, such as corn. If no in-season soil test (like the PSNT) is done, some preplant N should be applied (around 50 pounds/acre), some in the starter band at planting (about 15 pounds/acre) and some side-dressed (about 50 pounds).
4. One way to meet the needs of the crop is as follows:
   a. broadcast 500 pounds per acre of an 11-0-44 bulk blended fertilizer;
   b. use 300 pounds per acre of a 5-10-10 starter; and
   c. side-dress with 150 pounds per acre of ammonium nitrate. This will supply approximately 120 pounds of N, 30 pounds of phosphate, and 210 pounds of potash.

Recommendations for organic producers:

1. Apply 2 tons per acre of rock phosphate (to meet P needs) or about 5 to 8 tons of poultry manure (which would meet both phosphorus and nitrogen needs), or a combination of the two (1 ton rock phosphate and 3 to 4 tons of poultry manure).
2. Apply 400 pounds of potassium sulfate per acre broadcast preplant. (If poultry manure is used to meet phosphorus and nitrogen needs, use only 200 to 300 pounds of potassium sulfate per acre.)
3. Use manure with care. Although the application of uncomposted manure is allowed by organic-certifying organizations, there are restrictions. For example, four months may be needed between application of uncomposted manure and either harvest of crops with edible portions in contact with soil or planting of crops that accumulate nitrate, such as leafy greens or beets. A three-month period may be needed between uncomposted manure application and harvest of other food crops.

—SOIL TEST #4—
(Alabama)
Soil Test #4 Report Summary*

Field name: River A
Sample date: October
Soil type: sandy loam
Manure added: none
Cropping history: continuous cotton
Crop to be grown: cotton

MEASUREMENT	LBS/ACRE	PPM	Soil Test CATEGORY	Recommendation SUMMARY
P	102	51	very high	none
K	166	83	high	none
Mg	264	132	high	none
Ca	1,158	579		none
pH	6.5			no lime needed
CEC	4.2 me/100g			
OM	not requested			use legume cover crops, consider crop rotation
N	no N soil test			70–100 lbs N/acre

*All nutrient needs were determined using the Mehlich 1 solution (see table 21.3B).
Note: ppm = parts per million; P = phosphorus; K = potassium; Mg = magnesium; Ca = calcium; OM = organic matter; me = milliequivalent; PSNT = pre-sidedress nitrate test; N = nitrogen.

What can we tell about soil #4 based on the soil test?
- With a pH of 6.5, this soil does not need any lime.
- Phosphorus is very high, and potassium and magnesium are sufficient.
- Magnesium is high, compared with calcium (Mg occupies over 26% of the CEC).
- The low CEC at pH 6.5 indicates that the organic matter content is probably around 1–1.5%.

General recommendations:
1. No phosphate, potash, magnesium, or lime is needed.
2. Nitrogen should be applied, probably in a split application totaling about 70 to 100 pounds N per acre.
3. This field should be rotated to other crops and cover crops used regularly.

Recommendations for organic producer:
1. Although poultry or dairy manure can meet the crops' needs, that means applying phosphorus on an already high-P soil. If there is no possibility of growing an overwinter legume cover crop (see recommendation #2), about 15 to 20 tons of bedded dairy manure (wet weight) should be sufficient. Another option for supplying some of the crops' need for N without adding more P is to use Chilean nitrate until good rotations with legume cover crops are established.
2. If time permits, plant a high-N-producing legume cover crop, such as hairy vetch or crimson clover, to provide nitrogen to cash crops.
3. Develop a good rotation so that all the needed nitrogen will be supplied to nonlegumes between the rotation crops and cover crops.
4. Although the application of uncomposted manure is allowed by organic-certifying organizations, there are restrictions when growing food crops. Check with the person doing your certification to find out what restrictions apply to cotton.

—SOIL TEST #5—
(Semiarid Great Plains)

Soil Test #5 Report Summary*

	MEASUREMENT	LBS/ACRE	PPM	Soil Test CATEGORY	Recommendation SUMMARY
	P	14	7	low	20–40 lbs P$_2$O$_5$
Field name: Hill	K	716	358	very high	none
Sample date: April	Mg	340	170	high	none
Soil type: silt loam	Ca	not determined			none
Manure added: none indicated	pH	8.1			no lime needed
Cropping history: not indicated	CEC	not determined			
Crop to be grown: corn	OM	1.8%			use legume cover crops, consider rotation to other crops that produce large amounts of residues
	N	5.8 ppm		170 lbs N/acre	

*K and Mg extracted by neutral ammonium acetate, P by the Olsen solution (see table 21.3D).
Note: ppm = parts per million; P = phosphorus; K = potassium; Mg = magnesium; Ca = calcium; OM = organic matter; me = milliequivalent; PSNT = pre-sidedress nitrate test; N = nitrogen.

What can we tell about soil #5 based on the soil test?

- The pH of 8.1 indicates that this soil is most likely calcareous.
- Phosphorus is low, there is sufficient magnesium, and potassium is very high.
- Although calcium was not determined, there will be plenty in a calcareous soil.
- The organic matter at 1.8% is low for a silt loam soil.
- The nitrogen test indicates a low amount of residual nitrate (table 21.4B), and, given the low organic matter level, a low amount of N mineralization is expected.

General recommendations:

1. No potash, magnesium, or lime is needed.
2. About 170 pounds of N per acre should be applied. Because of the low amount of leaching in this region, most can be applied preplant, with perhaps 30 pounds as a starter (applied at planting). Using 300 pounds per acre of a 10-10-0 starter would supply all P needs (see recommendation #3) as well as provide some N near the developing seedling. Broadcasting and incorporating 300 pounds of urea or 420 pounds of ammonium nitrate will provide 140 pounds of N.
3. About 20 to 40 pounds of phosphate is needed per acre. Apply the lower rate as a starter, because localized placement results in more efficient use by the plant. If phosphate is broadcast, apply at the 40-pound rate.
4. The organic matter level of this soil should be increased. This field should be rotated to other crops and cover crops used regularly.

Recommendations for organic producers:

1. Because rock phosphate is so insoluble in high-pH soils, it would be a poor choice for adding P. Poultry manure (about 6 tons per acre) or dairy manure (about 25 tons wet weight per acre) can be used to meet the crop's needs for both N and P. However, that means applying more P than is needed, plus a lot of potash (which is already at very high levels). Fish meal might be a good source of N and P without adding K.
2. A long-term strategy needs to be developed to build soil organic matter—better rotations, use of cover crops, and importing organic residues onto the farm.
3. Use manure with care. Although the application of uncomposted manure is allowed by organic-certifying organizations, there are restrictions. For example, three months may be needed between application of uncomposted manure and either harvest of root crops or planting of crops that accumulate nitrate, such as leafy greens or beets. A two-month period may be needed between uncomposted manure application and harvest of other food crops.

ADJUSTING A SOIL TEST RECOMMENDATION

Specific recommendations must be tailored to the crops you want to grow, as well as other characteristics of the particular soil, climate, and cropping system. Most soil test reports use information that you supply about manure use and previous crops to adapt a general recommendation for your situation. However, once you feel comfortable with interpreting soil tests, you may also want to adjust the recommendations for a particular need. What happens if you decide to apply manure after you sent in the form along with the soil sample? Also, you usually don't get credit for the nitrogen produced by legume cover crops because most forms don't even ask about their use. The amount of available nutrients from legume cover crops and from manures is indicated in

table 21.5. If you don't test your soil annually, and the recommendations you receive are only for the current year, you need to figure out what to apply the next year or two, until the soil is tested again.

No single recommendation, based only on the soil test, makes sense for all situations. For example, your gut might tell you that a test is too low (and fertilizer recommendations are too high). Let's say that although you broadcast 100 pounds N per acre before planting, a high rate of N fertilizer is recommended by the in-season nitrate test (PSNT), even though there wasn't enough rainfall to leach out nitrate or cause much loss by denitrification. In that case, you might not want to apply the full amount recommended.

Another example: A low potassium level in a soil

Table 21.3
Soil Test Categories for Various Extracting Solutions

A. Modified Morgan's Solution (Vermont)

Category	Very Low	Low	Optimum	High	Excessive
Probability of response to added nutrient	Very High	High	Low	Very Low	
Available P (ppm)	0–2	2.1–4.0	4.1–7	7.1–20	
K (ppm)	0–50	51–100	101–130	131–160	>160
Mg (ppm)	0–35	36–50	51–100	>100	

B. Mehlich 1 Solution (Alabama)*

Category	Very Low	Low	Optimum	High	Excessive
Probability of response to added nutrient	Very High	High	Low	Very Low	
Available P (ppm)	0–6	7–12	13–25	26–50	>50
K (ppm)	0–22	23–45	46–90	>90	
Mg (ppm)**		0–25	>25		
Ca for tomatoes (ppm)***	0–150	151–250	>250		

*From Hanlon (1998).
**For corn, legumes, and vegetables on soils with CECs greater than 4.6 me/100g.
***For corn, legumes, and vegetables on soils with CECs from 4.6 to 9.0 me/100g.

C. Mehlich 3 Solution (North Carolina)*

Category	Very Low	Low	Optimum	High	Excessive
Probability of response to added nutrient	Very High	High	Low	Very Low	
Available P (ppm)	0–12	13–25	26–50	51–125	>125
K (ppm)	0–43	44–87	88–174	>174	
Mg (ppm)**		0–25		>25	

*From Hanlon (1998).
**Percent of CEC is also a consideration.

D. Neutral Ammonium Acetate Solution for K and Mg and Olsen or Bray-1 for P (Nebraska [P and K], Minnesota [Mg])

Category	Very Low	Low	Optimum	High	Excessive
Probability of response to added nutrient	Very High	High	Low	Very Low	
P (Olson, ppm)	0–3	4–10	11–16	17–20	>20
P (Bray-1, ppm)	0–5	6–15	16–24	25–30	>30
K (ppm)	0–40	41–74	75–124	125–150	>150
Mg (ppm)		0–50	51–100	>101	

Table 21.4
Soil Test Categories for Nitrogen Tests

A. Pre-Sidedress Nitrate Test (PSNT)*

Category	Very Low	Low	Optimum	High	Excessive
Probability of response to added nutrient	Very High	High	Low	Very Low	
Nitrate-N (ppm)	0–10	11–22	23–28	29–35	>35

*Soil sample taken to 1 foot when corn is 6–12 inches tall.

B. Deep (4-ft) Nitrate Test (Nebraska)

Category	Very Low	Low	Optimum	High	Excessive
Probability of response to added nutrient	Very High	High	Low	Very Low	
Nitrate-N (ppm)	0–6	7–15	15–18	19–25	>25

test (let's say around 40 ppm) will certainly mean that you should apply potassium. But how much should you use? When and how should you apply it? The answer to these two questions might be quite different on a low organic matter, sandy soil where high amounts of rainfall normally occur during the growing season (in which case, potassium may leach out if applied the previous fall or early spring) versus a high organic matter, clay loam soil that has a higher CEC and will hold on to potassium added in the fall. This is the type of situation that dictates using labs whose recommendations are developed for soils and cropping systems in your home state or region. It also is an indication that you may need to modify a recommendation for your specific situation.

MAKING ADJUSTMENTS TO FERTILIZER APPLICATION RATES

If information about cropping history, cover crops, and manure use is not provided to the soil testing laboratory, the report containing the fertilizer recommendation cannot take those factors into account. Below is an example of how you can modify the report's recommendations:

Table 21.5
Amounts of Available Nutrients from Manures and Legume Cover Crops

Legume cover crops*	N lbs/acre	
Hairy vetch	70–140	
Crimson clover	40–90	
Red and white clovers	40–90	
Medics	30–80	

Manures**	N	P_2O_5	K_2O
	lbs per ton manure		
Dairy	6	4	10
Poultry	20	15	10
Hog	6	3	9

*Amount of available N varies with amount of growth.
**Amount of nutrients varies with diet, storage, and application method.
Note: Quantities given in this table are somewhat less than for the total amounts given in table 12.1, p. 131.

Worksheet for Adjusting Fertilizer Recommendations

	N	P_2O_5	K_2O
Soil test recommendation (lbs/acre)	120	40	140
Accounts for contributions from the soil. Accounts for nutrients contributed from manure and previous crop only if information is included on form sent with soil sample.			
Credits			
(Use only if not taken into account in recommendation received from lab.)			
Previous crop (already taken into account)	-0		
Manure (10 tons @ 6 lbs N, 2.4 lbs P_2O_5, 9 lbs K_2O per ton, assuming that 60% of the nitrogen, 80% of the phosphorus, and 100% of the potassium in the manure will be available this year)	-60	-24	-90
Cover crop (medium-growth crimson clover)	-50		
Total nutrients needed from fertilizer	10	16	50

Past crop = corn

Cover crop = crimson clover, but small to medium amount of growth

Manure = 10 tons of dairy manure that tested at 10 lbs of N, 3 lbs of P_2O_5, and 9 lbs of K_2O per ton. (A decision to apply manure was made after the soil sample was sent, so the recommendation could not take those nutrients into account.)

MANAGING FIELD NUTRIENT VARIABILITY

Many large fields have considerable variation in soil types and fertility levels. Site-specific application of crop nutrients and lime using variable-rate technology may be economically and environmentally advantageous for these situations. Soil pH levels, P, and K often show considerable variability across a large field capacity because of nonuniform application of fertilizers and manures, natural variability, and differing crop yields. Soil N levels may also show some variation, but site-specific management of this nutrient is not warranted if the entire field has the same cropping and manure application history.

Site-specific management requires the collection of multiple soil samples within the field, which are then analyzed separately. This is most useful when the sampling and application are performed using precision agriculture technologies such as global positioning systems, geographic information systems, and variable-rate applicators. However, use of conventional application technology can also be effective.

Three- to 5-acre grid sampling (every 350 to 450 feet) is generally recommended, especially for fields that have received variable manure and fertilizer rates. The suggested sampling procedure is called unaligned because in order to get a better picture of the field as a whole, grid points do not follow a straight line. Grid points can be designed with the use of precision agriculture software packages or by insuring that sampling points are taken by moving a few feet off the regular grid

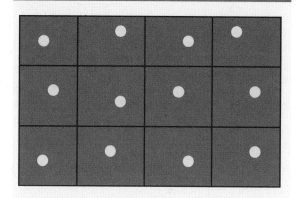

Figure 21.3. Unaligned sampling grid for variable-rate management. Squares indicate 3- to 5-acre management units, and circles are sampling areas for ten to fifteen soil cores.

in random directions (figure 21.3). Grid sampling still requires ten to fifteen individual cores to be taken within about a 30-foot area around each grid point. Sampling units within fields may also be defined by soil type (from soil survey maps) and landscape position, but fertility patterns do not always follow these features.

Grid soil testing may not be needed every time you sample the field—it is a time-consuming process—but it is recommended to evaluate site-specific nutrient levels in larger fields at least once in a rotation, each time lime application may be needed, or every five to eight years.

THE BASIC CATION SATURATION RATIO SYSTEM

This section deals with a somewhat complicated topic and is intended to clarify the issues for those interested in soil chemistry and a more in-depth look at the BCSR (or base ratio) system.

Background

The basic cation saturation ratio system, which attempts to balance the amount of Ca, Mg, and K in soils according to certain ratios, grew out of work in the 1940s and 1950s by Firman Bear and his coworkers in New Jersey and later by William Albrecht in Missouri. The early

With very little data, Firman Bear and his coworkers decided that the "ideal" soil was one in which the CEC was 10 me/100g; the pH was 6.5; and the CEC was occupied by 20% H, 65% Ca, 10% Mg, and 5% K. And the truth is, for most crops that's not a bad soil test. It would mean that it contains 2,600 pounds of Ca, 240 pounds of Mg, and 390 pounds of K per acre to a 6-inch depth in forms that are available to plants. While there is nothing wrong with that particular ratio (although to call it "ideal" was a mistake), the main reason the soil test is a good one is that the CEC is 10 me/100g (the effective CEC—the CEC the soil actually has—is 8 me/100g) and the amounts of Ca, Mg, and K are all sufficient.

concern of researchers was with the luxury consumption of K by alfalfa—that is, if K is present in very high levels, alfalfa will continue to take up much more K than it needs, and, to a certain extent, it does so at the expense of Ca and Mg. When looking with the hindsight provided by more than a half century of soil research after the work of Bear and Albrecht, the experiments carried out in New Jersey and Missouri were neither well designed nor well interpreted, by today's standards. The methods for determining cation ratios, as well as the suggested values that the cations should have, have been modified over the years. Recent work indicates that the system is actually of little value. When the cations are in the ratios usually found in soils, there is nothing to be gained by trying to make them conform to an "ideal" and fairly narrow range. On the other hand—as mentioned in the previous discussion—there are some, relatively infrequent, situations in which the problem of a high level of a particular cation needs to be addressed and can be addressed with either the BCSR or sufficiency system.

In addition to the lack of modern research indicating that it actually helps to use the BCSR system to make recommendations, and the problems that can arise when it (in contrast to the sufficiency system) is used, its use perpetuates a basic misunderstanding of what CEC and base saturation are all about.

Problems with the System

In addition to the practical problems with using the base ratio system, and the increased fertilizer it frequently calls for above the amount that will increase yields of crop quality, there is another issue: The system is based on a faulty understanding of CEC and soil acids, as well as a misuse of the greatly misunderstood term *percent base saturation*.

When percent base saturation (%BS) is defined, you usually see something like the following:

%BS = 100 x sum of exchangeable cations / CEC
= 100 x (Ca^{++} + Mg^{++} + K^+ + Na^+) / CEC

First off, what does CEC mean? It is the capacity of the soil to hold on to cations because of the presence of negative charges on the organic matter and clays, but also to exchange these cations for other cations. For example, a cation such as Mg, when added to soils in large quantities, can take the place of (that is, exchange for) a Ca or two K ions that were on the CEC. Thus, a cation held on the CEC can be removed relatively easily as another cation takes its place. But how is CEC estimated or determined? The only CEC that is of significance to a farmer is the one that the soil currently has. Once soils are much above pH 5.5 (and almost all agricultural soils are above this pH, making them moderately acid to neutral to alkaline), the entire CEC is occupied by Ca, Mg, and K (as well as some Na and ammonium). There are essentially no truly exchangeable acids (hydrogen or aluminum) in these soils. This means that the actual CEC of the soils in this normal pH range is just the sum of the exchangeable bases. The CEC is therefore 100% saturated with bases when the pH is over 5.5 because *there are no exchangeable acids.* Are you still with us?

As we discussed in chapter 20, liming a soil creates new exchange sites as the pH increases (see the section "Cation Exchange Capacity Management, p. 229). The hydrogen affected by the lime is strongly held on organic matter, and, although it is not "exchangeable," it does react with lime and is neutralized—creating new exchange sites in the process. So what does the percent base saturation reported on some soil test results actually mean? The labs either determine the CEC at a higher pH or use other methods to estimate the so-called exchangeable hydrogen—which, of course, is not really exchangeable. Originally, the amount of hydrogen that could be neutralized at pH 8.2 was used to estimate exchangeable hydrogen. In other words, the hydrogen that could be neutralized at pH 8.2 was added to the exchangeable bases, and the total was called the cation exchange capacity. But when your soil has a pH of 6.5, what does a CEC determined at pH 8.2 (or pH 7 or some other relatively high pH) mean to you? Actually, it has no usefulness at all. As the percent base saturation is usually determined and reported, it is nothing more than the current soil's CEC as the percent of CEC it *would have* if its pH were higher. In other words, the percent base saturation has no relevance whatsoever to the practical issues facing farmers as they manage the fertility of their soils. Why then even determine and report a percent base saturation and the percents of the fictitious CEC (one higher than the soil actually has) occupied by Ca, Mg, and K? Good question! Although we understand that many farmers believe that this system helps them to manage their soils better, it is our belief—based on research—that it would be best to stop using the system.

SUMMARY

The preponderance of research indicates that there is no "ideal" ratio of cations held on the CEC with which farmers should try to bring their soils into conformity. It also indicates that the percent base saturation has no usefulness for farmers. Professor E. O. McLean (a former student of Albrecht) and coworkers at Ohio State University summed up their research on this issue in a 1983 article as follows: "We conclude from the results of all aspects of this study that in fertilizer and lime practice, emphasis should be placed on providing sufficient, but nonexcessive levels of each basic cation rather than attempting to adjust to a favorable basic cation saturation ratio which evidently does not exist, as others have also reported..."

And as Kopittke and Menzies put it in a 2007 article that reviewed the older as well as newer research: "Our examination of data from numerous studies (particularly those of Albrecht and Bear themselves) would suggest that, within the ranges commonly found in soils, the chemical, physical, and biological fertility of a soil is generally not influenced by the ratios of Ca, Mg, and K. The data do not support the claims of the BCSR, and continued promotion of the BCSR will result in the inefficient use of resources in agriculture . . ."

If you would like to delve into this issue in more detail, see the articles by McLean et al. (1983), Rehm (1994), and Kopittke and Menzies (2007) listed in "Sources" below.

SOURCES

Allen, E.R., G.V. Johnson, and L.G. Unruh. 1994. Current approaches to soil testing methods: Problems and solutions. In *Soil Testing: Prospects for Improving Nutrient Recommendations,* ed. J.L. Havlin et al., pp. 203–220. Madison, WI: Soil Science Society of America.

Cornell Cooperative Extension. 2000. *Cornell Recommendations for Integrated Field Crop Production.* Ithaca, NY: Cornell Cooperative Extension.

Hanlon, E., ed. 1998. *Procedures Used by State Soil Testing Laboratories in the Southern Region of the United States.* Southern

Cooperative Series Bulletin No. 190, Revision B. Immokalee: University of Florida.

Herget, G.W., and E.J. Penas. 1993. *New Nitrogen Recommendations for Corn.* NebFacts NF 93-111. Lincoln: University of Nebraska Extension.

Jokela, B., F. Magdoff, R. Bartlett, S. Bosworth, and D. Ross. 1998. *Nutrient Recommendations for Field Crops in Vermont.* Brochure 1390. Burlington: University of Vermont Extension.

Kopittke, P.M., and N.W. Menzies. 2007. A review of the use of the basic cation saturation ratio and the "ideal" soil. *Soil Science Society of America Journal* 71: 259–265.

Laboski, C.A.M., J.E. Sawyer, D.T. Walters, L.G. Bundy, R.G. Hoeft, G.W. Randall, and T.W. Andraski. 2008. Evaluation of the Illinois Soil Nitrogen Test in the north central region of the United States. *Agronomy Journal* 100: 1070–1076.

McLean, E.O., R.C. Hartwig, D.J. Eckert, and G.B. Triplett. 1983. Basic cation saturation ratios as a basis for fertilizing and liming agronomic crops. II. Field studies. *Agronomy Journal* 75: 635–639.

Penas, E.J., and R.A. Wiese. 1987. *Fertilizer Suggestions for Soybeans.* NebGuide G87-859-A. Lincoln: University of Nebraska Cooperative Extension.

The Penn State Agronomy Guide. 2007–2008. University Station: Pennsylvania State University.

Recommended Chemical Soil Test Procedures for the North Central Region. 1998. North Central Regional Research Publication No. 221 (revised). Columbia: Missouri Agricultural Experiment Station SB1001.

Rehm, G. 1994. *Soil Cation Ratios for Crop Production.* North Central Regional Extension Publication 533. St. Paul: University of Minnesota Extension.

Rehm, G., M. Schmitt, and R. Munter. 1994. *Fertilizer Recommendations for Agronomic Crops in Minnesota.* BU-6240-E. St. Paul: University of Minnesota Extension.

SARE. *How to Conduct Research on Your Farm or Ranch.* 1999. Available online, along with other SARE bulletins, at http://www.sare.org/learning-center/bulletins.

Photo by Olha Sydorovych

Chapter 22

HOW GOOD ARE YOUR SOILS?
FIELD AND LABORATORY EVALUATION OF SOIL HEALTH

. . . the Garden of Eden, almost literally, lies under our feet almost anywhere on the earth we care to step.
We have not begun to tap the actual potentialities of the soil for producing crops.

—E.H. FAULKNER, 1943

Most farmers know that it is important to increase soil health. And by now, you should have some ideas about ways to increase soil health on your farm, but how can you identify the specific problems with your soil, and how can you tell if your soil's health is actually getting better?

Does your soil . . .

- allow water to infiltrate easily during a downpour and drain afterward to let air in?
- provide sufficient water to plants during dry spells?
- allow crops to fully develop healthy root systems?
- suppress root diseases and parasitic nematodes?
- have beneficial organisms like mycorrhizal fungi that promote healthy crops?
- supply nutrients from organic sources that reduce the need for fertilizer?

First ask yourself why you would do a soil health assessment. The most obvious reason is that it allows you to identify specific constraints, such as P deficiency or surface compaction, and target your management practices. A second reason might be to monitor the health of your soils over time. Is your soil improving after you start planting cover crops, beginning a new rotation, or switching to reduced tillage? While the goal of building soil health is to prevent problems from developing, it also helps to correct previous problems you might have had. A good soil health assessment done over a number of years allows you to see whether you are going in the right direction. Another reason might be to better valuate your soils. If they are in excellent health due to many years of good management, your land should be worth more when sold or rented than fields that have been worn out. After all, a healthy soil produces more and allows for reduced purchased inputs. Being able to effectively appraise soil health may be an additional incentive for farmers to invest in good management and build equity in their land.

We can generally approach soil health assessment

Photo courtesy Harold van Es

at four levels of detail: (1) general field observations; (2) field assessments using qualitative indicators; (3) comprehensive soil health tests; and (4) other targeted soil analyses. We'll discuss them each in some detail.

GENERAL FIELD OBSERVATIONS

A simple but very good place to start assessing a soil's health is to look at its general performance as you go about your normal practices. It's something like wondering about your own performance during the course of a day: Do you have less energy than usual? This might be an indication that something isn't quite right. Likewise, there are signs of poor soil health you might notice as part of the normal process of growing crops:

- Are yields declining?
- Do your crops perform less well than those on neighboring farms with similar soils?
- Do your crops quickly show signs of stress or stunted growth during wet or dry periods?
- Do you notice any symptoms of nutrient deficiencies?
- Is the soil obviously compacted, or does it plow up cloddy and take a lot of secondary tillage to prepare a fine seedbed?
- Does the soil crust over easily, or do you observe signs of runoff and erosion?
- Does it take more power than it used to to run tillage or planting equipment through the soil?
- Do you notice increased problems with diseases or nutrient stress?

These questions are all indicators of soil health, and any affirmative answers should prompt you to consider further action.

FIELD INDICATORS

The next approach is more specific. In several states, farmers and researchers have developed "soil health scorecards." The differences in soils and climates suggest that there is no uniform scorecard that can be used everywhere. Nor is there a magic number or index value

Figure 22.1. A soil penetrometer is a useful tool to assess soil compaction.

for soil health. The goal of these scorecards is to help you make changes and improve your soil's health over time by identifying key limitations or problems.

Whenever you try to become more quantitative, you should be aware that measurements naturally vary within a field or may change over the course of a year. For example, if you decide to evaluate soil hardness with a penetrometer (figure 22.1) or metal rod, you should perform at least ten penetrations in different parts of the field and be aware that your results also depend on the soil moisture conditions at the time of measurement. If you do this in June after a dry spring, you may find the soil quite hard. If you go back the next year following a wet spring, the soil may be much softer. You shouldn't then conclude that your soil's health has dramatically improved, because what you mostly would have measured was the effect of variable soil moisture on soil strength. Similarly, earthworms will be abundant in the plow layer when it's moist but tend to go deeper into the soil during dry periods. Make sure you select your locations well. Avoid unusual areas (e.g., where machinery turns) and aim to include areas with higher and lower yields.

This type of variability with time of year or climatic

Table 22.1
Qualitative Soil Health Indicators

Indicator	Best Assessed	Poor	Medium	Good
Earthworms	Spring/fall. Good soil moisture.	0–1 worms in shovelful of top foot of soil. No casts or holes.	2–10 in shovelful. Few casts, holes, or worms.	10+ in top foot of soil. Lots of casts and holes in tilled clods. Birds behind tillage.
Organic Matter Color	Moist soil.	Topsoil color similar to subsoil color.	Surface color closer to subsoil color.	Topsoil clearly defined, darker than subsoil.
Organic Matter Residues	Anytime.	No visible residues.	Some residues.	Noticeable residues.
Root Health	Late spring (rapid growth stage).	Few, thick roots. No subsoil penetration. Off color (staining) inside root.	Roots well branched. A few roots grow through cracks and reach into subsoil.	Roots fully branched and extended, reaching into subsoil. Root exterior and interior are white.
Subsurface Compaction	Best pre-tillage or post harvest. Good soil moisture.	Wire breaks or bends when inserting flag.	Have to push hard, need fist to push flag in.	Flag goes in easily with fingers to twice the depth of plow layer.
Soil Tilth Mellowness Friability	Good soil moisture.	Looks dead. Like brick or concrete, cloddy. Either blows apart or is hard to pull drill through.	Somewhat cloddy, balls up, requires multiple secondary tillage passes for good seedbed.	Soil crumbles well, can slice through, like cutting butter. Spongy when you walk on it.
Erosion	After heavy rainfall.	Large gullies over 2 inches deep joined to others, thin or no topsoil, rapid run-off the color of soil.	Few rills or gullies, gullies up to 2 inches deep. Some swift runoff, colored water.	No gullies or rills, clear or no runoff.
Water-Holding Capacity	After rainfall. During growing season.	Plant stress two days after a good rain.	Water runs out after a week or so.	Holds water for a long period of time without puddling.
Drainage, Infiltration	After rainfall.	Water sits for a long time, evaporates more than drains, always very wet ground.	Water sits for short period of time, eventually drains.	No ponding, no runoff, water moves through soil steadily. Soil not too wet, not too dry.
Crop Condition (how well it grows)	Growing season. Good soil moisture.	Problem growing throughout season, poor growth, yellow or purple color.	Fair growth, spots in field different, medium green color.	Normal healthy dark green color, excellent growth all season, across field.
pH	Anytime, but at same time of year each time.	Hard to correct for desired crop.	Easily correctable.	Proper pH for crop.
Nutrient-Holding Capacity	Over a five-year period, always at same time of year.	Soil tests dropping with more fertilizer applied than crops used.	Little change or slow downward trend.	Soil tests trending up in relation to fertilizer applied and crop harvested.

Source: Modified from USDA (1997).

conditions should not discourage you from starting to evaluate your soil's health—just keep in mind the limitations of certain measurements. Also, you can take advantage of the fact that soil health problems tend to be more obvious during extreme conditions. It's a good idea to spend some extra time in your fields during extended wet or dry periods.

The following paragraphs present some soil health

indicators developed for scorecards in Maryland, Oregon, and Wisconsin. They are not discussed in any special order—all are important to help you assess soil health as it relates to growing crops. Table 22.1 provides further guidance on good sampling times and interpretation of the measurements.

Soil color is an indicator of soil organic matter content, especially within the same general textural class. Darkness indicates the amount of organic matter (see chapter 2) in the soil. We generally associate black soils with high quality. However, don't expect a dramatic color change when you add organic matter; it may take years to notice a difference.

Crusting, ponding, runoff, and erosion can be observed from the soil surface. However, their extent depends on whether an intense rainstorm has occurred, and whether a crop canopy or mulch protects the soil. These symptoms are a sign of poor soil health, but the lack of visible signs doesn't necessarily mean that the soil is in good health—it must rain hard for these signs to occur. Try to get out into the field after heavy rainstorms, especially in the early growing season. Crusting can be recognized by a dense layer at the surface that becomes hard after it dries. Ponding can be recognized either directly when the water is still in a field depression, or afterward by small areas where the soil has slaked (that is, aggregates have disintegrated). Areas that were ponded often show cracks after drying. Slaked areas going down the slope are an indication that runoff and early erosion have occurred. When rills and gullies are present, a severe erosion problem is at hand. Another idea: Put on your raingear and go out during a rainstorm (not during lightning, of course), and you may actually see runoff and erosion in action. Compare fields with different crops, management, and soil types. This might give you ideas about changes you can make to reduce runoff and erosion.

You also can easily get an idea about **the stability of soil aggregates,** especially those near the surface. If the soil crusts readily, the aggregates are not very stable and break down completely when wet. If the soil doesn't usually form a crust, you might take a sample of aggregates from the top 3–4 inches of soil from fields that seem to have different soil quality. Gently drop a number of aggregates from each field into separate jars that are half filled with water—the aggregates should be covered with water. See whether they hold up or break apart (slake). You can swirl the water in the cups to see if that breaks up the aggregates. If the broken-up aggregates also disperse and stay in suspension, you may have an additional problem with high sodium content (a problem that usually occurs only in arid and semiarid regions).

Soil tilth and hardness can be assessed with an inexpensive penetrometer (the best tool), a tile finder, a spade, or a stiff wire (like those that come with wire flags). Tilth characteristics vary greatly during the growing season due to tillage, packing, settling (dependent on rainfall), crop canopy closure, and field traffic. It is therefore best to assess soil hardness several times during the growing season. If you do it only once, the best time is when the soil is moist but not too wet—it should be in the friable state. Make sure the penetrometer is pushed very slowly into the soil (figure 22.1). Also, keep in mind that stony soils may give you inaccurate results; the soil may appear hard, but in fact your tool may be hitting a rock.

Soil is generally considered too hard for root growth if penetrometer resistance is greater than 300 psi. Note also whether the soil is harder beneath the plow layer. It is common to measure a dramatic increase in resistance when the bottom of the plow layer is reached. This indicates subsoil compaction, or a plow pan, which may limit deep root growth. It's difficult to be quantitative with tile finders and wire, but the soil is generally too hard when you cannot easily push them in. If you use a spade when the soil is not too wet, evaluate how hard the soil is and also pay attention to the structure of the soil. Is the plow layer fluffy, and does it mostly consist of granules of about a quarter inch in size? Or does the soil dig up in large clumps? A good way to evaluate that is by lifting a spade full of soil and slowly dropping it from about waist height. Does the soil break apart into granules, or does it drop in large clumps? When you dig below the plow layer, take a spade full of soil and pull the soil clumps apart. They should generally come apart easily in well-defined aggregates of several inches in size. If the soil is compacted, it does not easily come apart in distinct units.

Soil organisms can be divided into six groups: bacteria, fungi, protozoa, nematodes, arthropods, and earthworms. Most are too small to see with the naked eye, but some larger ones like ants, termites, and earthworms are easily recognized. They are also important "ecosystem engineers" that assist the initial organic matter breakdown that allows other species to thrive, but their general abundance is strongly affected by temperature and moisture levels in the soil. Their presence is best assessed in mid-spring, after considerable soil warming, and in mid-fall during moist, but not excessively wet, conditions. Just take a full spade of soil from the surface layer and sift through it looking for bugs and worms. If the soil is teeming with life, this suggests that the soil is healthy. If few invertebrates are observed, the soil may be a poor environment for soil life, and organic matter processing is probably low. Earthworms are often used as an indicator species of soil biological activity (see table 22.1). The most common worm types, such as the garden and red worms, live in the surface layer when soils are warm and moist and feed on organic materials in the soil. The long nightcrawlers dig near-vertical holes that extend well into the subsoil, but they feed on residue at the surface. Look for the worms themselves as well as their casts (on the surface, for nightcrawlers) and holes to assess their presence, which is typically greatly enhanced in no-till systems. If you dig out a square foot of soil and find ten worms, the soil has a lot of earthworm activity.

With a little more effort, nematodes, arthropods, and earthworms can be removed from a soil sample and

Figure 22.2. A healthy corn root system with many fine laterals. Compare with figure 15.3, p. 163.

observed. Since these soil organisms like their environment to be cool, dark, and moist, they will crawl away when we add heat and light. With a simple desk lamp shining on soil in an inverted cut-off plastic soda bottle (called a Berlese funnel), you will see the organisms escape down the funnel, where they can be captured on an alcohol-soaked paper towel (the alcohol keeps them from escaping; see a description of the procedure at http://pnwsteep.wsu.edu/edsteep/SoilInvertebrates/Berlese.doc).

Root development can be evaluated by digging anytime after the crop has entered its rapid phase of growth. Have the roots properly branched, and are they extending in all directions to their fullest potential for the particular crop? Do they show many fine laterals and mycorrhizal fungal filaments, and will they hold on to the aggregates when you try to shake them off (figure 22.2)? Look for obvious signs of problems: short stubby roots, abrupt changes in direction when hitting hard layers, signs of rot or other diseases (dark-colored roots, fewer fine roots). Make sure to dig deep enough to get a full picture of the rooting environment, because many times there is a hard pan present.

The effects of soil health problems on general crop

performance are most obvious during extreme conditions. That's why it is worthwhile to occasionally walk your fields during a wet period (when a number of rains have fallen or just after a long, heavy rain) or during an extended drought. During prolonged wet periods, poor soils often remain saturated for an extended time. The lack of aeration stunts the growth of the crop, and leaf yellowing indicates loss of available N by denitrification. This may even happen with high-quality soils if the rainfall is excessive, but it is certainly aggravated by poor soil conditions. Dense, no-tilled soil may also show greater effects. Purple leaves indicate a phosphorus deficiency and are also often an indirect sign of stress on the crop. This may be related to soil health but also can be brought on by other causes, such as cold temperatures.

Watch for stunted crop growth during dry periods and also look for the onset of drought stress—leaf curling or sagging (depending on the crop type). Crops on soils that are in good health generally have delayed occurrence of drought stress. Poor soils, especially, may show problems when heavy rainfall, causing soil settling after tillage, is followed by a long drying period. Soils may hardset and completely stop crop growth under these circumstances. Extreme conditions are good times to look at crop performance and, at the same time, evaluate soil hardness and root growth.

Nutrient deficiency symptoms can appear on plant leaves when soils are low in a particular nutrient (table 22.2). However, many nutrient deficiency symptoms look similar, and they also may vary from crop to crop. In addition, typical symptoms may not occur if the plant is suffering from other stresses, including more than one nutrient deficiency. However, some symptoms on some crops are easy to pick out. For example, N-deficient plants are frequently a lighter shade of green than plants with sufficient N. Nitrogen deficiency on corn and other grasses appears on the lower leaves first as a yellowing around the central rib of the leaf. Later, the entire leaf yellows, and leaves further up the stem may be yellow. However, yellowing of the lower leaves near maturity is common with some plants. If the lower leaves of your corn plant are all nice and green

Table 22.2
Examples of Nutrient Deficiency Symptoms

Nutrient	Deficiency Symptoms
Calcium (Ca)	New leaves (at top of plant) are distorted or irregularly shaped. Causes blossom-end rot.
Nitrogen (N)	General yellowing of older leaves (at bottom of plant). The rest of the plant is often light green.
Magnesium (Mg)	Older leaves turn yellow at edge, leaving a green arrowhead shape in the center of the leaf.
Phosphorus (P)	Leaf tips look burnt, followed by older leaves turning a dark green or reddish purple.
Potassium (K)	Older leaves may wilt and look scorched. Loss of chlorophyll between veins begins at the base, scorching inward from leaf margins.
Sulfur (S)	Younger leaves turn yellow first, sometimes followed by older leaves.
Boron (B)	Terminal buds die; plant is stunted.
Copper (Cu)	Leaves are dark green; plant is stunted.
Iron (Fe)	Yellowing occurs between the veins of young leaves. Area between veins may also appear white.
Manganese (Mn)	Yellowing occurs between the veins of young leaves. These areas sometimes appear "puffy." Pattern is not as distinct as with iron deficiency. Reduction in size of plant parts (leaves, shoots, fruit) generally. Dead spots or patches.
Molybdenum (Mo)	General yellowing of older leaves (at bottom of plant). The rest of the plant is often light green.
Zinc (Zn)	Terminal leaves may be rosetted, and yellowing occurs between the veins of the new leaves. Area between veins on corn leaves may appear white.

Source: Modified from Hosier and Bradley (1999).

at the end of the season, there was more N than the plant needed. Potassium deficiencies on corn also show as yellowing on lower leaves, but in this case around the edges. Phosphorus deficiency is normally noted in young plants as stunted growth and reddish coloration. In corn, this may appear early in the season due to wet and cold weather. When the soil warms up, there may be plenty of P for the plants. For pictures of nutrient deficiencies on field crops, visit http://www.extension. iastate.edu/Publications/IPM42.pdf.

Using the simple tools and observations suggested above, you can evaluate your soil's health. Soil health scorecards or soil quality books provide a place to record field notes and assessment information to allow you to compare changes that occur over the years. You also can make up your own assessment sheets.

LABORATORY SOIL HEALTH TESTING
Comprehensive Soil Tests

Growers are used to taking soil samples and having them analyzed for available nutrients, pH, and total organic matter by a university or commercial lab. In arid regions it is common to also determine whether the soil is saline (too much salt) or sodic (too much sodium). This provides information on the soil's chemical health and potential imbalances. To get the most benefit from soil tests, sample soils frequently (at least every two years) and keep good records. Evaluate whether your soil test values are remaining in the optimal range, without adding large amounts of fertilizers. Also, make sure that you do not end up with excessive nutrient levels, especially phosphorus and potassium, due to over-application of organic materials. If your soil test report includes information on cation exchange capacity (CEC), you should expect that to increase with increasing organic matter levels. And, as discussed in chapter 20, soil CEC increases following liming a soil, even if there is no increase in organic matter.

The traditional soil test does not, however, make a

CORNELL SOIL HEALTH TEST REPORT (COMPREHENSIVE)

Name of Farmer: Beth Gugino   Sample ID: E231

Location: Plant Pathology, 630 W. North St. Geneva NY 14456   Agent: George Abawi

Field/Treatment: Gates 72   Agent's Email: 0

Tillage: 9+ INCHES   Given Soil Texture: LOAMY

Crops Grown: CLE/SWC/BNS   Date Sampled: 5/4/2007

	Indicators	Value	Rating	Constraint
PHYSICAL	Aggregate Stability (%)	26	32	
	Available Water Capacity (m/m)	0.13	29	water retention
	Surface Hardness (psi)	167	53	
	Subsurface Hardness (psi)	300	46	
BIOLOGICAL	Organic Matter (%)	2.3	18	energy storage, C sequestration, water retention
	Active Carbon (ppm) [Permanganate Oxidizable]	554	38	
	Potentially Mineralizable Nitrogen (µgN/ gdwsoil/week)	7.9	10	N Supply Capacity
	Root Health Rating (1-9)	4.3	63	
CHEMICAL	*pH	7.4	78	
	*Extractable Phosphorus (ppm) [Value <3.5 or >21.5 are downscored]	10.0	100	
	*Extractable Potassium (ppm)	50	72	
	*Minor Elements		100	
	OVERALL QUALITY SCORE (OUT OF 100):	53.3		**Low**

Measured Soil Textural Class:==> silt loam
SAND (%): 44.0   SILT (%): 50.0   CLAY (%): 6.0

Location (GPS): Latitude=> 42.866667   Longitude=> -77.05

* See Cornell Nutrient Analysis Laboratory report for recommendations

Figure 22.3. Sample Cornell Soil Health Test report.

comprehensive assessment of the health of a soil, which fact probably fed the "chemical bias" in soil management. In other words, the widespread availability of good chemical soil tests, although a very useful management tool, may also have encouraged the quick-fix use of chemical fertilizers over the longer-term holistic approach promoted in this book. The Cornell Soil Health Test was developed to provide a more comprehensive soil assessment through the inclusion of soil biological and physical indicators in addition to chemical ones (figure 22.3). Those indicators were selected based on their cost, consistency, and reproducibility and their relevance to soil management. The Cornell Soil Health Test also considers indicators that represent important soil processes. It provides information on four *physical* indicators:

- aggregate stability (relates to infiltration, crusting, and shallow rooting),
- available water capacity (relates to plant-available water),
- surface and subsurface hardness (relates to rooting), and
- soil texture (relates to most soil processes and is important for interpretation of other measurements);

and four *biological* indicators:

- soil organic matter content (relates to many soil processes, including water and nutrient retention),
- active carbon content (relates to organic material to support biological functions),
- potentially mineralizable nitrogen (relates to ability of organic matter to supply N), and
- root health (relates to soilborne pest problems).

In addition, nine *chemical* indicators, which indicate nutrient availability and pH balance and are part of the standard soil test, are included. Altogether, the Cornell Soil Health Test measures seventeen indicators related to relevant soil processes. The sampling procedure involves taking in-field penetrometer measurements and using a shovel to collect a disturbed sample, which is then submitted to a soil testing lab. A few indicators are especially noteworthy. The aggregate stability test is an excellent indicator of soil physical quality because aggregation is critical to many important processes such as aeration, water flow, rooting, and mobility of soil organisms. The test uses simulated rainfall energy to evaluate the strength of the aggregates, similar to conditions in the field. We have seen that soil management has a strong effect on aggregate stability, as seen in figure 22.4. Under organic management 70% of the aggregates of the silt loam soil remained on the sieve after application of energy from a rain simulator, while for a similar soil under conventional management only 20% of the aggregates remained.

Figure 22.4. Results of aggregate stability test for silt loam vegetable soils: organic (70% stable, left) and conventional (20% stable, right) management.

Active carbon is a relatively new indicator that assesses the fraction of soil organic matter that is believed to be the main supply for the soil food web and, during its decomposition by organisms, provides nutrients for plant uptake. Ray Weil of the University of Maryland has shown that it is easy to see changes in this test as management changes so that the results of the test can provide an early indication of soil health improvements. (It takes a long time to determine an increase in the total amount of organic matter in the soil.) Active C is assessed as the portion of soil organic matter that is oxidized by potassium permanganate, and the results can be measured with an inexpensive spectrophotometer (figure 22.5).

Another noteworthy indicator is the bean root rot bioassay, which provides a highly effective and inexpensive assessment of root health and overall disease pressure from various sources (plant-parasitic nematodes; the fungi *Fusarium*, *Pythium*, *Rhizoctonia*; etc.). Figure 22.6 shows examples from soil from a conventional field with bean root tissue containing lesions and decay, while the roots from beans growing in soil from an organic field are mostly white and are therefore more functional.

A soil health test report provides an integrative assessment and also identifies specific soil constraints; see figure 22.3. This particular report is for a soil that had been under intensive vegetable production for many years. For each indicator, the report provides a

Figure 22.5. Assessment of active carbon using permanganate oxidation and a portable spectrophotometer. Photo by David Wolfe.

measured value and the associated score (1 to 100), which is basically an interpretation of the measured result. If scores are low (less than 30), specific constraints are listed. An overall soil health score, standardized to a scale of 1 to 100, is provided at the bottom of the report, which is especially useful for tracking soil health changes over time.

The test report in figure 22.3 is somewhat typical for traditionally managed vegetable fields in the northeastern part of the U.S. It shows the soil to be in excellent shape in terms of the chemical indicators but severely underperforming with respect to the physical and biological indicators. Why is that the case? In this situation, the farmer was diligent about using the conventional (chemical) soil test and keeping nutrients and pH at optimal levels. But intensive vegetable cropping with conventional plow tillage without cover crops caused an unbalanced soil health profile for this field. The test identified these constraints and allows for more targeted management, which we'll discuss in the next chapter.

Microbial Soil Tests

Soils also can be tested for specific biological characteristics—for potentially harmful organisms relative to beneficial organisms (for example, nematodes that feed on plants vs. those that feed on dead soil organic matter)

or, more broadly, for macro- and microbiology. Since networks of mycorrhizal fungal filaments help plants absorb water and nutrients, their presence suggests more efficient nutrient and water use. Total and active bacterial and fungal biomass and various associated ratios are now offered on a commercial basis. These indicators tend to be sensitive to soil management and provide information on how biological functions are performing. Soils that are low in both bacterial and fungal counts are assumed to be biologically deficient and would gain from a variety of organic amendments.

The relative amounts or activities of each type of microorganism provide insights into the characteristics of the soil ecosystem. Bacterial-dominated soil microbial communities are generally associated with highly disturbed systems with external nutrient additions (organic or inorganic), fast nutrient cycling, and annual plants, while fungal-dominated soils are common in soils with low amounts of disturbance and are characterized by internal, slower nutrient cycling and high and

Figure 22.6. Examples of root rot bioassays on bean plants: conventional (left) and organic (right) soil management. Photos by George Abawi.

stable organic matter levels. Thus, the systems with more weight of bacteria than fungi are associated with intensive-production agriculture (especially soils that are frequently plowed), while systems with a greater weight of fungi than bacteria are typical of natural and less disturbed systems. The significance of these differences for the purposes of modifying practices is unclear, because there is no evidence that one should make changes in order to change the amount of bacteria versus the amount of fungi. On the other hand, modifying practices causes changes to occur. For example, adding organic matter, reducing tillage, and growing perennial crops all lead to a greater ratio of fungi to bacteria. But we generally want to do these practices for many other reasons—improving soil water infiltration and storage, increasing CEC, using less energy, etc.—that may or may not be related to the ratio of bacteria to fungi.

Other Tests and Measurements

Many other measurements can be made, either in the field or the laboratory: infiltration capacity, volume of large pores, etc. As we are writing this book, promising new molecular techniques, like microarray analysis, are being developed that allow for targeted biological analysis. Making such measurements in a meaningful way is challenging, and we recommend the involvement of a scientist or extension agent if you want to pursue more sophisticated methods.

There are geographical considerations to soil health assessment as well. High salinity and sodium levels should be assessed in arid and semiarid regions (especially when irrigated) and lands prone to coastal flooding. In some regions, soils may have high acidity (low pH) in the subsoil that limits root proliferation into deeper layers, and samples from the deeper layers may need to be chemically analyzed. If there are concerns about soil contamination, as may be the case in urban or industrial areas, or when sewage sludge or dredged materials have been applied, tests for heavy metals or

other contaminants are recommended. Laboratories that do these types of tests are listed in the "Resources" section at the end of the book.

SUMMARY

There are many things to be learned by regularly observing the soil and plants in your fields. These include being able to evaluate the severity of runoff, erosion, and compaction; root development; severe nutrient deficiencies; and the presence of earthworms, among other things. Laboratory evaluations of biological indicators, as well as more comprehensive evaluations of indicators of soil health, can also be employed. It is, of course, not enough to know whether a particular limitation exists. In the following (and last) chapter we will discuss both how to put together soil and crop management systems for building healthy soils and how to address particular issues that may arise from field observations or laboratory analyses.

SOURCES

Andrews, S.S., D.L. Karlen, and C.A. Cambardella. 2004. The soil management assessment framework: A quantitative soil quality evaluation method. *Soil Science Society of America Journal* 68: 1945–1962.

Gugino, B., O.J. Idowu, H. van Es, R. Schindelbeck, G. Abawi, D. Wolfe, J. Thies, and B. Moebius. 2009. *Cornell Soil Health Training Manual*. Cornell University. http://soilhealth.cals.cornell.edu.

Hosier, S., and L. Bradley. 1999. *Guide to Symptoms of Plant Nutrient Deficiencies*. Arizona Cooperative Extension Publication AZ1106. Tucson: University of Arizona Extension.

Soil Foodweb, Inc. 2008. http://www.soilfoodweb.com/.

U.S. Department of Agriculture. 1997. *Maryland Soil Quality Assessment Book*. Washington, DC: Author.

van der Heijden, M.G.A., R.D. Bardgett, and N.M. van Straalen. 2008. The unseen majority: Soil microbes as drivers of plant diversity and productivity in terrestrial ecosystems. *Ecology Letters* 11: 296–310.

Weil, R.R., K.R. Islam, M.A. Stine, J.B. Gruver, and S.E. Samson-Liebig. 2003. Estimating active carbon for soil quality assessment: A simplified method for lab and field use. *American Journal of Alternative Agriculture* 18: 3–17.

Chapter 23

PUTTING IT ALL TOGETHER

. . . generally, the type of soil management that gives the greatest immediate return leads to a deterioration of soil productivity, whereas the type that provides the highest income over the period of a generation leads to the maintenance or improvement of productivity.

—CHARLES KELLOGG, 1936

In this chapter, we'll provide some guidance on promoting high-quality soils through practices that maintain or increase organic matter, develop and maintain optimal physical and biological conditions, and promote top-notch nutrient management. In part 3, we discussed many different ways to manage soils, crops, and residues, but we looked at each one as a separate strategy. In the real world, you need to combine a number of these approaches and use them together. In fact, each practice is related to, or affects, other practices that promote soil health. The key is to modify and combine them in ways that make sense for your farm.

We hope that you don't feel as confused as the person on the left in figure 23.1. If the thought of making changes on your farm is overwhelming, you can start with only one or two practices that improve soil health. Not all of the suggestions in this book are meant to be used on every farm. Also, a learning period is probably needed to make new management practices work on

your farm. Experiment on one or two selected fields and permit yourself to make a few mistakes.

Decisions on the farm need to support the economic bottom line. Research shows that the practices that improve soil health generally also improve the economics of the farm, in some cases dramatically. Higher soil health tends to provide higher yields and more yield stability, while allowing for reduced crop inputs. However, you need to consider the fact that the increased returns may not be immediate. After you implement new practices, soil health may improve slowly, and it may take a few years to see improved yields or changes in the soil itself.

The bottom line also may not improve immediately. Changing management practices may involve an investment in new equipment; for example, changing tillage systems requires new tillage tools and planters. For many farmers, these short-term limitations may keep them from making changes, even though they are hurting the long-term viability of the farm. Big changes

Photo by Abram Kaplan

267

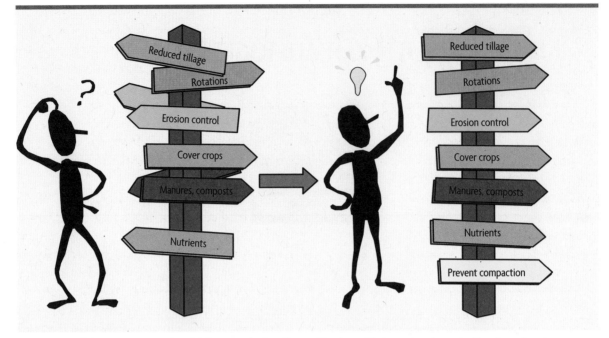

Figure 23.1. Are all the practices just confusing? Solutions can be found by matching them with the needs and opportunities of your farm.

are probably best implemented at strategic times. For example, when you are ready to buy a new planter, consider a whole new approach to tillage as well. Also, take advantage of flush times—for example, when you receive high prices for products—to invest in new management approaches. However, don't wait until that time to make decisions. Plan ahead, so you are ready to make the move at the right time. Remember that soil health management is a long-term commitment. There are no silver bullets or snake oils that will work to build soil health; it requires an integration of the concepts of physical, biological, and chemical processes we have discussed in this book.

GENERAL APPROACHES

Most types of agriculture soil health can be improved through six main approaches:
- reducing tillage
- avoiding soil compaction

- growing cover crops
- using better crop rotations
- applying organic amendments
- applying inorganic amendments

There are many options for making soil management changes in different types of farming systems. We have discussed these in the previous chapters with respect to helping remedy specific problems. A good analogy is to think of your soil as a bank account with credits and debits. The credits are management practices that improve soil health, like manure additions, reduced tillage, and cover crops. The debits are the ones that degrade the soil, like compaction from field traffic and intensive tillage (table 23.1). One farming system may result in a different balance sheet than another due to specific constraints. For example, a daily harvest schedule means that you cannot avoid traffic on wet soils, and small-seeded crops require intensive tillage at least in the planting row in order to prepare a seedbed. Still, strive to optimize the system: If a "bad" practice—such as harvesting in a wet field that contains ripe crops that might spoil if you wait for the soil to dry—is unavoidable, try to balance it with a "good" practice, thereby making your soil health account flush.

If at all possible, use rotations that use grass, legume, or a combination of grass and legume forage crops, or crops with large amounts of residue as important parts of the system. Leave residues from annual crops in the field, or, if you remove them for feed, composting, or bedding, return them to the soil as manure or compost. Use cover crops when soils would otherwise be bare to add organic matter, capture residual plant nutrients, and reduce erosion. Cover crops also help maintain soil organic matter in resource-scarce regions that lack possible substitutes for using crop residues for fuel or building materials.

Raising animals or having access to animal wastes from nearby farms gives you a wider choice of economically sound rotations. Those that include perennial forages make hay or pasture available for use by dairy and beef cows, sheep, and goats—and nowadays even poultry. In addition, on mixed crop-livestock farms, animal manures can be applied to cropland. It's easier to maintain organic matter on a diversified crop-and-livestock farm, where sod crops are fed to animals and manures returned to the soil. Compared to crop farms, fewer nutrients leave farms when livestock products are the main economic output. However, growing crops with high quantities of residues plus frequent use of green manures and composts from vegetative residues helps maintain soil organic matter and soil health even without animals.

You can maintain or increase soil organic matter more easily when you use reduced-tillage systems, especially no-till, strip-till, and zone-till. The decreased soil disturbance keeps biological activity and organic matter decomposition near the surface and helps maintain a soil structure that allows rainfall to infiltrate rapidly. Leaving residue on the surface, or applying mulches,

has a dramatic impact on soil biological activity. It encourages the development of earthworm populations, maintains soil moisture, and moderates temperature extremes. Compared with conventional tillage, soil erosion (water, wind, or tillage) is greatly reduced under minimum-tillage systems, which help keep organic matter and rich topsoil in place. Any other practices that reduce soil erosion, such as contour tillage, strip cropping along the contours, and terracing, also help maintain soil organic matter.

Even if you use minimum-tillage systems, you also should use sound crop rotations. In fact, it may be more important to rotate crops when large amounts of residue remain on the surface, as the residue may harbor insect

Table 23.1
Balance Sheet for Soil Health Management

Practice or Condition	Improves Soil Health	Reduces Soil Health
Tillage		
moldboard plowing		XX
chisel plowing		X
disking		X
harrowing		X
no/zone/ridge/strip tillage	X	
Compaction		
light		X
severe		XX
Organic matter additions		
bedded manure	XX	
liquid manure	X	
compost	XX	
Cover crops		
winter grain	XX	
winter legume	X	
summer grain	XX	
summer legume	XX	
Rotation crops		
3-year sod	XX	
1-year sod	X	

and disease organisms. These problems may be worse in monoculture with no-till practices than with conventional tillage.

WHAT MAKES SENSE ON *YOUR* FARM?

We strongly advocate a holistic management approach. As with human health, we have the ability to diagnose problems through observations and testing. If problems are identified, the patient and physician develop strategies to address them. This may include a change in diet, exercising, a pill, or even surgery. There are often multiple ways and combinations to reach the same goal, depending on personal preferences and circumstances. Similarly for soil health, what makes sense on any individual farm depends on the soils, the climate, the nature of the farm enterprise, the surrounding region, potential markets, and the farm's needs and goals. The tests and observations provide useful guidance to help target constraints, but there is rarely a simple recipe. We wish it was that easy. Holistic soil health management requires an integrative understanding of the processes, which is basically the purpose behind this book.

Start with regularly testing your soils, preferably using comprehensive soil health analyses, and applying amendments only when they are needed. Testing soils on each field every two or three years is one of the best investments you can make. If you keep the report forms, or record the results, you will be able to follow soil health changes over the years. Monitoring soil test changes will help you fine-tune your practices. Also, maintaining your pest scouting efforts and keeping records of those over the years will allow you to evaluate improvements in that area.

PRACTICES TO HELP REMEDY SPECIFIC CONSTRAINTS

Building soil health can help prevent problems from affecting the environment and the growth of plants. However, as good a job as you might do, specific problems may arise that require some sort of remedial action.

The choice of a practice or combinations of practices depends largely on specific soil health problems and possible constraints imposed by the farming system. We discussed in chapter 21 how traditional (chemical) soil tests are used to provide quantitative nutrient and lime recommendations. As discussed in chapter 22, newly available soil tests, as well as careful attention to your soils and crops, can help target management practices related to specific limitations. We cannot be quite as precise for making recommendations regarding physical and biological constraints as we can be for nutrient problems, because these systems are more complex and we don't have as strong a research base.

General management guidelines for specific constraints that may have been identified from soil health tests or field observations are presented in table 23.2. They are listed in terms of two time lines: short term or intermittent, and long term. The short-term recommendations provide relatively quick responses to soil health problems, and they may need to be repeated to prevent recurrence of the problem. The long-term approaches focus on management practices that don't provide quick fixes but address the concern more sustainably. You will probably note that the same practices are often recommended for different constraints, because they address multiple concerns at the same time.

Note that many of the management solutions listed in table 23.2 involve improving organic matter. As you probably realize at this stage of the book, we believe that improved organic matter management is key to sustainable soil management. But keep in mind that simply bringing in any type of organic material in any amount is not necessarily the solution. For one thing, organic additions that are too large may create problem nutrient surpluses. Second, some organic materials reduce disease levels, but others can increase them (see chapter 11 on rotations and chapter 13 on composting). Third, some constraints, like acidity, sodicity, and extremely low nutrient levels, are often more effectively approached

Table 23.2
Linking Soil Health Measurements to General Management Solutions

	Suggested Management Practices	
Physical Concerns	**Short-Term or Intermittent**	**Long-Term**
Low aggregate stability	Fresh organic materials (shallow-rooted cover/rotation crops, manure, green clippings)	Reduced tillage, surface mulch, rotation with sod crops
Low available water capacity	Stable organic materials (compost, crop residues high in lignin, biochar)	Reduced tillage, rotation with sod crops
High surface density	Limited mechanical soil loosening (e.g., strip tillage, aerators), shallow-rooted cover crops, biodrilling, fresh organic matter	Shallow-rooted cover/rotation crops, avoiding traffic on wet soils, controlled traffic
High subsurface density	Targeted deep tillage (zone building, etc.); deep-rooted cover crops	Avoiding plows/disks that create pans; reduced equipment loads and traffic on wet soils
Biological Concerns		
Low organic matter content	Stable organic matter (compost, crop residues high in lignin, biochar); cover and rotation crops	Reduced tillage, rotation with sod crops
Low active carbon	Fresh organic matter (shallow-rooted cover/rotation crops, manure, green clippings)	Reduced tillage, rotation
Low mineralizable N	N-rich organic matter (leguminous cover crops, manure, green clippings)	Cover crops, manure, rotations with forage legume sod crop, reduced tillage
High root rot rating	Disease-suppressive cover crops, disease-breaking rotations	Disease-suppressive cover crops, disease-breaking rotations, IPM practices
Chemical Concerns		
Low CEC	Stable organic matter (compost, lignaceous/cellulosic crop residues, biochar), cover and rotation crops	Reduced tillage, rotation
Unfavorable pH	Liming materials or acidifier (such as sulfur)	Repeated applications based on soil tests
Low P, K	Fertilizer, manure, compost, P-mining cover crops, mycorrhizae promotion	Repeated application of P, K materials based on soil tests; increased application of sources of organic matter; reduced tillage
High salinity	Subsurface drainage and leaching	Reduced irrigation rates, low-salinity water source, water table management
High sodium	Gypsum, subsurface drainage, and leaching	Reduced irrigation rates, water table management

with chemical amendments. Fourth, there are important considerations relating to the type of organic materials that are used. In chapters 9, 10, and 12 we discussed different organic residues and manures and their effects on soil health. One important distinction is whether the material is mostly "fresh" and easily decomposable or contains more stable compounds. Fresh materials like manure, cover crops, and green clippings are high in sugars, cellulose, and proteins and have relatively high N content (low C:N ratios). They immediately stimulate soil biological activity, especially bacteria, and provide

a lot of available N for crops. The organic materials that are dominated by stable materials that are high in lignin, like the residues of mature crops, and those that contain humic material, like composts, are critical to the long-term building of soil health. Biochar, which decomposes slowly over hundreds of years, is perhaps the most stable material. If, for example, aggregate stability or active carbon levels are low, the application of easily decomposable materials will be beneficial in the short term. However, these materials disappear quickly and need to be added regularly to maintain good aggregation. For

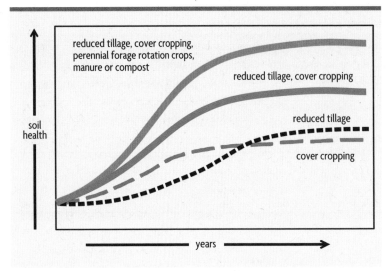

reduced tillage, cover cropping, perennial forage rotation crops, manure or compost

reduced tillage, cover cropping

reduced tillage

soil health

cover cropping

years

Figure 23.2. Combining practices that promote soil health has an additive effect.

longer-term effects it is recommended to include more stable organic compounds and use reduced tillage.

Grain Crop Farms

Most grain crop farms export a lot of nutrients and are managed with a net loss of organic matter. Nevertheless, these farms provide a great deal of flexibility in adopting alternative soil management systems because a wide range of equipment is available for grain production systems. You can promote soil health easily with reduced-tillage systems, especially no-till, strip-till, and zone-till. Well-drained, coarse-textured soils are especially well adapted to no-till systems, and the finer-textured soils do well with ridge-tillage or zone-tillage systems. Regardless of the tillage system that is used, travel on soils only when they're dry enough to resist compaction. However, managing no-till cropping on soils that are easily compacted is quite a challenge because there are few options to relieve compaction once it occurs. Controlled-traffic farming is a very promising approach, especially for such situations, although it may require adjustments of equipment and investment in a GPS guidance system.

Even if you use minimum-tillage systems that leave significant quantities of residue on the surface and decrease the severity of erosion, you also should use sound crop rotations. Consider rotations that use grass, legume, or a combination of grass and legume perennial forage crops. Raising animals on what previously were exclusively crop farms, cooperating on rotations and manure management with a nearby livestock farm, or growing forage crops for sale gives you a wider choice of economically sound rotations and at the same time helps to cycle nutrients better. Incorporating these innovations into a conventional grain farm often requires an investment in new equipment and creatively looking for new markets for your products. There also are many opportunities to use cover crops on grain farms, even in reduced-tillage systems.

Organic grain crop farms do not have the flexibility in soil management that conventional farms have. Their main challenges are typically providing adequate nitrogen and controlling weeds. Tillage choices are limited because of the reliance on mechanical methods, instead of herbicides, to control weeds. On the positive side, organic farms already rely heavily on organic inputs through green or animal manures and composts to provide adequate nutrients to their crops, so their balance sheet (table 23.1) is often very good despite the tillage. A well-managed organic farm usually uses many aspects of ecological soil management. However, erosion may remain a concern when you use clean and intensive tillage. It is important to think about reducing tillage intensity, using ridges or beds, controlling traffic, and perhaps investing in a good planter. New mechanical cultivators can generally handle higher residue and mulch levels and may still provide adequate weed control. Look into ways to increase surface cover, although this is a challenge without the use of chemical weed control. Alternatively, consider more traditional erosion control practices, such as strip cropping, as they work well with rotations involving sod and cover crops.

Crop-Livestock Farms

Diversified crop-and-livestock farms have an inherent advantage for improving soil health. Crops can be fed to animals and manures returned to the soil, thereby providing a continuous supply of organic materials. For many livestock operations, perennial forage crops are an integral part of the cropping system, thereby reducing erosion potential and improving soil physical and biological properties. Soil health tests conducted on dairy farms in New York consistently show good results for most soil health indicators, although compaction is still often a concern. Nevertheless, integrated crop-livestock farms have challenges. Silage harvests do not leave much crop residue, which needs to be compensated with manure application or cover crops. Minimizing tillage is also important and can be done by injecting the manure or gently incorporating it with aerators or harrows, rather than plowing it under. Soil pulverization can be minimized by reducing secondary tillage, using strip or zone tillage, and establishing the crops with no-tillage planters and seeders.

Preventing soil compaction is important on many livestock-based farms. Manure spreaders are typically heavy and frequently go over the land at unfavorable times, doing a lot of compaction damage. Think about ways to minimize this. In the spring, allow the fields to dry adequately (do the ball test) before taking spreaders out. If there is no manure storage, building a structure to hold it temporarily allows you to avoid the most damaging soil conditions. Frost manure injection completely avoids compacting the soil and, despite the generally narrow time window, should be considered in colder regions. Compaction can also result from animal grazing on wet

soil, although it is generally limited to shallow depths. On pastures, regular aeration helps reduce this problem.

Livestock farms require special attention to nutrient management and making sure that organic nutrient sources are optimally used around the farm and no negative environmental impacts occur. This requires a comprehensive look at all nutrient flows on the farm, finding ways to most efficiently use them, and preventing problems with excesses.

Vegetable Farms

Soil quality management is especially challenging on vegetable farms. Many vegetable crops are sensitive to soil compaction and often pose greater challenges in pest management. Vegetable lands have generally been worked hard over many years and have a long way to go toward improved soil health. Most vegetable farms are not integrated with livestock production, and it is difficult to maintain a continuous supply of fresh organic matter. Bringing manure, compost, or other locally available sources of organic materials to the farm should be seriously considered. In some cases, vegetable farms can economically use manure from nearby livestock

FINDING CREATIVE SOLUTIONS

Dairy farmers in Vermont were concerned about soil health on their corn lands. The colder continental climate of the state limits the time window for cover crop establishment before winter dormancy sets in. Working together with University of Vermont specialists, the farmers experimented with shorter-season corn varieties that mature seven to ten days earlier and increase the time window for cover crop establishment equivalently. They found that their corn yields were generally unaffected by the shorter growing season, but their ability to establish cover crops was greatly enhanced.

MORE IS NOT ALWAYS BETTER WITH GRAPEVINES

To establish healthy grapevines a good soil is needed in the early years. But the best wines generally come from soils that are not overly fertile and allow for some water stress during the season. High organic matter and nitrogen contents in vineyard soils create overly abundant vegetative growth in grapevines, reducing fruit set and requiring repeated pruning. Also, important traits of wines are enhanced by the presence of the grapes' anthocyanin pigments, which contribute to both the taste and the color of wine. Mild water stress and reduced root growth during the early summer (between bloom and the beginning of the ripening stage) increase the content of these pigments. Poor drainage and aeration are bad for wine quality. Some of the world's best wines are grown on soils that allow for deep rooting; are calcareous, sandy, or gravelly; and are low in organic matter. The best climates experience water deficits during the growing season, which can be supplemented by irrigation if needed. This complex interaction between soil, climate, and vine is referred to as *terroir*.

operations or swap land with them in a rotation. Farms near urban areas may benefit from leaves and grass clippings and municipal or food waste composts, which are increasingly becoming available. In such cases, care should be taken to ensure that the compost does not contain contaminants.

Vegetable cropping systems are often well adapted to the use of cover crops because the main cropping season is generally shorter than those for grain and forage crops. There is usually sufficient time for the growth of cover crops in the pre-, mid-, or post-season to gain real benefits, even in colder climates. Based on identified soil health constraints (see table 23.2) and growth windows, vegetable growers often have a multitude of cover cropping options. Using the cover crop as a mulch (or importing mulch materials from off the farm) appears to be a good system for certain fresh market vegetables, as it keeps the crop from direct contact with the ground, thereby reducing the potential for rot or disease.

But many vegetable crops are highly susceptible to diseases, and selection of the right cover or rotation crop is critical. For example, according to Cornell plant pathologist George Abawi, bean root rot is suppressed by rapeseed crown vetch, wheat, and rye but is actually enhanced by white clover. Sudan grass can effectively remediate compaction, control pathogenic nematodes,

and allelopathically control weeds, but it requires a long time window for sufficient growth.

The need to harvest crops during a very short period before quality declines regardless of soil conditions often results in severe compaction problems on large vegetable farms using large-scale equipment. Controlled-traffic systems, including permanent beds, should be given serious consideration. Limiting compaction to narrow lanes and using other soil-building practices between them is the best way to avoid compaction damage under those conditions.

Fruit Farms

Many fruit crops, such as bramble, citrus, grape, and stone fruits, are perennials that take several years to establish and may be harvested for twenty or more years. This means that mistakes made during the establishment years can have negative impacts on future years and places the emphasis on addressing soil health concerns in the establishment phase. Comprehensive soil health analyses and field surveys are worthwhile investments, considering the expense of establishing orchards and vineyards. For tree and vine crops, the reconnaissance should pay attention to deeper soil layers, especially the presence of hard pans, acidity, and shallow water tables, because the quality of the fruits is often strongly influenced by deep roots.

Any soil health concern should be addressed prior to transplanting. Depending on the results of tests and field analyses, it is often worthwhile to perform one-time investments like drainage installation, in-row deep ripping, and deep lime and compost incorporations, as these are difficult to perform after the establishment of trees, vines, or canes.

Post-establishment, the emphasis should be on managing the surface layer. Avoiding compaction is important, and maintaining good surface mulches is generally also beneficial, depending on the crop type.

SOME FINAL THOUGHTS

The old folk saying "The farmer's footprint is the best fertilizer" could be modified to "The farmer's footprint is the best path to improved soil health." If you don't already do so, begin to regularly observe and record the variability in crop yield across your fields. Take the time to track production from the various sections of your fields that seem different. Compare your observations with the results of your soil tests, so you can be sure that the various areas within a field are receiving optimum management. Each of the farming systems discussed above has its limitations and opportunities for building better soils, although the approaches and details may differ. Whatever crops you grow, when you creatively combine a reasonable number of practices that promote high-quality soils, most of your farm's soil health problems should be solved along the way, and the yield of your crops should improve. The soil will have more available nutrients, more water for plants to use, and better tilth. There should be fewer problems with diseases, nematodes, and insects, all resulting in reduced use of expensive inputs. By concentrating on the practices that build high-quality soils, you also will leave a legacy of land stewardship for your children and their children to inherit and follow.

GLOSSARY

Acid. A solution containing free hydrogen ions (H^+) or a chemical that will give off hydrogen ions into solution.

Acidic soil. A soil with a pH below 7. The lower the pH, the more acidic the soil.

Aggregates. The structures, crumbs, or clumps formed when soil minerals and organic matter are bound together with the help of organic molecules, plant roots, fungi, and clays.

Alkaline soil. A soil with a pH above 7, containing more base than acid.

Allelopathic effect. Suppression of the germination or growth of one plant by another. The chemicals responsible for this effect are produced during the growth of a plant or during its decomposition.

Ammonium. A form of nitrogen (NH_4^+) that is available to plants and is produced in the early stage of organic matter decomposition.

Anion. A negatively charged element or molecule such as chloride (Cl^-) or nitrate (NO_3^-).

Aquifer. A source of groundwater below the land surface.

Available nutrient. The form of a nutrient that a plant is able to use. Nutrients are commonly found in the soil in forms that the plant can't use (such as organic forms of nitrogen) and must be converted into forms that the plant is able to take into its roots and use (such as the nitrate form of nitrogen).

Ball test. A simple field test to determine soil readiness for tillage. A handful of soil is squeezed into a ball. If the soil holds together, it is in the plastic state and too wet for tillage or field traffic. If it crumbles, it is in the friable state.

Base. Something that will neutralize an acid, such as hydroxide or limestone.

Beds. Small hilled-up, or raised, zones where crops (usually vegetables) are planted. They provide better-drained and warmer soil conditions. They are similar to ridges but generally broader, and they are usually shaped after conventional tillage has occurred.

Buffering. Slowing or inhibiting changes. For example, buffering can slow pH changes by neutralizing acids or bases. A substance that can buffer a solution is also called a buffer.

Bulk density. The mass of dry soil per unit volume; an indicator of the density and compactness of the soil.

Calcareous soil. A soil in which finely divided lime is naturally distributed; it usually has a pH between 7 and slightly more than 8.

Cation. A positively charged ion such as calcium (Ca^{++}) or ammonium (NH_4^+).

Cation exchange capacity (CEC). The amount of negative charge that exists on humus and clays, allowing them to hold on to positively charged chemicals (cations).

Chelate. A molecule that uses more than one bond to attach strongly to certain elements such as iron (Fe^{++}) and zinc (Zn^{++}). These elements may later be released from the chelate and used by plants.

C:N ratio. The amount of carbon divided by the amount of nitrogen in a residue or soil. A high ratio results in low rates of decomposition and can also result in a temporary decrease in nitrogen nutrition for plants, as microorganisms use much of the available nitrogen.

Coarse-textured soil. Soil dominated by large mineral particles (the size of grains of sand); may also include gravels. Used to be called "light soil."

Colloid. A very small particle with a high surface area that can stay in a water suspension for a very long time. The colloids in soils—the clay and humus molecules—are usually found in larger aggregates and not as individual particles. These colloids are responsible for many of the chemical and physical properties of soils, including cation exchange capacity, chelation of micronutrients, and development of aggregates.

Compost. Organic material that has been well decomposed by organisms under conditions of good aeration and high temperature, often used as a soil amendment.

Controlled traffic. The restriction of field equipment to limited travel or access lanes in order to reduce compaction on the rest of the field.

Conventional tillage. Preparation of soil for planting by using a moldboard plow followed by disking or harrowing. It usually breaks down aggregates, buries most crop residues and manures, and leaves the soil smooth.

Coulter. A fluted or rippled disk mounted on the front of a planter to cut surface crop residues and perform minimal soil loosening prior to seed placement. Multiple coulters are used on zone-till planters to provide a wider band of loosened soil.

Cover crop. A crop grown to protect the soil from erosion during the time of the year when it would otherwise be bare. Sometimes called a green manure crop.

Crumb. A soft, porous, more or less round soil aggregate. Generally indicative of good soil tilth.

Crust. A thin, dense layer at the soil surface that becomes hard upon drying.

Deep tillage. Tillage that loosens the soil at a greater depth (usually more than 8 inches) than regular tillage.

Denitrification. The process by which soil organisms convert dissolved nitrate to gaseous nitrogen under anaerobic (low-oxygen) conditions. This occurs when soils become saturated and results in losses of nitrous oxide (a potent greenhouse gas) and dinitrogen (N_2, an inert gas).

Disk. An implement for harrowing, or breaking up, the soil. It is commonly used following a moldboard plow but is also used by itself to break down aggregates, help mix fertilizers and manures with the soil, and smooth the soil surface.

Drainage. The loss of soil water by percolation down through the soil as a result of the gravitational force. Also: Removal of excess soil water through the use of channels, ditches, soil shaping, or subsurface drain pipes.

Elements. Components of all matter. Seventeen elements are essential for plant growth; elements such as carbon, oxygen, and nitrogen combine to form larger molecules.

Erosion. The wearing away of soil by runoff water (water erosion), wind shear (wind erosion), or tillage (*tillage erosion*).

Evaporation. The loss of water from the soil surface as vapor.

Evapotranspiration. The combined processes of *evaporation* and *transpiration*.

Fertigation. The application of soluble fertilizers through an irrigation system, which allows for nutrient spoonfeeding of plants.

Field capacity. The water content of a soil following drainage by gravity.

Fine-textured soil. Soil dominated by small mineral particles (silt and clay). Sometimes called "heavy soil."

Friable soil. Soil that crumbles when force is applied. A soil generally goes from the plastic to the friable state when it dries.

Frost tillage. Tillage performed when a shallow (2–4 inch) frozen layer exists at the soil surface.

Full-field (full-width) tillage. Tillage that results in loosening soil over the entire width of the tillage pass—for example, moldboard plowing, chisel tillage, and disking.

Green manure. A crop grown for the main purpose of building up or maintaining soil organic matter; sometimes called a *cover crop.*

Groundwater. Water contained below the ground surface, typically in the pore spaces of underground geologic deposits.

Heavy soil. Nowadays usually called "fine-textured soil," it contains a lot of clay and is usually more difficult to work than coarse-textured soil. It normally drains slowly following rain.

Humus. The well-decomposed part of the soil organic matter. It has a high cation exchange capacity.

Infiltration. The process of water entering the soil at the surface.

Inorganic chemicals. Chemicals that are not made from chains or rings of carbon atoms—for example, soil clay minerals, nitrate, and calcium.

Irrigation. The application of water to soil to provide better moisture conditions for crop growth. *Flood and furrow irrigation* practices pond the soil with water for a limited time and allow it to infiltrate. *Micro-irrigation, including drip, trickle, and microsprinkler irrigation,* refers to a set of practices that apply localized irrigation water at low rates through small tubes and emitters and are generally water conserving. *Supplemental irrigation* refers to a practice used in humid regions where rainfall provides most crop water needs and irrigation is primarily used to maintain adequate soil moisture levels during limited drought periods. *Deficit irrigation* refers to a water-conserving practice whereby water supply is reduced below maximum levels and mild crop stress is allowed, with minimal effects on yield.

Landslide. The instantaneous downward fall of large soil volumes as a result of gravity. Landslides may occur on steep slopes when they become supersaturated with water.

Least-limiting water range. See *Optimum water range.*

Legume. Plants—including beans, peas, clovers, and alfalfa—that form a symbiotic relationship with nitrogen-fixing bacteria living in their roots. These bacteria help to supply the plants with an available source of nitrogen.

Lignin. A substance found in woody tissue and in the stems of plants that is difficult for soil organisms to decompose.

Lime or limestone. A mineral consisting of calcium carbonate ($CaCO_3$) that can neutralize acids and is commonly applied to acid soils.

Loess soil. Soil formed from windblown deposits of silty and fine-sand-size minerals; they are easily eroded by wind and water.

Micronutrient. An element, such as zinc, iron, copper, boron, or manganese, that is needed by plants in only small amounts.

Microorganisms. Very small and simple organisms such as bacteria and fungi.

Mineralization. The process by which soil organisms change organic elements into the "mineral" or inorganic form as they decompose organic matter; for example, organic forms of nitrogen are converted to nitrate.

Moldboard plow. A commonly used plow that completely turns over the soil and incorporates any surface residues, manures, or fertilizers deeper into the soil.

Mole drainage. A practice used on heavy clay soils whereby water is removed through subsurface channels 2–3 feet deep. This practice does not involve pipes; the channels are generated with the use of a bullet-type plow. Channels generally need to be rebuilt every four to six years.

Monoculture. Production of the same crop in the same field year after year.

Mulch. Organic materials like straw and wood chips that are applied to soil as a surface cover; generally also includes cover crop material left on the surface and heavy amounts of crop residues left at the soil surface after harvest.

Mycorrhizal relationship. The mutually beneficial relationship that develops between plant roots of most crops and fungi. The fungi help plants obtain water and phosphorus by acting like an extension of the root system and in return receive energy-containing chemical nutrients from the plant.

Nitrate (NO$_3^-$). The form of nitrogen that is most readily available to plants and is normally found in the greatest abundance in agricultural soils.

Nitrification. The process by which soil microorganisms convert ammonium into nitrate.

Nitrogen fixation. The conversion of atmospheric nitrogen by bacteria to a form that plants can use. A small number of bacteria, including the rhizobia living in the roots of legumes, are able to make this conversion.

Nitrogen immobilization. The transformation of available forms of nitrogen, such as nitrate and ammonium, into organic forms that are not readily available to plants.

No-till. A system of planting crops without tilling the soil with a plow, disk, chisel, or other tillage implement.

Optimum water range. The range of soil water content in which plants do not experience stress from drought, high soil strength, or lack of aeration.

Organic chemicals. Chemicals that contain chains or rings of carbon connected to one another. Most of the chemicals in plants, animals, microorganisms, and soil organic matter are organic.

Oxidation. The combining of a chemical such as carbon with oxygen, usually resulting in the release of energy.

Penetrometer. A device that measures soil resistance to penetration, which indicates the degree of compaction; it has a cone-tipped metal shaft that is slowly pushed into the soil while the resistance force is measured.

Perennial forage crops. Crops such as grasses, legumes, and grass-legume mixtures that form a complete soil cover (sod) and are grown for pasture or to make hay and haylage for animal feed.

pH. A way of expressing the acid status, or hydrogen ion (H$^+$) concentration, of a soil or a solution on a scale on which 7 is neutral, less than 7 is acidic, and greater than 7 is basic.

Photosynthesis. The process by which green plants capture the energy of sunlight and use carbon dioxide from the atmosphere to make molecules needed for growth and development.

Plastic. The state of a soil that molds easily when force is applied. Compare to *Friable*.

Plastic limit. The water content of soil at the transition from the plastic to the friable state; the upper limit of soil moisture at which tillage and field traffic do not result in excessive compaction damage.

Polyculture. The growth of more than one crop in a field at the same time.

PSNT. The pre-sidedress nitrate test is a soil test for nitrogen availability in which the soil is sampled to a depth of 1 foot during the early crop growth.

Raised beds. Crops grown in rows that are raised from the inter-row areas to provide better drainage and aeration and deeper topsoil. Raised beds are wider than ridges but aim to achieve the same benefits.

Recycled wastewater. Water derived from the treatment of municipal wastewater and used for crop irrigation.

Respiration. The biological process that allows living things to use the energy stored in organic chemicals. In this process, carbon dioxide is released as energy is made available to do all sorts of work.

Restricted tillage. Tillage that includes only limited and localized soil disturbance in bands where plant rows are to be established—for example, no-till, zone-till, strip-till, and ridge-till systems. Compare with *Full-field tillage*.

Rhizobia bacteria. Bacteria that live in the roots of legumes and have a mutually beneficial relationship with the plant. These bacteria fix nitrogen, providing it to the plant in an available form, and in return receive energy-rich molecules that the plant produces.

Ridge tillage. Planting crops on top of small ridges (usually 2–4 inches in height), which are generally re-formed annually with a special cultivator.

Rotation effect. The crop-yield benefit from rotations, which includes better nutrient availability, fewer pest problems, and better soil structure.

Runoff. Water lost by flow over the soil surface.

Saline soil. Soil that contains excess free salts, usually sodium and calcium chlorides.

Saturated soil. Soil whose pores are filled with water, resulting in a virtual absence of soil air.

Silage. A feed produced when chopped-up corn plants or wilted hay is put into airtight storage facilities (silos) and partially fermented by bacteria. The acidity produced by the fermentation and the lack of oxygen help preserve the quality of the feed during storage.

Slurry (manure). Manure that is between solid and liquid; it flows slowly and has the consistency of a very thick soup.

Sod crops. Grasses or legumes such as timothy and white clover that tend to grow very close together and form a dense cover over the entire soil surface.

Sodic soil. Soil containing excess amounts of sodium. If it is not also saline, clay particles disperse, and the soil structure may be poor.

Soil structure. The physical condition of the soil, which depends on the number of pores, the arrangement of soil solids into aggregates, and the degree of compaction.

Strip cropping. Growing two or more crops in alternating strips, usually along the contour or perpendicular to the prevailing wind direction.

Surface water. Water at the land surface, including streams, ponds, lakes, estuaries, seas, and oceans.

TDR (time-domain deflectometry). Method for assessing water contents of soils by measuring the medium's dielectric properties (its ability to conduct electromagnetic waves). Typically involves metal rods that are inserted into soil.

Texture. A soil's sand, silt, and clay content. "Coarse-textured" means that a soil has a high sand content, while "fine-textured" means that a soil has a high clay content.

Thermophilic bacteria. Bacteria that live and work best under high temperatures, around 110°–140°F. They are responsible for the most intense stage of decomposition that occurs during composting.

Tile drainage. Removal of excess soil water through pipes buried in the soil, typically 3–4 feet deep. Traditionally, the pipes were made of clay tile, but they are now corrugated flexible PVC pipes with perforations.

Tillage. The mechanical manipulation of soil, generally for the purpose of loosening the soil, creating a seedbed, controlling weeds, or incorporating amendments. *Primary tillage* (moldboard plowing, chiseling) is a more rigorous practice, primarily for loosening soil and incorporating amendments. *Secondary tillage* (disking, harrowing) is a less rigorous practice, following primary tillage, that creates a seedbed containing fine aggregates.

Tillage erosion. The downslope movement of soil caused by the action of tillage implements.

Tilth. The physical condition, or structure, of the soil as it influences plant growth. A soil with good tilth is very porous and allows rainfall to infiltrate easily, permits roots to grow without obstruction, and is easy to work.

Transpiration. The loss of water from the soil through plant uptake and evaporation from leaf surfaces.

Wilting point. The point at which a soil contains only water that is too tightly held to be available to plants.

Yield monitor. A computerized data acquisition system on a crop harvester—typically, a grain combine—that records and provides maps of crop yield in fields on the go.

Zone tillage. A restricted tillage system that establishes a narrow (4–6-inch) band of loosened soil with surface residues removed. This is accomplished using multiple coulters and row cleaners as attachments on a planter. It may include a separate "zone-building" practice that provides deep, narrow ripping without significant surface disturbance. It is a modification of no tillage, generally better adapted to cold and wet soils.

RESOURCES

GENERAL INFORMATION SOURCES

USDA supports three programs with the sole mission of promoting sustainable agriculture across America:

- *SARE—Sustainable Agriculture Research and Education,* the publisher of this book, is a grassroots grants and outreach program that advances sustainable innovations to the whole of American agriculture. Projects that explore practices to build better soils have been a cornerstone of SARE's grant-making portfolio since the organization was created in 1988. SARE also produces a wealth of information products, from books such as this one and *Managing Cover Crops Profitably* to bulletins on topics such as organic agriculture to online courses for ag educators. To find out about SARE grants or to download or order publications, visit www.sare.org.

- *ATTRA—The National Sustainable Agriculture Information Service* provides assistance and free publications and resources on topics such as sustainable soil management, drought-resistant soils, cover crops and green manures, farm-scale composting, and nutrient cycling in pastures. To download reports, visit www. attra.ncat.org or call 800-346-9140.

- *AFSIC—The Alternative Farming Systems Information Center* compiles bibliographies and resource lists on topics of current interest, such as soil quality, soil amendments and nutrient management, compost and composting, and much more. To view AFSIC's resources, visit afsic.nal.usda.gov or call 301-504-6559.

Further, most state Cooperative Extension offices publish leaflets and booklets on manures, soil fertility, cover crops, and other subjects described in this book. Request a list of publications from your county extension office. A number of states also have sustainable agriculture centers that publish newsletters.

NRAES, the Natural Resource, Agriculture, and Engineering Service (www.nraes.org) publishes practical books on most aspects of farming.

The Rodale Institute's New Farm website (rodaleinstitute.org/new_farm) offers practical information to farmers through a diverse collection of resources and web links on soil health, cover crops, composts, and related topics.

MANURES, FERTILIZERS, TILLAGE, AND ROTATIONS

Best Management Practices Series: Soil Management, Nutrient Management, and No-Till (http://www.omafra.gov.on.ca/english/environment/bmp/series.htm), Ontario Ministry of Agriculture, Food, and Rural Affairs. This website provides practical information on these subjects to farmers and crop advisers. Available from Ontario Federation of Agriculture, 416-326-5300, or online at https://www.publications.serviceontario.ca/ecom/.

Cedar Meadow Farms website (www.cedarmeadowfarm.com). Steve Groff maintains this site, which covers the practices he uses on his farm—especially using no-till and cover crops.

"Crop Rotations in Sustainable Production Systems," C.A. Francis and M.D. Clegg (1990), pp. 107–122 in *Sustainable Agricultural Systems,* C.A. Edwards, ed. CRC Press, Boca Raton, FL.

Diversifying Cropping Systems (2008). Sustainable Agriculture Research and Education (SARE). A 20-page bulletin on the soil and yield benefits of diversifying crops on farms and ranches. Download at www.sare.org.

The Farmer's Fertilizer Handbook, Craig Cramer and the editors of the New Farm (1986). Regenerative Agriculture Association, Emmaus, PA. This handbook contains lots of very good information on soil fertility, soil testing, use of manures, and use of fertilizers.

Fertile Soil: A Growers Guide to Organic and Inorganic Fertilizers, R. Parnes (1990). Fertile Ground Books, PO Box 2008, Davis, CA 95617, 800-540-0170.

Managing Cover Crops Profitably, 3rd ed., A. Clark, ed. (2007). Sustainable Agriculture Research and Education (SARE). An excellent, comprehensive source of practical information about when, where, and how to use cover crops in every region of the country. $19 plus $6.95 s/h to Sustainable Agriculture Publications, c/o International Fulfillment Corporation, 3570 Bladensburg Rd., Brentwood, MD 20722; www.sare.org.

Manures for Organic Crop Production, George Kuepper. ATTRA, http://attra.ncat.org/attra-pub/manures.html.

Michigan Field Crop Ecology: Managing Biological Processes for Productivity and Environmental Quality, M.A. Cavigelli, S.R. Deming, L.K. Probyn, and R. R. Harwood, eds. (1998). Extension Bulletin E- 2646. Michigan State University, East Lansing, MI.

Soil Fertility and Organic Matter as Critical Components of Production Systems, R.F. Follett, J.W.B. Stewart, and C.V. Cole, eds. (1987). SSSA Special Publication No. 19. Soil Science Society of America, American Society of Agronomy, Madison, WI.

Soil Management for Sustainability, R. Lal and F.J. Pierce, eds. (1991). Soil and Water Conservation Society, 7515 NE Ankeny Road, Ankeny, IA.

Soils for Management of Organic Wastes and Wastewaters, L.F. Elliott and F. J. Stevenson, eds. (1977). Soil Science Society of America, Madison, WI.

USDA Natural Resources Conservation Service / Soil Quality Institute—Agronomy Technical Notes Series. The NRCS Technical Notes Series provides an excellent introduction to cover crops, effect of conservation crop rotation on soil quality, effects of residue management and no-till on soil quality, legumes and soil quality, and related topics. http://soils.usda.gov/sqi/publications/publications.html#sq_tn.

SOILS, IMPORTANCE OF ORGANIC MATTER, SOIL ORGANISMS, AND COMPOSTING

Biological Approaches to Sustainable Soil Systems, N. Uphoff, A. Ball, E. Fernandes, H. Herren, O. Husson, M. Laing, C. Palm, J. Pretty, and P. Sanchez, eds. (2006). CRC Press / Taylor and Francis, Boca Raton, FL.

Cedar Meadow Farms website (www.cedarmeadowfarm.com). Steve Groff maintains this site, which covers the practices he uses on his farm—especially using no-till and cover crops.

Cornell Composting website (http://www.css.cornell.edu/compost/Composting_Homepage.html). Maintained by the Cornell Waste Management Institute, this site contains a wealth of information, including the science and engineering of compost.

Cornell Soil Health website (www.soilhealth.cals.cornell.edu) contains information about soil health and assessment.

Ecology of Compost, D. Dindal (1972). Office of News and Publications, 122 Bray Hall, SUNY College of Environmental Science and Forestry, 1 Forestry Drive, Syracuse, NY 13210-2778, 315-470-6644.

"Effects of Conversion to Organic Agricultural Practices on Soil Biota," M.R. Werner and D.L. Dindal (1990), *American Journal of Alternative Agriculture* 5(1): 24–32.

The Field Guide to On-Farm Composting, M. Dougherty, ed. (1999). NRAES-114. Natural Resource, Agriculture, and Engineering Service, 152 Riley Robb Hall, Cooperative Extension, Ithaca, NY 14853-5701, www.nraes.org.

The Nature and Properties of Soils, 14th ed., N.C. Brady and R.R. Weil (2007). Prentice Hall, Upper Saddle River, NJ.

NRCS Soil Quality website (soils.usda.gov/sqi/). The Soil Quality Institute identifies soil quality research findings and practical technologies that help conserve and improve soil, and enhance farming, ranching, forestry, and gardening enterprises.

On Farm Composting, R. Rynk, ed. (1992). NRAES-54. Natural Resource, Agriculture, and Engineering Service, 152 Riley Robb Hall, Cooperative Extension, Ithaca, NY 14853-5701 or www.nraes.org.

The Pedosphere and Its Dynamics: A Systems Approach to Soil Science, N.G. Juma (1999). Pedosphere.com, an award-winning website on soil science. University of Alberta, Canada, www.pedosphere.com.

Phytohormones in Soils: Microbial Production and Function, W.T. Frankenberger Jr. and M. Arshad (1995). Marcel Dekker, New York, NY.

The Rodale Book of Composting: Easy Methods for Every Gardener, D.L. Martin and G. Gershuny, eds. (1992). Rodale Press, Emmaus, PA.

"Soil Biology Primer" (http://soils.usda.gov/sqi/concepts/soil_biology/biology.html) by the USDA's Natural Resources Conservation Service presents an introduction to the living soil system for natural resource specialists, farmers, and others. This set of eight units describes the importance of soil organisms and the soil food web to soil productivity and water and air quality. Hard copies can be purchased at http://www.swcs.org/en/publications/soil_biology_primer/.

Soil Microbiology and Biochemistry, E.A. Paul and F.E. Clark (1989). Academic Press, San Diego, CA.

Soil Microbiology: An Exploratory Approach, M.S. Coyne (1999). Delmar Publishers, Albany, NY.

Soil Organic Matter in Sustainable Agriculture, F.R. Magdoff and R. Weil, eds. (2004). CRC Press, Boca Raton, FL.

COVER CROPS

Cover Crops for Clean Water, W.L. Hargrove, ed. (1991). Soil and Water Conservation Society, 7515 NE Ankeny Road, Ankeny, IA 50021, 515-289-2331; www.swcs.org/en/publications/cover_crops_for_clean_water.cfm.

"Crop Rotations in Sustainable Production Systems," C.A. Francis and M.D. Clegg (1990), pp. 107–122 in *Sustainable Agricultural Systems,* C.A. Edwards, ed. CRC Press, Boca Raton, FL.

Green Manuring Principles and Practices, A.J. Pieters (1927). John Wiley & Sons, New York, NY. An oldie but goody. This is an out-of-print book that can sometimes be located in college libraries or borrowed through an inter-library loan.

Managing Cover Crops Profitably, 3rd ed., A. Clark, ed. (2007). Sustainable Agriculture Research and Education (SARE). An excellent, comprehensive source of practical information about when, where, and how to use cover crops in every region of the country. $19 plus $6.95 s/h to Sustainable Agriculture Publications, c/o International Fulfillment Corporation, 3570 Bladensburg Rd., Brentwood, MD 20722; www.sare.org.

Northeast Cover Crop Handbook, M. Sarrantonio (1997). Soil Health Series. Rodale Institute, Kutztown, PA.

The Role of Cover Crops in Integrated Crop Production Systems, J.F. Power and V.O. Biederbeck. Soil and Water Conservation Society, 7515 NE Ankeny Road, Ankeny, IA 50021, 515-289-2331; http://www.swcs.org/documents/filelibrary/CCCW10.pdf.

The Role of Legumes in Conservation Tillage Systems, J.F. Power, ed. (1987). Soil and Water Conservation Society, 7515 NE Ankeny Road, Ankeny, IA 50021, 515-289-2331.

University of California's SAREP (Sustainable Agriculture Research and Education Program). The UC-SAREP Cover Crops Resource Page (www.sarep.ucdavis.edu/ccrop/) provides access to a host of online and print educational materials, including the very informative UC-SAREP Cover Crop Database.

DYNAMICS AND CHEMISTRY OF ORGANIC MATTER

Building Soils for Better Crops, 1st ed., F. Magdoff (1992). University of Nebraska Press, Lincoln, NE. The last two chapters of the first edition contain information on the chemistry and dynamics of soil organic matter.

Humic, Fulvic, and Microbial Balance: Organic Soil Conditioning, W.R. Jackson (1993). Jackson Research Center, Evergreen, CO.

Humus Chemistry: Genesis, Composition, Reactions, 2nd ed., F.J. Stevenson (1994). John Wiley & Sons, New York, NY.

"Soil Carbon Dynamics and Cropping Practices," R.E. Lucas, J.B. Holtman, and J.L. Connor (1977), pp. 333–351 in *Agriculture and Energy,* W. Lockeretz, ed. Academic Press, New York, NY.

Soil Organic Matter, M. Schnitzer and S.U. Kahn, eds. (1978). Developments in Soil Science 8. Elsevier Scientific Publishing, Amsterdam, Holland.

"Soil Organic Matter and Its Dynamics," D.S. Jenkinson (1988), pp. 564–607 in *Russell's Soil Conditions and Plant Growth,* A. Wild, ed. John Wiley & Sons, New York, NY.

SOIL TESTING

Laboratories

Most state land grant universities have soil testing laboratories that can be found through your local extension office or by searching online for your state laboratory. A number of commercial laboratories also perform routine soil analyses. The Soil Science Society of America administers a laboratory proficiency testing program (NAPT). A list of certified laboratories is available at http://www.naptprogram.org/. The ATTRA publication *Alternative Soil Testing Laboratories* is available online at www.attra.org/attra-pub/soil-lab.html, as well as in print.

Publications

Soil Testing: Prospects for Improving Nutrient Recommendations, J.L. Havlin et al., eds. (1994). Soil Science Society of America, Madison, WI.

Soil Testing: Sampling Correlation, Calibration, and Interpretation, J.R. Brown, T.E. Bates, and M.L. Vitosh (1987). Special Publication 21. Soil Science Society of America, Madison, WI.

INDEX